Acclaim for Susan Zakin's *Coyotes and Town Dogs*

"Zakin, a truly gifted writer, puts the reader smack into the scene . . . [and] it is this mythic element that Zakin catches so well in her evocation— an evocation of as odd a group of people, and as inspiring a collection of landscapes, as could be imagined."
　　　　　—Wilderness Magazine

"A vivid, comprehensive history . . . of a movement most Americans would probably consider crazy. . . . If we're still here 200 years from now, it will be due in no small part to groups like Earth First! and to writers like Susan Zakin who understand why we must heed their warnings."
　　　　　—Adam Hochschild, author of *The Mirror at Midnight*

"*Coyotes and Town Dogs* is one of those rare treasures that ends much too quickly . . . A superb contribution to the historical conservation literature of the past thirty years . . . Approaches pure genius in perception, integration, and presentation. The bookshelves of every dedicated conservationist should have a copy."　　　　　*—Conservation Biology*

"Zakin introduces us to the movement's principal movers and shakers, and her vivid prose captures the movement's excitement, occasional terror, and just as occasional triumph."
　　　　　—Outside magazine

"In crisp, clear and often sharply funny prose, Zakin alternates the Earth First! story with a knowledgeable overview of American environmentalism and judicious tidbits of gossip. It's a fascinating, sometimes hilarious, some- times appalling tale. Whatever you think about Earth First!, this book may well change your mind."
　　　　　—The Arizona Daily Star

COYOTES AND TOWN DOGS

COYOTES AND TOWN DOGS

EARTH FIRST! AND THE ENVIRONMENTAL MOVEMENT

Susan Zakin

The University of Arizona Press
Tucson

♾ This book is printed on acid-free, archival-quality paper.
Manufactured in the United States of America

07   06   05   04   03   02   6   5   4   3   2   1

Library of Congress Cataloging-in-Publication Data
Zakin, Susan.
Coyotes and town dogs : Earth First! and the environmental movement /
Susan Zakin.— 1st University of Arizona Press paperbound ed.
p. cm.
Originally published: New York : Viking, 1993.
Includes bibliographical references and index.
ISBN 0-8165-2185-9 (pbk. : acid-free paper)
1. Environmental policy—United States—Citizen participation.
2. Green movement—United States. 3. Earth First! (Organization) I. Title.
GE180 .Z35 2002
363.7'057'0973—dc21   2001052221

British Library Cataloguing-in-Publication Data
A catalogue record for this book is available from the British Library.

Here the land always makes promises of aching beauty and the people always fail the land.

—Charles Bowden
Blue Desert

Contents

COYOTES
AND
TOWN DOGS

Prologue

1989—Tucson, Arizona

ON THE LAST DAY OF MAY, the desert sky was a shade of gunmetal gray not often seen in late spring. Nancy Morton and Dave Foreman slept under a flowered sheet in their brick suburban tract house. Nancy had risen early and mixed a new batch of sugar water for the hummingbird feeders. But then she dozed off again, wearing her shorts and a T-shirt. It was that kind of morning, the air motionless, the neighborhood quiet.

At 7 A.M. someone knocked loudly at the front door. Nancy was the one who woke up. She walked barefoot through the dark hallway. When she opened the door, four men burst into the house, stiff-arming their guns in front of them.

"FBI!" one shouted. The agents rushed past her, heading straight for the master bedroom. They jerked the sheet off her husband, a bearded, balding environmental lobbyist, and aimed their cocked .357 Magnums at his naked body.

It was the couple's third wedding anniversary.

Eleven hours earlier and 200 miles to the northwest, Peg Millett crouched in a sandy wash. She kept her head down so the Blackhawk helicopter's sixty-million-candlepower spotlight couldn't home in on the reflection from her glasses. It was the first time she had stopped running since the FBI flare lit the night sky.

Millett could no longer see the place where the bust had gone down. But its afterimage was burned onto her eyelids. The eighty-foot power-line tower rose out of the desert like a giant insect in a Japanese horror film. FBI agents fanned out around it, an army of men wearing dark clothes to help them disappear at night. They wore plastic leggings, like medieval armor, to protect them from rattlesnakes. Most of all, she remembered their SWAT-team firepower: M-16 automatic rifles, 9-millimeter handguns, 12-gauge shotguns loaded with double-ought buck. She could not see the men or their guns anymore. But she could hear their voices. "Peg! Peggy Millett. Turn yourself in."

Peg was pretty sure she had broken through their circle. When the voices stopped, she listened for the sounds of men moving in the desert: a clatter of rocks being dislodged, the soft cry issued when cactus enters flesh. But there was nothing human. She heard only the occasional fluttering of a bat, the dive of a nighthawk, a subtle wind brushing catclaw acacia and desert broom. She waited for the helicopter to angle off into the night. She was perfectly still. Oddly, she was not frightened.

The wash was a good hiding place. It had been created by hundreds of purple and black monsoons ramming hard rain onto the desert floor. Repelled by the dry caliche, the waters had spun out and collided to carve the channel where Peg was holed up. The helicopter's explosive *chuk-chuk-chuk* made it easy to imagine another monsoon. It would dwarf all the previous storms that had etched these washes onto the desert like hieroglyphics of an unknown language. The summer rains started before the Spanish Jesuits, before the Sand Papago, even before the mysterious people, the Hohokam. Each civilization had left its mark, making it tougher to wring life out of the ground, causing the floods to become more violent. It was easy to imagine a flood to end all floods barreling through the wash, destroying its shallow borders. The brown water would sweep Millett and everyone she knew off the edge of the land like a broom disposing of human debris.

The helicopter's lights veered off, then disappeared. When Millett dared to look up, all she saw was the teeming Sonoran dark. She would spend the night alone, moving through the mountains toward home. The moon would not rise until about five, just in time to be blasted out by the desert sun.

Standing, she willed herself to regain her bearings.

Scorpio in the southern sky.

A barrel cactus near her right leg.

Coyotes yipping, answering the frantic, deep-throated cries of the German shepherds tracking her.

It was time to start walking.

By late morning news of the arrests was coursing over telephone wires, being spit out by fax machines, flashing on computer screens—sometimes even being transmitted face-to-face. Dave Foreman had been busted for conspiracy. The renegade environmentalist who founded Earth First! with his drinking buddies in the Mexican desert had been rousted buck naked from his bed by an FBI posse. He was still in the can, nobody knew where. Nobody knew why he had been arrested. All they knew was that on the previous night two other guys had been busted while cutting down a power line near the aptly named town of Salome, Arizona. Their names were Mark Davis and Marc Baker. Wags quickly dubbed them the Marx Brothers in honor of their misbegotten evening expedition. The power line they had been whaling away on was a microscopic part of the $3.5 billion Central Arizona Project, which diverts water from the already drained Colorado River to the air conditioners and swimming pools of Phoenix and Tucson. The CAP, as desert rats call it, would have been an

ambitious enough target for any self-respecting environmental sabo-
teur. But the FBI contended that the power-line fiasco was merely a
warm-up for a bigger enchilada, a conspiracy to take out power to
three nuclear facilities: the Palo Verde power plant in Arizona, the
Diablo Canyon plant in California, and a weapons-grade plutonium-
processing facility at Rocky Flats, Colorado.

As it turned out, the Marx Brothers were not staking out their
moves alone. A horse trainer and singer named Peggy Millett had gone
to Salome with them. Millett was a high-profile Earth First!er, a member in good standing of its Redneck Women's Caucus, and a friend
of Dave Foreman's. The fourth member of the group was the driver.
He was a shadowy man with deep-set brown eyes called Mike Tait.
Mike Tait's real name was Fain, which should have been spelled
"feign." Fain was an FBI agent who had spent the last year of his life
infiltrating Earth First! Peg Millett's trust was his opening wedge. But
when the FBI flare whited out the desert like a giant X ray, Fain's
federal bones popped out like a jitterbugging skeleton left over from
El Día de los Muertos. Peg Millett took one hard, fast look and ran
like hell. Eluding fifty FBI agents who were tracking her on foot, in
trucks, on horseback, and by helicopter, she disappeared into the
cactus-studded hills.

Long before agents got a fix on Millett, Dave Foreman's friends were
tracking down help. Some of the first calls went out to the Wyoming
law offices of Gerry Spence. The flamboyant "cowboy from Jackson"
had never lost a case. Spence earned his reputation as a defender of
the little guy by winning $1.8 million in damages for the family of
Karen Silkwood, a whistle-blower at a Kerr-McGee plutonium-
processing plant who had died under suspicious circumstances on her
way to meet a *New York Times* reporter. Not all of Spence's clients
were so sympathetic. He had won more than $1 million in damages
for a former Miss Wyoming who claimed to be personally maligned
by a *Penthouse* satire of the Miss America pageant, although the judgment was later reversed. A few years later, Spence punched a few

more holes in his white-hat persona when he represented Philippine dictatoress Imelda Marcos. But Spence proved that he hadn't lost his principles—or his ability to recognize a good platform—when he took on Foreman's case pro bono. Dave Foreman was the environmental movement's most charismatic figure. More than any other individual, he was responsible for linking the words *radical* and *environmentalist* in the public mind. Not to mention the minds of the people who ran the Federal Bureau of Investigation.

The FBI had been interested in Earth First! since 1981. The Weather Underground had long since been rained out and the G-men in J. C. Penney suits were stashing most of the gun-toting neo-Nazis of the radical right behind bars. By 1987, when the FBI admits it began a serious investigation of Earth First!, terrorists had become an endangered species on the American continent. Revolutionaries were even scarcer. Antiabortion fanatics who tried to blow up women's clinics were not considered fair game under official government policy. So apart from a few bomb-throwing Puerto Rican separatists, tough-talking nature lovers like Dave Foreman were the obvious choice when the agency had to justify its whopping $35 million a year counterterrorism budget. This fact was not lost on Gerry Spence. He would later thunder out in court that Foreman's bust was part of a blanket attempt to squelch the radical environmental movement. Since the domestic intelligence scandals of the 1960s and 1970s, the FBI had been officially prohibited from making direct political hits. Spence would do his best to put the FBI, not Dave Foreman, on trial.

In the meantime, the goal was to get Dave the hell out of jail. That was Jim Eaton's job. Eaton was a jovial, stocky blue-collar Californian who had left the Wilderness Society in the same 1970s purge as Foreman. When he heard about Foreman's arrest, Eaton activated an informal network called the wilderness grapevine. The grapevine was made up of about a hundred career environmentalists. They were westerners, by adoption if not by birth. Most had come of age in the 1970s, an era rich in both romantic turmoil and substance-abuse casualties. Usually the grapevine was little more than a long-distance substitute for the backyard laundry line. But in a genuine crisis, it was a crack organizing tool. The seventy-three character references that greeted U.S. Magistrate Morton Sitver at Dave Foreman's arraignment two days later were the grapevine's handiwork. They came from people like David Brower, aka the Archdruid, a white-haired visionary who had transformed the Sierra Club from a hokey hiking club into a political behemoth, creating in the process the template for a modern environmental group. There was even an affidavit from Foreman's ex-wife Debbie Sease, attesting to her belief that her former husband was not a flight risk. Since leaving the intense New Mexico cowboy who turned her on to politics, Sease had become a high-level Washington, D.C., lobbyist.

After a lengthy hearing, Dave Foreman was released on $50,000 bail. The other three defendants did not have similar clout. Characterized by the government as "terrorists," they would spend the next two months in jail. Six months later, a fifth indictment was handed down. Ilse Asplund, Mark Davis's lover and Peggy Millett's best friend, was also charged with felony crimes, although she had been home in Prescott on the night of the power-line expedition. These ecosaboteurs were not typical felony suspects. All but Davis were college graduates. They were intelligent, articulate, well mannered, and extraordinarily well read. They had been brought up on Dr. Spock and rock and roll. Until they were arrested, they thought that doing the right thing made them invulnerable.

Dave Foreman was the only exception. Since starting Earth First! in 1980, Dave Foreman had known this day might come. Later he admitted that his sense of danger had been rather abstract. But when he finally had a chance to reflect on the events surrounding his arrest, the only real surprise was the outpouring of support from the mainstream movement. He had traveled quite a ways up a dangerous, unmarked side canyon. But he was still a member of the tribe.

He hadn't always wanted to be. After leaving his high-powered Washington, D.C., lobbyist's job in the cold winter of 1979, Foreman did his best to make sure he could never go back. Inspired by Edward Abbey's 1975 novel *The Monkey Wrench Gang*, the founders of Earth First! made ecotage—burning bulldozers, spiking trees, yanking up survey stakes—an attention-grabbing tactic in their no-compromise approach to saving wilderness. But to a knowledgeable minority, monkeywrenching was almost beside the point. It was Earth First!'s willingness to cut through the sagebrush-scented bullshit of the western power elite that made the group truly radical. Foreman and his friends were among the first people to realize the true depth of the environmental crisis. All of them had read enough to understand that the land's ability to replenish itself was being choked off by industrial development. If only half of what they said was true, environmental issues were no longer a question of jobs vs. nature, snail darters vs. dams. Life itself was threatened.

For ten years, Earth First!'s proposals for biological preserves were pretty much ignored. But by the 1990s they had filtered out to mainstream environmental groups. In somewhat altered form, they were being debated in publications like *The New York Times* and *The Atlantic*. Slowly, suit-and-tie conservationists were rediscovering the maxim of Sierra Club founder John Muir: "To pick out anything by itself, we find it hitched to everything else in the universe." It was high time. Since the movement had become professionalized, most environmentalists lived in two worlds. In the real world of nature, salmon spawned in rivers beneath the soft russet bark of redwood trees and mountain lions took down the weakest of each year's deer herd. But in the "real" world, trees were being cut at a pace rapid enough to turn transparent mountain streams into channels of silt and mud. Because of government-sponsored extermination of predators, deer were overpopulating and becoming a "pest." Environmentalists found themselves agreeing to absurdities: everything from the ugly slaughter of buffalo migrating outside man-made park boundaries to wholesale destruction of the remaining 10 percent of the country's ancient forests. Ecologist Raymond Dasmann called it World War Three, industrial man's war on nature. As in any war, civilians were caught in the crossfire. Environmentalists found themselves seriously discussing the costs and benefits of environmental poisons. Was air conditioning worth .0125 human deaths per million?

It was insanity. Or at least schizophrenia. The founders of Earth First! took on the confusing task of integrating these contradictory worlds. Cowboys without illusions, they were determined to roll back the industrialized frontier. Beneath it were remnants of the American Eden, still plentiful, still possible. It was this wild, romantic idea that truly threatened the timber, mining, and ranching barons who had kept the politics of the American West on a tight rein since the closing of the frontier.

To men of their immense power, monkeywrenching was mostly an annoyance. But it was also an indication that the stakes in the environmental wars had risen. Skirmishes between nature lovers and the western business elite had gone on for at least a century. Now the conflict was escalating. The environmental movement had become increasingly powerful. At the same time, industrial development was cutting deeper into the heart of the West. Something had to give.

Another generation of environmentalists might have been content to redouble their lobbying efforts, push for better press coverage, or print yet another calendar with glossy color photographs. But the 1960s had shown even die-hard rednecks like Dave Foreman that you could influence the debate from the outside. And you could have a damn good time doing it.

For ten years, Earth First! did just that. By the late 1980s, the self-proclaimed anarchist "non-organization" boasted more than five thousand subscribers to its newspaper, the closest thing the group had to a membership roster. Earth First! activists dressed as bears kept popping up on the television news like *Wild Kingdom* reruns on LSD. Taking the term *photo opportunity* to lengths previously unknown in the environmental movement, they were doing everything from bicycle-locking their necks to bulldozers (the famed "Buggis Maneuver" named after the crazed Texan, now deceased, who invented it) to parading down Wall Street dressed as spotted owls.

And all around the country, there were quiet acts of sabotage.

Nachtwerke, Ed Abbey called it. Throwing a monkeywrench into the works of Demonic Progress. Dave Foreman's rabble-rousing, foot-stomping fundamentalist-preacher speechifying was more than an institution. It had become a virus.

The arrests in the desert on May 30, 1989, were only the first in a series of blows aimed at Earth First! Until then the group's most notable piece of crank mail had been a fan letter from prison-bound Manson groupie Squeaky Fromme. Suddenly Earth First! activists from California to New York were hit by repeated volleys of obscene, threatening hate mail. Faked inflammatory leaflets bearing the group's name mysteriously appeared in places where they could do the most harm, towns like Moab, Utah, where an annual off-road vehicle race attracted hordes of ham-fisted dirt bikers. Paranoia bubbled over as suspicious-acting newcomers tried to involve veteran members in violent acts. Ordinary stresses magnified, particularly those felt by Earth First! newsletter editors casting back to long-forgotten high-school French to figure out how to pluralize *agent provocateur*.

After the arrests a number of Earth First!ers asked for advice from people who had been active in radical groups in the 1960s and 1970s. Veterans of the antiwar movement and the American Indian Movement said they recognized a familiar tone in the harassment: incendiary and crude, peppered with racist and sexist epithets. Decades of lawsuits and reams of investigative reporting had identified the FBI as the source of similar harassment against antiwar activists in the Socialist Workers Party, the Black Panther Party, and other short-lived un-American institutions. Could the FBI itself be the origin of letters beginning "Dear Faggot"? Or was it someone in the Sahara Club, a bunch of thugs who promoted off-road vehicle use in the delicate, spooky moonscape of the California desert? There was neither time nor money to find out. As the trial of the Arizona Five began in the high desert town of Prescott, Arizona, the enemy remained invisible.

Or nearly so. In the late 1980s, a spate of right-wing, pro-industry groups rose up like dragon's teeth wrapped in yellow ribbons. They claimed to be homegrown, but many of these groups were quietly funded by industry. Some of these down-home folks even claimed their own brand of monkeywrenching. But they were utterly bereft of the wit and good humor that had characterized Earth First! Nobody knew who was to blame when Earth First! activist Judi Bari's pelvis was blown apart by a pipe bomb in Oakland, California, on May 24, 1990. But it was clear that someone had missed the joke entirely.

Judi Bari survived the bomb, but would walk with a painful limp for the rest of her life. Earth First!, too, was crippled by the abrupt escalation into violence. Even before the explosion, most of the Earth First! founders had begun to move on. They believed it was either time to let the locals take over or to cart Earth First! out to the desert and let the redheaded wattle-necked turkey vultures make it part of the food chain. Because Earth First! had succeeded. Beneath their beer-drinking, gonzo forays into guerrilla theater—and occasional lapses into guerrilla war—Earth First!'s founders shared the goals of the great innovative environmentalists who preceded them, people like Aldo Leopold, Bob Marshall, and David Brower. With these historic figures very much in mind, the hardscrabble Earth First! cowboys expanded the reach of the hundred-year-old environmental movement to include a truly ecological worldview. But many of them sacrificed their careers—and a few risked their lives—to do it.

The Buckaroos had a good run, longer than anyone could have expected. In a backhanded tribute, former Sierra Club conservation director Doug Scott sharply criticized Earth First! for "playing the Pied Piper of Hamelin." Their wild ways seduced an entire generation of environmentalists away from the dull, unglamorous work that is the engine of most environmental legislation. If Scott is right, then perhaps the environmental movement was like a lover stuck in a stale relationship. In their well-intentioned effort to ante up to a losing game, many career environmentalists had lost touch with the pure, transcendental rush that landed them at the table in the first place.

Scott was right about a lot of things, but he was wrong about at least one. This was not the first generation ripe for seduction. Dave Foreman's romantic vision had already captured the most daring intellectual environmentalists of a previous generation. Not the least of whom was Foreman himself, who started off his forty-fourth year facing the prospect of spending several decades in a federal pen.

The cottontail froze when Peg Millett dove beneath the acid-green paloverde tree. They stared at each other, the dun-colored rabbit and the woman trying to make herself invisible. A $16-million helicopter hovered above them. Inside it, men peered down through infrared goggles to spot anything warm and living on the desert floor.

Millett slowed her breathing. She waited. After several minutes, the sound of the machine died away. She lifted her head. Visions of Armageddon had subsided hours ago, when she yielded to the rhythm of flight. Now her life was measured by her own metronomic footsteps; by the sky; by the mountain passes and the miles; by hints and intimations carried on the subtle movements of desiccated air.

Before the night was over, Peg Millett would hike sixteen miles through the desert with no compass or flashlight. In the morning she would hitch a ride back to Prescott. She would spend most of the day at her office, shopping by phone for a lawyer. By late afternoon, FBI agents would come to arrest her.

But for now she was safe. The rabbit unfroze, a diorama figure come to life. Gingerly, it began nosing the triangle-leaf bur sage at the edge of the wash. It ignored Millett, as if she were just another creature going about her business in the dry, cracked landscape, under a sheet of stars.

The
Education of
an Environmentalist

The achieved West had given the United States something that no people had ever had before, an internal domestic empire.

—Bernard De Voto

I'm just a hick horseshoer who thinks he's a bronc rider.

—Dave Foreman, 1991

1960–Texas

TEXAS HILL COUNTRY starts northwest of San Antonio. Dry flat desert gives way to limestone hills engraved with meandering rivers; prickly pear yields pride of place to juniper and oak. From their southern edge, the rounded hillsides run right up through the middle of the state like a rumpled blanket. The towns here have more churches than bars; people are distinctly, but unoriginally, polite. Generally these towns do not hasten to accept strangers. But in Schertz, Texas, just outside Randolph Air Force Base, they welcome them. Military men and their families are favored guests. It is a patriotic town.

From a small, white-frame building on the corners of Curtis and Pfiel Streets comes the sound of singing. There is a congregation of about 150 inside the double doors. With their own hands, they built the uncomfortable wooden pews they're sitting on. They hammered up the joists, painted the walls a stark white, installed the venetian blinds. This is a frontier church, the Church of Christ. There is no figure of Jesus, no stained glass, no cross. In front of the simple wooden baptistery, there is a sunken tub. It measures about four feet by seven feet, like a mini swimming pool or a giant birdbath. A short, skinny kid named David with deep-dish blue eyes and a Leave It to Beaver haircut is standing in it, looking excited and nervous. The preacher strides into the pool, decked out in big rubber waders. In slow motion, intoning words from the Bible, he places his hand on the boy's head and pushes him all the way down into the water. It is a release; you can hear the congregation sigh. When the kid comes up for air, he breaks into a big, innocent thirteen-year-old smile and the congregation revs up into a hymn. Trust and Obey, they sing, for there's no other way to be happy with Jesus.

In 1907, Dave Foreman's great-grandparents drove their wagons across the wide Missouri to Tucumcari, New Mexico, becoming part of one of the great last waves of frontier migration. Later, Foreman would read in the books of Bernard De Voto about the historical currents that drove his family west. Nobody was better suited to unearthing the ironies of the American West than the brilliant and abrasive De Voto, a misfit who fled Mormon Utah for Harvard's intellectual high country in 1915. In De Voto's analysis, the western myth was stillborn, laced with nostalgia from the outset but no less poetic for all that. The West's ultimate irony, De Voto wrote in 1934, lay in the fact that it was the place where frontier culture broke down in the face of aridity. "The pioneer's tradition of brawn and courage, initiative, individualism, and self-help was unavailing here. He had, that is, to ally himself with the force which sentimental critics are sure he wanted to escape from: the Industrial Revolution."[1]

In the 1880s the Industrial Revolution began a century-long binge of dam building that would ultimately irrigate half a continent. It brought peaches, apricots, and oranges to the desert. It ripped copper from the heart of Arizona and the mountains of Montana, wrapped railroads like iron chains around the basin and range, made and lost fortunes for magnates in Pittsburgh and New York. It rerouted rivers and shaved the tops off mountains to get at the coal that lay beneath them. It built company towns where rugged individualists toiled year in and year out to live in company houses, shop in company stores, and send their kids to company schools.

But the myth of the frontier persisted. It persisted, not just because it came wrapped in the glamour of celluloid heroes, but because it was deeply embedded in the ethos of a people who sought out the hundredth meridian as if it were a stairway to heaven instead of merely a degree of longitude. From the 1830s until long after the turn of the century, tens of thousands of Scotch-Irish immigrants made their way west, bringing with them a religion founded on the romance of an untouched land. Like many of their fellow travelers, Dave Foreman's maternal grandparents, the Crawfords, were members of the Church of Christ, a fundamentalist frontier sect that split from traditional Presbyterian orthodoxy in the early 1800s. Its premier theologian was a Scottish immigrant named Thomas Campbell. Reviled as a heretic, Campbell wanted to heal divisions within Christianity by restoring the primitive church of the New Testament, to "recover the primordial past that stood behind the historical past."[2] In 1801, another renegade Presbyterian named Barton Stone had the same idea. Like Campbell, Stone believed that each local church should be completely independent, with no creed but the Bible. No bishops, no missionaries, no dogma, just the word of God. Stone, a charismatic preacher who thumped the Bible with reckless abandon, started holding outdoor revival meetings in Cane Ridge, Kentucky. It wasn't long before Cane Ridge looked as if the 82nd Airborne had landed. White tents billowed like abandoned parachutes on the open grass. Ten thousand people at a time came to the meetings; crowds overflowed into the fields. The wealthy brought their own tents, preferring not to mingle with the hoi polloi even at the gates of heaven. By 1811 the Stone movement had churches in twelve states. After a shaky alliance with the Baptists went bad in 1830, Thomas Campbell and his son Alexander linked up with Stone in 1832. The movement experienced its greatest growth over the next two decades, spreading West with covered wagons, domesticated cattle, and smallpox.

It was a uniquely American religion, a Huck-Finn-on-the-river church where the individual confronted God and his conscience *mano a mano*. Without an established creed, the Bible was not only the Word, but the Last Word. The lack of a central organization made the Church of Christ anarchistic in the purest sense. It was not chaotic, but organic, with each congregation growing out of a local community and culture. The "Christians in the West" were criticized for being "disorganizers, having no form of government, and aiming a destructive blow at all church government," explained their leader Barton Stone. Only if we're lucky, was the gist of Stone's response to his critics. Members of the Church of Christ ". . . simply did not concern themselves with organizations, new or old, or with systematic theological construction. Their concern, instead, was for freedom."

Freedom had its limits, of course. Christians were not allowed to drink or dance. Musical instruments were barred from church. Instead, the human voice became an instrument—in song, debate, and most of all, fiery preaching. These voices rang with a compelling vision. In a raw land that seemed to stand outside time, people dreamed of recovering their primal purity through strict self-abnegation and good works. Legends appeared suggesting that the Church of Christ sprang from an unbroken succession of Christian primitivist outcasts dating back to the time of Jesus. It was as if the church was calling back a sense of rightness, a primeval norm that had disappeared in the clouds of exhaust generated by the combustion engine. "Human time . . . embodied the disastrous aftermath of the fall" to the frontier Christians. They embraced "the idea of building anew in the American wilderness on the true and ancient foundations."

Baptism by total immersion was a rite to be taken seriously. When Dave Foreman took the plunge at age thirteen, he took it even more seriously than most. He had already decided that he would be a preacher when he grew up, just like Asa Lipscomb, the minister in Schertz. Lipscomb was a distinguished-looking man who had known David since he was in kindergarten. Not many outside the family had; the Foremans had already moved eleven times since David was born in 1946. His father, Benjamin "Skip" Foreman, was an Air Force pilot. Each time Skip was reassigned, his wife, Lorane, would pack up David, his younger brother, Steve, born in 1953, and their baby sister, Roxanne, who was born in 1955, and move them all to another town or maybe to another country. By the time the Foremans arrived in Schertz, they had lived in New Mexico, Arizona, Texas, Nevada, California, Bermuda, and the Philippines. Yet David's childhood had been spent in a single neocolonial milieu. Wherever they moved, the Foremans remained part of the military establishment, with its rows of whitewashed houses and PX privileges. Only the scenery changed, from the tropics, where loneliness mingled with exoticism, to culturally barren American towns where the only aesthetic was the magnificent, sculptured desert sky. It was really just a lucky coincidence that brought Asa Lipscomb into David's life again; as churchpeople, the Lipscombs were part of another gypsy work force and likely to disappear at a moment's notice. The Foremans and the Lipscombs had become friends while they all lived in Reno, Nevada, in 1951 and Asa Lipscomb had taken a liking to David. David wasn't a hard kid to like: intelligent, well behaved, and very gentle, especially with animals. With Skip away so much, David attached himself to the older man. Like many Church of Christ preachers, Lipscomb was a raftershaking orator. David wanted to be just like him when he grew up.

It wasn't that David didn't get enough attention. Lorane read to him all the time and indulged his fascination with animals. Each night they pored over *American Wildlife, Illustrated*, with its big, stylized color plates showing jaguars, mountain lions, and bison. David even got upset when Lorane vacuumed up spiderwebs. He was no less tough on himself, praying for weeks that it had been a stick, not a worm, that he accidentally trampled on the way to school. Having grown up on a farm in eastern New Mexico, Lorane shared David's interest in nature. But she had her limits. When they lived on Randolph Air Force Base, he captured a bull snake. Lorane let him keep it as a pet, but he was allowed to let it out of its cage only while she was out shopping or at church. Mother and son had a code: Lorane would honk her horn as she came up the driveway so that David could return the snake to captivity before she walked in the door.

Foreman may have been a bit of a mama's boy, but his shyness and sensitivity were tempered by a streak of rowdy self-confidence. He had become an Eagle Scout about the same time he was baptized and excelled at virtually all his Boy Scout activities. He liked to entertain his classmates by dancing on the top of his desk and was a good speaker in church. "He was shy among strangers but not before a crowd," recalled Lorane. His confidence was tested, though, by a sadistic fluke of the adolescent endocrine system. In fifth grade, he reached the unimpressive height of four feet ten and stayed there. And stayed there and stayed there.

By tenth grade, David still hadn't cracked five feet. That year, the family moved once again, this time to Blaine, Washington. When Lorane took him to register for his first day of school, the woman working behind the counter at the administration office took one look at him and said, "You must want the elementary school."

"Embarrassed David something awful," Lorane said. "He was so small and so smart, when he started school none of the kids would have anything to do with him because they thought he was a child prodigal or something. Oh, gosh. But they found out."

Foreman was good at turning inauspicious beginnings into triumphs. As a military brat, he had to be. In Blaine, he was helped by the long-awaited capitulation of his recalcitrant gene, which finally let him shoot up eight inches. In eleventh grade, having attained the borderline normal height of five feet six, he was elected class president. But that success was short-lived, because the family moved yet again, this time to Blythe, California, a bland, isolated agricultural community planted smack in the middle of the Mojave Desert.

"I think that that move hurt David more than any of the others ever had, because he was really starting to have some fun," said Lorane. "You know, and he had some really good friends and they weren't rough and tough or anything."

David seemed to bounce back from almost anything, but his younger brother, Steve, wasn't weathering the constant upheavals as well. Dave was shy and serious; Steve was a golden-haired charmer. In Blythe, Steve started hanging out with hoods. His parents worried that things came to him too easily, that he wasn't developing the right kind of character. But there seemed to be little they could do about it.

Foreman spent a miserable senior year in claustrophobic Blythe. He hiked a lot in the Mojave Desert. In contrast to the bleak town, the desert seemed surreal and full of life. It was the kind of life he liked best; fat chuckwallas doing push-ups on dry, superheated boulders and cactus wrens singing their ratchety tune from hiding places in the cream-colored leaves of yucca trees. Even in Blythe, he wasn't completely antisocial. His eleventh-grade electoral victory had strengthened his interest in politics. Instead of running for office in a brand-new high school where nobody knew him, he worked for Barry Goldwater in the Republican presidential primary. The family moved back to San Antonio, Texas, that summer. In the fall, David attended junior college there. But after his freshman year he decided to go to the University of New Mexico. New Mexico was where his mother's family lived. What roots he possessed were there. In the summer of 1965, he moved back to Bernalillo and took a dreadful job as an encyclopedia salesman. In the fall he started school.

In Albuquerque, Foreman thrived intellectually. He also began to rebel. His grades were lousy, but he continued a lifelong habit of reading anything that didn't have its covers hammered shut. At first he signed up as a biology major, but soon switched to anthropology, one of the school's strongest departments. After discovering the British historian Arnold Toynbee, he became a history major. These days Toynbee is regarded in academic circles as little more than a footnote, but his theory about the crash of industrial civilization made sense to Foreman. It resembled the Last Judgment, with machines doing the work of destruction.

That year, Foreman found another intellectual mentor. Just as some people may be susceptible to a certain virus, a certain number of college students in have a constitutional weakness for the work of novelist Ayn Rand. The 1940s Übermensch architect Howard Roark, Rand's protagonist in The Fountainhead, embodies one of the most extreme cases of a novelist falling in love with her creation. The passion was contagious. In Roark, Rand created not just a character but a cultural phenomenon, the enshrinement of a Nietzschean supercapitalist superman. Her cult of the individual won many converts in the late fifties and early sixties, when it seemed to some that the American capitalist system might hold the promise of utopia.

Like most viruses, enthusiasm for Rand's work generally struck hard, then disappeared. Foreman's ardor cooled when he discovered Rand's antipathy toward environmentalism. The only permanent effect of his infatuation was the loss of his religious beliefs. Foreman adopted Rand's philosophy of atheistic objectivism, almost too energetically. To put his newfound dogma into practice, Foreman gave his father's watered-down Nixon Republicanism a jolt of 190-proof libertarianism and joined the Young Americans for Freedom. By becoming a libertarian, Foreman stepped outside the traditional political spectrum of liberal and conservative. While conservatives believe in economic freedom and liberals value individual freedom, libertarians believe in maximizing both. In a sense, libertarians have more in common with anarchists than they do with most U.S. politicians. Barry Goldwater was an exception—Goldwater himself had libertarian inclinations and Rand had inspired a whole coven of Goldwater Republicans, including Foreman. In 1966 Foreman became state chair of Young Americans for Freedom, a libertarian youth organization with conservative overtones. Christianity was out. Freedom was in.

Or a new name for freedom. It was almost as if a department-store window dresser had changed a set of clothes, but left the mannequins in place. Despite his loss of faith, Foreman retained many of the ideas that he had learned as a churchgoing Christian in the intermountain West. He still believed in individual conscience crashing through the barriers of bureaucracy and dogma. After growing up in a place where the economy was based on raw materials exploited by rich eastern industrialists, he recoiled from any social organization that was not small and locally controlled, feeling that centralized power was anathema to freedom.

Foreman's own freedom was about to be severely curtailed by the Vietnam War. Brought up on tales of a global communist conspiracy, he had been mouthing off in support of the war in campus debates with the SDS. In 1967 he began to doubt his position, but he kept his reservations to himself. Besides, the military appealed to his competitive streak. He had started a fitness regime back in his ninety-seven-pound weakling days, running and lifting weights on alternate mornings. Now that he was a healthy six-footer, staying in good shape remained an almost obsessive concern. He was confident that he could breeze through basic training. The idea was to be a war hero, go to law school, then run for Congress.

Besides, Foreman didn't really feel that he had a choice. It was the height of the war and unless they were wealthy or well connected, young men of military age could either enlist, face the draft, or take up duck hunting in the north woods. Foreman chose to enroll in officer-candidate school. The Air Force and the Navy were booked, so he ended up with the Marines in Quantico, Virginia. As it turned out, Foreman and the Marine Corps were a match made in hell.

It took only a week for Foreman to realize he had made a terrible mistake. He might have been strong, but he was also clumsy and uncoordinated, always had been. To his dismay, he discovered that being in good shape didn't matter if you couldn't tell left from right on the parade ground. The shy kid who had overcome so many handicaps—being new in school, shorter than everybody else, and way too smart—suddenly found himself back in the role of the class doofus. But this time, the other kids didn't just ostracize him. The verbal abuse—unremitting and obscene—was followed by nightly raids. Foreman was awakened by a crowd of thugs who beat him up and, most humiliating of all, shaved his head.

Foreman knew when he was licked. On weekend leave, he went to the Library of Congress for help. In that august institution, he researched his way out of the military. The quickest fix, he discovered, was to declare yourself a communist. So Foreman sent a letter to his commanding officer telling him he was no longer loyal to the President of the United States or the Marine Corps. Not only was he a communist, but he was planning to join the SDS and the Progressive Labor Party and "dedicate [his] life to their crusade for true social justice." Foreman also wrote letters to the Communist Party and to the "Commandant and the Storm Troopers" (aka his base commander) announcing his commitment to "world revolution" and stating that "soon the Fascists will so [sic] against the wall and blood will flow." Leaving nothing to chance, he made an appointment with the drill instructor. Instead of giving him the Alice's Restaurant routine ("I want to kill. Keewl! Keewl!"), he took a surer route. I've been wrong about the war. I hope the Viet Cong win. Fuck the system, he rat-a-tat-tatted.

Foreman was transferred to casual company, a holding tank for Marine misfits. From there he would either be discharged or sent to the training center at Parris Island, South Carolina, as a regular enlisted man. Known for its brutal indoctrination of raw recruits, Parris Island made Quantico look like a finishing school. Along with its violence, it was renowned for its sand fleas, which swarmed up your sweaty trousers as you stood at attention in the broiling sun like a prisoner on Devil's Island. It was, in Foreman's words, "a place where you died."

One night Foreman was absently pushing a floor buffer across the battered linoleum of an office floor. Outside, a quartered yellow moon ticked off the days before some beefy-necked officer would decide if he was going to live or die. As he passed a desk, he caught sight of his name in a maze of manila folders. Not wanting to arouse suspicion, he kept the floor buffer on, propping it up against a wall while he snatched the folder and read its contents. His eyes moved frantically over the typewritten pages until, beneath the buffer's mechanical roar, he read the words *Parris Island*.

Skip was the one who got the call. It was David's friend Mike. His words rushed out like a clatter of falling rock. Dave was holed up in the Sandia Mountains outside Albuquerque, threatening to shoot anyone who came after him. Hungry and exhausted, Dave had stumbled to a telephone booth and called Mike, asking him to bring him food. Mike agonized over what to do. Finally he called the Foremans in Zuni, where Skip was working for the Federal Aviation Administration.

"God, we jumped in that old car fast," remembers Lorane. Skip drove up to the mountains with Mike, while Lorane spent a sleepless night with her relatives in Albuquerque. As dawn turned the Sandia range pink the next morning, Skip and Mike showed up with a pale, shaken David. Lorane wept at the sight of him.

After serving thirty-one days in the Marine Corps brig, David was released with an undesirable discharge. Years later, Foreman would say that his episode with the Marines was more than disillusioning. It caused his whole worldview to implode. "I was crazy as a bedbug throughout this period and for a year afterwards," he said.

Not knowing what else to do, he moved in with his parents in Zuni. Father and son were barely speaking. Skip and Lorane's brother, another career military man, had turned David in to the MPs. So angry he could barely look his son in the eye, Skip blurted out that he wished David had gotten killed in Vietnam; it would have been less dishonorable. It took years for father and son to reestablish their relationship. In some ways, they had never really had one, because Skip was absent so much. When he was home, he tried to reassert his authority, but instead ended up alternating unpredictably between strictness and laxity. The equally arbitrary but far more violent discipline of the Marine Corps—"Their educational philosophy is to destroy a person's individuality and turn them into hamburger" became Foreman's standard mot on the subject—couldn't have been better designed to push Skip Foreman's oldest son into finding out just how far he could stray from his family's military roots.

At first Dave didn't go very far, just down the hill to his cousin's trading post where he worked at the undemanding job of night manager from the spring of 1969 until the summer of 1970. He became friends with a guy named Jack Dembs, a big hunk of a cowboy who worked with Skip at the FAA. At thirty, Jack was seven years older than Foreman. But both men had things to learn from each other. Foreman had been changing fast. In college, Foreman was a stomp, not a hippie. Even though he went to school at the height of the counterculture, he hadn't smoked pot until after he graduated; he was such a redneck nobody would sell it to him. But by 1970, Foreman was turning into a hippie, albeit a short-haired one. He turned Jack on to marijuana. One night, the two guys drove up to Albuquerque to see *Easy Rider,* which really blew their minds. Later Foreman would affectionately say he had created a monster. In less than a year, Jack's hair was long, he was divorced, and he had quit his nice, secure job at the FAA. Jack and Foreman picked up two motorcycles, old BSA 600 cc thumpers, and hit the road in late spring. They toured Yellowstone, then veered west, where they roared down the California coast to Big Sur, searching for the totemic upside-down camera angles and low-budget special effects of the authentic American experience, 1960s-style.

They returned to Zuni in the fall, but the trip seemed to go on and on. An old friend of Jack's had a surreal subcontracting job for the Air Force and he farmed out much of his work to Jack and Dave. They'd drive 400 miles into the middle of nowhere, lay out an acre of canvas panels in a specific pattern, and leave them there to bake for six hours while a distant satellite snapped a photo. Then they would pick up the panels, drive 400 miles, and repeat the whole process. It reeked of Lewis Mumford, the twentieth-century political philosopher who dated the debasement of the human race to the days of the pyramids, when people first became mere cogs subordinated to a grandiose, inhuman technic. But instead of being crushed beneath the wheels of progress, Jack and Dave scurried happily around the West's basin and range like bearded, dope-smoking worker ants, the all-seeing eye of the megamachine hovering invisibly above them.

Jack went to horseshoeing school in the spring of 1971 and Dave followed him that summer. Still uncoordinated, Dave was a lousy horseshoer. But he was elected president of his horseshoeing class, which may have been a sign that politics really were his métier, especially because he hadn't even run for the office. The cowboys all voted for him because he had been helping them with their book work. After the eight-week course was over, Jack and Dave moved up to an old adobe with no running water that Jack's family owned in the Jemez Mountains outside Santa Fe. They supported themselves with the canvas-humping job and occasional horseshoeing gigs.

The Jemez Mountains were once active volcanoes. Today cattle graze in the bowl of a giant, grassy caldera. Hot springs and waterfalls lie hidden in the folds of steep, reddish hills. When he lived in the mountains in the summer and fall of 1971 Foreman did a lot of back-packing and river running. On days when the solitude of the mountains became too much, he'd drive down to Albuquerque and hang out with his friends from college. One of them, Dave Seeley, was bartending at a joint next door to a Pizza Hut. He introduced Dave to some folks from the Black Mesa Defense Fund, which was based in Santa Fe. Soon Dave added Santa Fe to his usual peregrinations, stopping in at the Black Mesa office to volunteer every couple of weeks.

At Black Mesa, Foreman was introduced to a unique species of anarcho-environmentalism native to the American Southwest. The Black Mesa Defense Fund was formed in 1970 to stop construction of a coal mine atop a brooding desert highland inhabited by Hopi and Navajo Indians. Its founders were artists, musicians, and rich kids. They were educated roughnecks with a bohemian bent and a political passion that for a while, at least, became all-consuming. Piece by piece, the activists amassed information revealing that the mesa was the black heart of a massive, politically interconnected series of public-works projects that stretched from Los Angeles to Wyoming. The fight over Black Mesa became the ultimate environmental David-and-Goliath story. Black Mesa Defense's puny slingshots ranged from filing lawsuits to vandalizing heavy equipment. It was a frenetic, free-form, whole-hearted effort that lasted an exhausting three years, a spindly eccentric cactus with wild magenta flowers but very sharp spines. An aberration, an art form, and a rescue mission all in one, Black Mesa Defense was to the Sierra Club what John Coltrane was to Bach. It was a hell of an introduction to the environmental movement.

In characteristic entrepreneurial fashion, Foreman decided to start his own version of Black Mesa Defense. In late 1971 he moved back to Albuquerque to open a satellite office for River Defense, a Black Mesa offshoot. But River Defense was just the beginning. Dave Foreman had figured out what he wanted to do with his life. To prepare for a career as a conservationist, he enrolled in undergraduate science classes at the University of New Mexico, planning to apply to a master's program in biology.

As usual, Foreman's studies took a backseat to politics. Right away, he joined a student conservation group and began writing an environmental column for the school newspaper. He cajoled his way onto the New Mexico Wilderness Study Committee, which was run by a group of hoary old geezers who looked as if they had been working on outdoor issues since territorial days. Realizing volunteer labor was in short supply, the Wilderness Committee reluctantly signed up the scruffy-looking student to coordinate the environmentalist response to the review of the Gila National Forest.

In Albuquerque, Foreman started hanging around a pretty, part-Cherokee bartender named Debbie Sease. Like Foreman, Sease had been a student at the University of New Mexico. She possessed the impenetrable steadiness of an outdoor guide and later became one for a few years. But beneath her steely river-runner's facade, she was as shy as Foreman. From across the bar, Foreman's blue eyes and sandy, dark blond hair blended in with a thousand other eager-looking male faces of Anglo-Saxon persuasion. But when they met a little more formally on a wilderness study trip, Foreman was able to make a stronger impression. She gave him a copy of Edward Abbey's book *Desert Solitaire*, a loosely connected series of essays that were a lazy seduction, a roar of anger, and a religious offering to wilderness in the Southwest. "It was the first book I'd ever read that I totally agreed with," said Foreman.[3] By the spring of 1972, they were living together and organizing the third Earth Day at the University of New Mexico. Partway through the semester, Foreman dropped out of school, too busy with environmental work to keep up with his studies. He began the compulsive work schedule that would give him a sense of order in the midst of chaos for the next twenty years.

The geezers on the Wilderness Study Committee were unprepared for this onslaught of obsessive hippie redneck energy. Foreman took over the Gila wilderness campaign, arranging for a poster to be made, putting together a slide show to get people worked up about the region's beauty, and organizing raiding parties of environmentalists to testify at Forest Service hearings. His work caught the attention of Jerry Mallett, the youthful éminence grise of the Wilderness Society's Denver office. Mallett spoke to his boss Clif Merritt and in January 1973, Foreman was invited back to Washington, D.C., for a Wilderness Society lobbying seminar. Another young hotshot named Doug Scott showed Foreman around town. Neither was particularly impressed with the other. But Scott's lack of enthusiasm didn't prevent seasoned lobbyist Harry Crandell from offering Foreman a job as the group's New Mexico field consultant. The pay was minimal, even for those days—$250 a month, plus $50 expenses. But money was the last thing on Foreman's mind. He accepted the offer. And he was thrilled.

In the flush of his exalted new position, Foreman and Sease moved to the tiny town of Glenwood, New Mexico. The best thing about Glenwood was the country that surrounded it. The Gila Wilderness Area and the Gila Primitive Area were made up of nearly 600,000 acres of juniper-clad mountains where you could lose yourself for days at a time. They lived in the town's oldest house, a tin-roofed farmhouse with foot-and-a-half adobe walls, exposed wood beams, and a corral for Nellie Belle Queen Bee Junebug, their prized mule. They paid only $40 a month to live there—rent even an environmentalist could afford. In October of 1975, they were married in Debbie's stepsister's backyard in Albuquerque. They bought land in Glenwood with two other couples. Eventually they hoped to build an adobe of their own. Debbie spent hours sketching its elaborate plan.

Glenwood was the real West, where the past is all recent and the line between myth and reality is weaker than truck-stop coffee. On a lucid day, Foreman's landlord could be persuaded to reminisce about Butch Cassidy and the Sundance Kid. The two outlaws had spent a few months working at French's ranch, about three miles away in the town of Alma. The landlord didn't remember much about them, just that neither looked a stitch like Paul Newman. But Foreman was enchanted by the thought of the outlaws huddled around a gas lamp on some wintry night a century ago. Who knows? They might have sat in his very own living room, oiling their pistols and listening for the sound of federales' hooves.

More recently the area around Glenwood had been a stomping ground for a law-abiding transplant from the Midwest named Aldo Leopold. Leopold arrived in the Southwest in 1909, a greenhorn fresh out of Yale forestry school. His superiors praised his intelligence. But the experienced hands who worked under him found the well-heeled college boy an irritating know-it-all. Luckily, even a rich boy could earn his spurs. By the 1920s, after suffering a serious illness that kept him out of the field for over a year, Leopold had matured. His ideas were evolving into the philosophy that would emerge in the century's most important book on the environment, *A Sand County Almanac*. Foreman would call it the century's most important book, period. The *Almanac* wasn't released until after Leopold's death in 1948, but during his lifetime he published a veritable army of essays. They trace the development of Leopold's great contribution: the idea of land as community, rather than commodity. A ground-breaking essay was published in 1921 in the *Journal of Forestry*. "The Wilderness and Its Place in Forest Recreation Policy" was the forestry profession's first formal discussion of the wilderness idea. In the essay, Leopold suggested cordoning off half a million acres of national forestland surrounding the headwaters of the Gila River. All signs of civilization would be barred from the region, which consisted of high mountains and box canyons in New Mexico's Mogollon Mountains.

Five days after Leopold left the southwest for a new job in Wisconsin, his supervisor at the Forest Service bestowed a parting tribute. On June 3, 1924, the Gila Wilderness Area was established. It was the first wilderness area in the national forest system. Leopold's biographer noted: "No European nation ever could, or ever would, proclaim such a wilderness."[4] And, he might have added, no red-blooded young American could live in such a wilderness and not fall desperately, romantically in love with it. More important than any single human being's joy, sorrow, or neurosis, wilderness existed in a place beyond boundaries. Its preservation was central to the illusion that America was pure at heart, free of the claustrophobic satin-upholstered decadence of the Old World. At least so it seemed to the young couple living in their frontier adobe, with the Gila Wilderness right outside the front door.

EAST:
Burn On

There's a red moon rising
On the Cuyahoga River
Rolling into Cleveland to the lake

There's an oil barge winding
Down the Cuyahoga River
Rolling into Cleveland to the lake

Cleveland, city of light, city of magic
Cleveland, city of light, you're calling me
Cleveland, even now I can remember
'Cause the Cuyahoga River
Goes smokin' through my dreams

Burn on, big river, burn on
Burn on, big river, burn on
Now the Lord can make you tumble
And the Lord can make you turn
And the Lord can make you overflow
But the Lord can't make you burn . . .

—Randy Newman
"Burn On," 1972

1970–The City

THE FIRST EARTH DAY, April 22, 1970, gave New York City mayor John Vliet Lindsay a novel feeling: relief. The epithet most commonly attached to Lindsay's name was Kennedyesque. The tall, good-looking aristocrat was descended from the Dutch patroons who were the first in a distinguished line of New York City discount shoppers, having purchased the island for a few knickknacks from its native inhabitants. But Lindsay possessed neither the Kennedys' back-room savvy nor his

Dutch forebears' negotiating skills. By 1970, he was vehemently despised by every union sanitation man and taxi driver in the city of New York. These were not people one enjoyed having as enemies. They sputtered saliva in your face when they yelled at you; they made threats you felt certain they were capable of carrying out. At various times during the Lindsay administration, they did. The city became paralyzed. Cabs wouldn't pick up passengers. Trash piled up on street corners in the dead stinking heat of summer. Lindsay's union troubles were a presentiment of New York City's future as a second Calcutta. So John Lindsay enjoyed the hell out of Earth Day. The city was one giant, pulsing good vibe. The blue-eyed aristocrat marched down Fifth Avenue with 100,000 of the city's masses. It was the first day he could remember appearing on the street without getting booed.[1]

It was a time of unanimity, brief but sweet. Pollution was the common enemy and victory still seemed possible. The righteous energy had started pumping up back in 1969, a banner year for environmental disasters. The season opener was the Santa Barbara oil spill, a drilling platform leak that washed oil-slicked waves onto a stretch of heavily populated shoreline in late January. Television flashed powerful images of dying grebes, gulls, and murrelets, a macabre Surfin' Safari on the coast of southern California.

By summer, Cleveland's Cuyahoga River was providing more sensational entertainment for America's television screens. The Cuyahoga, which bisects Cleveland and pours into Lake Erie, had become so polluted that even the leeches and sludge worms deserted it. The Cuyahoga didn't flow: it oozed. On June 22, it did something else. It ignited. A burning slick of oil and kerosene floated through the city, exhaling a five-story fireball that took out two railroad bridges like a surge of napalm. The incident made Cleveland the butt of jokes for years afterward.[2] It also inspired a Randy Newman song which suggested that not only was God dead, but maybe Nature was, too. Twenty years later *New Yorker* writer Bill McKibben would expound this compelling idea more soberly, although with less brevity, in his book *The End of Nature.*

What few people outside Cleveland realized was that this wasn't the pyromaniac river's first inflammatory episode. The Cuyahoga had also caught fire in 1936 and 1952. But by 1969, a new epoch had begun. Television news had become the American family's equivalent of saying grace before dinner. This time, when the Cuyahoga burned, its flames illuminated the poisons lurking at the edges of the American landscape. Soon every major magazine was trumpeting pollution stories. *Time* and *The Saturday Evening Post* both began regular sections covering the environment.

With the media jumping on the bandwagon, politicians couldn't be far behind. The enthusiasm started all the way at the top. President Richard Nixon, happy to be asked about something other than the Vietnam War, called for Americans to "make peace with nature" and "make reparations for the damage we have done to our air, to our land and to our water." In a heated race for reelection, California Governor Ronald Reagan announced, ". . . there is no subject more on our minds than the preservation of our environment."* Reagan's gubernatorial challenger, Jesse Unruh, the sloppy, overweight Tammany Hall–style boss of the California legislature, said it best: "Ecology has become the political substitute for the word 'mother.' "[3]

If doggedly conservative Ronald Reagan was giving lip service to ecology back in '69, the liberal community was in a positive tizzy. Senator Ed Muskie tried to shift part of the federal highway fund to pollution control and mass transit. Senator Gaylord Nelson of Wisconsin, the strongest conservationist in the U.S. Congress, called for the elimination of all nonreturnable bottles, cans, and jars. Why not come up with a practically pollution-free auto while you're at it? asked Nelson.

In Ann Arbor, at the University of Michigan, a twenty-three-year-old named Doug Scott joined a group of students planning an environmental teach-in. Scott had avoided the draft by enrolling in the school's graduate program in forestry. He had done his share of antiwar demonstrating, hanging out with the freaks shouting "Fuck

---

* This apparently became one of many subjects Reagan "could not recall" once he assumed the office of president.

Nixon" on the Capitol mall. Eventually Scott decided that levitating the Pentagon wasn't his style. Still, he didn't see why some of the antiwar movement's tactics couldn't be adapted to conservation, which had been a mania with him since the two summers he spent as a park ranger at Carlsbad Caverns.

As it turned out, the same idea had occurred to Senator Gaylord Nelson. Scott remembers that the synchronicity was a little, well, deflating. "I remember how . . . hurt, in a sense, we were, when somebody brought in *Time* magazine, which in mid-October of '69, in their Miscellany column, had a little thing saying the senator from Wisconsin, who was a great conservationist, and whom I had met on and off by that time, had this idea. Because we had it, too. We were the first people who walked in his door and said, Hey, we're doing this at the University of Michigan," said Scott.

Nelson and the Michigan students weren't the only ones suddenly shouting "Eureka!" at the sight of a tree. By the end of the year, little green triangles were appearing on lapel buttons everywhere. Their genesis was obscure, but the meaning was clear. Antiwar activists were realizing that their support for Vietnamese peasants wasn't just a rebellion against America's latest clubfooted attempt at manifest destiny in a foreign jungle. It was also a rebellion against the alienating, materialistic, Third World–exploiting American Way of Life. Once they figured this out, college students turned their raging hormones and undemanding schedules to good account. In a *Reader's Digest* article drumming up support for the April 22 "Teach-In," which came to be called Earth Day, Senator Nelson detailed a succession of "small miracles" on college campuses.

"Whether they are *burning billboards* [author's italics], burying an internal combustion engine or giving out 'dishonor awards' ('Smokestack of the Month'), students everywhere have shown a flair for spotlighting the issue," Nelson wrote. "At the University of Washington, conservation militants put out a bucket of oil and invited onlookers to dip their hands in it so they'd know how it felt to be a bird caught in an offshore oil slick. A 19-year-old coed put dye and peanut hulls into the toilets of Miami's shoreline hotels to see if raw sewage was going into Biscayne Bay; it was. On April 22, a group at the University of Minnesota plans to march to the Minneapolis Mall, where they will set up tents and hand out free oxygen."[4]

In the early 1980s, Earth First! would refine these guerrilla-theater tactics, outraging their opponents and amusing viewers of TV news. Later in the decade, AIDS activists in ACT-UP and Queer Nation would adopt a harsher brand of guerrilla theater, appropriate to a situation where the results of institutionalized callousness were more immediate.

On Earth Day, things did not seem so bleak. Except for the Daughters of the American Revolution ("Subversive elements plan to make American children live in an environment that is good for them," warned a Mississippi matron in early April),[5] Earth Day had very few enemies. Much as they would twenty years later, corporations jumped on the environmental bandwagon. Putting their mouths where their money was supposedly going to follow, they snatched public-relations victory from the jaws of potential stock-dividend disaster. For example, the president of General Motors committed his company "to eliminating the automobile as a factor in the nation's air-pollution problem," even if it took abandoning the gasoline engine itself.* Other companies announced pollution-control projects: less-polluting grades of oil and biodegradable containers. When all else failed, they ran antilittering advertisements.[6]

The energetic Scott quickly hitched a ride on the Earth Day caravan. He was in line for a prime position, having already talked himself into a series of summer jobs with big environmental groups. Along with another "token student," he was placed on the board of directors of Environmental Teach-In, Inc., the group organizing Earth Day.[7] At first, the teach-in depended on handouts from other liberal nonprofit groups. But Earth Day soon grew beyond a volunteer effort. Denis Hayes, an intense prelaw student from Harvard, convinced Gaylord Nelson to hire him as Earth Day's coordinator. Hayes had an unusual background for a Harvard student. His father, a Washington

---

* Presumably, he didn't give himself a deadline.

State paper-mill worker, had been partially deafened by the noise of the mill's heavy machinery. At twenty-five, the working-class Hayes already felt pushed to the wall by overindustrialization. He saw its effects, not just on his family, but on his hometown of Camas, Washington, set in the green foothills of the Cascade range, where the local pulp mill had polluted the Columbia River and belched sulfur into the air. After serving as president of his undergraduate student body at Stanford, Hayes did the requisite Third World hippie stint before gracing Harvard's prelaw program. With blue eyes set deep in his bony face, he struck a *New York Times* reporter as the quintessential angry young man.[8] Calling for Earth Day to "bypass the traditional political process,"[9] Hayes took one disdainful look at the plush, wall-to-wall carpeting in the Common Cause offices and told everyone to start packing. He moved the teach-in over to a building on Dupont Circle, which Scott remembers as a "crummy old rat-infested place that was full of little movement groups." It was the perfect stage for the bloodless coup Hayes and the others were trying to pull off.

Through the weird chemistry of the times, they did it. Earth Day was a resounding success. Twenty million people either marched, demonstrated, or participated in "happenings" and "teach-ins" at 1,500 campuses and 10,000 schools. It was fitting that Cleveland's demonstrators wound up on the banks of the Cuyahoga River. It was no longer burning, but the river still oozed rather than doing a proper meander through the midwestern city. Standing at the spot where founding father Moses Cleaveland allegedly landed in 1796, one student flourished a plastic sack full of garbage, groovily intoning, "This is my bag."[10]

In a slightly more impressive gesture, New York City banned combustion engines from Fifth Avenue for two hours. It was eerily quiet as 100,000 New Yorkers marched down Manhattan's central artery. Despite a marathon Frisbee game and the ubiquitous haze of marijuana smoke, one reporter characterized Earth Day in New York as "a secular revival meeting." Speakers urged participants to think more deeply about what they could do to fight pollution. The Environmental Action Coalition handed out a "New York Pollution

Survival Kit" with forty things that an individual could do to fight noise, waste, and dirt—or in 1990s hypespeak, forty things they could do to save the earth.[11]

It was going to take more than a laundry list to slay the mega-machine. Even on a day that contained much of the hopeful side of the activism sparked by the Vietnam War, something unpleasant was in the air, both literally and figuratively. At an Alaska Earth Day gathering, Interior Secretary Walter Hickel rather undiplomatically announced plans to construct an 800-mile hot-oil pipeline that would slash through the Arctic tundra from one end of the state to the other. In Washington, D.C., as 10,000 longhairs rocked out on the mall, the U.S. Department of Commerce chose April 22 to announce that it was granting a permit for a major new oil refinery outside Honolulu.[12]

But Earth Day participants accomplished many of their immediate goals. Since the founding of the Sierra Club in 1892, the conservation movement's sole mission had been preserving bits and pieces of the open frontier. With the advent of ecologists like Aldo Leopold and Robert Marshall in the 1920s, the movement haltingly expanded its agenda and ideology. But for the most part, it remained in the doughty realm of sensible shoes and funny hats favored by women who would rather slog around a swamp than eat at "21." One of those women, Rachel Carson, became the link between old-style conservation and the contemporary environmental movement. With the publication of her book *Silent Spring* in 1962, Carson alerted the country to the dangers of pesticides. This new awareness widened the movement to include crusaders like Barry Commoner and Ralph Nader, ethnic, highly politicized urbanites characterized as populist pollution fighters by historian Stephen Fox. When the children of the sixties tentatively pulled the two strands of old-style wilderness conservation and populist pollution fighting together on April 22, 1970, they created what is now considered the contemporary environmental movement. Both the environmental agenda and its constituency had broadened. The twenty million people who turned out for Earth Day made sure that the environment would never again be considered a special interest.

This new diversity was reflected in Earth Day's participants, who ranged from Nelson Rockefeller to Abbie Hoffman. If Earth Day was a benchmark for the environmental movement, it was also a benchmark for its participants, many of whom date the beginning of their environmental consciousness to April 22, 1970. In fact, Earth Day was just the most visible manifestation of a groundswell of feeling that was already propelling far-reaching legislation through Congress. In a single year, 1970, the Clean Air Act and Clean Water Act were strengthened, the Environmental Protection Agency was created by executive order, and the National Environmental Policy Act was signed into law. Innumerable environmental laws were also enacted at the state level. The momentum continued through the 1970s, which has been called "the decade of environmental legislation."

But a mere eight days after Earth Day, the U.S. Air Force began bombing raids on Cambodia. Four days later, four students demonstrating against the war at Kent State University in Ohio were shot and killed by the National Guard. The country was riveted by the emblematic photograph of a young woman crying over the body of a fallen protester. Not long afterward, a majority of Americans turned against the war.

The Kent State killings yanked public attention away from the environment and back to the war. Hard-core antiwar activists argued that it should have remained there all along. From the beginning, they had accused Earth Day organizers of being government dupes. It was true that the environment provided a new focus for the energy of antiwar activists. For some it was temporary. Others found a lifelong cause.

As the Earth Day crowds dispersed, its organizers wondered if a mass movement could truly embody the intellectual and spiritual ideals of twentieth-century environmentalism. Two decades later, Denis Hayes talked about his disappointment with the results of the first Earth Day, even as he prepared to launch the second. "We hoped it would lead to a new kind of ideology, a new value system based on ecology and a reverence for life," said Hayes. Instead, Hayes charged, the movement was ideologically and geographically fragmented. Dominated by the upper middle class, it ignored the grass roots, labor, and minorities. Its provincialism left it ill equipped to function on the global level, where the most significant conservation issues would be decided in the 1990s and beyond.[13]

Oddly, few of the people who later played important roles in Earth First! remember Earth Day as an important event in their lives. Earth Day was only tangentially related to their romantic vision of wilderness. Most of Earth Day's momentum came from outside the wilderness movement—from concern over pollution problems that had grown severe enough to warrant a special issue of *Newsweek* in January 1969, and from the frantic energy of the antiwar movement. In contrast to Doug Scott, most of the people who later joined Earth First! were not active in the antiwar movement. Either they were right-wingers, gung-ho to join the Marines like Dave Foreman, or they weren't yet of draft age. Born just a few years apart, Doug Scott and the members of Earth First! seemed to belong to different generations. Scott and others like him had been formed by the stable, affluent society of the 1950s and early 1960s. But to the teenagers who grew up in the 1970s and 1980s, a disintegrated social order was the only reality. Fed on post-Vietnam cynicism instead of outraged liberal optimism, Earth First!ers turned toward the green tunnel of wilderness.[14]

It was only natural that Earth Day would have marginal appeal to these kids. Denis Hayes said that the overarching purpose of Earth Day was to reform society, not escape from it. Organizers hoped to achieve this by consolidating the antiwar, women's, civil-rights, and conservation movements. It was a good strategy, at least in theory. For decades, the crabby, brilliant eco-anarchist Murray Bookchin had been trying to make common cause among these social movements. Domination of the environment came from the same nasty mind-set that oppressed women and the Third World, said Bookchin.

Bookchin was right. But there was a big problem with his idea. No matter how much you stirred them, the political ingredients never quite seemed to mix into a viable coalition. Most career environmentalists scoff at the very idea of an environmental "movement." In a sense, the environmental movement is not political at heart, they say. It is a collection of individuals with very different experiences and agendas: old-line WASP Republicans who like to shoot ducks, lower-middle-class blacks living downwind from a refinery, housewives who turn into ecowarriors when their kids get leukemia. Not exactly a unified bloc. Even the hipster mountain climbers who fancy themselves born-again John Muirs aren't particularly ideological. They tend to have an aversion to soiling the wilderness ethic with the selfish, grotty needs of human beings. It wasn't just that environmentalists disagreed about politics; most simply didn't care.

In the 1980s, Earth First! would inherit a piece of the environmental movement's traditional apolitical base. But as Earth First! grew, it would attract a second generation. Like the organizers of Earth Day—who were the second generation of the movement as a whole—the new wave of Earth First!ers found the idea of reforming human society more attractive than the idea of dispensing with it. Initially fueled by Dave Foreman's backslid-fundamentalist vision of apocalypse, most members of Earth First! eventually found they wanted something to hold on to, even if it was only a pipe dream that industrial society could somehow be reoriented toward an ecologically saner system. Foreman and his friends got jazzed about animals; the new generation of Earth First!ers actually thought people could be interesting, too.

This crevasse, which eventually would obsess the left wing of the environmental movement, began as a barely perceptible crack in the sidewalk on Earth Day in New York City. Even then, some left-wing environmentalists were frustrated by the way the rest of the movement turned ideology into Wonder Bread. They worried that conservation's broad constituency and essentially apolitical nature left it vulnerable to corporate depredations. This situation was particularly galling for Fred Kent, coordinator of New York's Environmental Action Coalition. Kent was the first spoilsport to criticize the business community's attempt to turn Earth Day into a public-relations bonanza. "It is irresponsible for business to say that they support us. They are just trying to co-opt us," Kent said as Earth Day participants frolicked under ecology banners erected by New York utility Consolidated Edison. "The apparent unanimity on the issue of environment disturbs many who fear that genuine progress will be lost amid a flurry of superficial reforms," the article went on to explain.[15]

Unknown to Kent, new seeds had already fallen into those cracks in the sidewalk. Soon strange plants would grow in them, between Fred Kent and Doug Scott, between the old-line aristocrats and the ethnic peasants, between the Lefties and the hard-faced mountaineers. Already, unshaven ecosaboteurs were hiding in the seashell-colored hills of northern Arizona. In the 1980s, these weird hybrids would liven up a movement that had been coasting on the brief spurt of energy commandeered by Earth Day.

WEST:
Phantoms

1959–The Desert

MARC WAS THE YOUNGEST ONE. Blue crystal air held him in its arms as he threw a Molotov cocktail at the dish-shaped billboard advertising Meteor Crater, tourist attraction, Come one, Come all. *THUNK*. The Coke bottle rolled to the ground, perfectly intact—except for the gasoline seeping out. So was the Meteor Crater billboard, which seemed to mock him as it cast its shadow under the full, bright moon.

The next night Marc came back carrying a cold chisel in the pocket of his Levi's. He cracked the bolts that held the billboard to its steel legs, watching with satisfaction as it toppled to the ground. After he finished his night's work there was nothing left but a spindly forest of naked posts. To make sure the billboard couldn't be repaired, he sawed it into firewood.

It was hard work, but Marc had help. There was his friend from seventh grade, Ted Danson. And then there were the big kids. Some nights there were more than a dozen: graduate students in archaeology who were visiting the Museum of Northern Arizona from Princeton and Harvard, geologists, a couple of Indians. Once in a while they'd detour onto Route 66 to get their kicks. They'd hold a billboard pigout along the old commercial highway. In a single night, relay teams could down as many as thirty.

But mostly they hit Route 180, the road that turned and twisted between Flagstaff and the Grand Canyon. "It was protection of the entryway to the Grand Canyon, protecting an area that was pristine-looking, so that people wouldn't have to look at all this garbage on the way to the canyon," said Bill Breed, a Museum of Northern Arizona curator who took part in the raids. Marc's favorite target was a housing development that a certain Mr. Harold Butts was inflicting on the road to the Grand Canyon. It was called Fort Valley, a scattering of ranchettes built on a floodplain before zoning laws were introduced in the mid-1960s. The land was impressive, a vista Clint Eastwood could squint across. But when the winter snows melted, the Butts ranchettes looked like a Monopoly set that had been unceremoniously dunked in a swimming pool.

It was 1959. The tsunami of uncontrolled development was ramming its high, blind edge up against an old way of life. Los Angeles native and student of Americana Randy Newman wrote about it in the song "Dayton, Ohio—1903" on the 1972 album Sail Away. "Let's sing a song of long ago/When things could grow/And days flowed quietly/The air was clean and you could see/And folks were nice to you," Newman sang in mock simplicity. In the cities, young people were wearing green lapel buttons and marching to stem the tide. In the Southwest, people are less likely to join groups, carry signs, discuss political philosophy. Marc's friends were desert rats. They did what they could to make things right.

To Harold Butts, Marc and his friends were criminals. To Stanford University professor Iain Boal, they were populist defenders of the status quo—Luddites. Luddites were rebellious nineteenth-century Nottingham weavers who began losing their jobs because of automation. They called themselves followers of "King Ludd," or Ned

Ludd. Nobody knows if King Ludd was real or mythical. But the Luddites were real enough. Their midnight raids were effective—for a short time—in destroying the new looms that were putting them out of work.

The popular conception of Luddites is that they were angry, infantile vandals whose attempt to stop progress was doomed to failure. Boal suggests something different. Citing the work of British historians Eric Hobsbawm and E. P. Thompson, Boal believes that the Nottingham weavers—and the followers of Captain Swing who destroyed threshing machines for similar reasons in the 1830s—were engaging in a primitive form of collective bargaining at a time when unions were outlawed. Food riots in England served a similar purpose. When wheat prices became unbearably high, a peasant, usually a woman, would go to the town square and call out for a riot. The peasants would seize the wheat from millers. They would agree on a fair price among themselves, which they paid to the owners of the wheat. Food riots, like Luddism, were a way for ordinary people to gain a measure of authority over their lives at a time when technology and social organization were growing increasingly complex, centrally controlled, and unresponsive. In the twentieth century, the Guerrilla Girls borrowed from both Luddism and guerrilla theater to protest discrimination in the art world. They donned masks, just as the early Luddites had, and sneaked into art shows, where they exhibited pointed, well-researched statements about the art establishment.

Contrary to popular belief, the Luddites did not fail. The new technology eventually took hold in the Nottingham mills, but King Ludd's followers slowed its adoption long enough for the work force to adapt. Appropriate-technology supporters like Boal—people who believe technology is not intrinsically bad, but that new forms of technology must emerge organically from less destructive social values— tend to believe that Luddism is not antitechnology per se. In the publication *Utne Reader*, Daniel Grossman described a phenomenon called Neo-Luddism. He contended that today's Neo-Luddites don't believe in saying no to all changes, just the ones that "threaten valued traditions, customs, and institutions."[1]

Grossman may be right. But then again, some people say no a lot more loudly and frequently than others. From 1959 to 1964, Marc and his monkeywrenching team were in a defensive frenzy. Real-life Beaver Cleavers, they gnawed at the supports of billboard commercialism. Driven by the demon of Babbittry, they turned the work ethic on its head as they sweated through the nights outside Flagstaff, speeding the death of their own Puritanism as the country flew toward sex, drugs, and rock and roll.

Even though he was only twelve when he started monkeywrenching, Marc Gaede was sophisticated beyond his years. He was a unique species of archaeology brat, a child who could only have been produced by a landscape of dark monsoon clouds over high red mesas. Marc's father was an alcoholic reporter back in the bad old days when those two words were still synonymous. The elder Gaede had checked out of Marc's life years before and Marc's mother wasn't far behind. Marc was raised by his sister and her husband, an archaeologist named Alan Olson. From the age of eleven, Gaede spent his summers working on archaeology crews, surveying Glen Canyon before it was flooded by the big dam, getting to know Monument Valley the way a suburban kid knew his own backyard. He developed a reverence for the skeletal landscape of the Southwest, its bony canyon walls, the honeycombed eye sockets of its cliff dwellings. Everywhere he looked he saw white men chipping away at the stone that knitted the landscape together, dynamiting a canyon here, blasting away at a mountain there, building dams, digging mines, turning rivers into sandy wastes. He became a German shepherd protecting his home, a pack rat counting coups. He stacked his trophies—the remains of enemy billboards —in the woods outside Flagstaff. Maybe protecting nature was in his genes. Marc's maternal grandfather was Irving Brant, a newspaperman who had been an adviser to both Franklin Roosevelt and Roosevelt's secretary of the interior, Harold Ickes. Brant also was a crony of the National Audubon Society's Rosalie Edge, the only woman in the early conservation movement with real clout. He played an important role in preservation issues, including the establishment of Olympic National Park.

Irving Brant was not your average skeptical journalist. He was attracted to pantheism and subscribed to John Muir's central belief, which he characterized as "the idea that the world exists in part for its non-human inhabitants." Brant was no revolutionary, but if he had been born later in the century he might have been. By then some of the most dynamic and literate members of the conservation elite were considered radicals, including Sierra Club Executive Director David Brower, authors Edward Abbey and William Eastlake, and the social theorist and writer Joseph Wood Krutch. The virus of radicalism was most prevalent among people who had become intimate with the delicate landscape of the Southwest, a place where even a brief touch of civilization leaves an ugly, visible scar. But Marc Gaede was the first of a new generation. For him, going underground was not an agonizing mid-life transition, but a rite of passage into adulthood. Before he and his friend Ted reached voting age, they shared credit for helping to topple virtually every billboard between Flagstaff and the Grand Canyon. More than five hundred unsightly road signs ate dirt before the rampage was over.

By the late sixties, Marc Gaede and Ted Danson had both moved on to other pursuits. Ted became an actor, with a sideline in Hollywood-style environmental activism. After a stint as a Marine paratrooper, Marc immersed himself in the drug culture. He became a nomad, staying at hippie houses all over the West. Several times, he visited the canyon at Laguna, where orange sunshine was being manufactured by the Brotherhood, a confederation of drug manufacturers that included the famed LSD pioneer Augustus Owsley Stanley III, also known simply as Owsley. Marc was even there the day Timothy Leary wandered outside to announce his candidacy for president in front of a crowd of stoned hippies.

Being a flower child was great. The girls were pretty and the dope was good. But by the end of the decade Marc found himself living in his own private Altamont, which arrived wearing a blue uniform at the crash pad in Tucson where he spent the majority of his time. One by one, his friends got busted. Paranoia seeped out of the adobe walls;

it shot out of cactus spines; it vibrated along the power lines that were beginning to march in unhealthy military formation across the Sonoran desert. Everything felt poisoned.

In the spring of 1970 Marc drove from Tucson to visit friends in Aspen. He dropped a hit of acid with them and suddenly he couldn't stand being there anymore. Leaving Aspen in the middle of a snowstorm, he headed south. By the time he reached the dreamscape of southern Utah canyon country he was coming down from his high. Driving his VW bug into Moab, Utah, Marc recognized familiar landmarks. In the early-morning light the serrated ridges of Deadhorse Point looked apricot colored; they stretched for hundreds of miles, a fleet of barks and brigantines bigger than the imagination of any sixteenth-century Spanish monarch. He nearly cried when he saw the old stone house at Arches National Park where park superintendent Bates Wilson lived. He was stunned by the brightness of sunlight reflecting off the last of the spring snow; he was bowled over by the intensity of Moab's blue sky deepening against warm, red rock. In the midst of all this, Marc Gaede had a revelation. A simple one. He was home.

"When I came into Moab I didn't necessarily want to be an environmentalist. I just wanted to be with gentle people, to live in beauty," he said.

"This was southern Utah. It was beautiful. The people were beautiful and the country was spectacular. The cliffs were clean. Everything was clean. There were no more drugs. There was no more paranoia. I can't tell you the joy I felt coming into that place."

Leaving Moab, Marc passed through the Navajo reservation, where mesas rise out of the flat plains like startling, elegant altars. He passed all the places he had worked as a kid. Navajo Mountain. Shiprock. Monument Valley. Kayenta. And just outside of Kayenta, Black Mesa.

Since the early 1960s Marc had known that the Peabody Coal Company had plans for the mesa. News like this always hit the archaeology crews first. Because of the Federal Antiquities Act of 1906 they were called in to do surveys before the draglines lumbered across the land. And in this case, there was no doubt that the draglines, sooner or later, would be coming. Black Mesa, a brooding 3,300-foot-tall highland, scrubby and overgrazed, contained the largest coal deposit in Arizona. It was inhabited almost exclusively by Navajo families and their sheep. But the situation was complicated by the fact that both Navajo and Hopi tribes had rights to the mesa. Before the coal company could come in and dig up the earth, the mesa's ownership had to be clarified.

By the mid-sixties, Peabody Coal had a clear field. The land rights had been determined by a U.S. Supreme Court case in 1963. The following year, mining permits were secretly granted by the Hopi and Navajo councils, with the encouragement of the Bureau of Indian Affairs.[2] The Navajo sold their coal rights for a royalty of twenty-five cents a ton, which turned out to be less than one tenth of market value once the coal was mined. Peabody also made a highly advantageous deal with the Hopi, who were even less capable of protecting their interests. Most of the Hopi did not even participate in the tribal government, which had been established by the Bureau of Indian Affairs and did not reflect the village-based structure of Hopi society, with its local leaders, called Kikmongwi (pronounced *Kee-mung-wee*).

Black Mesa's fate was decided once and for all in 1968. On February 1, Secretary of the Interior Stewart Udall announced the cancellation of two dams slated for the Grand Canyon. The controversial dams had been designed to power the Central Arizona Project (CAP), the multibillion-dollar Rube Goldberg water-diversion scheme that would pump Colorado River water over a 1,200-foot mountain pass to Udall's home state of Arizona. But when the Sierra Club brought out the heavy artillery, the secretary's advisers were forced to come up with an alternative. Instead of building the dams, the federal government would help fund construction of the Navajo Generating Station, one of six enormous coal plants planned for the Four Corners region of the Southwest. In return, a portion of the plant's generating capacity would be used for hauling CAP water over the mountains. The coal deposits under the mesa would be the Central Arizona Project's black, dusty lifeblood.[3]

By the time Marc Gaede began working as the staff photographer for the Museum of Northern Arizona, the Black Mesa deal was a fait accompli, at least as far as everyone in Washington, D.C., was concerned. But in Arizona and New Mexico, it was a different story.

"That whole summer of 1970 the Black Mesa thing was cranking up. Everybody was talking about it," Gaede said. "Then I started going up there. When I saw those first cuts that they had made I was blown away. I mean, the open ground just ripped open and all that black, ugly coal . . . You just *looked* at it and you knew it was wrong."

All of a sudden the world had become ugly again, this time without the aid of artificial stimulants. The ugliness was seeping into Gaede's home, his new life, his hope for the future. He took pictures of the mesa, documenting each slice of land hauled away. In October, he started the Black Mesa Defense Fund. It was pretty much a one-man show, although he had help from a Navajo named Bill Lee and Bob Lomadapki, a Hopi jewelry maker. Around the same time, Alice Luna, a Navajo who had ties to the American Indian Movement, organized The Committee to Save Black Mesa. Together, Gaede and members of the committee spoke at Navajo chapter houses, trying to gain support for stopping the mine.

"I never lectured to Hopis. Hopis are like, kind of, people you can't really tell something. Hopis know it, you see. You don't *tell* a Hopi. . . . Most of the Hopis are very much against strip-mining, about 80 percent of them are traditionalists, they believe in Hopi kachinas. But they don't run the tribal council because they don't vote. It wouldn't do me any good to talk to a bunch of Mormon converts at New Oraibi. And the traditionalists don't want to hear me talk anyway, they know more than I do. They know all the spirits live here and there and you shouldn't do that and they have their own protests going.

"But the Navajos, I'll tell you what, it made a big impression on them. But you know what they really liked, I think? They liked that here was a white guy, and a couple of white guys sometimes, or a girl would come with me, with the Indians I was with, that paid attention to them, that would come to their chapter house. Nobody else did. Not even the strip miners.

"They knew the issues, but I think they considered it an honor that we were there. Most of their chapter meetings are nothing. It's just a feast with fry bread and the kids run around, the same old thing. Most of these places didn't even have electricity, so we had to bring our own generator to run the slide show.

"I think they felt powerless to do anything about it. Most of them didn't like it. Money didn't seem that important to these people. They didn't want the strip mine. But they didn't know what to do about it. It didn't fit into their political process to protest it so much except for AIM.

"But the lectures were greatly appreciated from an entertainment point of view. Here we were bringing slides, you know? I mean, they get to look at Black Mesa, all these color slides."

Marc didn't know how much good it was doing, but he felt compelled to keep trying. Soon he heard about a group of bohemians in Santa Fe who were putting on their own show. In the spring, when Marc had been rediscovering the Southwest, a jazz musician named Jack Loeffler had been making the rounds of the region, too. When Loeffler visited the town of Shonto, on the Navajo reservation, a school principal told him about the mine at Black Mesa. And Loeffler, too, decided to do something about it. But he did it in his own unique way.

Born just a hundred miles from Home, Pennsylvania, the birthplace of *The Monkey Wrench Gang* author Edward Abbey, Jack Loeffler migrated west under the auspices of the U.S. Army. In 1957, he found himself playing his trumpet in the cold dawn of the Nevada Proving Grounds while an atom bomb exploded overhead. It was just a test, of course. But after the third one, the U.S. military-industrial complex had most definitely failed, at least as far as Private Loeffler was concerned. "I performed three bombsworth before the Army relinquished me to the streets, my horn in my hand, my mind thoroughly blown, unstuck from mainstream American values but definitely not unhinged," he wrote many years later.[4] And like succeeding generations of young Americans who became similarly unstuck, Loeffler took his blown mind and his musical instrument to California. San Francisco, to be exact.

It was the beatnik era. Loeffler smoked pot and played jazz. He hung out with poets like Gary Snyder and Philip Whalen. Sometimes he lived on the beach. At night he cuddled a tire iron for protection; during the day he used it to pry abalone from the rocks at low tide. He learned to meditate at Esalen. And he read political philosophy. Struck by Prince Peter Kropotkin's 1902 book, *Mutual Aid*, Loeffler became an anarchist. Unlike the bomb-throwing species of anarchist exemplified by Mikhail Bakunin, Prince Kropotkin was a gentle fellow who loved nature. Resisting the entreaties of his ambitious family, who wanted him to accept a military appointment to the court at St. Petersburg, Kropotkin chose instead to do his military service in Siberia. Siberia was a biological island, a Noah's ark of nature before the advent of man. There Kropotkin made an observation that few in Western civilization had ever made. He noticed that although different species may compete for a biological niche, animals of the same species usually help one another to survive. It was a sweet and compelling argument against nasty, brutish social Darwinism. Unjustly ignored in recent years, Kropotkin's book was a landmark in the post-Darwinian debate over meaning and morality. Along with Darwin's work, it was one of the earliest social theories to grow directly from observations of animal behavior.

As Loeffler's feeling for nature grew stronger, he was increasingly drawn to Kropotkin's ideas. He became peripatetic, traveling constantly between California and the Southwest. He wandered through the ancient Indian kivas and cliff dwellings of northern New Mexico. On long hikes, he lost himself in the sandstone fins and needles, molded turrets, and sheer canyon walls of the Colorado Plateau. Eventually he came to believe that the cultures that had grown up in these places—both Native American peoples and the old Hispanic settlements of the Rio Grande del Norte—exemplified Kropotkin's anarchist ideal. These societies had been formed in response to the realities of an arid landscape. Isolated from any central government, they operated on a small scale. Most of them had succeeded for centuries because of voluntary cooperation that did not seem to rob individuals of their dignity or sense of freedom. It made sense to ex–Private Loeffler—especially compared with being forced to stand at attention and play nationalistic claptrap on your trumpet as giant mushroom clouds exploded overhead, dosing you with cancer-causing radiation. In 1962, he moved to Santa Fe, resolving that he would do whatever it took to stay there.

Two years later, the artist John Dupuy introduced Loeffler to Ed Abbey. In the next quarter century Abbey, Dupuy, and Loeffler would hike together across the equivalent of the length of the United States, "talking all the time" according to Loeffler. When Loeffler decided to work full-time on environmental issues, Abbey stayed behind the scenes. But he developed a knack for appearing at the moments when Jack needed him most. These moments started coming more frequently once Loeffler started Black Mesa Defense Fund.

In 1968, when Loeffler learned that a mine was planned for Black Mesa, he imagined "a small coal mine so that the Navajo families would burn coal instead of pinyon and juniper." Eventually he discovered that Peabody was planning a huge operation. The strip mine would cover 26,000 acres. It would mine eight million tons of coal a year for thirty-five years, earning an estimated $750 million for the company. The mesa was at the heart of a development scheme hatched by WEST (Western Energy Supply and Transmission Associates), a consortium of twenty-three utilities. Energy from the coal plants would be linked to a grid stretching from Wyoming to Southern California.

In 1970, Loeffler began a frenetic campaign to keep the coal company off the mesa. He called in friends to help, people like Dennis Hopper's brother Jimmy and photographer Terry Moore. Eventually Gaede found out about Loeffler's group and suggested that they work together. In theory it was a good idea. Practice was something else.

"Loeffler kept his phone in the freezer," Gaede remembered. "He figured it was tapped and if it was in the freezer they couldn't hear anything. That isn't how phone taps work, but he thought with the phone just sitting there, they could hear you. So he'd put the goddamn phone in the freezer. So you'd try to call Jack, goddamn him, he couldn't hear the phone in the fucking freezer. And I've got important shit to talk over with Jack. Jack, I've got to talk to you.

"But when he doesn't answer, I know the phone's in the goddamn freezer again. You go into his house and the wire goes up through the kitchen and into the freezer."

In contrast to Marc Gaede's local-boy roughhouse style, Loeffler's group was sophisticated, if unconventional. Despite the occasional difficulty of reaching them by telephone, they were expert at public relations. Loeffler appeared on network television several times and was one of the first people to be interviewed on the National Public Radio show *All Things Considered*. Articles quoting members of Black Mesa Defense appeared in *Newsweek*, *Time*, and *Life*. The twenty-four-year-old Dave Foreman, on his occasional visits to the Santa Fe office to stuff envelopes and run errands, was impressed with the publicity bang that Loeffler and the others got for virtually no bucks.

There was so much press that even politicians in Washington, D.C., began to pay attention, according to Brant Calkin, a legendary southwestern environmentalist who recently retired as director of the Southern Utah Wilderness Alliance. "When Black Mesa got all this publicity, it was not lost on Congress. The Senate held five hearings on the Four Corners," said Calkin. "It was the Sierra Club that talked to Congress and got the hearings going. The Sierra Club was good at gathering information and doing that sort of thing. But when it came to getting the attention, frankly, it was Loeffler and Terry Moore."

The reason for all the publicity—and all the commitment—was that the issue was bigger than Black Mesa. In the go-go years of the late sixties, utilities were predicting an increase in energy use of 5 percent a year. *Forever.* As they madly rushed to build power plants, many utilities overextended themselves. In the 1980s, the worst of these pyramids collapsed when a string of nuclear plants turned into a multibillion-dollar catastrophe for the Washington Public Power Supply System or WPPSS (ironically pronounced "*Whoops*"). In the

Southwest, utilities also ran into financial trouble as the country's appetite for electricity slowed.

In retrospect, a 5 percent annual increase in energy consumption seems not only unbelievable but horrifying. But in the late sixties and early seventies, Black Mesa Defense was one of the few groups trying to pull leather on the utilities' runaway horse. Terry Moore, the photographer who worked on the Black Mesa issue in Santa Fe, recalled, "We were fighting not just the mine; we were fighting all of those power plants and all of those mines,"—the six coal-burning plants planned for the Four Corners region and the many strip mines slated to supply them with coal.

Slowly, awareness of the energy issue spread. Black Mesa became a rallying point for this new consciousness. Support groups formed in Tucson, San Francisco, Los Angeles, and San Diego, all calling themselves Black Mesa Defense Fund. They operated autonomously, checking in now and then with Moore or Loeffler, or whomever they happened to know in Santa Fe. "What I tried to say was, if you have something you'd like to do, you're welcome to do it with us," Loeffler said. "We were really a bunch of anarchists."

In 1970, Moore and Loeffler recruited advertising genius Jerry Mander. In 1965, Mander and his partner, Howard Gossage, had pioneered full-page ads with clip-out coupons in the fight to save the Grand Canyon. Mander came up with a similar one for Black Mesa. Mining on Black Mesa was "like ripping apart St. Peter's to get the marble." The copy explained how Black Mesa was just a small part of the country's misguided energy policy.

In the space of two years, Black Mesa Defense Fund participated in six separate lawsuits, made a film that was shown to the New Mexico state legislature, and lobbied every governmental body from Congress to the United Nations. They also tried—and in true anarchist fashion, failed—to blow up a coal slurry line. By the end, Loeffler was so emotionally and physically drained that he almost collapsed after testifying at the last Senate hearing on the issue, held in Page, Arizona. Ed Abbey had to hold him up as he walked away from the microphone.

"I was reading testimony of Hopi people who couldn't speak in the microphone," Loeffler said. "And the next thing I knew, it was over. That whole period of concentration was over and I was utterly wasted. It just all hit. I felt myself start to go. I was standing onstage. I felt a hand on my arm and somebody literally just lifted me off the stage. And it was Ed. He got me out of there."

As they sat around a campfire that night, the two friends made a pact. They agreed that when either one of them died, the other would give him a proper burial. That meant burying his body in the desert, illegally, at midnight.

With the drama of the Black Mesa fight, musing about death didn't seem out of place. The Southwest seemed to be overflowing with Rhett Butlers gung-ho to join the Confederate Army after Atlanta had already fallen. Practical-minded people like Sierra Clubber and billboard bandit Bill Breed, Marc Gaede's boss at the Museum of Northern Arizona, couldn't see what the fuss was about. Black Mesa was hardly pristine wilderness; the Navajos' hoofed locusts had taken care of that. But even Breed admitted that something about Black Mesa inspired revolutionary fervor.

To most of the people who tried to save it, Black Mesa's mystical significance was as important as its political role. Traditional Hopis believed that Black Mesa was the final refuge on earth. Its destruction would signal the coming of environmental Armageddon.

The mesa also figured in Navajo mythology, although it was not as central as it was to the Hopi. The Navajo called Black Mesa the female mountain. Lukachukai was the male mountain, and the two together were symbols of harmony, which, along with beauty, is the Navajo Way. If the balance were lost, the Navajo Way would be destroyed. According to historian Alvin Josephy, "Even the unbelieving white man visiting the mesa can feel the truth of the warning, for it is an awesome and timeless region of solitude, wonder, and beauty."[5]

For rationalists, the mesa's strategic importance was equally compelling. Even before its role in the Central Arizona Project was clear to them, both Gaede and Loeffler were aware of Black Mesa's connection to the network of six noxious power plants planned for the Four Corners area. It galled Gaede that almost half the output of the Four Corners and Mojave plants would be fueling the rapid growth of Los Angeles at the expense of air quality in the Southwest. By the mid-seventies, scientists at Los Alamos National Laboratory estimated that emissions from the plants had cut the region's visibility in half. Air pollution engulfing the Four Corners was the only sign of civilization in the Southwest visible from space. Jack Loeffler and Ed Abbey took turns appropriating the National Academy of Sciences description: "a national sacrifice area."

The mine on Black Mesa also signaled the last major depredation of the Colorado River, a once-terrifying wild river that had become an inkwell for the industrial West to write checks against the future —checks that were starting to look suspiciously rubbery. To run the slurry line that would transport Black Mesa coal 200 miles away to the Mojave power plant, Peabody would be draining water from the Colorado, plus pumping 2,200 gallons of scarce groundwater out of the mesa each day. In return for approximately 300 mining jobs, the Navajo had donated rights to 34,100 acre-feet of the Colorado, leaving less than 16,000 acre-feet for their own needs. This donation, helpfully drafted by the Interior Department, is now estimated to be worth $6.8 million a year.[6]

Soon Black Mesa became a symbol of everything that was wrong with development in the West. In his book *Indian Country*, Peter Matthiessen called Black Mesa "the ugliest ecological disaster of our time." Jack Loeffler was blunter, saying, "It is the most complete model of an environmental fuck-up in the world." Matthiessen wrote that a year after the strip-mining started, a Navajo living on Black Mesa told the photojournalist Dan Budnick, "I think as I walk this earth, what will next summer bring? Since the company started their work, people began to change. The air began to change. The plants seem to have no life. When the wind blows our way, the dust covers the whole ground—the food, the animals, the hogans, the water."

In Flagstaff, Marc Gaede joined Native American demonstrators to stop the mine. First, in the winter of 1970, Hopi elders peacefully protested in the Peabody Coal office. In the spring, AIM staged a more militant protest. Several hundred Navajos camped out on the mesa for days, chanting and drumming. About thirty wore the red shirts and Levi jackets that were the AIM uniform. Marc Gaede was excited. Things were finally starting to happen. He drove out to the mesa in a van borrowed from the Museum of Northern Arizona, where he was the staff photographer. The owner of a local trading post lent him an unloaded rifle to use as a prop. He was going to take a picture of a young Navajo named Leroy Keams. Keams would hold the gun aloft in a gesture of defiance, with the Peabody Coal dragline in the background. But something went wrong. When Marc started clicking away, the dragline operator swung a bucketful of dirt toward them. Marc, Leroy, and the others ran for the van, which, in rather impolitic fashion, had the museum's name on the door. They raced away, but the dragline cut them off. Thinking fast, Marc swerved into the shelter of a cluster of parked pickup trucks that belonged to coal company employees. Surely, they wouldn't attack their own vehicles. For a few moments, Marc and the Indians were safe. Then Marc saw an opening and made a break for it. The dragline followed in lumbering pursuit. Behind them a half dozen police cruisers appeared. Dust trails crisscrossed the mesa like Isadora Duncan's scarves, as the van, the dragline, and the cop cars performed their awkward dance.

Marc was arrested that day, along with a handful of others. But his photo turned out to be a classic. It was made into a poster that showed Leroy Keams, complete with high Navajo cheekbones and western hat, brandishing the rifle in front of the Peabody Coal dragline. The AIM-inspired headline "INDIAN POWER" on the poster's first press run was eventually changed to "SAVE BLACK MESA."

Public demonstrations were not the only form of protest used by Black Mesa Defense Fund. Luddites were surfacing again in northern Arizona, and they were doing more than failing to blow up the slurry line. A ghostly figure called the Arizona Phantom was making the rounds of Peabody Coal after dark. Night after night, he was tearing up the tracks of the Black Mesa railroad. Heavy equipment suffered, too. A scraper, a grader, and a battalion of Caterpillar tractors fell to the Phantom, who had a knack for getting to their vital parts.

But neither guerrilla warfare nor lobbying could save the mesa. Construction of the mine went forward, and by 1972 Black Mesa Defense Fund had quietly expired. It would have been out of character for the southwestern anarchists to hook up with an established environmental group—a bit of political maneuvering that might have given them greater longevity and success. But reforming U.S. energy policy was probably too big a job for anyone, including President Jimmy Carter. When they tackled the issue in the mid-1970s, the big national groups didn't meet with much success, either. They discovered that they usually had to be satisfied with mitigation, rather than redirecting policy. But at least the big groups were trying. Black Mesa's publicity helped get them focused on the energy issue.

"Black Mesa became a cause célèbre for the emerging ranks of environmentalists across the country through articles in the *New York Times*, *Washington Post*, *Audubon*, and *Wassaja* and shows on CBS and ABC. Although the publicity did not stop the mining of Black Mesa, it had repercussions among both Indians and non-Indians that are still felt today," wrote historian Marjane Ambler in her book *Breaking the Iron Bonds: Indian Control of Energy Development*.

Black Mesa Defense did manage to wrest a few concessions from Peabody. The company agreed to reclaim land on Black Mesa after strip-mining it. Black Mesa Defense was less successful in forcing the utilities to install pollution-control devices on the power plants. "I get sick when I hear about the Navajo plant with its eight-hundred-foot stacks," said Terry Moore. "They slipped in this high stack theory. We said, 'High stack, high shmack.' You're not solving a problem, you're creating one." Twenty years later, the federal government would agree, requiring new pollution-control devices on the enormous Navajo Generating Station.

But the environmentalists' biggest victory was forcing a reconsideration of at least one of the six proposed power plants in the Four Corners region. Ultimately, Southern California Edison dropped out of the consortium which was planning to build an enormous coal plant on the wild Kaiparowits Plateau. The utility's decision effectively shut down the project. Even utilities were starting to realize that the boom was ending.

When Peabody tried to open a strip mine on the Cheyenne reservation in Montana, there was a brief revival of activity. In 1972, The Committee to Save Black Mesa invited a delegation of Cheyenne to the Four Corners to see what had happened to the mesa. For the Cheyenne who couldn't visit Black Mesa, Terry Moore and Alvin Josephy, a former editor of *American Heritage*, took a slide show up to the reservation. According to historian Marjane Ambler, the fate of the Northern Plains tribes was radically changed by what they learned.

The Phantom disappeared in 1972. Nobody from the daytime crew of the Black Mesa Defense Fund ever figured out who he was. Marc Gaede speculates that the Phantom might have been one of his old billboarding pals, but even he is not sure. The Phantom would reappear later . . . but perhaps that is not the right word. He would leave invisible traces of his presence buried in tree trunks along certain forest roads. In a few select basements and garages, neophyte monkeywrenchers would find gifts: hammers, tool belts, ten-penny nails in bulk—the tools and supplies for tree spiking. He would even write to the *Earth First! Journal* with tips on shooting cows and euthanizing billboards. But nobody—not even the reporter he would finally tell about his exploits—would ever see his face.

The same was true of a shadowy figure in the Midwest who called himself the Fox, after the Fox River in Illinois. The Fox's existence was one more piece of evidence that monkeywrenching was not isolated criminal activity but an allergic response to runaway technology. In 1970 the Fox plugged the illegal drains of soap companies and capped their smoking chimneys to protest water and air pollution. Hounded by police and shot at by guards, the Fox courted further danger by sending notes to the media to make his point. He was even interviewed on television wearing a black mask. The Fox's most publicized action was the presentation of the "Fox Foundation for Conservation Action Award," a fifty-pound jar of sludge that he poured onto the office carpet of a U.S. Steel executive. "They keep saying that they aren't really polluting our water. If that is true, then it shouldn't hurt the rug, right?" he remarked. Then he disappeared, apparently forever.[7]

The Tucson Eco-Raiders should have borrowed a few more gizmos from the Fox's Houdini bag of tricks. In the summer of 1971, a group of college-age boys got fed up with the shopping center mania that was eating their hometown of Tucson, Arizona. At that time the city had no comprehensive planning legislation. Tacky housing developments and convenience stores were mowing down the Sonoran desert landscape that made the city unique. Stripped of saguaro cactus, delicate-branched paloverde, and the smoky scent of creosote after a rain, Tucson was turning into a last chance trailer park on the road to hell.

"We bear a particular grudge against developers who go in and flatten out everything," one of the Eco-Raiders told *Berkeley Barb* correspondent Tom Miller. "In general, if we see a nice area of the desert being destroyed, we'll do something about it."

"Something" encompassed a whole palette of vandalism techniques. The Eco-Raiders had a fine time cutting billboards, claiming hundreds during their two-year run. But that was just the beginning. The Eco-Raiders pulled up survey stakes from housing sites, poured lead in the locks of developers' offices, ripped out electrical and plumbing fixtures in unsold houses, broke windows, sabotaged bulldozers, and, in Miller's words, trashed "any object representing the outer edges of urban sprawl."

Occasionally the Eco-Raiders instructed Tucsonans on other environmental issues. "One time they carefully piled up thousands of aluminum cans and broken bottles at the doorstep of the Kalil Company, a local soft-drink bottler. They left an accompanying note: 'A little non-returnable glass: Kalil makes it Tucson's problem. We make it Kalil's problem.—Eco-Raiders.' "

The Eco-Raiders had a good run. But in 1973 the developers struck back. They pressured county officials until the sheriff's department agreed to put nine investigators on the Eco-Raiders case. Six weeks later it was a done deal. After profiling their suspects, the cops busted an Eco-Raider named Chris Morrison, correctly guessing that he would talk. The other four were rounded up within forty-eight hours. The phantoms of Southern Arizona had been made flesh.[8]

They would be made flesh again, but only after Edward Abbey, a seasonal park ranger who spent his winters in Tucson, made them fictional. The Eco-Raiders had no idea that more than half a million people would read Abbey's 1975 novel *The Monkey Wrench Gang*, which was loosely based on the Eco-Raiders' approach to citizen activism, along with a healthy dose of scenes borrowed from the Black Mesa bandits. And they could never have guessed that five years later, five disillusioned refugees from the mainstream environmental movement would decide to become another real-life monkey wrench gang.

Abbey wasn't the only one to take the craziness of the Eco-Raiders and Black Mesa Defense Fund to heart. Dave Foreman, former stomp and ex-nerd, considered the Santa Fe bohemians one of his biggest influences. Foreman had done his share of monkeywrenching up in the national forests in New Mexico, pouring sand in the odd bulldozer crankcase, yanking up survey stakes, retiring a power line here and there. But that was kid stuff. Foreman always thought big. Black Mesa Defense Fund, a collection of bright, talented people all doing their own thing without a boss or a committee: now *that* seemed like the right way to run an environmental group.

Foreman's unseemly departure from the Marines had fostered a real change. It wasn't just that he took a toke off a joint now and then. The years in Zuni had given Foreman a new respect for his own intuition. On the reservation, he found a way of looking at things he had never experienced in hick military towns.

"The Zuni rituals probably had more effect on me than I realized," he said later. "Just coming into contact with that whole different approach that was so different from the Church of Christ."

In 1967, Foreman had spent his first summer in the pueblo, teaching in the local Head Start program. When a sixteen-year-old Zuni girl drowned in a nearby lake, someone was needed to retrieve the body. None of the Zunis could swim, and only a few whites lived on the reservation. Police came to the whitewashed house on the hill where Foreman lived with his parents and asked him to do it. It would be baptism by total immersion all over again. But this time the result would be different.

Foreman and a friend from college slid on snorkeling masks and flippers. They found the body, still lifelike at the lake bottom. When they dragged it up on the shore, the Zunis stepped back in fear. They believed there was a water monster in the lake. Because Foreman had recaptured the girl's body before the monster was willing to give it up, he had become a marked man. They held a purifying ceremony for him, using a proxy because a white was not allowed in the ceremonial stone kiva. Even so, the next day Foreman's Head Start class was empty. Stay away from the lake, he was told. The water monster is after you. Foreman, who claimed to be an atheist, never went near the lake again.

Maybe it was the long tentacles of the water monster that brought Foreman closer to life and death in Zuni. He made a practice of going on solo hikes around the big mesa east of the pueblo. All alone, he free-climbed rock walls, risking his life for no particular reason. Floating on a handhold or on a boot tip lodged in a crack, he felt unmoored but not unhappy. He stumbled on cave paintings, including a multi-colored parrot five feet high. Investigating crevices and caves, he discovered etched stones and altars made with prayer feathers. These holy places were still used by the Zunis, whose pueblo dates from the 1300s and is one of the oldest continuously inhabited settlements in North America.

Foreman went drinking with the Zunis, which gave him another view of the culture. Ever the adaptable military brat, Foreman found he could get into their mind-set. "There was a different worldview, a different basis for relationships," he said. "I'd go out in a car full of Zunis, be the only Anglo in there. I mean, their sense of humor is very strange. You wouldn't get one of their jokes. But it was as though my head could make a shift and get in their frame of reference. And I could even start telling Zuni-type jokes."

Like Jack Loeffler, who had lived for a year in a forked-stick hogan on the Navajo reservation, Foreman was experiencing a different way of life. This culture took its rituals from the changing seasons, from the rocks and rain and blood and growth and the births and deaths of humans and animals. It was a far cry from the political realities that filtered into your brain with the dirty air you breathed in the East. Out here, something else was alive. Loeffler's anarchism was just a word for it, a white man's construct for something innate. It promised a way to make complete freedom work on a social scale, by setting up a community that would be small and tribal, with its own rituals and agreements, spoken and unspoken, shifting if necessary, but never coerced. No one would ever have to take an order. As Foreman later would be reminded, no one could give one either.

Coyotes
and
Town Dogs

1973—New Smyrna Beach, Florida

BY TWENTY-FIVE, Bart Koehler had done a lot of hard shifting from reverse into overdrive. High-school athlete. College fuck-up. Top student in his graduate program at the University of Wyoming. After he fell, he always climbed back up. He went higher each time, using signs and symbols from his personal mythology as handholds. Place names—obscure ones like Otto Road—surfaced with uncanny regularity in his wanderings. Grizzly bears changed his life. Peak experiences were all he knew.

But that winter, Koehler was uncharacteristically stuck in neutral. When Clif Merritt called him from the Wilderness Society's Denver office, Bart was living with his parents in Florida, saving money from his construction job so he could travel to Alaska. His April 21 departure date was carefully chosen. April 21 was Bart's birthday; it also was the birthday of John Muir, the brilliant and eccentric transcendentalist who had founded the Sierra Club. Even spookier, the exact day Koehler was born, April 21, 1948, was the day Aldo Leopold had died. Bart couldn't help thinking all this synchronicity must mean something. Maybe he was destined to save a great wilderness or something. Whatever it was, April 21, 1973, felt like the right day to start a new life.

In the meantime, Koehler was the only guy on the construction crew with a master's degree and "Help Save the American Bald Eagle" plastered on his hardhat. Each morning he'd gulp down his orange juice, then hump it at work for eight hours. At night he would run home across miles of flat white beach, plant himself in front of the TV, pound down a six-pack, wolf down his dinner, and pass out. In the mirror he saw a beefy guy with the dulled sensibilities of a farm animal.

So when Merritt asked if Bart would consider working for the Wilderness Society, Bart was speechless. Well, almost. "Fuckin' A, Clif!" were his exact words, or at least how he remembered them a decade later. All his carefully laid plans for April 21 went out the window. The negotiations were simple. Merritt told him that the Wilderness Society could pay him $400 a month for three months. Koehler made a counterproposal, asking if he could reduce his monthly pay to $300 and lengthen his job to four months. Offer accepted. Five years later, Koehler still hadn't learned his lesson. When the Wilderness Society was having financial problems, Bart and Dave Foreman offered to take a pay cut so that an additional staff person could be hired. Bart believes that this selfless gesture forever stamped the two cowboys as blatantly unprofessional in the eyes of William Turnage, who had recently taken over as the Wilderness Society's executive director.

"We didn't care," he said. "We didn't care at all. Our job was to go out and defend the country and save the world. As long as we had enough money to get gas, beer, and cheeseburgers, we'd sleep on the floor or outside. Screw it. I was twenty-five and ready to rock and roll."

Since the 1960s, Clifton Merritt had been building the perfect beast, the best field staff ever assembled by an environmental group.

Merritt's Buckaroos were a new breed of environmentalist. They weren't really hippies. Yeah, their hair was kind of long, but they were just as likely to trail the odor of mule shit as marijuana smoke. They were some kind of weird hybrid. Redneck hippies, you might call them. Tough, a little rough, almost low class, the Buckaroos were cut from a more homespun cloth than their predecessors. They were the scruffy coyotes in Mark Twain's *Roughing It*, a collection of archetypal tales filled with pathetically ignorant eastern dudes and savvy westerners of all species. Merritt's populist approach was distinctly western; its rough edges concealed a smooth intelligence. He said he looked for three things in his employees: education, an ability to work with people, and "a gut feeling for wilderness."

Merritt was a Montana boy with more than his share of gut feeling for wilderness. In 1956, he had founded the Montana Wilderness Association. It wasn't long before he faced the western conservationist's usual dilemma. Success in his home state led to an offer to work in Washington, D.C., light years away from the land that he was devoting his life to fighting for. Reluctantly, in 1964 he took a job at the Wilderness Society's Washington, D.C., office. But he kept his ear to the ground back at home. What he heard were the words "Copper Creek." It was a name he and his twin brother, Don, both remembered from their grandfather's hunting and fishing trips.

"I had it rumored to me that they were surveying a road up there," said Merritt. Sure enough, on a trip home, he hiked up the creek bed and saw a road stake planted in his family's old base camp. Roads meant logging, or even worse, seismic blasting for oil exploration. Merritt followed the trail of stakes over a rise leading up to a fishing spot named Heart Lake. As he walked, he came to the "violent" conclusion that they "would build a road there over my dead body."[1]

Merritt joined forces with an ex–forest ranger named Cecil Garland, who had been trying to whip up the citizenry to save 70,000 acres of backcountry outside Lincoln, Montana. The Lincoln backcountry wasn't full of big timber; what it had in abundance was fish. And bears. More than 10 percent of the grizzly bears killed each year came from the backcountry.[2] The term *biodiversity* hadn't been invented yet, but anyone who grew up fishing and hunting knew this was a hell of a place.

Merritt persuaded Garland to add Copper Creek to his proposal. In deference to local people who resented the federal government's "locking up" their land, he convinced him not to try to add the land to the Bob Marshall Wilderness. Instead, Merritt's strategy was to gain protection for the Lincoln-Scapegoat Wilderness separately, to avoid looking "hoggish."[3] It took them eight years to convince Congress to designate the wilderness area, which eventually consisted of 300,000 acres. Two decades later, Clif and Don Merritt were getting ready for a trip into the Lincoln-Scapegoat. By then, they were in their seventies. "There are still grizzly bears there, and wolves come through," Merritt said proudly.

When he assembled the Wilderness Society field staff with his lieutenant Jerry Mallett, Merritt found plenty of candidates with the requisite gut feeling for wilderness. The time was right. California may have led the 1960s cultural revolution, but the Rocky Mountain West was setting its sagebrush stamp on the pop culture of the 1970s. In Denver, the *Mountain Gazette*'s Western hipster New Journalism was setting the tone of a fleeting cultural renaissance. Gary Hart and Dick Lamm, good-looking Colorado cowboys with a progressive slant, were elected on a promise that environmental responsibility would replace rape-and-run.

But the old guard wasn't going down without a fight. A group of born-again privatizers called the Sagebrush Rebels wrapped themselves in the Marlboro man's mantle to cloak their true goal—keeping western resources flowing into corporate coffers. When he was elected president in 1980, Ronald Reagan chose one of their foot soldiers, James Watt, to be his Secretary of the Interior. Watt was affiliated with the Mountain States Legal Foundation, an antienvironmental bastion bankrolled by the right-wing union buster Joseph Coors, owner of the Coors Brewing Co. The southern Californian president who liked to play cowboy knew that the Sagebrush Rebels were the front men for the West's monied class, which happened to include some of his biggest campaign contributors. To be fair, Congress was hardly immune to their influence, either. For their parts, environmentalists were prostrated by the Reagan landslide. At first, even the powerful Sierra Club didn't oppose Watt's appointment.* Eventually a small-scale mutiny in the club's Washington, D.C., office generated opposition. But with Reagan's strong backing, Watt was confirmed.

Merritt's Buckaroos were sickened by the sight of the wimpish James Watt brandishing spurs and a ten-gallon hat. The cowboy image was their domain. They *owned* it. People like Bart Koehler and Dave Foreman had fallen deeply and irremediably in love with the American West. They were smitten with its sunset colors and prehistoric size, with the way empty spaces on the map translated into a long, lonely horizon. They were western heroes themselves, marked by the classic signs: macho flair, undying loyalty, and hearts of mush. The Buckaroos might have been naive in the ways of Washington, D.C., but their vision was right on target on their home turf, where a new generation was reclaiming the western myth.

"We were people who didn't make much money, and were, you know, sort of proud of being redneck wilderness people," said Tim Mahoney, a New England–born convert to the frontier who spent his twenties hanging around the Wilderness Society's Denver office until Clif Merritt finally had no choice but to hire him. "We drank beer and listened to country music and hit the bars and wore cowboy boots and things like that. We did not like the wine and Brie stereotype. And we didn't like the stereotype that was being used by wilderness opponents, that we were somehow effete Californians or easterners or city dwellers who were coming after their [turf]. . . . We felt like we were descendants of the frontier ethic, not them."

---

* The Sierra Club made a short-lived attempt to jockey for position after Reagan's election by appointing a Republican, Doug Wheeler, to the post of executive director. Since the ouster of firebrand David Brower in 1969, the job expectancy of Sierra Club executive directors has generally been short. Wheeler's tenure was briefer and less glorious than most. He left after most of the club's top executives threatened to resign.

For Mahoney, Foreman, and Koehler, the soundtrack of the 1970s wasn't the mechanized disco beat that was terrorizing the Top 40, but the reborn country-western twang of Willie Nelson, Waylon Jennings, and Jerry Jeff Walker. Even their name for themselves, the Buckaroos, came from a song on a Jerry Jeff Walker album titled, with self-conscious irony, *Viva Terlingua.*

"At the time in the 1970s, country music was going through one of its Nashville glitter kind of showbiz ways, really saccharine stuff," said Mahoney. "Willie Nelson and Waylon Jennings put out an album called *Outlaws* and it was a big hit. It was sort of Austin-oriented as opposed to Nashville-oriented. These were long-haired rednecks. They weren't Merle Haggard types who talked about the flag. They talked about drinking, pickup trucks, and having a good time. We liked that image, outlaws."

It all rubbed Doug Scott the wrong way, this messy, enthusiastic coup at the Wilderness Society. Scott had become the consummate Washington, D.C., insider. He left the Wilderness Society in 1973, after failing to convince Stewart Brandborg, the society's executive director, to set him up in Seattle as the West Coast counterpart to Clif Merritt. Anticipating the problems that would later cause major upheavals at the Wilderness Society, Scott landed a job as the Sierra Club's Northwest representative. He soon became known for his ability to maneuver legislation through Congress. Amateur hour was what Scott called the Buckaroos' Wilderness Society. Amateur hour.

It must have irked Scott that the legacy of his shadowy mentor, Howard Zahniser, was the real reason that the Buckaroos were embarrassing him with their crude humor and tacky clothes. Zahnie, as he was affectionately called, was a former civil servant who had succeeded biologist Olaus Murie as head of the Wilderness Society in the 1950s. Scott had written his graduate thesis on Zahniser's life work, the twenty-year effort to enact the Wilderness Act. In fact, the summer he spent researching his thesis at the Wilderness Society had been Scott's entree into the world of professional environmentalism. It would not be too much to say that Zahniser, who died before Doug

Scott could meet him, became a father figure to the young environmentalist. Scott laboriously traced Zahniser's strategy of compromise and consensus building, which he would use as a model for his own career. Over and over, Scott saw how Zahniser, like a benign, bookish spider, made delicate and not-so-delicate adjustments to the bill's language. There were sixty-six rewrites before the Wilderness Act finally passed Congress.

Zahniser's achievement was a turning point for the wilderness movement, and possibly for the American land ethic. Before its passage, wilderness had been only feebly protected by administrative designations. These could be subverted or overturned on a bureaucratic whim. The Wilderness Act gave *legislative* protection to nine million acres of wilderness and introduced a mechanism to protect more wilderness in the future. It was the terminal moraine left by the closing of the frontier, the mark left by a slow transformation of America's attitude toward its landscape. Seventy-five years after the frontier slid finally and forever into the Pacific Ocean, Americans decided that islands of wilderness in the United States had a right to exist.

For environmentalists, the Wilderness Act completely changed the ball game. It gave three of the four largest federal land-management agencies—the U.S. Park Service, the U.S. Forest Service, and the U.S. Fish and Wildlife Service—the enormous task of reviewing potential wilderness areas in their jurisdiction. The agencies were expected to make recommendations based on these reviews, but Congress had the ultimate power to designate wilderness. The Federal Land Policy Management Act, or FLPMA, also known as the BLM Organic Act of 1976, later set up a timetable for the U.S. Bureau of Land Management, which administers more land than any other federal agency, to go through the same process.

This was not exactly the way Zahniser had envisioned the law. Originally Zahniser intended wilderness designation to be a presidential prerogative. The right president could create the kind of national wilderness system that environmentalists dreamed about, reasoned Zahniser. Look at what Teddy Roosevelt had done with the national parks. But a last-minute deal brokered by President John F. Kennedy gave Congress the right to designate wilderness. Kennedy agreed to the change in order to appease a powerful legislator, Congressman Wayne Aspinall of Colorado. Aspinall had killed the bill in committee for eight years running. Kennedy's move may have been the only way to break the logjam.

Giving Congress the power to declare wilderness was only one of a series of significant compromises in the Wilderness Act. Some were truly awful. For instance, existing mining claims could be worked in wilderness areas until December 31, 1983, which led to an attempted fire sale under the Watt regime. Cattle grazing was also allowed in certain wilderness areas.

Weeks before the Wilderness Act passed, Zahniser died of a heart attack. The legend was that he died of a broken heart. A similar myth had grown up about the death of Sierra Club founder, John Muir, who died not long after Congress ignored his pleas to save a beautiful Sierra canyon named Hetch Hetchy. But although overwork may have contributed to Zahnie's early death—he was in his fifties—Doug Scott believes that Zahniser was far too resourceful a politician to regard Kennedy's deal as a defeat. Zahniser was not a mad Scot like Muir, careening off a battered childhood into an ecstatic world of nature and poetry. He died knowing that his life's work was about to become a reality, even if the price for victory was high. It may have been a fitting end for this master of strategic compromise.

It was left to Stewart Brandborg, Zahniser's successor at the Wilderness Society, to turn the expanded role of Congress into an advantage. After all, Congress could be lobbied. But it was a daunting, multifarious task. Federal agencies administered hundreds of *millions* of acres of federal land, most of it in the West. The tiny, underpaid staffs of environmental groups simply couldn't ride herd on all the places that would be hauled onto the chopping block in the next ten years. Brandborg's vision could be achieved only by tapping into a reservoir of volunteer labor.

Under Brandborg's regime, the Wilderness Society took the revolutionary step of forming citizens' wilderness committees. While the Sierra Club's highly politicized volunteer hierarchy rivaled the Boy

Scout merit-badge system in complexity, the Wilderness Society ran on seat-of-the-pants esprit. Sometimes it wasn't safe to be seen lurking in the hallways unless you were ready to become a star witness. Doug Scott worked for Brandborg in these early days. He remembers Brandborg closing down the office and chartering a bus to bring his entire staff, including secretaries and receptionists, to speak at a wilderness hearing for Shenandoah National Park. Somehow Brandborg even persuaded the bus driver to testify.

This was a whole new way of doing business. Historically, conservationists had relied on an old-boy network to get their message to government officials. Even the movement's noisy public crusades to keep dams out of Dinosaur National Monument and the Grand Canyon in the 1950s and early 1960s had been orchestrated by a select few. Now the old boys couldn't do it alone. As pressure mounted to divvy up the public lands, a whole raft of professional field organizers was needed to stage-manage the efforts of citizen activists. That's where people like Dave Foreman, Bart Koehler, and Tim Mahoney came in. By the mid-1970s they were in Doug Scott's face, on *his* turf in Washington, D.C., like a low-budget movie of his former life. And the soundtrack was the roar of thousands of students yelling "Fuck Nixon!" straight into his delicate, early-middle-aged eardrums. Or maybe it was "Earth First!"

Even the most arrogant New West hipster had the feeling that if Waylon Jennings or Willie Nelson ran into Dave Foreman at a Texas honky-tonk, they'd have a lot to talk about. Women, booze, putting up fence, or maybe, in Foreman's case, cutting it. All the young field staffers wore dusty cowboy boots and sported bandannas, but Foreman, well, Dave was the real thing, down to the Texas twang and the squint when he smiled. He had that ineffable quality, that *presence,* that made people seek his approval. Charisma, it was usually called. Foreman had joined Merritt's band of Buckaroos in the fall of 1973. He didn't have the most impressive credentials in the bunch, but he had a solid track record on national-forest issues in New Mexico. He and Debbie Sease had spent the previous summer camping out in the basement of the Albuquerque Environmental Center, learning the intricacies of U.S. Forest Service bureaucracy. Mostly, they were trying to get the agency to expand Aldo Leopold's prized Gila wilderness. In the process, they found themselves watchdogging the agency's first Roadless Area Review and Evaluation, known as RARE. When they weren't convincing people to write letters or attend hearings, Foreman and Sease were backpacking, checking maps to make sure the Forest Service was giving out accurate reports about the areas that it was studying. Like environmentalists all over the West, they were startled by how little the agency knew about the land that it managed.

Forest Service officials knew they had a problem and RARE was their first attempt to solve it. The inventory was kicked off in 1971, after an official suddenly realized that the new environmental laws passed around the time of Earth Day would be coming home to roost under the eaves of the agency's roof. Foremost among these was the National Environmental Policy Act, which for the first time required government agencies to consider the environmental impacts of their actions. The passage of NEPA was the biggest environmental victory of the decade, perhaps of several decades. But when Richard Nixon signed the act into law on January 1, 1970, it went virtually unnoticed.

Most environmentalists believe that two men, at most, understood what the president was signing that day. Ironically, the president wasn't one of them. One of the few people who may have understood the bill's ramifications was its Senate sponsor, Senator Henry "Scoop" Jackson. Jackson's support for the Vietnam War had earned him the epithet Henry Hawk, but he also was an ardent conservationist. It was Jackson who recruited an Indiana University professor named Lynton Caldwell to write NEPA. Caldwell became the legislative equivalent of a sniper behind enemy lines when he included the revolutionary "action enforcer" provision. This section required government agencies to assess the environmental impacts of major projects in a document called an Environmental Impact Statement, or EIS. Then the American public could comment on the agency's plans. If an interested party didn't get satisfaction through administrative challenges, a lawsuit could be brought.

NEPA was the equivalent of handing over a fleet of F-14s to a scrawny bunch of guerrilla fighters. The law was put to the test fairly quickly. Stewart Brandborg at the Wilderness Society and Brock Evans at the Sierra Club, two of the environmental movement's top leaders, decided to use NEPA to stop the Trans-Alaska pipeline that Interior Secretary Wally Hickel had so proudly announced on Earth Day. It was a lopsided battle, with the environmentalists on one side and oil companies, the federal government, and most of the media on the other. Even Brock Evans, the eloquent, Princeton-educated attorney who ran the Sierra Club's Washington, D.C., office, wasn't surprised when NEPA's godfather, Scoop Jackson, dumped his own law by refusing to oppose the pipeline. Evans had once been the Sierra Club's Northwest field representative and he had worked closely with Jackson. One of the arguments for the pipeline was national security, and Jackson wasn't called Hawk for nothing.

"Besides, when the two conflicted, NEPA being a symbol and the oil being real . . . nobody's gonna let ten billion barrels of oil go," Evans said.

Despite an all-out effort that virtually broke the bank at the Wilderness Society, the pipeline was approved. On July 17, 1973, Alaska Senator Mike Gravel pushed through an amendment that exempted the pipeline from the provisions of NEPA. The Senate was deadlocked forty-nine to forty-nine; Spiro Agnew cast the tiebreaking vote.

Today Evans claims that the administration's reliance on a vice-presidential tiebreaker indicated its desperation. "Spiro Agnew!" he expostulates. "They had to resort to *Spiro Agnew.*" But that was scant comfort in 1973. Chafing in defeat beneath the "pale sun" and the "cold mountains" of Alaska's magnificent Brooks Range, Evans wrote a heartbroken dispatch that was published in the *Sierra Club Bulletin*:

At that moment I came completely under the spell of the North; and for the first time I understood what Jack London and the others who came before us had written. There is a silence to this vast empty land, a special feeling that comes

only from being so far away from people or roads. It is something of the human spirit, touched by ancient memories of
what it once must have been like for the entire race so long
ago. . . . What really has happened—even more than the physical damage—is damage to the spirit of this land. This road
has broken that spirit, forever. . . .[4]

The Alaska pipeline battle set a pattern that was to be repeated
with other strong environmental laws, most notably the Endangered
Species Act. In cases where "social consensus," as Doug Scott calls it,
is lacking, or the interests of oil companies—or so-called national
security—appear to outweigh the rights of snail darters or red squirrels,
Congress simply overrules the law. Critics charge that the environmental movement has an unfortunate tendency to pass legislation that
is ahead of the mainstream. But it may simply be that Americans think
that squirrels and snail darters have rights most of the time, but not if
a major public-works project is on the line. Democracy, to paraphrase
James Madison, is sloppy.

So sloppy, in fact, that what appeared to be a devastating loss
turned out to be one of the environmental movement's greatest victories. The environmentalists' hard line ensured that the pipeline received more supervision than any oil project in history.* The
environmentalists routed the pipeline away from the Arctic National
Wildlife Refuge's coastal plain, a tundra at the foot of the remote
Brooks Range that has been compared to Africa's Serengeti. Most

---

* But not tough enough, apparently. A provision that would have required
double-hulled tankers (and probably would have prevented the *Exxon Valdez*
oil spill) was defeated. By 1987, out of twenty-nine federal and state inspec-
tions of the pipeline, eleven had revealed hazardous-waste violations. The oil
industry itself had reported more than 17,000 oil spills. In one case, 58,000
gallons of toxic liquid were spilled. Tundra ponds, which are essential com-
ponents of the fragile Arctic web of caribou, insects, and migratory birds,
were found to contain toxic metals and hydrocarbons. Nevertheless, the oil
industry continues to campaign to open the coastal plain of the Arctic National Wildlife Refuge to oil drilling.

important, the pipeline battle established the parameters of NEPA, "the environmental Magna Carta."

Under this new rule of law, even the U.S. Forest Service needed a rationale for its actions, or lawsuits would hail down from all quarters. For decades, the Forest Service had enjoyed an unprecedented degree of freedom from political controls. Unlike the national parks, which were lined with roads and tacky concessions, large sections of the national forests looked as if they had been frozen in a nineteenth-century landscape painting. The agency itself had a tradition of professionalism that sometimes bordered on arrogance. But as population increased and resources dwindled, developers began to gnaw away at the painting's edges. The Forest Service became the lightning rod for a conflict that involved ideology as well as land. From 1970 to 1990, the wilderness movement was caught in the long, convoluted, and frequently bitter process of imposing a new land ethic on a deeply entrenched federal bureaucracy. A more confrontational relationship between conservationists and government emerged out of this process. For people like Doug Scott, Bart Koehler, and Dave Foreman, it redefined not only their philosophies, but also the directions of their lives.

The storm was already brewing. With behind-the-scenes coaching from people like Clif Merritt, citizen activists—nobodies like eighth-grade dropout Cecil Garland and Alabama housewife Mary Burks— were propelling wilderness bills through Congress. Hell, these people weren't *professionals,* complained the Forest Service. But Congress didn't care. After all, the Forest Service doesn't vote, as veteran lobbyist Ernie Dickerman once pointed out. It wasn't enough for the self-important men in green to tell an irate Montana senator named Lee Metcalf to hold off on preserving the Lincoln-Scapegoat because they hadn't studied it yet. If they didn't get their maps and compasses out—and do it soon—the great unwashed would do it for them. Between the fall of 1971 and the summer of 1972, the Forest Service defensively launched RARE, the Roadless Area Review and Evaluation. The agency studied almost 1,500 roadless areas totaling 55.9 million acres, held 300 public meetings, and received more than

50,000 comments. It was the biggest public-involvement effort ever conducted by the federal government.

But it wasn't good enough. The Forest Service attitude toward wilderness was still in a Neanderthal stage—or as Dave Foreman might say, not Neanderthal enough. Absurd as it sounds, the agency insisted on writing environmental-impact statements on *protecting* roadless areas. Not too many detrimental effects there. But the agency refused to study the impacts of logging and mining. The logging practice called clearcutting, in which all the trees in one section of a forest are leveled, was especially controversial. In the 1960s clearcutting had become the method of choice for foresters. All over the country, logging companies were leasing tracts of national forest at bargain-basement prices and chopping down every tree in sight. Entire watersheds were left looking like scarred, dying victims of triple-canopy napalming.

Environmentalists had taken on this issue before. In 1973, a lawsuit over the Monongahela National Forest culminated in a decision that outlawed clearcutting. Once again, Congress responded by changing the law. The 1976 National Forest Management Act made clearcutting legal, but required replanting.

But foresters soon learned that it was impossible to re-create a dense, varied old-growth forest. Spraying herbicides and planting neat, orderly single-species tree farms just wasn't the same. Sometimes even replanting didn't work, especially on steep, eroded hillsides where seedlings had problems surviving. By the 1970s, less than 10 percent of the country's old-growth forest remained. Losing the remainder to clearcutting meant more erosion, a smaller gene pool, the loss of many species of birds, mammals, insects, and endemic plants. Yet another frontier would be closed.[5]

Environmentalists were determined that the Forest Service inventory reflect a commitment to preserving the frontier. The agency's first attempt was not reassuring. RARE set aside 12.3 million acres for further study, thereby opening the other approximately 67 million acres of roadless land to development. After the results were announced, the Sierra Club prepared to sue. But first environmentalists had to deal with dissension in their own ranks. Wilderness Society honchos were counseling the Sierra Club Legal Defense Fund against bringing the lawsuit; they considered it hopeless. Certain members of the Sierra Club also argued against it. They didn't want to damage the good working relationship that they had with the Forest Service. Like other venerable environmental organizations, the Sierra Club had a tradition of working with government agencies, not confronting them as adversaries.

The tough-minded SCLDF attorneys prevailed. *Sierra Club* v. *Butz* charged that logging or otherwise developing a potential wilderness area was indeed "a major federal action" that required an environmental-impact statement under NEPA. Before the judge could make a final ruling, the Forest Service backed down. This lawsuit, settled in 1972, gave environmentalists a handle for saving wilderness for the next 20 years.[6]

Once this question was settled, the Forest Service tried again. This time, the agency instituted a decentralized review process called unit planning. Because its implementation was left almost entirely up to the forest supervisors, unit planning was extremely inconsistent. In one case, a 400,000-acre roadless area was divided into twenty separate unit plans. In another case, three enormous roadless areas were lumped together for consideration. The process dragged on for years, inspiring innumerable lawsuits and administrative appeals. As the review process limped forward, it drew increased public scrutiny. Even Congress began to question the Forest Service. For its part, industry wised up, adopting the grass-roots tactics pioneered by environmental groups in the early sixties.

As wrangles in the sticks became increasingly nasty and chaotic, the Washington, D.C., pros were busy figuring out a way to turn the carnage to their advantage. In 1976, Doug Scott and Chuck Clusen, who were both working for the Sierra Club, came up with the artful concept of introducing an omnibus wilderness bill. They carefully selected potential wilderness areas that had enough political support to make it through Congress, packaging them under the label Endangered American Wilderness. The second criterion Scott and Clusen used to select places was how they had fared in the RARE process.

Certain places were included to show how wrong the RARE evaluations were. It was a brilliant move from the point of view of Washington, D.C., a massive wilderness coup that would at least partially preempt the Forest Service.

But a blue-eyed nurse named Nancy Morton thought it stank. Morton had just spent several years of her relatively young life trying to protect 61,000 acres of oak-studded foothills outside Lassen National Park in northern California. The area was named for a Yahi Indian named Ishi, the last Native American to grow up isolated from whites. In 1911 Ishi had emerged from these hills, a lonely ghost in search of a vanished civilization. Even today, the place conveys a sense of mystery, its curving, lion-colored hillsides marked by drifts of chaparral. But like many other areas suggested by local activists, Ishi's land was not included in the Endangered American Wilderness bill. Because it had only lukewarm support from its congressman, an infamous wilderness opponent named Harold "Bizz" Johnson, it didn't fit into the sure-thing strategy.

All over the country, grass-roots activists were finding out that the Endangered American Wilderness Act was merely a postponement of battle. In Oregon, an articulate, aggressive college dropout named Andy Kerr had been trying to include in the bill an old-growth forest called the Kalmiopsis. Kerr's attempt failed in the face of opposition from Sen. Mark Hatfield. The Oregon Republican was a liberal, Kerr discovered, except when it came to confronting the timber companies that had clearcut the state's politics for generations. But the Kalmiopsis—and Kerr—would surface again in national environmental politics.

Several places in New Mexico were also aced out of the bill, which galled Dave Foreman. Maybe he had been spending too many days in the hot southwestern sun, baling hay and turning on the charm with local ranchers. His patience with the laggards in Washington, D.C., was slowly draining away. He and Scott had never hit it off anyway, and Scott's glitzy PR approach to Endangered American Wilderness irked Foreman. He took pleasure in pointing out that Scott had actually chosen the *least* endangered wilderness to box and package in the bill.

In the following years, Scott was more than happy to cop to this strategy. His reasoning was that a bill that couldn't pass would merely confirm the Forest Service's faulty RARE II diagnosis. It was better to let those issues ripen, concentrating on areas around which consensus had already formed, the A Number One Easies, as Brandborg called them. "Each area was ready to go but didn't look it—that was the stroke of genius about it," Scott proudly told Forest Service historian Dennis Roth.[7] In any case, not all environmentalists were so critical of Scott. Steve Evans, Nancy Morton's partner in the late 1970s, worked with her on the Ishi wilderness proposal. Scott's strategy was effective, but it set an unfortunate precedent, said Evans, who is now conservation director of the environmental group Friends of the River. "The Endangered American Wilderness Act was the first big omnibus bill, so it showed it could be done. But it set the tone of future wilderness bills. It meant that areas that were very endangered, with lots of conflict, tended to be dropped."

That was tough, as far as Doug Scott was concerned. True, Jimmy Carter's 1976 election had created a friendlier climate for environmental legislation. But why take chances? So far things were looking pretty good. For one thing, the lanky Mo Udall had risen to even greater heights of power in the Democratic election sweep. When the six-foot-five Arizonan found out he had become chair of the House Interior Committee, he hugged the much smaller Chuck Clusen, Scott's colleague at the Sierra Club, saying heartily, "Now let's pass that Endangered Bill." You could almost hear the word *pardner* dangling in the air like a promise of environmental victories to come.[8]

But the forces of darkness never rested. One day, Doug Scott was listening to the drone of voices in a stuffy hearing room, waiting for Rupert Cutler to give testimony on behalf of the Endangered American Wilderness bill. Cutler had recently been appointed by Carter to a high post in the U.S. Department of Agriculture, the government agency that included the Forest Service. Scott knew he could count on support from Cutler, who had been assistant executive director of the Wilderness Society in the 1960s. When he took the microphone, Scott didn't expect any surprises.

Scott wasn't reckoning on the pressure Cutler was facing from powerful timber and mining interests. Before his confirmation hearing, he had met with timber industry officials and listened to their fears about the "uncertainties" plaguing the national forests. Cutler agreed to speed up the inventory process.

Cutler duly testified on behalf of the Endangered American Wilderness Act. But then he dropped a bombshell, announcing that the Forest Service would be undertaking one gigantic programmatic EIS to determine the fate of the nation's forests.

Doug Scott was floored. The next morning, he ran over to the Forest Service. The chief showed him the sketchy outline of the six-month inventory that was to become RARE II, the Second Roadless Area Review and Evaluation. Scott says his first thought was: "Here's another quick and dirty attempt to get rid of the wilderness issue."[9] Nevertheless, swayed by his friendship for Rupe Cutler, Scott decided to support RARE II. As it turned out, the inventory process would last not six, but eighteen months. And its results would be even worse than Scott feared.

Scott's support for the project was important. The eager graduate student had become one of the most powerful environmentalists in the country. Doug Scott was a Horatio Alger figure. The son of a kitchen-cabinet salesman, he grew up camping in the national forests of his native Pacific Northwest. In the early days of his career he had handed out copies of Saul Alinsky's *Rules for Radicals* like candy to children. Like Alinsky, Scott never lost his belief that the system worked—if you knew how to work it. That was what Howard Zahniser had done. Now Scott was doing it, too. In the 1970s, Scott became recognized as the environmental movement's foremost strategist. But critics charged that his tactical brilliance prevented him from seeing the big picture. Scott spoke in a moving fashion about the little people, the volunteers in Iowa and South Dakota. But his hardheaded practicality—like his decision on the Ishi wilderness—sometimes left them feeling betrayed.

When Scott moved over to the Sierra Club, he and Clusen edged out the more passionate, emotional Brock Evans. Evans was a hold-over from the regime of David Brower, the "archdruid" who had almost singlehandedly steered the Sierra Club to national prominence. Brower was ousted in 1969 when his difficult management style and fiscal freehandedness alienated the club's board. But many of his hand-picked staff remained. Like Brower, Evans had an expansive view of his mission. Even when he lost the first round, he was confident of eventual victory because he believed history—if not God Himself— was on his side. If he could nudge the tide forward, so much the better. But this wasn't good enough for the new pragmatists at the Sierra Club, who considered Evans more style than substance. It wasn't long after Scott moved up in the ranks that the charismatic, if somewhat manic, Evans was kicked upstairs. Soon he accepted a high-level job at the Natonal Audubon Society, where he continued to take aggressive stands on controversial issues.

Doug Scott prided himself not so much on his idealism as on his ability to get things done. He felt it was his responsibility to the bal-looning membership of the Sierra Club. Many of the club's members were volunteers who devoted significant portions of their lives and incomes to its activities. By the mid-1980s, when he became the club's conservation director, Scott's power was enormous. With a few mach-inations and a stroke of a pen, he could get tens of thousands of letters fluttering their way into congressional mailboxes. Political wisdom holds that when an elected official receives one letter, it represents the views of one hundred like-minded but lazier people. Scott had no intention of diluting the Sierra Club's substantial clout by enrolling his precious letter writers in a lost cause—nor was he willing to risk losing their loyalty by being branded a loser. "I used to suggest that, Doug, you want to always consider the ethical approach, too," said Merritt. "He said, 'Well, as a youngster I had to grow up as the smallest and youngest of four brothers. I had to fight to survive and that's all I know.' " Scott's career had become a perfectly tuned aesthetic response to the forms and rituals of Washington, to the symmetry of the game.

By 1978, Scott's approach seemed to be vindicated, not just by his legislative successes, but by disarray at the more gung-ho Wilderness Society. In the early 1970s, Stewart Brandborg had dipped into the group's endowment to fight the Alaska pipeline. For a short time, it had actually looked as if Brandborg's troops had stopped the military-industrial complex dead in its giant tire tracks. At this heady point, the Wilderness Society made a disastrous effort to computerize. Membership figures became a guessing game as a dozen keypunch operators sent membership lists into an electronic twilight zone, where the Red Queen of magnetic tape bestowed no privileges, but rained down renewal notices at a hectic nonsensical clip. This failed attempt to go high-tech multiplied the society's financial woes.

As money got tight, Brandborg's administration became erratic. Finally he sparked an all-out war by firing the editor of the organization's magazine, *The Living Wilderness*. Appalled at the change of attitude at the Wilderness Society, which had always functioned more like a family than an employer, Harry Crandell quit. His fellow lobbyist Ernie Dickerman stayed loyal to Brandborg.

The uproar reached all the way to the Wilderness Society's governing council. After a period of agonized soul-searching and frantic bean-counting, Brandborg left the organization in late 1975. Clif Merritt once again agreed to camp out in Washington, filling in as executive director. But Merritt's heart was always in fieldwork. He used his temporary elevation to juggle a few budget items so that he could rebuild the western field staff gutted by Brandborg in an earlier cost-cutting move. After two and a half months, the board sent Merritt back to Denver. George Davis, a conservationist from the Adirondacks, was hired as executive director. But Davis, too, was unable to get the organization's financial or administrative problems under control. In 1977, the Wilderness Society governing council took the unprecedented step of asking a woman to rescue the once-thriving conservation group. To this day, Celia Hunter remains one of the few females to have headed a major U.S. conservation organization. But that was not the only thing that made her tenure at the Wilderness Society revolutionary. Hunter was an Alaskan frontierswoman with a progressive bent. She hauled the Buckaroos into Washington, D.C., like a band of dirty, thirsty, saddle-sore cowboys in from the range. Washington might be the same again, but the Buckaroos wouldn't.

5

West
Meets
East

I went back to Ohio
But my pretty countryside
Had been paved down the middle
By a government that had no pride

—Chrissie Hynde of the Pretenders
"My City Was Gone," 1982

1978—Rosslyn, Virginia

THE RAT SWAYED in the breeze. Gently, because it was an eastern breeze. A wimpy current of air, not likely to push the dead rodent out of his hangman's noose onto the nests of newspapers, catcher's mitts, old boots, and dirty socks that lined the back porch. He was safe up there. Safer than he had ever been before, probably.

The rat proved one thing: it wasn't easy being a Buckaroo in the big city. Certain accommodations had to be made. For instance, when they moved into the bilious-green house, Dave Foreman, Debbie Sease, and Tim Mahoney christened it the Bunkhouse. The Buckaroo Bunkhouse. Of course, they had a sacred mission to make it live up to its name. When the varmints railroaded out from behind the kitchen stove, there was only one thing to do. String them up on the back porch the same way ranchers strung up dead coyotes, a crude warning to their furry kin. The effect on other rats may have been negligible, but the dangling rodents added a pungent *je ne sais quoi* to the Bunkhouse mystique.

Not that it needed much help. The Buckaroo Bunkhouse quickly became a rowdy safe house for western environmentalists on their periodic D.C. trips. Most of the regulars worked for the Wilderness Society. There was Jim Eaton, a stocky, unassuming guy who was mastering the sleazy art of California's backroom politics. Sweet-voiced Susan Morgan, the education director at the Denver office, was also a frequent flier to Washington. All the women who hung out with the Buckaroos had to win their spurs as Buckarettes, and Morgan was no exception. But she refused to participate in the Buckarette initiation ceremony. "Sorry, guys," she explained. "I'm just not going to pee off a bridge." Fortunately, the requirements were flexible. The only things you needed to qualify were balls, or some reasonable facsimile thereof. Morgan became a Buckarette. Eventually they all decided Buckarette was sexist and she became a Buckaroo.

Bart Koehler was another welcome visitor. Bart was the one who had spotted the Bunkhouse, which seemed appropriate to everyone. Bart, who had that funky, magical touch, a guy who played howling rock and roll, drew funny, quirky, little pictures, and saw signs and portents everywhere. Years later, talismans kept his morale up as he achieved the impossible: stopping logging in over one million acres of old-growth habitat in the Tongass National Forest, a piece of Alaskan rain forest bigger than Rhode Island. By then, nobody was cracking a smile at Bart Koehler's rodeo-star-sized belt buckle with a grizzly bear on it or the howling coyotes on his red power tie. They just swallowed hard and begged him to make their cause his next congressional end run.

But in 1978, Bart was still in the chorus line. His buddy Dave Foreman was the one with the big promotion. The fifth-generation New Mexico redneck with the near-genius IQ had agreed to move to Washington for just one year. He would be the liaison between the Wilderness Society's entire field operation and its lobbying staff, although his title—Coordinator of Wilderness Affairs—inspired him to describe his duties as "making sure everybody got laid out in the boonies."

At times, Foreman probably wished his new job were that easy. Washington, D.C., was a tougher league than Foreman had ever played. Like the other western wilderness freaks, Foreman felt penned up in the airless, shuttered rooms of the capital. In the concrete bull's-eye of Pierre L'Enfant boulevards, jaded bureaucrats decided the lives and deaths of uncounted species, of timber rattlers, elk, and caribou, grizzly bears, timber wolves, coyotes, trumpeter swans, and whooping cranes. The city hummed with power; the opportunities were staggering compared to what you could accomplish in Laramie, Wyoming, or Phoenix, Arizona. Whether they saw it as a political mecca or an urban hell, it was hard for a serious environmentalist *not* to be drawn to Washington, D.C.

That snowy January, the raw recruits to urban hell were being mysteriously beckoned not by the capital itself but by "the dismal canyons of Rosslyn, Virginia," to quote an unsung tabloid poet. Bart had agreed to keep Dave and Debbie company while they searched for a suitable habitat for themselves and Tim Mahoney, who was moving to Washington in a few weeks. Should any landlord question the morality of their living arrangement, Foreman was prepared to pass Mahoney off as Debbie's ne'er-do-well brother, although he neglected to devise an explanation for why their checking accounts bore three different names. Leaving such minor details for later, Bart, Debbie, and Dave squeezed into the front seat of Foreman's pickup and started scoping. The requirements were simple. No Formica in the kitchen. (Dave insisted that Formica reeked of urban life.) With a yard. (Obviously.) Cheap, because none of them made more than $14,000 a year, not even Foreman.

Minimal as these demands were, Washington, D.C., couldn't seem to satisfy them. Ergo unglamorous Rosslyn. Because it lay just over the border in Virginia, it had weaseled out of the rule that buildings in the nation's capital could not exceed the height of the Washington Monument. Once upon a time Rosslyn might have been a nice, if unpretentious, town. But skyscraper office buildings and luxury high rises were swallowing up any modest claim to all-American ambience Rosslyn might have boasted. Only a few scattered remnants of it remained, including a decrepit farmhouse painted a bizarre shade of chartreuse.

"That's your house!" roared Koehler. "It's straight out of American Gothic!" Foreman made a quick turn, parking in front of the house with the wraparound porch. A sleazy used-car dealership shouted polyester and vinyl on one side, a vacant lot died quietly on the other, and a For Rent sign was planted haphazardly out front. They piled out of the truck and walked up to the front door. Inside was a thicket of lath. A fine mist of plaster dust swam in the air.

"No Formica," said Sease.

Koehler pointed to the bombed-out vacant lot next door. "Yard," he said.

They took it.

A trust-fund beneficiary might have balked at their lifestyle, but the young environmentalists were rich in what really mattered: political capital. The decade preceding their arrival in Washington had transformed environmentalism into a mass movement by combining the traditional wilderness-preservation agenda with antipollution activism. Historically, the conservation movement had been a creature of the romantic sensibility, an elitist, primitivist reaction to the frontier's closing in 1890. When the noose of barbed wire tightened around the American West, wilderness ceased to be the dark, satanic force of the Puritan imagination. Instead of being threatening, wilderness itself became threatened. As the wheels of the machine hummed closer in the latter half of the twentieth century, the wilderness ethic filtered out of country clubs and into barrooms and truck stops. The Buckaroos were the link between the two stages of the movement, blue-jeaned, beer-drinking ambassadors to the trailer park.

A new culture was evolving with this consciousness. Dave Foreman, the onetime anthropology major in cowboy boots, called the people who shared it the wilderness tribe. These were the people who knew they were losing ground every time a mall developer plowed up a Joshua tree or a "nuisance" grizzly bear was shot in Yellowstone. Foreman didn't go so far as to call the Buckaroos a loudmouthed subset of the tribe, young braves out for the kill. But he could have. Their leader was just as much of an outsider, an uppity, unconventional woman. Like them, the woman was not disheartened even though she knew the entire throw weight of industrial society was aimed at the things she cared about most. Every inch of lost ground just made her more determined to kick ass. Politely.

The daughter of a Washington State stump farmer, Celia Hunter arrived in Alaska in 1948, after flying pursuit planes as a World War II WASP (Women's Air Force Service Pilots). She and her fellow WASP Ginny Wood staked land outside Mount McKinley National Park, constructing a few tent cabins for tourists seeking an out-of-the-ordinary wilderness vacation. Anticipating the Park Service, they named their resort Camp Denali. The two women ran it successfully for twenty-five years before selling out in 1975, when wilderness travel had become a luxury commodity.

But Hunter was more than a frontier entrepreneur. She had grown up as a Quaker and felt strongly about a wide array of liberal causes. By the time she retired from the tourist trade, Hunter had become a power in Alaska's new, embattled conservation movement. The Wilderness Society had deep roots in Alaska, where Olaus Murie, one of its founders, had conducted pioneering studies of predator/prey relationships. In 1969, Hunter joined the society's governing council. In 1976, she became its president.

Within six months of Hunter's accession to the post of acting executive director of the Wilderness Society in June of 1977, the organization's structure had changed dramatically. The biggest change was that field representatives were no longer reporting only to Clif Merritt. The lines of authority had gotten murky. More often than not, they were answering to a new coordinator in Washington, D.C., who was being used by Celia to consolidate her power. His name was Dave Foreman. Along with Foreman, most of the Denver office staff had been transferred to Washington or out to the field.

By agreeing to the transfers, the field staff was reluctantly supporting Hunter's decision to gut the Denver office. Although Merritt would always be revered, a personality clash between Hunter and Jerry Mallett, Merritt's lieutenant, had caused a rift that was threatening to destroy the organization. Even Foreman believed that leadership had to be centralized if the Wilderness Society was going to survive.

Merritt and Mallett remained in the Denver office for a few months, while nearly everyone else moved on. Tim Mahoney was given the choice of becoming a field representative or moving to Washington. He sweated over the decision, but finally resolved that he could do the most good by using his RARE II expertise in the largest possible arena. Foreman had already been promoted to the D.C. office. Mahoney joined him there in early January. The pressure on the two rookies was enormous. Celia Hunter and the other staff members were consumed with the organization's financial and administrative problems. Foreman and Mahoney found themselves making policy decisions formerly handled by men twice their age.

If Clif Merritt's flannel-shirted field reps were ugly ducklings to Doug Scott, they were swans-in-waiting to Hunter. "We loved Celia because Celia loved and valued us," remembers Tim Mahoney. "She saw us as talented and deserving of more support than we had been getting. She promoted us—we didn't have any money so there wasn't much salary—and brought us to Washington and really let us run the program."

By the end of their climactic first year in Washington, Foreman and Mahoney had gone in separate directions, although they remained close friends. Foreman was moving toward an emotional center that lay somewhere west of the hundredth meridian. Mahoney was learning how to be a high-functioning schizophrenic: keeping his heart pure, but getting his hands dirty.

Foreman had learned his formative lessons from the unabashedly populist Clif Merritt. He wasn't about to change his style just because he was going back east. For instance, his mother, Lorane, had insisted that he buy a suit after his big promotion. Skip, finally proud of his son, anted up the cash. Foreman strutted home wearing a western-cut suit and a big ten-gallon hat. This egregious outfit proved that it was a long way from Albuquerque, New Mexico, to the carpeted environs of Brooks Brothers or J. Press, those stalwarts of bureaucratic mufti. To be fair, Foreman's clothes weren't any worse than those of the other Wilderness Society staff members, who had an unfortunate propensity for polyester leisure suits particularly ill chosen for those formal lobbying occasions.

But Foreman wasn't just an awkward dresser; he was openly rebellious. Confined by the neoclassical lines of official architecture and systematic deal-making of Washington, D.C., Foreman reacted by becoming more redneck-than-thou. Even before his promotion, he had a habit of flying in from New Mexico for lobbying trips wearing cowboy boots caked with mule shit, courtesy of Nellie Belle Queen Bee Junebug. Then he'd make sure to cross his legs elaborately in the Senate hearing room, just to let them know he was the real thing, not some Robert Redford cowboy. Not that they couldn't see him coming a mile off. They might even have smelled him.

Like most of the Buckaroos, Foreman wasn't the least bit embarrassed when rough edges poked out from beneath his too-tight collar. Back in his field-rep days, Foreman had designed a slide show on the history of wilderness in America. Ron Kezar, a Texas medical librarian and Sierra Club conservation chair, got a kick out of the hokey presentation, particularly when Foreman referred to those "effete easterners" while flashing a slide of Gainsborough's curly-locked and beribbonned Blue Boy. The next slide revealed the stirring sight of a mountain man on horseback, representing the virile West. It was a myth Foreman would cling to for a long time.

More comfortable with giving orders (genially, of course) than taking them, Foreman found his perfect boss in Celia Hunter. "We got along well because I left him alone. He did his thing and I did mine," Hunter said. "Dave's a rugged individualist. He always kidded himself about being—what was it?—a male chauvinist. He really can play the role beautifully, but he isn't that at all. I think he's very respectful of women in many ways. He certainly gives them credit for having brains. But he's not a political animal. He'd be fine in New Mexico, in the local rough-and-tumble of politics at that level. But he doesn't like this whole slick thing of how you buy your way into power you don't earn."

Hunter was right about one thing. Foreman was out of his element. Like Mahoney and the others, he was still learning how to negotiate with the horse traders in Congress. The New Mexico delegation wasn't caving in to him the way he'd hoped. In fact, Dave was being forced to lobby for a New Mexico wilderness bill that actually contained *less* land than the Forest Service had recommended. Exhausted by a decade of seventy-hour work weeks and frustrated by the trade-offs he was making, Dave Foreman fantasized about resurrecting the Striders. Whimsically named after the woodland scouts in J. R. R. Tolkien's books, the Striders were an off-the-cuff political group organized by Bill Mounsey, a Denver-based outdoor guide who occasionally worked for the Wilderness Society. The Striders crashed a few hearings in the mid-seventies, making outlandish proposals that reflected the spirit of true wilderness freaks. In Foreman's view, these proposals weren't any more extreme than the ideas being tossed around by the Sagebrush Rebels. Yet the poisonous little nerds in cowboy hats were considered *normal*. Mounsey's idea was to provide a counterweight to the phony cowboys by offering a radical environmental alternative. That way, the Striders would move the parameters of the debate and come up with a truly fair compromise. It was a strategic way of thinking, but very different from the clockmaker's art of internal springs and levers that Tim Mahoney was learning. It was an outsider's strategy, an obvious choice for the perennial new kid in town—and for a grown-up whose guiding passion was to change the politics of the American West. After all, nobody knew exactly where Middle Earth was supposed to be, but it sure as hell wasn't inside the Beltway.

It was ironic that of all the Buckaroos, it was the house radical, Tim Mahoney, who learned the lessons of Washington, D.C., best. As the Rocky Mountain range wars grew increasingly bloody, Mahoney emerged as one of the environmental movement's toughest gunfighters. Shy, but with a core of self-confidence, Mahoney grew up Irish Catholic in a hardscrabble central New Hampshire town called Contoocook. When he moved to Denver in 1975, he felt a strong physical affinity for the Colorado high country. Its steep granite mountains and dark pine trees were an idealized portrait of the White Mountains of New Hampshire, where he had spent the happiest summers of his youth. When he moved to Denver he immediately became, in his own words, "a western chauvinist." After a few discouraging years of beating on the door, Mahoney carved himself a job as a hired gun for the Wilderness Society. He specialized in fighting Forest Service logging plans, traveling from state to state in the West to coach local environmentalists. Later Mahoney would reflect that the beginning of his career was more similar to Doug Scott's than to Dave Foreman's. Like Scott, he started with a big national group, rather than as a citizen activist on his native turf. Educated at Tufts University outside Boston and the University of Michigan, where he earned a master's degree in plant ecology, Mahoney was also more sophisticated than most of the Buckaroos. As an easterner, he was familiar with how formidable the opposition really was, its tightly woven strands of power and influence stretching from prep school to global corporate monopolies. And like Doug Scott, Mahoney began his career steeped in left-wing politics. He was young and emotional, a street fighter.

But when Mahoney came to Washington, he discovered that the schtick that played to a packed house in Boise laid an egg in the Senate lunchroom. It hit Mahoney like a bolt of white light when he heard a presentation by veteran lobbyist Ernie Dickerman at a Wilderness Society conference. "I had never lobbied. All my work had been with the Forest Service in a very confrontational way. I would analyze their plans; they were terrible. I would attack them venomously, threaten to undo them, threaten to go to court, file administrative appeals. We changed a great number of plans throughout the Rocky Mountain region. In a very confrontational way, not the way you lobby Congress.

"Ernie Dickerman, in an hour of explaining to a group of green people—I was just sitting there eavesdropping—explained more about how to lobby . . . he explained what simpleminded, malleable people members of Congress were. If you would just treat them nicely, really all they wanted to do was get reelected. If you remembered that, and that they really wanted to be kind of popular and that they didn't really want to fight, in fact would go to great lengths to avoid fighting . . . it all kind of clicked into place."

Eventually Mahoney came to believe that it was the "uncompromising" local activists who got creamed in Washington. Dickerman's soft-sell technique concealed negotiating skills equal to those of the toughest used-car dealer—or politician. Modulation was the key: knowing when to push harder and when to back down. Mahoney found himself intrigued by the subtleties of the game. Eventually he would play it better than anyone else. But that didn't solve the immediate problem. In 1978, the Wilderness Society was long on guts, but short on the most valuable commodity of all—experience.

By the summer of 1978, the furor over RARE II was building. But for the Buckaroos it was nearly eclipsed by the furor at the Wilderness Society. Hunter had been able to do little more than hold the line in the red zone. Finances and membership, the two vital signs for any environmental group, were disastrous. The group's original endowment, left to them by Bob Marshall, had vanished. For eight of the previous ten years the society had run a deficit. The computer operation was such a mess that for a long time nobody knew how many members there were. But as Celia Hunter and her staff struggled to make sense of the data-entry nightmare, they realized that the figures seeping out from the system's cracked silicon innards didn't look good. They indicated that the group's enrollment had dropped from 70,000 to something like 40,000.

Around Labor Day, the governing council cleaned house in a big way. They told Celia to book her passage back to Alaska; they had hired a Yale- and Oxford-educated mountain climber from the exotic enclave of Big Sur, California, to replace her. His name was Bill Turnage. His claim to fame was that he had worked as a business manager for Ansel Adams, the photographer whose black-and-white panoramas of Yosemite had indelibly etched the park's image in the public's imagination. Turnage was a well-heeled hit man, the result of a seventeen-month search to find someone with sufficient toughness to turn the organization around. Arrogant, blunt-spoken, and unremittingly upper-class, with a mouth so full of marbles he sounded like he was choking, Turnage couldn't have been better chosen to infuriate the Buckaroos.

Despite his pretentiousness, Turnage was not a lightweight. He had an intelligently conceived idea of the niche he wanted the Wilderness Society to fill in the environmental movement. It was somewhere between the Natural Resources Defense Council and the Sierra Club, a think tank with political teeth. So far, no environmental organization had combined hard science with the Sierra Club's legislative clout. Turnage wanted to return the Wilderness Society to the glory days of Bob Marshall and Aldo Leopold. In the 1930s and 1940s, the Wilderness Society had been the most influential conservation group in national politics, as well as the movement's intellectual and philosophical leader. At the very least, Turnage was determined to keep the organization alive—and to leave his stamp on it.

Their den mother may have been gone, but the young coyotes weren't going to leave the den without a fight. At first, the conflict was discernible only as a subtle tension that permeated the office and gave an interesting edge to social occasions. Ron Tipton, a staff member hired after the purge, vividly remembers his first meeting with both Turnage and Foreman. It was a social evening; the guests even took a sauna together. But Tipton says he could sense the two men preparing for war.

In fact, Tipton remembers a special dynamic existing between Turnage and Foreman. They seemed to like each other, although Foreman later remarked that the idea of Bill Turnage liking him caused him "undying uneasiness." But Tipton believes there was an odd attraction between the two, an intensity that neither experienced with other people on the staff. "Dave always respected people who were intelligent," Tipton said. "Bill has a first-class mind. Bill and Dave were very formidable adversaries. They took each other on in a very interesting way." He paused before adding, "It was an unfair fight, of course, because Bill was running the show."

Before the struggle over the future of the Wilderness Society could erupt into full-scale war, RARE II did. On January 4, 1979, Rupert Cutler announced the results of the survey. Only ten million acres in the Lower 48 states were recommended for wilderness. Thirty-six million acres were opened for development and eleven million acres were set aside for further planning. In addition, Cutler had succeeded in getting five million acres of Alaska's Tongass National Forest recommended for wilderness preservation. Dave Foreman and his friend Howie Wolke, a Friends of the Earth representative in Wyoming, believed there were an additional eighteen million acres of roadless land throughout the West that had not even been included in the study, either because of bad map work or bureaucratic finagling. That land would be open to development, too.

A hasty summit meeting was called. The Wilderness Society was represented by Dave Foreman, Tim Mahoney, and Roger Scholl, Celia Hunter's former second-in-command. But Doug Scott and John McComb, who were working for the Sierra Club, dominated the talks. Doug Scott expressed himself in his usual vehement way. His position was that a RARE II lawsuit would provoke a violent anti-environmental backlash. Still working on Zahniser's model, Scott wanted to "control the politics" in the way that environmentalists had in years past, when small-scale wilderness bills were maneuvered through Congress. After hours of unhappy negotiations, Foreman and the others quelled their doubts and agreed not to sue over RARE II. Instead, they resolved to work on several bills that would repair some of the damage.

But as the months passed and no significant bill left the starting gate, Huey Johnson got restless. Johnson was California's commissioner of natural resources under Zen governor Jerry Brown. California had fared particularly badly in RARE II, and Johnson wanted to sue. In the summer, the Wilderness Society dispatched its California representative, Jim Eaton, to talk sense to Johnson. Tim Mahoney flew out from Washington to lend weight to the argument and Trent Orr of the Natural Resources Defense Council drove up to Sacramento from San Francisco. Eaton remembers orbiting in a rattan chair that hung from the ceiling in Johnson's office, wondering what strait-laced industry people thought when they entered this garden of countercultural artifacts. If they underestimated Johnson, they were wrong. Johnson was a tough customer who had pioneered successful land-preservation schemes when most of the conservation movement was still bouncing around in tennis shoes. Eaton, Mahoney, and Orr extracted a promise that Johnson would give the environmentalists thirty days to pull together a response to RARE II that didn't involve litigation. Five days later, with no warning, Johnson sued the Forest Service.

The political impact of Johnson's suit was enormous. Not only did he win, but the precedent left the Forest Service RARE II recommendations in every western state open to similar challenges. The political landscape was changing very rapidly. In Johnson's case, *California v. Bergland*, the court decided that site-specific environmental-impact statements were required before a roadless area could be developed. The court also ruled that RARE II did not fulfill this requirement. Once again, the Forest Service had blown a chance to meet the requirements of NEPA.

After the Johnson suit, statewide wilderness bills became the political medium through which management of the national forests was filtered. The new statewide system had a number of disadvantages. Environmentalists often were forced to negotiate on the basis of over-all acreage instead of on the merits of individual areas. Even worse, the price for passing virtually every bill was something called "release language," which meant that environmentalists couldn't bring a Huey Johnson–style lawsuit in that state. The days when a lobbyist could patiently let political consensus ripen around each wilderness area were over. It was the antithesis of the slow, strategic Zahniser style; now everything was on the block. Whether this meant less or more wilderness protection in the long run is still an open question. Whatever the answer, the change to hard-fought statewide bills became inevitable as wilderness issues attained a higher profile.

But in 1978, nobody knew if Johnson's suit would stick. All that environmentalists knew for sure was that they had lost big on RARE II, despite Rupert Cutler's being on the inside. And inside the Wilderness Society, Dave Foreman was getting the same sick feeling of defeat. His biggest humiliation occurred around Christmas at a staff retreat in Coolfont, West Virginia. Foreman's presentation was the first item on the agenda. He was given two-and-a-half days of the three-day retreat to make an eloquent appeal to the entire staff, and to Bill Turnage in particular. Summoning Asa Lipscomb's penetrating preacher's voice from the deep recesses of his childhood, Foreman made his case for keeping intact the romantic, egalitarian style of the Hunter era. Sitting with the staff in a circle on the floor, Foreman talked about how they were a family, a tribe united by a common belief in wilderness. Debbie Sease, Tim Mahoney, and Bart Koehler chimed in when Foreman talked about the value of the consensus approach that they had developed over the past year.

Nobody wanted it to be over.

But the fix was in. Soon after he began work, Turnage had been shocked by the news that the society's endowment had been siphoned off into day-to-day operating expenses. Not long afterward, he paid a call on Brock Evans at the Sierra Club. Evans called in Doug Scott and John McComb, who had both recently left the Wilderness Society. They proceeded to give Turnage a thorough rundown on every staff member at the society, calling practically every one of them radical, undisciplined, and unprofessional. Turnage's attitude hardened. It wasn't long before he was at loggerheads with the staff. "No one wanted to take orders. No one wanted to do anything, except what they wanted to do," he complained. A female Yale graduate with good fund-raising credentials who had been referred to him via the school's old boy network was rejected by the staff for the absurd reason that she didn't look outdoorsy enough. Turnage huffily replied that she was one of the best squash players in the country. Clearly, the Buckaroos were living on borrowed time.

Turnage had already gotten the message to close the Denver office. Even without his staff, Clif Merritt was too strong a counterweight to the Washington, D.C., operation. It was a measure of the organization's dire circumstances that even Margaret Murie, the universally respected widow of Society cofounder Olaus Murie, acquiesced in this decision. Merritt's head wasn't the only one about to roll. A war over the environment was beginning—soon the Sagebrush Rebels would lay siege to Washington—and Turnage was determined to assure the Wilderness Society's survival, even if it meant canning the whole flannel-shirted staff and replacing them with Ivy League graduates who knew how to fill in a balance sheet. He proceeded to do just that. The Wilderness Society became solvent, although it never regained the position of political and intellectual leadership that it had once held.

Of all the holdovers from the Hunter era, Turnage was amenable to keeping only Tim Mahoney, a former congressional staffer named Joe Hooper, and Dave Foreman. Foreman was bound to be difficult. If Turnage couldn't keep him at his right hand like some bound-and gagged Lucifer, he would let him take a six-month sabbatical before resuming his previous duties as New Mexico field representative.

As 1979 approached, Foreman made plans to leave Washington. He had no idea yet how far he would travel. The end of the decade would bring enormous changes that would push Foreman to the edge of the political landscape. These changes went deeper than ideology or economics, according to the Pulitzer Prize–winning poet Gary Snyder. Snyder, who has thought deeply about human society's relationship to nature, believes that the 1980 election of Ronald Reagan signaled no less than a turning point in the national mythology. At that moment, the corporate warrior replaced the cowboy as the country's dominant archetype. As the CEO ascended the mythological ladder, the cowboy became an outlaw. It was merely ironic that Ronald Reagan, an actor who liked to play dress-up in cowboy clothes, presided over the archetype's demotion.

When he examined the tangible roots of the western myth, Snyder discovered that the cowboy is heir to an aesthetic of living close to the land. The tradition began in Arabia, where the finest horses were bred. The Moors carried it to Spain. From Spain, it sailed with the conquistadores to the New World, where it found its way into the callused hands of Mexican vaqueros.

The cowboy moved north to the United States in the 1800s, as the giant buffalo herds were slaughtered. This inglorious, politically motivated massacre cleared the way for domesticated cattle, but its real purpose was to destroy the power of the Plains Indians. Despite this ignoble genesis, the American cowboy is a preindustrial hero, Thomas Jefferson's natural aristocrat.

"No matter how poor you might be, no matter what other kind of social status you have, it was part of the preindustrial world that a man who knew horses and a man who could ride horses had a certain kind of automatic status. Regardless," says Snyder.

"The next phase is that the cowboy becomes the finally crystallized version of the frontier. The frontier is the embodiment of a certain kind of self-sufficiency, self-reliance, the egalitarianism of people whose esteem is based on nothing more than their ability and their capacity, a kind of camaraderie and conviviality and humor and distance from authority."

It was as good an epitaph as any for the Bunkhouse crew. The anointing of Bill Turnage was a minor footnote to the apparent triumph of corporate culture on the larger stage of American society at the close of the 1970s. If an alien from outer space relied on *Time* or *Newsweek* to learn about America over most of the following decade, he would believe the public narcotized by the repetitive hammerlock of a disco beat, bored and brainwashed into believing the happy talk of an aged and possibly senile president who made them feel that the bills for a consumptive lifestyle would never come due, and that life was full of limitless Levittown possibility, just as it had been circa 1959.

But beneath the shiny, four-color surface of New York and Washington, D.C., journalism, a sea change was taking place in small towns and cities all over the country. By the middle of the 1980s, hundreds of grass-roots groups—nobody knew exactly how many—had formed to work on local environmental issues, from cleaning up a toxic-waste site on the poor side of town to establishing a wilderness preserve. The members of these groups were double-knit people: cowboys, working-class blacks, hardware-store owners, housewives, long-haired, dope-smoking construction workers. If you weren't living in Glenwood, New Mexico, or Lander, Wyoming, or Austin, Texas, these people were probably invisible to you.

When they were still living in the old Glenwood adobe, Foreman and Sease had agreed to spend a single year in Washington, D.C. That year was over. Foreman was ready to heft his belongings into the back of his pickup truck and head home. But Debbie told her husband she wasn't ready to move. As his quid pro quo for moving to Washington, Dave had insisted that the Wilderness Society give Debbie a job trying to reform the Bureau of Land Management. Finally, Debbie had found work that gave her a chance to use her brain, not just her hands on a set of oars or her legs pumping up a mountain. She wanted to stay.

Now Foreman had lost everything.

Trouble Waiting to Happen

6

I turned on the news to the Third World War
Opened up the paper to World War IV
Just when I thought it was safe to be bored
Trouble waiting to happen

—Warren Zevon
and J. D. Souther
"Trouble Waiting to Happen," 1987

1979—Wyoming

THE PICTURE WINDOW in his office makes a satisfying crash as Bart smashes it. Rain flies in through the hole. He kicks out the jagged glass to the percussive sound of thunder overhead. The phone rings. He rips it out of the wall. Stepping out onto the ledge, he sees lightning fork down behind the domed statehouse. Rain soaks his hair and makes his face shine like the moon. He throws his head back and roars.

"Come and get me, you motherfuckers! C'mon, Exxon. Fuck you, Arco! I'll take you all!!!!"

Sirens cut through the cacophony of thunder and screaming. Up on his wet pigeon's perch, Bart looks into the faraway black gun barrels of five Cheyenne, Wyoming, cops. One cop shouts to him, but his voice is lost in the wind. Bart stares. With the politeness he can't seem to shake even when he's freaking out, he gently tells the cop to hang on just a minute. He hops back into his office, runs a hand through his rainy tangled dark hair, and opens the door so that they can arrest him. His seven-year tenure as the Wyoming representative of the Wilderness Society was over.

It was the end of the environmental decade and Bart Koehler was self-destructing. Koehler had just been through his seventh session of the Wyoming legislature, forty days and forty nights of what he called "hell on wheels." For the past seven years, Koehler's big heart and manic energy had attracted dozens of smart young volunteers. During the legislative session, they all crashed at the same house, downing cases of beer and pulling all-nighters in what *High Country News* called "The Children's Crusade." The Children's Crusade helped pass landmark environmental laws in a tough, conservative state. But by 1980, Koehler was fraying badly. The new regime at the Wilderness Society was nothing but a source of frustration to him. His whole approach to public lands was built on fending off industry's attempts to colonize BLM lands and the national forests. A staggering majority of the country's wild land was administered by these agencies. This was the *Wilderness* Society, wasn't it? Then this snotty guy named Turnage who drinks Perrier out of a fancy French canteen gets hired. The new guy wants to do something about national parks. (Well, sure, he used to work for Ansel Adams. All those tasteful scenic views of Half Dome with the little scratchy trees lurking in the lower edges of the photo.) Who cares about national parks? They're already protected. Not to mention full of tourists. This guy Turnage is into playing an acreage game. Who cares about acreage if you're taking it up the ass on the important stuff like wildlife habitat? It worked for funders, maybe, but Koehler just didn't see the point. On April 21—his thirty-first birthday—he got very drunk. From a bar's pay phone he dictated a telegram to Bill Turnage. "I'm leaving the reservation," he grandly announced. "Your blankets are thin and your meat is rotten." Then he repeated the telegram's contents to a drinking buddy who happened to be a reporter. There was no going back. Bart became the first Buckaroo to quit the Wilderness Society. April 21, again. John

Muir's birthday. The anniversary of Aldo Leopold's death. It must have seemed like a good day for Bart to take a powder himself.

In all fairness, it wasn't just Turnage. Seven years of hard work and hard play were starting to catch up with Bart. Unfortunately, he had a chink in his physiology that most people didn't have, a deficiency of something called lithium that kept you from going manic. The problem was, Koehler didn't know about the deficiency. He just kept getting more and more pumped up. By the spring of 1979, he was so pumped up that the Cheyenne cops couldn't get the tranquilizer needle into his arm when they busted him; it was like a steel rod. Koehler's mania would reach flashpoint several times before a South Dakota psychiatrist finally figured out what was wrong and gave him a better life through chemistry. In the meantime, Koehler was lucky. He had spent seven years being generous to his friends. Now his friends stood by him, fastening their seat belts when they saw him getting hyper. They knew it was going to be a bumpy night, but for Koehler's sake, they'd do whatever it took to help him make it through.

Barton Koehler had traveled a long way to get to this particular nadir. All the way from Great Neck, Long Island, a crass New York City suburb. Koehler's parents were always a little different. They weren't accountants or real estate wheeler-dealers or hyper-manicured bleached-blond housewives like his friends' parents. His mother was an art teacher, and his father commuted into the city at night to work as an assistant conductor at the New York Philharmonic. They didn't really belong in Great Neck and neither did their son. So Bart Koehler's journey really began when he was thirteen and the family moved to Mayfield, a small town at the very southern edge of the Adirondack Mountains. At six million acres, the Adirondack Park is the largest wilderness east of the Mississippi. The old, worn-down mountain range has recovered gracefully from turn-of-the-century logging. By the 1960s, its tall spruce and fir trees had recaptured the dark, cubist shadows of primeval forest. Bart steeped himself in the dark green quiet. But at the tumultuous age of thirteen, learning the land proved to be easier than learning local culture. When classes began at the tiny Mayfield school, Koehler quickly realized he'd better stop saying "Pass the bawl" in Long Islandese if he wanted to fit in at soccer practice.

Fortunately for Koehler, the musician's ear he inherited from his father got him talking like an upstater pretty fast. By the time he reached high school, he didn't just fit in, he excelled. He was an honor student and an athlete. College was a different story. After he entered the State University of New York at Albany in 1966, Koehler followed in an older brother's footsteps, majoring in booze and spending his nights playing in a rock-and-roll band. It was the first in a tumultuous series of ups and downs that would characterize Koehler's life. This time, a trip across the country turned things around.

It was 1971 and Koehler and his friends were driving an old beat-up Chevy to Alaska, hoping to find the last frontier. On the way, they stopped for a hike in Montana's Glacier National Park. The park is famous for its classic Rocky Mountain scenery, a Coors commercial in Sensurround. It is also known for having the largest concentration of fatal grizzly bear attacks in the United States, including the case of a young woman who was ripped apart as she lay asleep in her tent. Even if you never saw them in the flesh, silver-tipped grizzlies roamed through your mind when you hiked in Glacier. They hung out there, picking blackberries, turning slowly as they caught your scent on the wind. At night they kept you awake in your sleeping bag, the way their ancestors kept your ancestors awake ten thousand years ago.

Bart and his friends were no exception. They hiked up to a mountain pass, where they spent the late afternoon watching a family of mountain goats poking their way down a scree slope. That night they were so spooked by the prospect of running into a bear that they all jammed into a steel hut for an uncomfortable night's sleep. None of them had traveled farther west than Pennsylvania before. "I mean, you get out in this country and they say climb a tree if you see a bear . . ." Koehler laughs. "I mean, there are no trees anywhere and the wind's blowing the wrong way and the hairs are standing on the back of my neck and we're going, wait a minute. So we came walking back and a grizzly was just coming around the other side—we had just gotten out of there in time. So I thought, well, you know, that's as close as I want to get to a bear for now. I didn't know anything about grizzlies except I knew they were serious."

Koehler and his friends hiked back to the car singing a song they called "The Grizzly Bear Blues" to make up for the bells and whistles that they hadn't brought along to scare off the bears. Koehler was terrified but exhilarated. Most of all, he was hooked. He wanted to spend the rest of his life here. The way to do it, he figured, was to work for the U.S. Park Service.

Despite his bad grades in college, Koehler talked his way into the graduate program in outdoor recreation, resource management and planning at the University of Wyoming. On probation. By the end of his first year, he had the highest average in the department. When it came time to choose a thesis topic, Koehler stumbled onto an attempt by local foresters to do their bit for RARE I and decided he would help out. Almost twenty years later, his thesis, catchily titled *An Evaluation of Roadless Areas in the Medicine Bow National Forest*, was still being used by local environmentalists in their disputes with the Forest Service. It was a monumental piece of work, three master's projects in one. First, it offered a critique of how the Forest Service was conducting its review of the roadless areas in the Medicine Bow National Forest. Second, Koehler conducted a targeted survey of leaders of various interest groups, asking for their opinions on wilderness versus timber cutting. Third, Koehler, who had majored in geography as an undergraduate, hiked through every roadless area in the Medicine Bow forest. He mapped them and inventoried their resources, using the criteria set out by the Wilderness Act of 1964 to evaluate their suitability for wilderness designation. It was a tour de force, a letter-perfect example of what the Forest Service should have been doing.

Koehler was a graduate student working part-time as a boatman on the North Platte River when he ran into Clif Merritt. A year later, when the Wilderness Society gave Merritt the go-ahead to hire more staff, he immediately thought of Koehler. In his first year with the society, Bart spent a lot of time flying back and forth to Washington,

D.C., serving an apprenticeship that would pay off later on. "It's a very tough league," said Koehler. "My two mentors when I got here, the guys who taught me to work the Hill—I don't like to call it lobbying because lobbyists are sleaze buckets who work for oil companies. We work in the public interest. Anyway, I learned from the good old boys, from Harry Crandell and Ernie Dickerman. They just had a marvelous way of being straightforward and open and honest with people and not being your typical charge-ahead pushy person on the Hill."

Koehler was a good student. In fact, he was so good that after a year at the Denver office, he got a call from the Wyoming Outdoor Council. They wanted to hire him as executive director. He wrestled with the idea for a while—he liked his job, but he hated Denver. And he loved Wyoming. So he turned in his resignation. But Clif Merritt had a better idea. He asked Koehler to become the Wilderness Society's half-time Wyoming representative, a job he could do while he was working at the outdoor council. Koehler's salary climbed to a whopping $400 a month. Out of that, he paid the rent on an office next door to the historic Buckhorn Bar in downtown Laramie. Laramie was a minor countercultural hub, a graceful western college town that had kept both its architecture and its nineteenth-century atmosphere intact. Naturally, there was no money left over for his own rent, so Koehler slept in the back of the office. With no home to escape to, things got pretty intense during the state legislature's forty-day session. "We started out just easygoing, with a case of normal-sized beers. And then by the end we were drinkin' cases of quarts. And we'd play a lot of music and be bad. We were very effective," said Koehler, grinning.

After a year and a half, the Wyoming Outdoor Council was running out of money and Koehler was running out of a job. He was kicking ass in the statehouse, but his rowdy ways were starting to alienate the more conservative members of the outdoor council's board. Once again, Clif Merritt materialized. Like the good witch in *The Wizard of Oz*, Merritt waved his magic wand and Bart became a full-time representative for the Wilderness Society. He moved up to

Jackson in the winter of 1975 and opened a field office. He was new in town, but Jackson was a happening place, an enclave of the young and hip and old and rich, so Koehler got along. Then in July he met someone he could *really* get along with. Howie Wolke became the second in the eventual trio of Wyoming Buckaroos.

Howie was a huge guy with pretty blue eyes and dark blond hair, a gorgeous hunk with the social graces of Sasquatch under a full moon. He had been born in Brooklyn, New York, but when he was five years old, his father, a traveling salesman, moved the family to the outskirts of Nashville. "I come from a working-class family. You can write the American dream and it's my family. There's no indication, no wilderness there," said Wolke. But Wolke remembers spending summers driving through the countryside with his father, straining to see what lay behind the green curtain flashing past the car window. Back home, he explored the woods and streams and hills near his house. He decided that the only thing he wanted to do in the world was be a forest ranger.

Wolke achieved the first part of his dream, attending classes at the University of New Hampshire's forestry department. What he found there depressed him. His professors were teaching the same brand of U.S. Forest Service–approved industrial forestry being taught in forestry schools around the country. The schools were turning out platoons of tree farmers. Maximizing yield was the goal, even if it meant turning the forest into the outdoor equivalent of a mini-mall. Soon the whole country would be a giant Kmart.

Wolke stuck it out as long as he could. But in his junior year he was glumly watching a computer spit out timber-yield tables when a friend told him about a new program in conservation studies. Relieved, Wolke switched his major, finished up his degree in 1974, and headed west. He wound up in the town of Dubois, Wyoming, because he had read somewhere that the Sierra Club had an office there. After he had worked as a volunteer for a while, the Sierra Clubbers tactfully suggested he look up Bart Koehler in Jackson.

"He was a wild-eyed college student and wanted to save the West," says Koehler. "He was doing some national forest work for these two women and they couldn't deal with him. He crawled out from under a rock, he was like a caveman to them. So they said, well, we know a guy who you ought to meet, maybe he can put you to work. I met him in a bar, which he thought was a good sign. We got to like each other right off."

When Howie got to Jackson, both the Forest Service and the Bureau of Land Management were inventorying their roadless areas. Environmentalists were analyzing the inventories, trying to influence decisions as much as they could on the local level before the agencies turned in their formal recommendations to Congress. Koehler was splitting the work with the Sierra Club's local representative, a soft-spoken, red-haired guy named Bruce Hamilton. Koehler handled the Forest Service RARE II work, while Hamilton tried to keep the BLM honest. Even dividing the work this way, there was a lot of it.

Koehler not only liked Wolke, he could keep him busy. "I said, look, you know, I don't have a lot of money and I'm not getting paid much but I'm willing to give you a hundred bucks here and there whenever you need it, food and beer, and I need somebody to do a bunch of fieldwork. We've got a lot of country to understand before we take this thing to the wall."

Under Koehler's tutelage, Wolke disappeared into the mountains for weeks at a time. He was ecstatic. This was the whole reason he had come out West. Every few weeks he would wander into town like a lost elk: dirty, smelly, hungry, and very thirsty. Koehler would feed him and the two would spend hours on bar stools, taking meetings and drinking beer. Through Koehler, Wolke was hired by Friends of the Earth, the group David Brower had founded after leaving the Sierra Club. In true Brower fashion, FOE was chaotically managed but intellectual and creative, a vehicle for turning cutting-edge ideas into reality. Wolke was hired—although he claims that "hired" may not be the right word, given his $50-a-month salary—to assume the title of FOE's Wyoming representative.

Wolke worked at a variety of menial jobs to supplement this tiny stipend. In the winter of 1975, he was employed as a busboy at a restaurant called Cache Creek Station on Jackson's town square. He was in the back room squirreling away a couple of pastries, trying to beat the rush, when the next shift arrived to do their bit of minor theft. Wolke found himself competing with a tall, skinny guy who looked as if he could eat the whole restaurant. He turned out to be Mike Roselle, just twenty years old, a refugee from the counterculture who Wolke described as "a skinny vegetarian" and "a walking left-wing slogan." Roselle was a stray dog with a gleaming intelligence, a self-educated runaway from a poor, violent, alcoholic family in Los Angeles.

Wolke adopted Mike Roselle the same way Bart Koehler had adopted him. Roselle's girlfriend had just left town, so he was available for Wolke's gonzo winter camping trips, excursions Roselle later called "breakneck endurance hikes." Roselle was eager to learn about environmentalism. As a runaway teenager, he had attached himself to the Yippies at the historic, bloody 1968 Democratic convention in Chicago. After the Vietnam war ended, he hitchhiked back east. He ended up in Great Smoky Mountains National Park. "I'm a pretty urban kid," Roselle said. "My parents never took me into the wilderness. I think that's probably why when I got there it was the closest thing to a religious experience I ever had."

Wolke lost no time getting Roselle into the environmental movement. He even made him the front man for a quasi-imaginary group called "Construction Workers for Wilderness." Still struggling to make ends meet, Wolke was working a day job on a construction crew. At night and on weekends, he was helping Bart Koehler organize environmentalist testimony for a public hearing on the DuNoir section of the Shoshone National Forest. The DuNoir, which already had limited protection, was a place some mainstream environmentalists considered "trading stock" in negotiations over the Wyoming Wilderness bill. But the DuNoir was one of the first places Howie had explored in Wyoming; neither he nor Bart nor Bruce Hamilton was willing to give it up. He drew up a petition, typed "Construction Workers for Wilderness" at the top of the page, and persuaded the guys on his crew to sign it. At the hearing Wolke testified for Friends of the Earth. Then he introduced the petition from Construction

Workers for Wilderness, Mike Roselle, chairperson. The press ate it up. Years later, Mike Roselle managed to keep a straight face when he told reporters about the ground-breaking alliance of construction workers, hunters, and sportsmen that he and Howie had organized back in Wyoming.

Roselle's theatrical skills didn't develop overnight. He was shy and tall, a gangly six-foot-six giraffe. At public hearings, he tended to mumble indistinctly into the microphone, stooping his shoulders like a professor peering over a pair of spectacles. Behind-the-scenes action was Roselle's forte. He had read *The Monkey Wrench Gang* and he liked the general idea. He bought a collapsible saw and started harvesting billboards outside Jackson. Soon it became a regular thing. On Sunday nights Roselle would hang out at the Stagecoach Bar, which had a live band. After the bar closed at ten, he would hit the highway. For months, he tried to get Wolke to come out with him. Wolke resisted, thinking that he would be too obvious a suspect because of his connection with Friends of the Earth. He actually preferred Randall Gloege's idea of leaving Friends of the Earth entirely and starting an underground movement. Right now, he wasn't even going for *that*. He still believed in doing things the responsible way, working for mainstream conservation groups. But after a particularly noisy, drunken night at the Stagecoach, he somehow found himself on a late-night expedition to the billboard funeral parlor.

In 1979, Howie finally became disillusioned with mainstream politics. That was when he showed Roselle *real* monkeywrenching. Knocking down billboards barely qualified as a minor form of vigilante justice. Through hands-on learning, he showed Roselle how disabling expensive machinery might actually have some effect when applied strategically to a political issue, namely oil exploration in the Gros Ventre section of the Bridger-Teton National Forest. The Gros Ventre was an ark of endangered species, including grizzly bears, bison, elk, trumpeter swans, and eagles. By the time Getty Oil decided to search for oil there, the two Buckaroos also had figured out that, when all else failed, a combination of monkeywrenching and public relations could provide a satisfying palliative to losing the battle against environmental destruction. They got a chance to exercise their skills on a "show-me" tour Getty organized in 1979.

Wolke and Roselle got wind of Getty's propaganda tour a few days before it was going to be held. They had plenty of time to paint big wooden signs with slogans like "Getty Out of the Gros Ventre Wilderness!" and "Stop Forest Service Oil Industry Destruction!" Standing on each other's not insignificant shoulders, they hammered the signs to trees that lined the trail, placing them too high to be removed in time for the press tour. After the tour arrived, they hung around long enough to watch the photographers click away, then scurried off to a local bar to celebrate.

That night at the public hearing, Wolke gave his sincere, wholesome, I'm-a-nice-young-crusading-environmentalist testimony. He cited facts, figures, even *science,* for Chrissake. Afterward, Roselle took the microphone. He started off in his usual low tones, but then a strange thing happened. Roselle became forceful. Wolke listened openmouthed as his protégé spewed forth brilliance, fueled by a combination of vast quantities of alcohol and the morning's excitement. But as Roselle's momentum increased, he couldn't seem to stop. "All of a sudden he's up there just ripping the oil industry a new asshole. He's going on and on about how the future economics of Jackson is in tourism and not oil and gas extraction. And he goes, 'And you know what? We got hunters, we got fishers. We don't need any fuckin' oil rigs.' " Wolke said. "This is in front of the whole hearing room. And nobody said 'fuck' at these public hearings. Mike broke the ice on that. So he's a true linguistic pioneer in Wyoming.

"So he's going on and on, 'We don't need any fuckin' oil rigs. These fuckin' people think that they can come over here and take over our fuckin' country!' I was just . . . it was hilarious. The director of the chamber of commerce is sitting right next to me. He says, 'Howie, where'd you get this guy?' 'Oh, he's a good friend of mine, Bob.'

"At the end of the hearing, your basic public hearing, everybody mills around. Roselle stands on top of a chair—you've got to remember, I'm the only one in the room who knows how much he drank during the day, how shitfaced he was—he stands up on top of a chair and goes, 'Long Live the Gros Ventre Wilderness and Death to Its Destructors!' And he kind of slips off the chair onto the floor, regains his balance, and goes staggering out the door. Everybody goes, whoa, who was that guy?

"I think Roselle lost a lot of his shyness that night. It's kind of like the second losing of his virginity or something like that."

It didn't end there. Later that night, Wolke and Roselle were drinking at the same bar with the Forest Service officials and the Getty Oil people. When one of the Forest Service guys came over to their table, Wolke told him that he'd like him better if he came right out and took his paycheck from the oil companies. Roselle went even further, striding over to a table of Getty Oil executives and challenging them to a fistfight. Roselle may have been skinny, but he *was* six feet six. Wolke was built like a Clydesdale. Needless to say, the Getty men declined Roselle's offer. And the odds are they never thought of environmentalists as wimpy bird-watchers again.

When he wasn't telling off the Forest Service, Wolke was working with somewhat greater seriousness on a wilderness proposal for Wyoming. As the Forest Service conducted RARE II, environmentalists were scrambling to produce their own recommendations, hoping that negotiations would eventually land somewhere in the middle. Wolke drafted Alternative W, along with Bart Koehler, Sierra Club staffer Bruce Hamilton, and Sierra Club activist Phil Hocker. Hocker, who would later found the Mineral Policy Center in Washington, D.C., knew more than any sane person would ever want to about the country's outdated, environmentally destructive mining laws. If you lived in Wyoming during the oil boom it was easy to become obsessive. Oil rigs were as ubiquitous on the basin and range as prairie dogs, passenger pigeons, and buffalo had been a century earlier. Any attempt to bring land into the wilderness system threatened the way these giant steel grasshoppers continually expanded their range.

After the details were hammered out, Alternative W proposed wilderness designation for 2.4 million acres out of 4 million acres of roadless land managed by the Forest Service in Wyoming. But that wasn't enough for Wolke. He supported Alternative W but issued a statement that Friends of the Earth also endorsed wilderness protection for another half million acres.

When the Forest Service released its RARE II recommendations on January 4, 1979, Bart Koehler, Howie Wolke, and Mike Roselle joined Dave Foreman in the ranks of newly minted cynics. The RARE II proposal for Wyoming totaled fewer than 700,000 acres. It was mostly alpine country that Howie Wolke called "rock and ice." The other half of the ecosystem, the productive valleys that provided winter range for deer, antelope, and elk, usually contained timber as well. Strange to say, the Forest Service wasn't recommending many of these places for wilderness protection.

"We made moderate proposals," said Wolke. "We showed up at the hearings with facts, data. . . . I looked at the loggers who had organized. Didn't follow the Forest Service's parameters. They shouted down their buddies in the Forest Service. They bused loads of loggers down to public meetings, telling them, if this RARE II wilderness thing goes through, you'll lose your job. And they won. They kicked our butts."

Maybe Roselle's spontaneous eruption at the public hearing wasn't exactly the model Wolke wanted to use. But his method didn't seem to work, either. On top of that, Friends of the Earth was faltering financially. Wolke was informed that even his lousy $50 salary was too much. The folks at FOE headquarters in San Francisco magnanimously offered him a chance to keep on working without pay. He declined. God, it was frustrating. Friends of the Earth was the only organization whose staff people seemed to understand the ecosystem approach that Wolke believed in. If they hit the skids financially, the rest of the environmental movement would blithely go on with its archaic emphasis on scenery and recreation. In the meantime, elk and grizzlies would lose ground to drilling rigs and logging roads, leaving the northern Rockies a gorgeous stage set with no actors. The oil companies that had been unleashed by the so-called "energy crisis" were reaping a bonanza on the public lands, particularly in the northern Rockies that Howie loved. Even though the environmental movement was gaining cash and membership every day, Howie believed that on an intellectual level things were slowing down just when they should be speeding up.

The Buckaroos in the northern Rockies weren't the only ones who were discouraged. By the spring of 1979, just about everybody was at loose ends. Foreman was back at the old adobe moping over Debbie. Occasionally he would rouse himself to go on a death-march hike with his friends. The group usually included Ron Kezar, the Sierra Club guy he had met down in Texas. Kezar had invested in land near Glenwood and was hanging around pretty regularly. A local environmentalist named Bob Langsenkamp came along pretty often, too. So did Wes Leonard, a honcho with the El Paso Sierra Club. The four men would sit around the campfire, get shitfaced, and fantasize. Sometimes the talk turned to weird paramilitary eco-commandos, Green Beret tree-huggers. At other times, they day-dreamed about initiation to a wilderness elite via a painful ritual inspired by the Plains Indians. "Ordeal of suffering . . ." Leonard would mutter semi-incoherently, as the fire burned low and the smell of stale alcohol exuded from his pores. Prowling around the Southwest, they were "lonely, ornery, and mean," as Waylon Jennings sang it. They looked like trouble—or maybe a new environmental group —waiting to happen.

Desert Heart,
Devil's
Highway

On a whizzing cold night in January, 1907, Dr. Daniel Trembly MacDougal said to me: "Look here! I wish you to go with me on a fine desert trip, in the near future; and I also wish you to know that there are mighty few men whom I ever invite to go with me into the deserts."

—William T. Hornaday
Camp-Fires on Desert and Lava, 1908

1980–Sonora

CERTAIN PLACES ON EARTH attract more than their fair share of strange occurrences. The unfortunate thing is, word usually gets out. Ojai, California, is that kind of place. Around 1900, devotees of Eastern religion were drawn to this town on a high plateau of the San Gabriel Mountains. It was rumored that Ojai was some kind of energy magnet, nearer my Krishna to thee. Sedona, Arizona, is another case in point, a once-charming village in redrock canyon country overrun in the 1980s by rich Texans and stoned-looking counterculture types brandishing crystals.

A scattering of these spooky places remains undiscovered. Some are even uninhabited. In this select group is Mexico's Pinacate Desert, where, legend has it, Earth First! was founded. The Pinacate is a blank spot on the map just east of the Sea of Cortez. For centuries, it was a dehydrated Bermuda Triangle, blocking travel for 600 square miles between the main part of Mexico and the long, dangling province of Baja California. A blue-black spine of mountains divides the desert into two parts. To the east, waves of lava spread across the desert, frozen in a moment of geologic time that occurred a mere 5,000 years ago. Occasionally the waves part to reveal long stretches of sand pocked by giant craters. Some are more than 500 feet deep: huge cave-ins blasted into the sand, volcanoes gone awry. In other places the volcanoes blew cinders into the air, heaving black cones on the desert floor like spent hourglass sands. Pinacate Peak and its near-twin, Carnegie Peak, are large enough to be called mountains.

The western section of the Pinacate is a light-skinned cousin to the rugged lava of the east. It is *Lawrence of Arabia* blown up to 300-millimeter, a Sahara-like configuration the Mexicans respectfully call El Gran Desierto. Wind-scored drifts of sand susurrate down the west flank of Pinacate Peak. Dunes dip and eddy for a hundred miles, glowing an unearthly pink in the distance, nearly vacant of life. They taper off into the silty remains of the much-abused Colorado River as it trickles into the Sea of Cortez. Geologists call El Gran Desierto an *erg*, a term borrowed from the Arabic. It is rumored to be the only erg on the continent and that, said Edward Abbey, is probably a good thing.

It was Dave Foreman's idea to go to the Pinacate. A big fan of Ed Abbey's, he had read about the region in 1973's *Cactus Country*. The book was written for the Time-Life American Wilderness series, an obvious bread-and-butter job. But even the tedious patina of Time-Life editing hadn't stolen Abbey's voice. He brought the desert as close as a cactus spine lodged in your thumb. Foreman liked to quote Abbey on the Pinacate. "Abbey once said Saguaro National Monument is high school, Organ Pipe Cactus National Monument is undergraduate, Cabeza Prieta is graduate school, and Pinacate is post doc, as far as the Sonoran desert goes."

Foreman was eager to prove himself once more. During his six-month sabbatical he had divorced himself from the national political scene, aimlessly roaming the West while the RARE II bloodletting occurred at a far distant point over the horizon. He did his best to divorce himself from the Wilderness Society, too. But the rift was more a fractious separation than a divorce. In early June, Foreman met with newly appointed executive director Bill Turnage and the rest of the field staff at Claire Tappan Lodge in the California Sierra. After the meeting, they went on a sketchily planned overnight backpack into a proposed wilderness area called Granite Chief. It was one of those camping trips where everyone rushes into a grocery store and grabs whatever catches his eye. Foreman thought that each person's choice revealed something about his personality. His dinner was a T-bone steak. He joked to the others that if they were real men, they'd buy steaks, too, and eat them raw. Foreman remembers Bill Turnage being unmoved by his bluster and laying in a schizophrenic repast of SpaghettiOs and French mineral water.

It was already dark when they got to their campsite. According to Foreman, Turnage and a field rep named Joe Walicki laid plans to break into a cross-country ski hut to sleep for the night. Foreman was annoyed. Why come to the Sierra if you were going to shut out the sight of flat-faced granite batholiths cast in silver by the moon? His irritation was compounded by hunger. When Eaton and the others teased him about his real-men jibes, Foreman thought, what the hell? It was too late to build a fire. He ripped the raw steak out of its cellophane package and tore into it with his teeth, horrifying everyone except Jim Eaton. Eaton joined in and they both did a caveman jig, grunting and hopping around in front of Bill Turnage, who seemed more hurt than disgusted. Foreman didn't know or didn't care. Jim Eaton always made a good audience and Jim's dog, Stickeen, the beneficiary of Foreman's T-bone scraps, was even more appreciative.

This caveman telegraph failed to discourage Turnage from his enthusiasm for Foreman's less denticulate talents. On July 1, Foreman resumed work as the Wilderness Society's New Mexico representative. His parents were living in Rio Rancho, a suburb of Albuquerque. Foreman moved in with them once again and opened a Wilderness Society office nearby in the old Spanish town of Bernalillo. In the wake of Huey Johnson's lawsuit, environmentalists were scram-

bling to develop statewide wilderness bills. Foreman duly began draft-
ing one for New Mexico. But part of his mind was off somewhere
else, casting issues in thematic terms. Ronald Reagan was headed for
the White House and the Sagebrush Rebels were riding behind him
in a cloud of expensive rose-colored dust. An ideological counter-
offensive was desperately needed. In the fall of 1979, Foreman organized a conference in Denver where environmentalists could plot
anti-Sagebrush strategy. They would have to play a lot of catch-up.
Soon, the media would be headlining stories on Reagan's cuts in social
services. But only sporadic attention would be paid to the equally
energetic effort to gut a less visible sector of the public trust. Reagan
made plain his commitment to dismantling wilderness when he appointed card-carrying Sagebrush Rebel James Watt as Secretary of the
Interior. Until he was forced out of office in disgrace, Watt worked
to implement an agenda that was part radical-right, part pork-barrel
giveaway. From the environmentalist perspective, his sins were staggering. They ranged from trying to strip-mine national parks to selling
federal coal leases to Colorado wheeler-dealers at a staggering loss to
taxpayers. On top of everything else, the guy looked like a total geek,
with a cue-ball head, thick glasses, and an idiot grin blaring out from
beneath his beaver Stetson. It was enough to give cowboys a bad
name.

In one way, at least, Watt was a true democrat. He gave equal
time to all the West's vested interests. That included ranchers. Cattle
grazing on federal land became a major topic at the anti-Sagebrush
conference, marking the first time environmentalists seriously took on
the task of ranching reform. Overgrazing had caused an environmental
disaster in the West, but generations of conservationists had felt compelled to tiptoe pragmatically around the problem. Foreman and some
of the others who attended the conference, like Howie and Bart and
Johanna Wald of the Natural Resources Defense Council, were unhappy that the environmental movement had taken, at best, a defensive position. The most effective action on grazing had been taken by
an outsider, journalist Bernard De Voto. In 1946, De Voto received
an assignment to travel to the West. With his wife and son, he drove

his old Buick from Cambridge, Massachusetts, to the landscape of "dry grass and stiff sage" which he had fled many years before.[1] Now that he was middle-aged and successful, De Voto fell in love with the West he had once despised. In typical reporter fashion, he managed to squeeze a few lucrative travel articles out of the trip. He also scored an investigative coup by uncovering a plot by stockmen to privatize federal grazing lands. One of their more subtle maneuvers was the introduction of a bill that would have shifted ownership of federal grazing land to the states. It was a slick move that would have allowed states to auction off public land. Almost singlehandedly, De Voto turned back this attempted coup with a series of powerful, well-documented articles in the pages of *Harper's*, including the aptly titled "Sacred Cows and Public Lands."[2]

The Utah-bred De Voto was a misfit who had grown up as a Roman Catholic intellectual surrounded by the middle-brow regimentation of the Land of Mormon. He found fame in Cambridge and New York by exposing the hypocrisies of the western booboisie. Conservationists, on the other hand, tended to stick around town. So they played their cards a little closer to the vest when it came to facing down ranchers. Like De Voto, they knew that it wasn't just money at stake, but mythology, too. The western myth was a baseline, not just for people who lived in the arid region west of the hundredth meridian, but for Americans in general. Freedom lay at the heart of the American ideal and the cowboy was its living, ranching, roping, and tobacco-chewing embodiment. The frontier was his stage set, a place where the restraining hand of Tom Sawyer's Aunt Polly couldn't reach. It was a good myth. It was just too bad that cows came along with it. This minor detail dated from the 1880s, when the West was a preindustrial society and lack of refrigeration meant that beef had to be produced on the western range. But in the twentieth century, western cattle ranching was just plain stupid. The American West was so arid that it took almost thirty acres in a state like Nevada to feed one cow. In Alabama a cow could live on fewer than four acres and think it was at a Howard Johnson's All You Can Eat Night.

Economically, raising cattle on federal land was a disaster. Low grazing fees had been institutionalized since the last free-roaming buffalo shuffled off to ungulate heaven. As late as 1992, grazing fees were only $1.92 per cow. A minor scandal occurred when it was discovered that ranchers were subleasing their grazing rights for a profit of between $2.76 and $8.34 a head.[3]

All in all, the government was paying more for range maintenance than it was getting in grazing fees, subsidizing cattle grazing on federal lands to the ratchety tune of approximately $14 per animal. This inspired the term *welfare ranching* among antigrazing activists.[4]

But the cost to taxpayers was not solely economic. "Range maintenance" doubled as a euphemism for destruction of native ecosystems: hauling down native pinyon pine and juniper trees with chains and bulldozers; spraying pesticides to eradicate native grasses. Once they had scraped the landscape into a tabula rasa, government officials planted non-native species like crested wheatgrass—cow food.

Foreman and other environmentalists saw clearly how cattle ranching had transformed the western landscape. The range had been cowburnt since the 1880s and things were not improving. By 1975, the Bureau of Land Management reported that only 17 percent of its range was in good condition. When the subject of grazing comes up, Howie Wolke likes to quote Aldo Leopold, who wrote: "One of the penalties of an ecological education is that one lives alone in a world of wounds."[5] To the Buckaroos' educated eyes, the consequences of overgrazing stood out in sharp relief all over the intermountain West, where erosion had flattened rivers into muddy channels, or dried them up completely. Streams that once had been lined by birds, trees, and grasses looked like vacant lots in the South Bronx, minus the graffiti —usually.

The costs of western cattle ranching seemed even more outlandish when you considered that no more than 10 percent of the nation's beef ever set hoof west of the Mississippi, whether to graze for a few months, or to spend a week in a feedlot before being shipped out. Only 2 to 3 percent actually spent their entire truncated lives on the range. These figures held steady despite the best efforts of federal land managers, who by the 1980s were allowing grazing on 250 million acres of federal land, an area more than three times the size of the entire national park system.[6] As cottonwoods wilted along streambeds, it seemed that the cattle industry's imprint on the settlement and character of the West would never be erased, even when winter winds lifted the dry, desertified soil into whirling dust devils.

Despite all this evidence, the immense power of ranchers—the West's version of a landed aristocracy—promised to stymie any efforts to make grazing a political issue for years to come. Even in less aristocratic western circles, ranching was not unpopular. It still had the aura of the cowboy—the "grasslands biome technician" of Gary Snyder's rodeo-inspired poem "Grand Entry."[7] And it was true that the nineteenth-century cowboy tradition had been kept up by a few hardy souls, including a fair number of sun-browned women with tough, stringy biceps and a self-contained manner. Some of these ranchers were too proud to graze their cattle on public land. But most cattle operations were geared to turning as much federal land as possible into the brown, trampled equivalent of a war zone. To loosen your grip on the myth, you might have to sit next to a potbellied rancher in his V-8 as it rumbled over hills and gullies of destroyed meadows and eroded washes. In the summer of 1979, Dave Foreman was back to watching the emperor's red neck frying in the sun, as he fruitlessly tried to convince stockmen that it was okay to fence cows out of a few places in the West. It was a frustrating job. Years later, there would be an edge in his voice when he asked, "How does looking at the hind end of a cow make you a great romantic lover of the West?"

The 1979 Anti-Sagebrush conference was a step forward. But taking a hard look at the grazing issue merely strengthened Foreman's belief that nature would quit before the BLM (aka Bureau of Livestock and Mining) would. The New Mexico wilderness bill was limping in at just over 700,000 acres. In May 1980, after making one last attempt to work for Bill Turnage, Foreman himself quit. Always loyal to his friends, Foreman announced that he was leaving to protest Turnage's wholesale firing of the other Buckaroos. But it was more than that. Foreman was burned out. Burned out on fighting the lie that westerners were a race of hardy, independent souls when they were really just a bunch of welfare crooks. He was sick of the assumption, which environmentalists pretended to share, that the western grasslands had been created as a convenience for man. He had spent way too much time quarreling over how best to *use* the land. Most of the time, he didn't believe in *using* it at all.

Foreman's frustrations were not born entirely from altruism. His personal ambitions had been torn apart by his departure from Washington. In his early thirties, he was at the point where the curves of knowledge and energy intersect. He knew more than he ever had before, and he still had the nonstop drive to pound this knowledge home to other people. He was at his peak. He could *feel* it. But what the hell was he supposed to do? Leaving Washington had seemed like the right thing at the time. But ditching the Wilderness Society entirely meant he had no arena for his ideas. And there wasn't another job in the whole environmental movement that appealed to him. Who would be his audience now? It wasn't as simple as it had been back in sixth grade, when he could fly up onto his schoolroom desk and dance around like a happy voodoo penitent.

After his trip to the Pinacate, Foreman found his niche. The desert—the black lava mother desert of them all—gave him the raw material to invent Earth First! In classic frontier fashion, Foreman also managed, in the dark cinder cones and soft pink desert sands, to reinvent himself.

The funny thing was, not a whole hell of a lot actually happened on the trip.

One of the first things that Foreman did after returning to the Southwest in late 1979 was trade in his beat-up, bent-up pickup. The old Ford had seen good service transporting him to Washington, D.C., and then safely back to his native Southwest. But baling wire and chewing gum only hold things together for so long. Besides, Foreman's image was changing. He bought the classic desert-rat vehicle, a 1960s Volkswagen minibus. Its paint was rubbed raw by sandstorms and beating sun, and its mechanical aptitude was rated as far below normal as Foreman's. Because of its starter problems, the VW acquired the nickname "Parks on a Hill." Despite its decrepitude, in the spring of 1980 Foreman and Ron Kezar planned the bus's maiden voyage to the desert's black heart. Howie Wolke and Mike Roselle lassoed a still whacked-out Bart Koehler and scissored their extra-long legs into the cramped seats of a Greyhound headed for Tucson. At twenty-four, Roselle was eight years younger than Foreman. Ron Kezar was the oldest one in the group; he was already thirty-seven. There were a few generational differences, not the least of which was that Roselle's drug of choice was marijuana, not beer. But after Foreman and Kezar picked up the Northern Buckaroos at the bus station on March 29, their first stop was a loud party that lasted most of the night. Roselle lost any qualms he might have had about the trip or his companions.

The next morning a bleary-eyed Foreman piloted the VW south. As they left the outskirts of Tucson, the Buckaroos entered the country's second-largest Indian reservation. The Papago tribe, or, as they are now called, the Tohono O'odham, own 4,600 square miles of prime Sonoran desert, an area larger than the state of New Jersey. For some mysterious reason, known perhaps by elders of the tribe, the reservation is lusher and greener than most of the surrounding desert. Looking at the roadside passing by, the Buckaroos were each, in his own way, awed by the sight of the Sonoran desert, with its long-armed saguaro cactus, its gold-lit cholla, and unexpected grassy stretches. With some relief, they realized that they had chosen the perfect time for their trip. Temperatures were mild and the winter rains had sent the creosote and brittlebush into bloom. Hanging a left at the town of Why (population 135, one gas station, a ramshackle cafe, and a boarded-up but still functioning post office), they cruised through Organ Pipe Cactus National Monument, past the iron-lit Ajo Mountains and into Mexico. They crossed the border at Sonoyta, a funky but relatively sleepy border town. After the ritual pit stop at the *cervecería*, they were on the road again.

Within forty-five minutes, the Buckaroos had entered another world. It was as if a door had opened and someone were whispering the word "Away." The rusty crushed cans and signal flags of white toilet paper, standard detritus of civilization on both sides of the border, disappeared almost immediately after they hung a left into the Pinacate. The quiet was immense.

There are several ways to enter the Pinacate, which is a Mexican National Park. But once you are in it, you are caught in a maze of sandy washboard roads that curve and intersect like the tracks of a quail feeding on scattered seeds. The only signs marking your way are old wooden posts jammed crookedly into the dirt. At one time they were painted white. You can almost make out the faded Spanish words scrawled on them.

Because it is so far from any substantial amount of civilization and crammed with things like rattlesnakes and loose blocks of ankle-crunching black rock and no water, the Pinacate might sound like a threatening place. It is wise to be cautious there, but it is more spell-binding than scary. As the Buckaroos rattled down the cactus-lined roads, each started to feel the excitement of the place, the funny catch in the throat, the sensation that an ordinary lens has been replaced by another one. They were not the first to have this experience. People tell stories about doing crazy things in the Pinacate, falling in love with someone they just met, hiking forty-three miles down to the Sea of Cortez and back in a mere twelve and a half hours just to get a glimpse of water, going down alone into the lava tube called I'Itoi's Cave. Abbey called the Pinacate "the final test of desert rathood."[8] Astronomer William Hartmann characterizes it as something else: the heart of the Sonoran Desert. Once you enter the Pinacate lavas, writes Hartmann, you sense that something is different. "The spatial scale of variety is small—yards. That is part of its strange charm. There is a fierce intimacy. Volcanoes form enclaves where variety occurs on a human scale. A path encountered leads not in a line for miles toward a vanishing point, but around the next corner, behind a cinder cone, into some unexpected cavity. The lava cannot seem to flow without forming nooks for soil, crannies for flowers, folds and crenulations, vesicles, cracks filled with seeds."[9]

The mystery that lies at the heart of all deserts is particularly strong here. Between 1936 and 1945 most of the Pinacate's animal life vanished. Pronghorn antelope, desert bighorn, even jackrabbits became scarce.[10] Nobody knows why. It was as if the erg had swallowed them whole. Secret atomic tests, of course, would explain the disappearances. But there is no evidence, no hint, that such tests took place. And atomic tests could not explain the drift of a distilled, invisible essence . . . the mystery. It emanates from Pinacate Peak and Carnegie Peak and from the saddle that dips between them like a delicate female concavity. In this low country, the blue-black mountain range follows you everywhere. It lies at the corner of your sightline as you crouch in the shade of a crater listening to a curve-billed thrasher. It is a distant, unapproachable god you bow to, rubbing raw your knees and hands on a stumbling hike over reddish black lava. The mystery ("Mystery itself, with a capital 'M,' " Abbey called it) is by definition unquantifiable and nearly indescribable. It goes something like this: by binding himself to physical survival, the desert rat finds the transcendence that lies at the core of the real world. (Not that he would ever say anything so pretentious.) It is the old law of alchemy, of shamans and psychologists: If you're looking for something, immerse yourself in its opposite. Then go as far as you possibly can.

The American desert has a venerable tradition of eccentrics who did just that. John C. Van Dyke was the first white man to dive into the furnace of the American desert and see the face of God. He returned to write about it in the archetypal book *The Desert,* published in 1901. Van Dyke was an asthmatic forty-two-year-old art historian from New Jersey, a college professor, and a friend of the Victorian art critic John Ruskin. In 1898 he rode his Indian pony into the California desert, accompanied by a fox terrier named Cappy. Over the next three years, he would crisscross the Mojave, Sonoran, and Colorado deserts, traveling from Oaxaca to Oregon with no apparent plan. "He came to the Southwest and ultimately to the desert because of illness, but there is a great discrepancy between his subsequent behavior and any recognized cure for asthma," writes the poet Richard Shelton. "And there are repeated references in his autobiography which suggest that he later recognized his behavior for what it probably was—compulsive and out of control. He was on a binge, possibly the greatest binge of his life, an enormous flirtation with death and a love affair with the desert's beauty."[11]

Van Dyke's training gave him tools to translate his passion into the art of seeing. An entire chapter of *The Desert* is devoted to the subjects of light and color. Van Dyke combines a technician's exactitude with a metaphysician's awe. "I mean now that the air itself is colored," he tells you, grabbing your shirtfront.[12] Desert air contains a greater concentration of dust than ordinary air, he explains. More dust means more refraction. More refraction means more color. This is why, in the space of a few hours, an island off the coast of Baja will turn from greenish blue to salmon pink to purple. Pyrotechnics alone, however, are not the genesis of the desert's beauty. Color is born from light and Van Dyke is at his best when describing this dynamic relationship. "All color—local, reflected, translucent, complementary —is, of course, made possible by light and has no existence apart from it. Through the long desert day the sunbeams are weaving skeins of color across the sands, along the sides of the canyons, and about the tops of the mountains. They stain the ledges of copper with turquoise, they burn the buttes to a terra-cotta red, they paint the sands with rose and violet, and they key the air to the hue of the opal. The reek of color that splashes the western sky at sunset is but the climax of the sun's endeavor."[13]

Even to a half-mad aesthete, beauty was not an end in itself. It was a means to an end, the sugar coating for an idea that most people can't swallow. Van Dyke's illness pushed him into seeing how closely life and death are linked. It is only through accepting death that one can truly be alive. This is what Van Dyke discovered and it is the desert's ultimate lesson, the true desert heart. A desert journey is a nearly universal metaphor for a near-death experience, for a prolonged period of spiritual and emotional isolation. To reveal oneself to another person during this journey is excruciatingly painful—only those who have traveled there before you can understand your utter despair. Even they cannot join you. There is no comfort. At times, there is no hope.

Not everyone is called on this journey. And the people who take it almost invariably experience long periods during which they wish to be someplace else. McDonald's. A Motel 6. Anywhere. But that's too bad. Turning back is impossible. And it should be. There are no second chances. Take Jesus, for instance, who visited the desert for purification. Only after forty days and forty nights of thirst and hunger was he ready to climb a mountain to confront Satan, who personified the biggest sin of all—spiritual pride. The desert defies such pride. Even Father Kino, the Italian Jesuit who may have been the first European to enter the Pinacate region, left only a few traces of colonialism behind him. Far better known than any of Kino's whitewashed missions is the road out of the desert. It is called the Devil's Highway.

To the godless humanists of contemporary society, the desert journey translates into a confrontation with the false self; the symbolic death of the alcoholic hitting bottom, the stockbroker losing it all in a crash. Or a rather bizarre art history professor facing his own loneliness. Provoked by his subconscious, Van Dyke sought out this mythic death-seeking and life-seeking ritual in the desert. "He had heard all the horror stories about the desert," Richard Shelton writes, "knew its dangers, but chose to go into it anyway. 'I was just ill enough,' he says, 'not to care about the perils and morbid enough to prefer dying in the sand, alone, to passing out in a hotel with a room-maid weeping at the foot of the bed.' "[14] When Van Dyke surfaced, he used his first choking, asthmatic breath to speak of what he had learned. He described the depths and pinnacles of isolation and beauty. He wrote that man's attempts to break the stillness of the desert night—to conquer the world with steel and smoke, to rise above his own animal nature, *to live forever*—are ugly and intrusive, a rent in the fabric. "A cry in the night! Overhead the planets in their courses make no sound, the earth is still, the very animals are mute. Why then the cry of the human? How it jars the harmonies! How it breaks in discord upon the unities of earth and air and sky! Century after century that cry has gone up, mobbing high heaven; and always insanity in the cry, insanity in the crier. What folly to protest when none shall hear! There is no appeal from the law of nature. It was made for beast and bird and creeping thing. Will the human never learn that in the eye of the law he is not different from the things that creep?"[15]

The same vision grew in the mind of a ragged hiker during his first lonely, ecstatic days in the humid wilderness of the American South. "The world, we are told, was made especially for man—a presumption not supported by all the facts," wrote John Muir in 1916.[16] Virtually anyone who has spent significant time alone in nature has arrived at the same belief. The desert has its own fierce way of teaching it. And the Pinacate is the ultimate desert.

It is a good place to die, or to be reborn.

That first afternoon, the Buckaroos visited the 722-foot-deep Sykes Crater. The crater was named after Godfrey Sykes, one of the legendary Pinacate Pirates who had explored the desert in 1907. Though he was a desert rat of mythic proportions, Sykes was not the most colorful of the pirates. That honor was reserved for the Pirates' guide, a dubious local lawman named Jefferson Davis Milton. Round-cheeked and squint-eyed, Milton might have been Dave Foreman's granddaddy or black-sheep uncle. In fact, the two men shared not only a physical resemblance but also the rumpled flair of good-natured macho poseurs. Milton staked out the territory early with a vintage photo that showed him sardonically eyeing a rattlesnake coiled fatly near his bedroll. Like Foreman, Milton later created his own myth by writing his memoirs. "Hell must have boiled over at the Pinacate," he intoned in the 1936 account of his Old West adventures. This particular trip, however, was anything but hellish. The Pinacate Pirates included the most well-known conservationist of his day, the irascible animal-rights activist and head of the New York Zoological Society, William T. Hornaday. The other pirates were desert botanist Daniel Trembly MacDougal, a photographer named John Phillips, the local explorer Sykes, an Indian guide named Charlie Foster, and the least popular member of the expedition, a young friend of Milton's named

Rube Daniels, who had the unsettling habit of whipping out his gun and blistering the nearest cactus with bullets for reasons known only to himself. The Pirates made several new discoveries, which gave them the liberating feeling of being completely unconstrained by civilization. In the 1850s the Irish explorer Sir Richard Burton had traveled all the way to Africa for such an experience. But on the American continent in 1907, these things were still possible—and joyful. After discovering his crater, Godfrey Sykes was immortalized in a snapshot even goofier than Milton's. The lanky desert rat is standing on his head at the summit of Pinacate Peak, doing a completely uncreditable imitation of a Pinacate beetle. If you turn the photo upside down, you can see that Sykes has a slightly glazed look in his eye and a shit-eating grin on his face. It was a tradition that Foreman, Wolke, Kezar, Koehler, and Roselle did their best to keep up on their trip seventy-three years later.

To a man, the Buckaroos have terrific memories of the Pinacate trip. None remember its details. You could say that the ultimate desert cast its spell on them. But in the interests of accuracy, it might be fair to mention that large quantities of beer dim the memory. The outlines of the trip remain because Kezar, the ex-librarian, was a meticulous, if disarmingly inclusive, diarist.

On March 31, the Buckaroos woke up just as the early-morning haze was burning off to reveal yellow brittlebush, the high, scruffy *Encelia farinosa* of the Sonoran desert, veering into negative space against the black lava hillsides. A few cups of strong coffee ate away the previous day's beer residue. The Buckaroos tossed supplies into their packs and set out for the Pinacate volcanic shield, dark blue in the distance like a misplaced slice of night sky.

Kezar estimates that the Buckaroos hiked about ten miles, approaching the mountains from the northeast. It was the more difficult route, but they didn't know any better. Progress across the lava was slow. The Buckaroos scraped their knees and hands and tore up their hiking boots on the jagged vesicular rock. But it was late March, the gentlest time in the desert. Temperatures stayed in the nineties. The sky was bright blue except for a few ostrich feathers of cloud fanning the summits of the peaks. The Buckaroos reached the base of Carnegie and Pinacate Peaks by mid-afternoon. Squinting up at the nearly identical mountains, they tried to figure out which was the taller one. That would be Pinacate Peak. They made their choice and trudged on, rubble showering from their boots. Years later, a park ranger from Organ Pipe Cactus National Monument discovered their names in the hiker's register at the Pinacate summit. "Up from Rd. to E via false summit. Long walk! Ron Kezar Glenwood, N.M." The scribbled entry also noted that Kezar had abandoned "Howie Wolke, Mike Rosell [sic], Bart Kohler [sic], and Dave Foreman" back on Carnegie Peak. Sucking down brews, they lounged among the black cinders and competed to see who could stand on his head longer, à la Sykes, as the spry Kezar dropped down into the saddle and scrambled up Pinacate Peak. They had climbed the wrong mountain. And they didn't care. Except for Kezar, who had a thing about peak-bagging.

It was rough stuff, this journey to the grim and forbidding desert heart. And the next day was even rougher. They piled back into the VW bus and drove an hour south to Puerto Peñasco, a Mexican beach town and shrimping port catering to gringos. They bodysurfed in the warm waters of the Sea of Cortez. That night, they scarfed down two shrimp dinners each at a local restaurant, taking full advantage of the imperialist exchange rate. The next day, April 2, the Buckaroos drove 120 miles west along Route 2 to the vaguely industrialized city of San Luis. When it grew dark, Ron Kezar led them on a tour of the Zona Roja, the Red Zone where the city stashed its whorehouses. Kezar was an odd duck, a brainy bachelor with varied and arcane interests. A photo of the Buckaroos taken in one of the whorehouses shows Kezar as the odd man out, at least physically. Small, serious, and smart-looking, Kezar sits at the table like an accountant who's just signed a pile of lucrative contracts with an unusually hairy band of football jocks. Kezar was eccentric, but well liked by nearly everyone. The ties between Kezar and Foreman ran particularly deep. Like Foreman, Kezar had grown up in a fundamentalist household. Only Kezar's was more repressive. He grew up in Stockton, California, the mean Central Valley town of John Huston's movie *Fat City*. The stale grayness of truck-stop air permeated his earliest memories. As soon as he left home, Kezar rebelled. Unlike Foreman, whose emotional style was vulnerable and actorish, Kezar's rebellion was quiet. But it was consistent and it colored his intellectual interests. His enthusiasms— anarchism, the radical union activists of the IWW—painted the political banners of Earth First! And his interest in prostitution, probably a lingering hangover from his religious upbringing, made him a handy tour guide.

It was in the Zona Roja that the differences between Roselle and the other Buckaroos first became apparent. Kezar noticed it at the first cantina. At this joint, the whores were young. Real young. One by one, most of the Buckaroos got drunk enough to wander off with the dark-eyed teenager of their choice. But not Roselle. He was drunk, sure, but not drunk enough for that.

At the next place they went to, the girls were a few years older. Howie Wolke later thought that Kezar, in his methodical way, had figured out the age level at all the different whorehouses and geared them to the Buckaroos' projected level of drunkenness. (Assuming, in a most politically incorrect manner, the younger the better. Further assuming that by 2 A.M. anything looked good.) At this whorehouse, the Buckaroos met Marta, a pretty woman in her early thirties. Marta was middle class and had a couple of kids, just like someone they all might have known in the States. Marta sat with the Buckaroos most of the night and even had her picture taken with them. But eventually she slipped off with Dave, and later Bart.[17] Howie and Ron Kezar took turns with another girl. At one point or another all the Buckaroos left the table. Except Roselle.

By the time they got to the third place, the prices had dropped and the whores' ages had risen. The oldest and most garishly made-up woman glued herself to the table loaded with brawny Americans. They bought her drinks and let her stay, nicknaming her Big Blue; they were just out for laughs at this point. Inevitably someone started teasing Roselle about his failure to sufficiently improve Mexico's trade deficit. Knowing he was sensitive about being one of the boys, they ganged up on him unmercifully. Roselle, pink-cheeked and pie-eyed, just stared down at the table and took it, his arms crossed awkwardly and his cowboy hat askew.

Then he smiled. He grabbed the most pathetic whore of all, Big Blue, the high-mileage harridan who had become a fixture at their table, and whirled her upstairs. The Buckaroos sat openmouthed, their empties strewn across the table like downed bowling pins. If Roselle was making a point about their attitudes toward women, it was lost on them. But like Foreman's raw-steak maneuver, it was a piece of histrionics that everyone would remember. Howie Wolke had already noticed Roselle's sense of sudden theater. A penchant for breakneck gestures would make him a good man on the barricades.

Around 5 A.M., the booze-soaked Buckaroos crossed the border into Arizona. With the odors of the night still on them, they were easy targets for the border guards who forced them to give up their stores of cheap Mexican liquor. They grumbled all the way to a turnoff outside Yuma, where they passed out into seamless drunken sleep.

They made it to Tucson by the night of April 3. After a nostalgic stop at a strip joint, they dropped Bart Koehler off at Saguaro National Monument. He was planning to hang around Arizona to pursue a practical-minded female attorney on whom he had a hopeless, demented crush. Foreman, Kezar, Wolke, and Roselle drove on until they reached a rest stop on the interstate between Tucson and Lordsburg where they slept that night. It wasn't until Friday, after Kezar's departure for Glenwood, that anyone remembers talking about starting a radical environmental group. They were headed toward Albuquerque. Roselle was lying in the back of the bus, stoned. Wolke and Foreman were cruising in front, popping cans of Bud and talking nonstop. It was serious stuff they were talking about, not moaning and bitching about hangovers. Things got like that with Howie.

Wolke was crude, bordering on truculent, but he also was the most scientifically minded of the bunch. In his dogged way, he was completely focused on inserting a biological alternative into the political process.

Nobody remembers how it happened, but suddenly everything made sense. *The Monkey Wrench Gang,* the Striders, even the Kachina Mudheads, who weren't *supposed* to make sense. Put them all together and you had the obvious move. It was Lesson One of negotiating: Ask for more than you think you can get. They had all learned it over the last few years of fieldwork. Foreman had learned it again—painfully—in Washington, D.C. Now they were ready to bring it all back home. But how? Each one of them had talked about the idea with different people over the years. Now it was Foreman who said it. The guy had a relationship with words like Van Gogh's with paint. He shot out the name: "Earth First!" and it was perfect; it worked, it exemplified everything they believed. The vibe was strong. Even Roselle caught it, stirring in the back like a funky-smelling griz in the spring. He drew a crude fist in a circle, just like the one on Foreman's motorcycle helmet. The logo. No Compromise in Defense of Mother Earth. Who thought of that? Nobody remembers, nobody cares anymore. Just go on. We're gonna write a manifesto. Have a newspaper. Big wilderness proposals. What about all the fuckin' land that got left out of RARE II? The mystery acreage? Bring back the wolf. Darken the plains with buffalo. Yeah. We're really gonna do it. Maybe. No, really. You call Susan Morgan. We'll get Rose. You call Debbie. Hmm. Well, okay, Wes. Bob. Hell, we'll get Mo Fuckin' Udall.

Much later, when Dave Foreman was asked if the Pinacate played any role in creating Earth First!, he quite rationally replied that RARE II had a lot more to do with it. But for the first decade of the group's existence, Foreman would unfurl the myth of the group's formation in the desert crucible as if it were a fiery scroll handed down by saints and mystics. And the myth may be as true as the bureaucratic reality. It takes a while to sink in, but time in the wilderness can put a spin on your life. And there is that terrible, seductive Mystery, the blue-black presence in the Pinacate that you can't quite put your finger on.

Doubtless it was just coincidence, but long after Earth First!'s founding, the same ranger from Organ Pipe Cactus National Monument discovered another interesting entry in the Pinacate Peak register. Dated exactly nine years to the day before Kezar's, it was written in loose-jointed handwriting, the kind a man with big hands and an Appalachian drawl might slap on a page after a long hike. It said: "Clumb up from Tule Tank. <u>Gawd</u> knows why. Neat view." Signed, Edward Abbey.

"Dear Monkeyfucker"

It was a time of pushing limits. How can you take Aldo Leopold one step further? Or Henry David Thoreau? How can you make those kinds of people relevant—not that they're irrelevant, but more relevant—for the twentieth and the twenty-first century?

—Louisa Willcox

1981–Salt Lake City

THE VOICE ON THE PHONE was the human equivalent of a flat-bottomed boat scraping on river rocks.

"Ken, this is Ed. There are some sort of spring rites going on at Lake Foul. It might be a good time if you want to get together."

Ken Sanders was surprised and a little flattered. Edward Abbey rarely used the telephone, preferring pithy messages written on cheap postcards. Occasionally there was a letter—one written to his friend Jack Loeffler had been fondly addressed: "Dear Monkeyfucker." The editorial pages of daily newspapers also were recipients of Abbey's epistolary largesse. But rarely, if ever, a phone call. It was all part of the mystique. And Abbey had plenty of that. As David Quammen wrote of Abbey's 1968 book, *Desert Solitaire,* "A man wrote a book, and lives were changed. That doesn't happen often."[1] In fact, Ed Abbey did more than change people's lives. He created a new kind of nature writing. He may not have been a hippie, but Ed Abbey did some of his best writing in the 1960s and 1970s, when the outer layer of sexless, well-bred conventionality was lifting off American life. In everything from movies to comic books, sentimentality was being trounced. The new role models were Peter Fonda and Dennis Hopper playing bikers on a drug-laden odyssey across America. Antiheroes like the neurotic Spiderman were replacing square-jawed Superman and Captain America. The gritty *Cabaret* blew apart the conventional Broadway musical—after all, people do not unaccountably launch into uplifting song-and-dance numbers at the most stressful points in their lives. For at least a decade, irreverence was the only sure sign of artistic integrity.

By the time *Desert Solitaire* was published in 1968, John Muir's transcendental maunderings seemed hopelessly sugarcoated, only most nature writers hadn't figured it out yet. Abbey almost singlehandedly made it impossible for nature writing to lapse back into babbling brooks and heavenly birdsong. In his books, real people made love, got mad, and threw beer cans out of car windows. They did it all in the midst of devastating natural beauty, which was under siege by fat Mormon developers and, invariably, the United States government. Ironically, it took a writer who believed in biocentrism—the idea that nature, not humanity, is the measure of all things—to take Nature off its pedestal and populate it with memorable characters. Ponderousness and poetic mawkishness, the bane of most nature writing, were completely foreign to Abbey. So was self-righteousness. Abbey merged the personal and the political like a maestro conducting the ultimate orchestra: the world itself. (The real world, *muchachos,* as he might have paraphrased B. Traven.) Readers—and critics—either loved him or they hated him.

Ken Sanders fell into the first category. But in his case, it wasn't love at first sight. Sanders's first reaction to the 1975 bestseller *The Monkey Wrench Gang* was shocked disapproval. It wasn't the book's hearty endorsement of ecosabotage that rubbed Sanders the wrong way; it was George Washington Hayduke's pesky propensity for littering. But Sanders's attitude changed after Abbey made a few appearances at the Cosmic Airplane, the bookstore Sanders owned in Salt Lake City in the 1970s. Sanders had a soft, mushy spot in his heart for writers, anyway. Descended from Mormon aristocracy—one of his great-greats was a heavyweight capo of patriarch Joseph Smith—he had relinquished any claim to respectability in the state of Utah when he grew his hair down to his waist and failed to attend college. But Sanders was far from illiterate. He had the sort of reverence for books that only the self-educated possess. His friendship with Abbey, while occasionally volatile, was an important part of his life.

So it didn't take much convincing for Sanders to accept Abbey's invitation to attend the mysterious spring rites. It was their location that floored Sanders: Lake Powell—the aforementioned Lake Foul—a giant artificial blob of Colorado River backed up behind white-walled Glen Canyon Dam. The campground Abbey had mentioned, Lone Rock, wasn't bad. Its distinguishing feature was a cigar-shaped sandstone monolith typical of the ones nearby that were used as a backdrop for a partially bare-chested and equally monolithic Charlton Heston in *The Greatest Story Ever Told*.

But Sanders couldn't figure out what the hell Ed, of all people, was doing up at Lake Powell. Rites of spring? Nobody hated Glen Canyon Dam more than Abbey. Certainly nobody wrote more beautifully about the canyon that it had flooded. A hundred miles from any town, the turrets and minarets of Glen Canyon exemplified wilderness to Edward Abbey. Just months before the dam's sluice gates folded shut, Abbey had navigated the stretch of Colorado River that ribboned along the canyon floor. "Down the River," Abbey's essay on Glen Canyon in *Desert Solitaire,* was one of the best pieces he ever wrote. Memoir and diatribe run seamlessly side by side in its pages, twin currents in a Colorado still big and wild enough to contain a soul. Abbey knew that Glen Canyon wasn't just archetypal wilderness; it was archetypal *American* wilderness. Eden violated by Progress. In this instance, Progress was the last giant water project built by the

U.S. Bureau of Reclamation, a soaring 587-foot dinosaur called the Glen Canyon Dam, an ugly concrete canker sore left over from the winning of the West.

Sanders, of course, had read *Desert Solitaire,* as well as *The Monkey Wrench Gang.* In both books Abbey fantasized about "some unknown hero with a rucksack full of dynamite strapped to his back" who would descend into the bowels of the Glen Canyon Damn [*sic*], depositing his charges where they would do the most good. Abbey's imaginary hero would enter the abomination's concrete core on the most public occasion possible, the dam's dedication ceremony. Maximum effect.

In reality that dark day had passed some eighteen years ago. Sanders noted, however, that the scheduled date of the so-called rite of spring was not lacking in significance. March 21, 1981. The equinox. It sounded dramatic and druidical, intriguing enough for Sanders to delay a backpacking trip into the Maze at Canyonlands National Park.

Louisa Willcox was also making plans to be in Glen Canyon on the twenty-first. She had been one of the first people to hitch up with the Buckaroos when they poured themselves back into Wyoming after their spiritual debauch in the Pinacate the year before. Louisa was working as a reporter for *High Country News* at the time, living in Lander, a medium-sized town north of the Wind River range. News traveled so fast in Lander that Louisa heard about Earth First! practically before the Buckaroos limped homeward. "When they came back from the trip—that sort of seminal backpack—it was buzzing around Lander. It was sort of like, yeah, this great idea [Earth First!] . . . The Sierra Club was talking about it and other people were talking about it.

"At that point it wasn't a confusing discussion of violence versus nonviolence. It was, 'There needs to be a benchmark on the Left.' There needs to be a voice which speaks for the rights of wild country, wild critters, just for themselves," said Louisa.

"The Wilderness Society was eliminating that whole cadre of people that grew up in the trenches. There was this sense in the Watt years that the groups were getting too top heavy, concentrated in the Beltway, concentrated in the cloakrooms of Washington and maybe a bit forgetful of the grass roots.''

It might have been a good concept, but it was pretty clear that the Buckaroos hadn't figured out how to make it work yet.

"I mean, really, it was just a camping trip," said Louisa. "A group of people basically sat there and said there's a time and a place for earth to come first in our minds and in our actions. That's all it was initially, this sort of funny idea."

In Lander, Wyoming, in the 1970s and early 1980s, all you really needed was an idea. Lander was a happening place if you were an environmentalist. For one thing, Bruce Hamilton was running the Northern Plains office of the Sierra Club there, right across the hall from *High Country News*. *High Country News* was a center for subversion itself, a newsprint flagship for environmental consciousness in the New West. Before joining the Sierra Club staff, Bruce had worked as the paper's news editor. Bruce's wife, Joan Nice, still worked there as managing editor. Later, when Bruce was promoted to the club's national office in San Francisco, she became an editor at *Sierra* magazine. It was a conflict of interest typical of the clubby, amateur-laden world of environmental publishing. Joan was an Amelia Earhart look-alike whose gaze always seemed to be fixed on a distant and very icy mountain range. Together, the Hamiltons made the perfect environmentalist couple, both willowy, long-limbed, soft-spoken, and Anglo-Saxon in a pained sort of way. Their home was a magnet not just for Louisa, but for Bart, too. Although Bart's romantic streak was the antithesis of Bruce's hardheadedness, there was a tender loyalty between the two men. More often than not it was Bruce and Joan's floor where Bart would end up sleeping when his mania had worn him out—and driven everyone else to ground.

To Louisa, Joan and Bruce were a New Age Ozzie and Harriet, too. They helped her believe that marriage and family were still possible as she rode through her share of the roller-coaster love affairs that everyone was living through those days. With all the craziness, she sometimes wondered what she was doing out there, climbing mountains and drinking in cowboy bars. Louisa's life had begun in a different milieu, as distant from the squat military houses of Dave Foreman's youth as it was possible to imagine. She was a good-natured jock from an affluent Quaker family whose Main Line roots stretched back to the 1600s. As a teenager she rode in fox hunts in the green hills outside her hometown. Crouched into a jump, she wore the de rigueur tight tan jodhpurs and tailored riding coat, her curls pressed flat under a hard velvet hat. She was a good girl and she was expected to go to college and get married in fairly orderly progression. As a Quaker, she might want to give back to the community some of the benefits that she had received, perhaps by tutoring disadvantaged youth or volunteering at a local hospital. But Louisa Willcox ended up trying to save a different corner of the world. Something in her was freed instead of shackled by her advantages. Adventure was easy; without being self-destructive, she breezed through physical danger the way her horses flew over fences. When she was fourteen, she spent the summer at her uncle's ranch in Sunlight Basin on the Shoshone National Forest in Wyoming and then she was hooked, not on horses anymore, but on the West. At sixteen, she scaled the Grand Teton, gripping nylon ropes as she pressed her body against blue-gray ice and granite. A few years later she laughed off macho jibes to become one of the early female mountaineering instructors at NOLS, the National Outdoor Leadership School, which was based in Lander. Eventually she would become one of the top grass-roots environmentalists in the northern Rockies.

In fact, the Lander environmental scene was even bigger than NOLS and Joan and Bruce and the *High Country News*. The Wyoming Outdoor Council, where Bart Koehler launched the Children's Crusade, had an office in town. So did the Wyoming Wilderness Association, the group that Howie had helped start. This was one of many statewide groups that came together—often sponsored by the nationals—to push through RARE II wilderness bills. Louisa was volunteering as newsletter editor for the wilderness association. She knew the turf; not only had she hiked through many of the wilderness areas, but she also had worked with Bart and Howie on Alternative W, the environmentalist proposal for a RARE II wilderness bill. Coincidentally she had interviewed Dave Foreman a year or two previously for *High Country News*. Even then he enjoyed a mild kind of celebrity among the cognoscenti. Here he was, a Buckaroo who had made good in Washington.

Louisa's sense of adventure made her a perfect candidate for Foreman's new endeavor. Foreman had learned that one of the keys to organizing was giving people the chance to do things they wanted to do anyway. Now was the time to push it a little further, to find out how the ideal of individual freedom worked in a social context. It would be anarchism made real, the wilderness tribe reborn. Being in the tribe meant that you shared a worldview—but it also meant that you had the freedom to choose how to put it into action. The whole thing was so laid-back and hip, it was enough to make you cringe if you weren't captured by the romance of it all. Or if you didn't know that beneath that western hipster drawl a certain amount of intellectual intensity was assumed. It might not be cool, not quite macho cowboy, but you were supposed to be asking the hard questions. This was the structure underlying it all, the common culture of smart young environmentalists who had seen enough of the world to make them angry, but weren't jaded yet. There was something eternal about it, at least eternally youthful, this never-ending late-night bullshit session of hard-core idealists. "It was a time of pushing limits," Willcox said. "How can you take Aldo Leopold one step further? Or Henry David Thoreau? How can you make those kinds of people relevant—not that they're irrelevant, but more relevant—for the twentieth and the twenty-first century?"

So they talked philosophy for a while, usually via memo. Foreman, in particular, gave stellar memo, shooting them off like fireworks from his parents' home in Bernalillo. By the late spring of 1980 the memos were tumbling into action. With the help of Koehler, Wolke, and Roselle, Foreman organized the first Earth First! rendezvous in Dubois, Wyoming (egregiously pronounced "Doo-boys"), at the T-Cross Ranch at the edge of the Washakie wilderness. He scheduled it for July fourth, 1980. Koehler came up with the name Round River

Rendezvous, after Aldo Leopold's metaphor for an ecological world-view. "For years some of us had realized that the best work at every conference got done informally, not in the formal sessions, but in the bullshitting around afterwards," Foreman said. The Buckaroos decided to have a conference that was all bullshit session.

The flyer for the campout was written in a bad imitation of western branding lettering and ran down the event this way: "WHY: To reinvigorate, enthuse, inspire wilderness activists in the West; to bring passion, humor, joy, and fervency of purpose back into the cause; to forge friendships, cooperation, and alliances throughout the West; to get drunk together, spark a few romances, and howl at the moon."

Participants were told to bring "camping equipment, food, booze (lots), weird wilderness outfits, musical instruments, bizarre toys, imagination, a good and gonzo attitude," but sensibly, no pets. Mindful of the popularity of movement gossip, Foreman dangled hints of hot info to come, plus an opportunity to learn the trade from the pros. "WHO: Wilderness warriors, shamans, and chiefs from around the West and a few honorary westerners from Washington, DC. A few of the grey-hairs of the tribe to pass on the torch. Meet people you've only heard rumors about before (are ——— and ——— really together? does ——— really drink that much? is ——— really such a jerk?)." Finally, he wrote: "Plan to sleep out or wherever you pass out."

Not surprisingly, the new Earth First! looked a lot like the old Wilderness Society. In fact, Foreman and the other Buckaroos hedged their bets by holding the Rendezvous at the same place the Wilderness Society staff had celebrated the Bicentennial and billing the event as a combination Earth First! gathering and Wilderness Society reunion. Foreman published a crude mimeographed newsletter, Number 0, which came out a few weeks before the Rendezvous. He gave it the horrible name *Nature More,* from a Byron poem that was quoted on the first page. "I love not man the less, but nature more," read the poem, perhaps the best of a succession of feeble and rather disingenuous attempts to grapple with the charge that the group was misanthropic.

The founders soon realized that *Nature More* had the honor of being the worst name of any environmental publication. It was quite an achievement to beat *Not Man Apart,* the Friends of the Earth newspaper. David Brower, FOE's founder, had lifted the phrase from a poem by Robinson Jeffers. After the organization grew, Brower successfully defended the name to his board despite overwhelming statistical evidence that readers—and his own staff—hated it. Fortunately, the Earth First!ers didn't have to deal with someone of Brower's sizeable stature, ego, or stubbornness. The name of the second issue of the Earth First! newsletter, edited by Susan Morgan, uneventfully became *Earth First.* (The exclamation point had not yet made its appearance.) By then, Foreman had found a Stephen Crane poem that expressed the group's goofy vision of apocalypse.

Many workmen
Built a huge ball of masonry
Upon a mountaintop
Then they went to the valley below,
And they turned to behold their work.
"It is grand," they said;
They loved the thing.

Of a sudden, it moved;
It came upon them swiftly;
It crushed them all to blood.
But some had opportunity to squeal.

The second issue—Number 1, Volume 1—announced that Earth First! was ready and willing to squeal. "Like Pallas Athena springing fully armed from the brow of Zeus, Earth First enters the wilderness fray . . ." trumpeted the mimeographed sheet. " 'What!?' you say. 'Another wilderness group? There are more wilderness groups than plague fleas on a New Mexico prairie dog! I already belong to nine of the damn things. Why another one? Why Earth First?'

"Because," it continued, "we're different."

And they were. *Earth First* No. 1 set a tone—satirical but still serious enough to rally the troops—that helped give the group its unique role in the environmental movement. The agenda set by the Buckaroos in *Earth First* No. 1 was the substance behind the satire, the group's real contribution to the environmental movement.

The Earth First! platform, laid out in the first newsletter and in many subsequent editions of the *Earth First! Journal,* consisted of a plan to preserve one major wilderness area in every ecosystem in the United States. To the Buckaroos, that meant setting aside forty-four wilderness areas of 1 million acres or more. Slices of ecosystems had already been preserved, such as Maine's Baxter State Park, the Florida Everglades, and Big Bend National Park. The Buckaroos proposed major, mind-blowing expansions of those parks. In fact, very few parks or forests met their criteria for big wilderness—tracts of wild land large enough for natural processes to go on undisturbed. The only places that did were the Bob Marshall Wilderness and nearby Glacier National Park. In these areas, the Buckaroos proposed closing down merely a road or two.

The high desert of Oregon, the red desert of southern Wyoming, the prairie and floodplains that lined the Missouri River in Montana. A one-million-acre preserve in southern California for the California condor. One million acres of South Texas brush country to keep ocelots and jaguarundis slinking and mating in peace and harmony. Reading Earth First!'s list, one could almost see the Hieronymus Bosch landscape that swarmed and slithered in the overheated prose of sixteenth-century Jesuits who had come to the New World to convert the heathen Indians. Often the Jesuit accounts were wildly inaccurate; the elephant that had been seen by one priest was either a figment of his imagination or a very early circus runaway. But the tone of wonder—along with the salesmanship—in these early dispatches is genuine. Frightening as it sometimes was, precolonial America was the closest thing the priests could imagine to Eden. Reading the less poetic but more amusing *Earth First!* newspaper, one could almost believe it was possible to restore it.

The word *restoration* had not yet become a buzz word in the environmental movement. But the Buckaroos were already running with the idea. In *Earth First* No. 1, they announced that they didn't just want to stop development; they wanted to turn it around. "It is time to *recreate* wilderness; identify key areas, close roads, remove developments, and reintroduce extirpated wildlife."

It was not until 1988, when former Friends of the Earth staffer John Berger organized the first national conference on ecosystem restoration in Berkeley, California, that the mainstream environmental movement would start tossing around the ideas that Earth First! had proposed almost a decade earlier. Even with Earth First!'s outrageous, attention-grabbing tactics—or perhaps because of them—their serious message had a hard time getting through. "It's time to be passionate. It's time to be tough," Foreman wrote in an early newsletter. "It's time to have the courage of the civil rights workers who went to jail." Of all of them, he best understood the inertia that they were up against. His experience had made him angry; it had also built his determination to do things differently.

With the preppy shadow of Bill Turnage looming offstage, the newsletter promised that Earth First! would not get hung up on organizational politics. It proudly announced that the group did not own a photocopy machine. But an environmental group is an environmental group. Later issues would establish another Earth First! tradition: the "usual disgusting plea for money."

In the meantime the Buckaroos were pleading for bodies, not cash. They urged everyone to show up at the first Round River Rendezvous. They weren't disappointed. All the old friends rallied around. Faithful Susan Morgan agreed to produce the *Earth First!* newsletter. Even Debbie Sease put in a guest appearance, making an entrance with her new boyfriend, Sierra Club field representative Russ Shay. Other missionaries from the straight world arrived. Bruce Hamilton came, accompanied by a cohort of Sierra Club activists. The federal land management agencies were thoroughly, if surreptitiously, represented: the National Park Service, the National Forest Service, even the Bureau of Land Management. Not to mention the white-collar government guys who had known Koehler and Foreman during hard-charging legislative sessions. Why shouldn't they be friends? They were all about the same age and had chosen their careers for the same basic reason, crackbrained idealism. Usually it was only a fine shade of personality difference that kept them on opposite sides of the fence. One sympathetic official even adopted the nom de monkeywrench Big Don Schwarzenegger and ascended to the Circle of Darkness— Earth First!'s unofficial board of directors. Debbie, on the other hand, was relegated to La Manta Mojada, the Wet Blankets. This was Foreman's idea of separation of powers. The Wet Blankets were charged with the task of preventing the Circle of Darkness from going too far. Needless to say, Debbie was appointed to her post by the smartass— and still smarting—Dave Foreman.

By the end of the first Round River Rendezvous, the skeleton of Earth First! had pretty much formed. But what would animate it? Back in April, Foreman and about a dozen friends had moved their Frankenstein's feet a few tentative steps. They schlepped a heavy wooden plaque into Cooney, a New Mexico ghost town north of Glenwood. Sweating and laughing, they seated the phony historical marker in a hole. It was a monument to Victorio, an Apache Indian who led a raid on the Cooney mining camp on April 28, 1880. The message on the marker explained the reason Victorio was being honored. "Victorio strove to protect these mountains from mining and other destructive activities of the white race."

It wasn't exactly a public-relations coup. The *Silver City Daily Press,* which billed itself the "Gateway to the Gila Wilderness," ran a photo. Victorio's monument was about one notch up from your basic Associated Press novelty item, like the man with 36,000 library books or the bony mare that found its way home across ten states.

Despite his gutsy facade, the winter after the Rendezvous was a boring and vaguely desperate time for Foreman. In the fall, he returned briefly to Washington to lobby the New Mexico wilderness bill through Congress. The rest of the time he was stuck in Bernalillo, firing off memo after memo. Funds were low to nonexistent. Foreman was digging into what was left of his savings and trying to sell off the land in Glenwood that he had been saving for his retirement. In the meantime, if this thing was going to work, the Buckaroos would have to act fast. They couldn't organize a political campaign. That would cost too much money. What they had to do was stage the ultimate PR coup. It had to be sharp, it had to be funny, it had to be big. Most of all, it had to be on TV. In other words, a simple, easy-to-read declaration of independence. Along with playing to the masses, the event would send a special message to the initiate. The message was: *We're not gonna take it.* The medium would send shock waves though the arrogant, ramrod-up-their-butts honchos at the Wilderness Society and the Sierra Club.

Finally Foreman hit on the idea that would bust Earth First! loose from the puny typewriter he had borrowed from his kid sister. The answer was simple, when you really thought about it. Especially if you had read every word Edward Abbey ever wrote. What was the ulti-mate symbol of the greed and stupidity that were destroying the West? The biggest visual aid on the planet? It had to be Glen Canyon Dam. Three million cubic feet of concrete had destroyed a place that existed outside time. Starting with the 1869 account written by one-armed explorer John Wesley Powell, visitors to the canyon had described with awe its stone amphitheaters and alcoves; the turrets and spires that rose from the canyon floor like visions of a lost city; and the canyon's odd, secret places, like the storm-carved hollow Powell named Music Temple for the sound of the wind running through it. In 1963, Glen Canyon began its slow death by drowning as water filled the 186-mile reservoir sacrilegiously named after the late ex-plorer. Foreman's generation, and all the generations that came after it, would never see the canyon.

Foreman ran the idea of a Glen Canyon shindig past the Circle of Darkness. They were enthusiastic. His next move was to recruit Edward Abbey. The two men had never met, but lack of chutzpah was never Foreman's problem. He figured that the guy who wrote *The Monkey Wrench Gang* would like the idea of having his fictional characters come to life. Hell, after writing a book that was a goddamn call to arms, Abbey couldn't fail to come through. Could he? It turned out that Foreman was right. Abbey agreed to meet Foreman and his band of ecofreaks at the spring rites. He even invited a few friends, like Ken Sanders.

Sanders blasted into Lone Rock campground on the afternoon of March 30. No Abbey. Instead, a grim-looking bunch of guys blocking a VW bus. Big and bearded, they stood with their legs splayed, arms crossed over their chests, staring straight at him. Sanders noticed that there was this black plastic *thing* draped over the bus. This unidentifiable thing. The guys were acting totally paranoid, but Sanders stonewalled. A friend had sent him, he told them. "No way. I wasn't going to drop Abbey's name," he said, shaking his head and laughing. "No fucking way."

The Buckaroos circled Sanders like a mean bunch of wolves. The face-off went on for hours, Foreman giving Sanders the worst of his hooded stares, Koehler wobbling over to him like a Mexican soccer player after a ten-day gutter binge, Howie Wolke flexing his muscles with a wholesome, athletic sort of menace, and Mike Roselle, with his rubbery basketball player's body, looming over Sanders's airspace in a leering, maniacal way.

Finally some gesture was made, a beer proffered. By the time Abbey showed up with Clarke Cartwright, the latest in a series of young girlfriends, Sanders knew all about the weird thing on top of the VW bus. It wasn't *that* mysterious, just a 300-foot sheet of black polyurethane, the kind used more commonly as a weed killer in organic gardens than as a prop. But performance art was probably the best explanation for how this piece of plastic was going to be used. Foreman said as much to the clerk at Babbitt's hardware in Flagstaff, who wanted to know why anyone would need such a big piece of plastic.

"We're art students," said Foreman. "This here is our master's thesis."

"Sure like to see it when you're done," the clerk replied.

"Just look in the paper Monday morning," Foreman told him.

Louisa Willcox was amused by the testosterone-induced face-off between Sanders and the Buckaroos. Sanders, with his long hair and funky '54 Chevy truck, sure didn't look like a spy. But paranoia was part of the game. It was a game she was heartily enjoying. She had driven down with Howie Wolke and Mike Roselle, red-rock Utah a blur of beer, fast driving, and nonstop talk. By morning, when about seventy-five people had shown up at Lone Rock campground, things started moving even faster. Louisa was in demand and not just for her feminine charms—the knot-tying skills she had learned in mountaineering school were needed for the Buckaroos' "art project." Other people were being recruited, too. Cagey Ron Kezar was deemed the perfect getaway-car driver. There were new faces, too. Just like Ken Sanders, Toby McLeod and Randy Hayes had been lured to the scene by Ed Abbey. They had telephoned to ask if they could interview him for a documentary. He suggested that they meet at Lone Rock. When they showed up, they were briefed on the art project and quickly agreed to immortalize it on film.

Foreman was in his element. His wispy ginger hair flew in all directions as he ran around like a combination mad scientist and D. W. Griffith. (He and Bart were having a contest to see who could grow his hair longer. Foreman, already slightly balding, was losing.) Dave made quite a picture, dressed in a cheesy red, white, and blue polyester warm-up jacket with USA splashed all over it. Both Foreman and his jacket looked like factory seconds from the '76 Olympics. But you couldn't miss the message. Goddammit, it was time to wrest the land of the free away from the Marines.

The guests who turned out for Earth First!'s coming out party were a little less likely to wave the flag. A cross between standard-issue hippie and the young, freshly scrubbed western outdoorsy type, they stood by discreetly as the black polyurethane "art" was borne away to its destiny. Most were content merely to smile as they rubbed their hands and stamped their feet against the cold.

Part exorcism, part lunacy, the whole thing went off almost too easily, despite the fact that the authorities had been tipped off that something, they didn't know what, was going to happen at the dam. Louisa, Howie Wolke, Bart Koehler, Dave Foreman, and a guy from Montana named Tony Moore had no trouble getting to the top of the dam. They simply bypassed the generator room, where police were waiting for them, walked to the top of the dam, and clambered over a fence. Using the climbers' knots she had mastered at NOLS, Louisa fastened the plastic to a series of grates running across the walkway. Not far away, from a steel bridge spanning the remains of Glen Canyon, Ed Abbey and the crowd of sixty or seventy Earth First! supporters hooted and applauded as a 300-foot ersatz crack— that very same sheet of black plastic—unfurled down the dam's eyeless machine face. "Earth First!" shouted Abbey. "Free the Colorado!"

The Monkey Wrench Gang had come to life.

The monument to Victorio hadn't exactly rocked the nation, but the cracking of Glen Canyon Dam certainly grabbed people's attention. The first person to sit up and take notice was Ed White. White was the deputy sheriff of Page, Arizona, the town created by the Bureau of Reclamation in 1957 out of a sandy, barely populated mesa that happened to be near Glen Canyon. White showed up just as Ed Abbey, speech in hand, was hoisting his six-foot-three frame up onto the tailgate of Ken Sanders's pickup. It was an auspicious debut for Alfonso the Chevy's career as the official Earth First! stage. More than that, it was a moment of sadness and anger, a moment of hope. A golden moment, as the network programmers say. The plastic crack was flapping in the breeze. The dam crackers had coolly taken the elevator down to the visitors' center parking lot, where Bart Koehler, masquerading as country-and-western star Johnny Sagebrush, warmed up the crowd with a few tunes. Toby McLeod and Randy Hayes were still rolling their cameras, after capturing shots of the scurrying figures on the dam and the unfurling of the dramatic crack now officially loosed on the media world.

"Oppose the destruction of our homeland. If resistance is not enough, subvert!" Abbey read from a sheet of paper. Ed White was busy taking down information from Howie Wolke and Dave Foreman's drivers' licenses when he realized what he was hearing. "Is that Ed Abbey?" he asked, his pen stalled in midair. Foreman, who had been rather overzealously using the word *sir* in his dealings with the deputy sheriff, merely smiled.

There were no arrests at Glen Canyon that day. But in the Earth First! archives a photograph of the two Eds, Abbey and White, floats around like a stray remnant of black plastic bobbing on the artifical blue waters of Lake Powell. And somewhere the man named Ed White, a true fan, probably still has the autograph personally given to him by the author of *The Monkey Wrench Gang* on a rather memorable day of the deputy sheriff's life.

David Brower was another person who paid serious attention when the Glen Canyon dam cracked. The prematurely white-haired mountaineer was the environmental movement's high priest, its resident genius, patriarch, and bad boy rolled into one. The writer John McPhee had given him the double-edged moniker "the archdruid," which conveyed both vision and intransigence. So when Foreman wrote his letter to Edward Abbey, something significant happened in the environmental movement. Or didn't happen. Because Foreman chose not to write to the archdruid. His reasons were sound. After all, Brower, the century's premier conservationist, had sold out Glen Canyon.

In one way, at least Brower's story was typical. David Brower was drawn to conservation work, where he would have to deal with people almost every waking hour, because he was shy. The son of an engineer, Brower felt more at home in the natural world than in the boxy buildings of his hometown of Berkeley, California. The young David Brower had ample reason to be timid. An accident had knocked out his teeth while he was an infant. By the time his grown-up teeth grew in he was twelve years old. Cruel fellow students already had nicknamed him "The Toothless Boob." Brower spent his youth roaming the hills on the eastern outskirts of town, either alone or accompanied by his mother, who was blind. Brower's belief in the power of words began with the experience of describing the dark-green oaks and golden grasses of the East Bay hills to his mother. Because she could not see, he had to expand his own vision.[2]

At age twelve Brower read *My First Summer in the Sierra,* the book John Muir had written as a young man. Not long afterward, he began exploring Muir's territory. By the time he entered the University of California at Berkeley, he had adopted the Sierra as his second home. To his later regret, he didn't last long in college. Too shy, too independent, or both. After a year or two, Brower gave in to the allure of the mountains. He dropped out and began spending as much time as he could in the Sierra. According to Stephen Fox's excellent book *The American Conservation Movement: John Muir and His Legacy,* Brower made thirty-three first ascents in the Sierra in the 1930s. Once he climbed three 14,000-foot peaks in twelve hours. In 1935 he began living in Yosemite National Park.[3] "In those days—the late 1920s—backpacking and mountaineering were considered the oddest of preoccupations, the province of slightly deranged British peers," writes Marc Reisner in his book about western water issues, *Cadillac Desert.* "The Sierra Nevada, which is invaded by so many hikers today that it feels like a zoo, was virtually devoid of humanity. The rapture Brower experienced there transported him to a mystic state; it became a dependency, a drug. He had food and supplies cached all over the place; he could return to one weeks after laying it in and it would still be there. Like his hero John Muir, Brower grew intimate with vast proportions of that range."[4]

One of the ways conservation groups thrive is by adopting bright, talented misfits like Brower and turning their eccentricities to good account. In Brower's case, it was quite naturally the Sierra Club that brought him into the fold. In the summer of 1933, when Brower was twenty-one years old, he met photographer Ansel Adams. Adams sponsored him for club membership. Brower also became friends with attorney Dick Leonard, a tough mountaineer who was a mover and shaker in Sierra Club politics. His most important mentor, though, was the gentle Francis Farquhar. Leonard and Adams both represented parts of Brower's own character. Leonard was a mountaineer, a man of action. Adams and Brower shared an aesthetic sensibility. But Farquhar was an old-world gentleman. Like a father, he welcomed Brower into his family, his library, his darkroom, and finally into his magazine, the *Sierra Club Bulletin*. Brower inherited the editorship from him in 1946.

Until he was drafted in World War II, Brower led the Sierra Club's high-country hiking trips. People fell in love with his airy good looks, his creative mind, and the sense of freedom he brought to the Sierra Club's well-appointed mass excursions into the wilderness. In the mountains, Brower lost his shyness; he was incandescent. "Once in the company of people who shared his devotion to alpine country, to climbing and skiing and waxing theological about the meaning of nature, Brower grew steadily more self-confident," writes Russell Martin in *A Story That Stands Like a Dam: Glen Canyon and the Struggle for the Soul of the West*.[5] His insecurity ebbing under the glow of approval, Brower entered Sierra Club mythology as the reincarnation of its founder, John Muir. Engineers, lawyers, and college professors provided the Sierra Club's financial and organizational backbone. But Muir, a self-taught scientist, abused child, poet, inventor, gentleman farmer, writer, and eccentric, had given the club its heart. Cornball as his prose was, Muir's transcendental vision was the animating dream for hundreds, if not thousands, of people whose lives revolved around the Sierra Club. The Sierra Club always had a split personality. When Brower stepped in, Muir's romantic vision was once again in ascendancy.

Brower's tenure at the Sierra Club was a wrinkle in the usual organizational pattern. Environmental groups and businesses alike are generally started by charismatic visionaries. If the organization survives, the visionaries give way, peacefully or not so peacefully, to the managerial class of executive. But rarely does a visionary take hold for a second time. After its initial forays into national politics around the time of the Hetch Hetchy debate in 1914, the Sierra Club had lapsed into being a provincial and fairly apolitical California hiking club. When David Brower became head of the Sierra Club, the group was reborn into a passionate, political idealism.

But the club's lawyers and engineers remained their stolid selves and it wasn't long before Brower found himself bucking traditional club politics. Brower had started off fairly conservative himself. But after a brief skirmish with anti-FDR Republicanism, his politics became more liberal. In conservation matters, he was radical, making wilderness his guiding principle rather than gearing policies toward human use. Brower's wilderness orientation was a big leap for the Sierra Club. In the beginning, he moved carefully. In the 1930s he worked almost exclusively for the *Sierra Club Bulletin,* where he could not directly influence policy. Then World War II interrupted his career. Brower won three battle stars and a bronze star during his World War II service with the elite Tenth Mountain Division, where he instructed troops in climbing techniques and served as a battalion intelligence officer. In 1949 the conquering hero was appointed to the club's board of directors.

That year also marked a high point for the U.S. Bureau of Reclamation, whose officials would soon come to consider David Brower their worst enemy. The agency had been created in 1902 to aid settlers along the western frontier. Twenty years later its political role was solidified by the Colorado River Storage Compact, which divided the water of the Colorado River among the western states like poker chips. Shortly after the agreement was made, it became apparent that the game was far from over. The Colorado had swollen to unusual heights in the teens and twenties. As the river subsided—and population grew—too many states were left fighting over too little water. Los Angeles, with its obscene growth rate and nonexistent resources, would have been enough to tip the balance. But everybody wanted a piece of the action. Water was the currency of development and development equaled money. Local and state pols squabbled over the Colorado River like pigs jockeying for position at a rapidly emptying trough. Out of the free-for-all of water politics, the U.S. Bureau of Reclamation grew into an empire. It was a remarkable story, well-told in *Cadillac Desert.* But the conservation movement played a fairly small role in it until the dispute over Dinosaur National Monument rolled around in the 1950s.

By then, Floyd Dominy, the J. Edgar Hoover of Western water, had consolidated so much power that BuRec engineers no longer thought about measly little dams, but about *projects.* The year Brower became a Sierra Club board member, the first of these megabuck water-diversion schemes was floating around Congress. The $1-billion contraption was called the Colorado River Storage Project. It included four dams, one of which would inundate a section of Grand Canyon National Monument. If the plan went through it would stitch up the Escalante—canyon country—like an overly ambitious seamstress.

It was a mark of the times that the Sierra Club did not oppose the Colorado project. The club's board endorsed Dominy's plan, despite the fact that it would intrude on national parkland. Some people, like David Brower, felt the club's approval contradicted its own history. In the early 1900s the club had lost a protracted, brutal conflict over the proposal to dam Hetch Hetchy canyon in Yosemite National Park. So much blood was spilled in the fight over Hetch Hetchy that fairly little industrial development was allowed in the national parks for the next forty years. But as the bustling Bureau of Reclamation started running out of good dam sites, the agency's greedy eyes became fixed on the park system.

In the first go-round, Brower was able to pass a resolution delaying formal Sierra Club approval until a dam was built in Glen Canyon, which was not on federal land. Only if Glen Canyon Dam proved inadequate would the Sierra Club endorse shutting off the Colorado as it roared through the Grand Canyon.

The real issue was far greater than one canyon, no matter how beautiful. The integrity of the national park system was at stake. The U.S. Park Service had a double mandate: to preserve land and to render it accessible. This contradictory mission was causing enough problems in the age of the automobile. But parks legislation made no mention of industrial development, either pro or con. Several times, the Park Service had allowed utilities to cross park boundaries. But most of this development was hidden, like the water-diversion tunnel in Rocky Mountain National Park, which had been built in the 1930s. A dam in the Grand Canyon was far more serious. It would mean that parks and monuments were no different from the national forests, just another part of the industrial landscape.

By 1952, the issue stood out in sharper relief. A squabble between

Arizona and California had nixed the Grand Canyon dam, but the giant Colorado River Storage Project was still being bounced around. These days the BuRec boys were training their slide rules on a section of Dinosaur National Monument called Echo Park. Alerted to the threat, Bernard De Voto arose like a squat intellectual genie created for the sole purpose of bedeviling western businessmen. In 1950, De Voto wrote an article for *The Saturday Evening Post* called "Shall We Let Them Ruin Our National Parks?" which criticized the more egregious aspects of the CRSP. The article was a hit. After it was reprinted in *Reader's Digest,* it drew new visitors to the remote Escalante region. Suddenly the Bureau of Reclamation's entire mission was in question. The Bureau was no longer universally viewed as the savior of struggling pioneers. Increasingly it was seen for what it had become: a political giant handing out multimillion-dollar plums to private industries like Bechtel, Standard Oil, and Del Monte.

It was around this time that David Brower discovered the Southwest. The region became the love of his mature years. The deserts of the Four Corners, with their long vistas, flat mesas, and dark clouds, were conducive to reflection. More can be seen; the loneliness of the landscape is a source of strength. It was an appropriate place to be at a time when death starts to seem real, when life is taking on sharper contours. Yet Brower the mountaineer was not slowed by middle age. He made many technical climbs when he was in his forties, including pioneering a climbing route up Shiprock in Navajo country. In 1953 he took a trip on the Green River. Floating through Dinosaur National Monument was a life-changing experience for Brower. Living on river time, the particulars of existence were determined by the relative heat of sun on sandstone, by the river's current. After a few days, Brower was no longer even moving on river time; he was in sync with geology. The year before, he had been hired as the Sierra Club's first paid executive director. Struck hard by canyon country, Brower was determined to use his new position to save it.

Brower's interest in the Southwest was shared by a wealthy Sierra Club member named Edward Mallinckrodt, Jr. Mallinckrodt was a chemical manufacturer who loved nature, an irony less apparent in the days before *Silent Spring*. He already had been tapped by Howard Zahniser over at the Wilderness Society to foment rebellion against the Bureau of Reclamation in Washington, D.C. Characteristically, the Beltway-bound Zahniser hadn't even heard about Dinosaur National Monument until it was touted as a potential dam site. But he got the point in a hurry. In 1950, he set up a committee to protect Dinosaur, appointing Mallinckrodt one of its members. The Izaak Walton League, the Audubon Society, and even the National Wildlife Federation all joined. Only the Sierra Club hung back. Mallinckrodt, a devoted Sierra Clubber, became determined to dislodge the club from its California provincialism.

With Mallinckrodt's backing, Brower took on the Dinosaur issue. Brower had little experience as a political activist, so his first foray was on familiar turf—the wilderness. In the summer of 1953, he organized three float trips down the Green River, inviting along a few dozen influential conservationists. This was a tactic the Sierra Club had used since its inception in 1892. John Muir had been convinced that people who experienced the wilderness would want to save it. By 1989, this tradition would climb to new heights of media sophistication as Los Angeles staffers led perennial starlet Morgan Fairchild and Sen. Alan Cranston on cushy forays into the California desert accompanied by as many reporters as they could muster. It was all for a good cause. Cranston had introduced a sweeping desert-protection bill endorsed by the conservationists. As always, visuals made a difference.

Under the direction of David Brower, however, the club's political and aesthetic arsenals expanded well beyond celebrity-studded wilderness outings. Dinosaur National Monument became the focus of Brower's power to mythologize, to pull together the strands of biology and history to form a coherent message. With Brower's help, the environmentally concerned publisher Alfred Knopf rushed through a book called *This Is Dinosaur*. Edited by Brower's friend, the western novelist, biographer, and essayist Wallace Stegner, with essays by Olaus Murie and others, the book nonetheless bore Brower's creative stamp. The publication history of *This Is Dinosaur* also was marked by Brower's growing political sophistication—the first copies landed on the desks of congressmen. With Brower's passion and the coalition-building skills of Howard Zahniser, opposition to the Echo Park dam became more widespread. The strategy was this: Conservationists would not oppose the whole Colorado River Storage Project. They might threaten to scuttle it, but in reality they simply didn't have enough clout to do it successfully. Nor could they achieve unanimity among themselves on such a sweeping antidevelopment stand. But they could knock Echo Park out of the proposal. To make things easier, they could throw the Bureau of Reclamation a bone—Glen Canyon. Glen Canyon was on Navajo land, not in a park or a monument. Few people outside of the Southwest had ever heard of it.

When hearings convened on January 18, 1954, Brower was ready. The engineer's son was armed with passion, but he also had a secret weapon. His secret weapon was Walter Huber, the president of the American Society of Civil Engineers. Primed by Huber, Brower followed Howard Zahniser, who rather ineffectually quoted from the Robert Southey poem "The Cataract of Lodore" because one of the side canyons which would be flooded was named after it. By contrast, Brower began by comparing Echo Park to Hetch Hetchy, the dam built in the California Sierra in 1914. In Sierra Club lore, the damming of Hetch Hetchy had assumed the proportions of Greek tragedy. Not only had it drowned a beautiful valley, which Brower showed his Congressional audience in a still-montage film, but it had also reputedly caused John Muir to die of a broken heart. This story handily ignores the fact that the Sierra Club patriarch was seventy-six years old when the dam was built and had lost his wife and daughter in the preceding decade.

That was legend. This was fact: the dam at Hetch Hetchy was unnecessary. There were many other possible sources of water for the city of San Francisco. (In the 1980s, Donald Hodel, James Watt's successor as Secretary of the Interior, would even propose dismantling it, an unexpected suggestion that mostly got environmentalists suspicious.) More facts. A dam at Echo Park was equally unnecessary. Brower whipped out a blackboard and, using Huber's figures, corrected the Bureau of Reclamation math. He proved that a dam in

Glen Canyon would cause less evaporation than one in Dinosaur National Monument. He also proved that a dam in Glen Canyon would store more water. To be exact, 700,000 acre-feet more. Brower recited these figures with amiable sarcasm, calling his arithmetic "the simple, ninth-grade variety."[6]

There were several skirmishes before everybody showed their hands. In the fall, Zahniser pulled out all the stops, using a publicity ploy that would develop into one of the primary weapons in the environmental movement's tactical repertoire. He placed an open letter in the October 31 *Denver Post* threatening to oppose the entire Colorado River Storage Project if the Dinosaur dam wasn't deleted from the bill. A flurry of meetings and letters followed, culminating in the conservationists' winning their main point. The House of Representatives revised the bill to preclude the construction of any dam or reservoir in a national park or monument. They also added language mandating "adequate protective measures to preclude impairment of the Rainbow Bridge National Monument," which lay in the path of the water that would back up behind the Glen Canyon Dam. On January 23, 1956, Brower, Zahniser, and the other members of the conservation bloc anted up their quid pro quo. They wrote a letter to Wayne Aspinall, chairman of the House Subcommittee on Irrigation and Reclamation, withdrawing their opposition to the Colorado Storage Project. The $900-million water project, sans Dinosaur National Monument, was passed by the House on March 1, 1956.

Letter writing, wilderness outings, dazzling congressional testimony, and full-page ads would become standard issue for hotshot environmental groups in the seventies and eighties. But before the Dinosaur fight, they had never been used on a mass political scale. Urged on by senators and congressman who wanted to stop the whole Colorado River Storage Project, Brower stayed in Washington. But in 1959 the Sierra Club recoiled from its own athleticism. The board yanked Brower back to San Francisco and adopted an official policy of cooperation with government officials. Brower felt hog-tied and turned much of his attention to the club's growing publishing business. But not permanently. His biggest battle still lay ahead.

First, though, Brower had to deal with aftershocks of the Dinosaur fight. Although Dinosaur was considered a victory, it spawned yet another threat to national parkland. All along, everyone knew that unless an innovative solution was found, water from the Glen Canyon Dam would seep into Rainbow Bridge National Monument. This was the same problem that everyone had been trying to avoid in the first place. The day Rainbow Bridge flooded would be the most visible encroachment of nontourist development into land administered by the National Park Service since Hetch Hetchy.

In 1957, David Brower had floated through Glen Canyon with his family. "Drifting here, you learned to perceive, not to preconceive, what makes a land beautiful," he wrote in text that accompanied photographs by Phillip Hyde in the *Sierra Club Bulletin:*

Beauty is where you see it and you saw it often where the big river, thin-edged with green, slid along under the pastel tapestries. An old river had built the stone grain by grain, and the new river was shaping it—imperceptibly aided by artists who left long ago. You didn't quite catch the river in the act of sculpturing, but the color of the Colorado assured you that creation was still going on. . . . Down in the main gorge the vista was fine enough, but what really counted was what you could seek out in a hundred tributary clefts. Georgie White knew when the big boats should be tied up and people should start walking, and you learned to know Warm Springs, the silence of Moki Canyon, and the strangeness of Hole-in-the-Rock. There were the antiquities that you discovered, and some that would never be. . . . High above the noonday twilight of Hidden Passage you might have looked small but you felt big. For all the massiveness and height, your own good feet could put you there and had. There was time to rest in shady silence, to wonder how, to begin to understand why, once again, to know yourself.

Brower was aghast at his role in the canyon's destruction—destruction he had not just allowed, but promoted, for God's sake. "Glen Canyon died in 1963 and I was partly responsible for its death," Brower would write in the introduction to *The Place No One Knew*. Before he wrote those words, he made one last attempt to correct his mistake. On January 21, 1963, he spent the morning fidgeting in the anteroom of the Secretary of the Interior like a kid outside the principal's office. He wanted to ask Stewart Udall to delay sealing the diversion tunnel at Glen Canyon Dam. If the tunnel was sealed on schedule, tourists would be able to row their boats up to Rainbow Bridge, a natural arch made of eroded desert sandstone, despite the government's pledge to protect it. Millions of dollars and untold hours of human labor were all pressing the project forward. It was a hopeless cause.

Brower waited and waited. With the death of Howard Zahniser, he had become the most powerful man in the environmental movement. But he waited in vain. Stewart Udall refused to see him. Udall was busy preparing for a press conference. He was getting ready to announce a plan that would make a few feet of water at Rainbow Bridge look like kid stuff. Floyd Dominy, the cigar-chomping chief of the U.S. Bureau of Reclamation, had gone back to his original idea: constructing two big cash-register dams in the Grand Canyon. They would be part of yet another Bureau of Reclamation behemoth, the Pacific Southwest Water Plan. And Stew Udall, the conservation conscience of President Kennedy's cabinet, was going to let him. The Pacific Southwest Water Plan promised to bring a hefty increase in water to Udall's home state of Arizona. Udall may have been a conservationist, but he was also a native son, the descendant of Mormon pioneers who had struck it rich in an arid land. One year before the founding of Salt Lake City, Udall's great-grandfather, John D. Lee, had traveled to New Mexico to learn irrigation techniques from the Mexicans who had been living there since the 1500s. He reported back to Brigham Young, helping to make possible the Mormon empire in Utah.[7] Udall understood the quasi-religious significance of water in a dry land. A modern-day John D. Lee, Udall had traveled to the faraway city of Washington, D.C. Now he was ready to do his duty to the clan.

More than the fate of the Grand Canyon was riding on the Southwest water project, as Marc Reisner reported in *Cadillac Desert*. The two big dams on the Grand Canyon were cash-register dams. They would pay for the construction of two dams on the Trinity River in northern California, which would supply water to Los Angeles and the agricultural San Joaquin Valley. By creating a new supply of water for southern California, the Colorado could be diverted to the long-awaited Central Arizona Project, a series of dams, canals, and pumping stations that would siphon off Arizona's portion of the Colorado River. Finally, Arizona would get its share out of the Colorado. Udall was not entirely enthusiastic about damming the canyon, but as an Arizona home boy, he couldn't pass up an opportunity to get his state in on the Colorado River bonanza before it went bust.

In the afternoon, Brower joined the crowd in the conference room. He sat stunned as Udall announced the new water project. Several years before, when novelist Wallace Stegner questioned the sacrifice of Glen Canyon, Brower had argued practicality. He had talked about the conservation movement's limited resources. He had talked about compromise, about being reasonable. Never again would he make these arguments.

After Stewart Udall announced the Grand Canyon scheme, Brower took the conservationist movement into unmarked territory. The lobbying blitz to save the Grand Canyon would form the character of the modern environmental movement.

Howard Zahniser had died in June 1964, just three months before formal passage of the Wilderness Act. Stewart Brandborg, who had taken Zahniser's place at the Wilderness Society, was still finding his feet. It was Brower's show. Like his fellow aesthetes John Muir and the gonzo environmentalists of Earth First! ("Poetry must be in advance of action" read a quote from the French Symbolist poet Rimbaud in the Earth First! newsletter), Brower's style combined confrontational politics with highly creative propaganda. In many ways, the Grand Canyon debate was similar to the one over Echo Park. Once again, a national monument was threatened. But the whole scale was different. As a Sierra Club ad printed in the thick of battle read: "This time it's the Grand Canyon they want to flood. *The Grand Canyon.*" The two proposed dam sites, Marble Gorge and Bridge Canyon, actually were located in Grand Canyon National Monument, which surrounded Grand Canyon National Park. The dams would have backed up water ninety-three miles, flooding the monument's bottom. But they also would have affected the park itself in two ways. Lower Havasu Creek, which Reisner calls the canyon's most beautiful side stream, would have been completely flooded. The dams also would have submerged Lava Falls, the biggest, roughest white water in the canyon. According to Reisner, the entire ecosystem of the Grand Canyon would have been altered by the dams. Once again, the nineteenth-century scenic approach to land preservation was running aground on twentieth-century technology.

The Pacific Southwest Water Plan was truly grandiose, even by the standards of the mid-twentieth century. It was enough to keep even the hard-drinking, whoremongering BuRec Commissioner Floyd Dominy interested in a job that was threatening to get stale. In addition to nailing down the Arizona situation, it called for two major water projects in Utah and construction of the Hooker Dam, which would inundate part of Aldo Leopold's legacy, New Mexico's Gila Wilderness.

As it turned out, it was not the job that was getting stale; it was Dominy. He misjudged the temperament of the American people. Even some of the industrial megamachine's high priests were finding that they preferred hot, harsh canyons to pork-barrel water projects. The Pacific Southwest Water Project probably marks the first time that a dam failed to win the full support of its state delegation. Wildcard libertarian Republican Barry Goldwater flat out refused to back a dam in Marble Canyon, where he had traveled six times. Nuking the Vietnamese was one thing, but blowing away prime cowboy mythmaking apparatus was another. Marble Canyon was exactly what a canyon should be, said Goldwater. According to Russell Martin: "Marble Canyon . . . for reasons the senator had a hard time making abundantly clear, was different. *Its* scenic beauty, its grandeur, its towering cliffs of Redwall limestone surely ought to be preserved in their pristine state. . . . Reflecting on Marble Canyon, the senator said, made him long for the future day when new technologies would make it unnecessary to dam any more free-flowing rivers."[8]

David Brower felt the same way. He drafted a trio of MIT boys —a mathematician, an economist, and a nuclear engineer—to explain to Congress why the Central Arizona Project could just as easily run on coal or nuclear energy. Both were thought to be panaceas in those naive days. Even Floyd Dominy was forced to testify that it was "theoretically possible" to build CAP without damming the Grand Canyon.

Brower's tour de force was not limited to Washington, D.C. While he testified to Congress, Brower simultaneously staged an unprecedented media campaign. Sierra Club members around the country argued their cause with editorial boards of their local newspapers. Club publications carried citizen alerts, asking members to write to their congressmen and senators. Thousands of letters poured in, then hundreds of thousands. It wasn't hard to capture the American imagination when you had something as iconic as the Grand Canyon. In Washington, Brower entered copies of *The Place No One Knew* into the Congressional record, along with a new book, *Time and the River Flowing: Grand Canyon*. He loaned out copies of a Sierra Club film on Glen Canyon. When questioned on his previous advocacy of Glen Canyon Dam and the Sierra Club's long-ago support for Bridge Canyon dam, Brower replied that the current opposition to Grand Canyon dams represented an "evolution in our own thinking."

"Ten years ago I was testifying in favor of a higher Glen Canyon Dam and I wish I had been struck dead at the time," he said. "We found out how wrong we had been. I would just stress that over these years our own thinking has evolved, and I still hope that Mr. Udall's will."[9]

Well, Mr. Udall's did, but it took more work on Brower's part.★ After the hearings ended, conservationists got a tip that dam supporters might try to railroad through a piece of legislation. Brower was convinced that his opponents were running scared. He decided to press his advantage. On June 9, 1966, *The New York Times, The Washington Post,* the *San Francisco Chronicle,* and the *Los Angeles Times* all carried full-page ads placed by the Sierra Club. Each paper split its press run so that Brower could see which idea worked better, his straightforward open letter to Stewart Udall, or the ad written by San Francisco consultants Howard Gossage and Jerry Mander. (Mander, a critic of technology, later became known for his books *Four Arguments for the Elimination of Television* and *In the Absence of the Sacred.*) It was Mander and Gossage's splashy ad, hands down. "NOW ONLY YOU CAN SAVE GRAND CANYON FROM BEING FLOODED . . . FOR PROFIT" read the ad. The body copy went into more detail, but the ending came back to the issue's emotional core. "Remember, with all the complexities of Washington politics and Arizona politics, and the ins and outs of committees and procedures, there is only one simple, incredible issue here: This time it's the Grand Canyon they want to flood. *The Grand Canyon.*"

Response to the ad was so overwhelming that the ad itself became news. But Morris Udall, who not only was a congressman from Arizona but also happened to be Stewart Udall's younger brother, was furious. He thought the ad was tremendously unfair to his brother, who had been responsible for setting aside a great deal of wilderness in the West. He still hadn't cooled off by cocktail hour, when he had arranged to meet Sheldon Cohen at the Congressional Hotel. Cohen

---

★ Udall's thinking continued to evolve after he left public office. In 1981 he wrote: "Myths die hard . . . it is not easy to take a country conditioned to believe that every problem has a technical solution and to persuade its citizens that a major change of orientation has become necessary." This passage comes from a foreword Udall wrote for *Overshoot,* by William R. Catton, Jr., University of Illinois Press, 1982. Catton's book is a Neo-Malthusian Bible to deep ecologists.

just happened to be commissioner of the Internal Revenue Service. Less than twenty-four hours later—four o'clock in the afternoon on June 10, according to Russell Martin's account in *A Story That Stands Like a Dam*—the Sierra Club received a letter from the IRS threatening its tax-exempt status. The letter also became front-page news.

Despite the misgivings of the Sierra Club board of directors, Brower was buoyant. Hell, this was better publicity than the club had ever been flush enough to purchase. A second ad followed in July. In August ad whizzes Mander and Gossage outdid themselves. "SHOULD WE ALSO FLOOD THE SISTINE CHAPEL SO TOURISTS CAN GET NEAR THE CEILING?" ran the full-page ad in *The New York Times*. After decades of pussyfooting around, the aesthete conservationists were taking on Babbittry full force.

And they were winning. According to Reisner, the writing on the wall was clear to everyone but Floyd Dominy, who was "bullheaded, willful," and "obsessed with defeating Brower." But in early 1967 the Okie czar of the Bureau of Reclamation was forced to leave Washington on his annual inspection of international water projects being built with U.S. assistance. After Dominy's plane lifted off the tarmac, Udall directed his aides to come up with an alternative to the Grand Canyon dams. At that point, their main concern was revving up enough energy for the Central Arizona Project. To get the water to Arizona, engineers had to figure out how to pump it over a 1,200-foot mountain pass. The solution was coal, which had already been tacitly approved by the environmentalists. Dirty, unglamorous coal, no engineering feat or tourist attraction. Just smokestacks. Six plants perched at the edge of canyon country, on the high plateaus of the Four Corners area in the land of the Navajo and the Hopi. They would pollute a region known for the clarity of its air, the brightness of the blue sky that framed its deep-red mesas. The federal government would kick in $81 million to partially fund one of the plants, the Navajo Generating Station. In return, the plant would allocate 24.3 percent of its generating capacity to the government. The Central Arizona Project, first approved by Congress eighteen years before, could finally be built. And environmentalists like Marc Gaede, Terry

Moore, and Jack Loeffler would have something to occupy them for the next few years: fighting the Black Mesa mine. They were probably the only ones who thought it could be stopped. Even Dominy recognized a fait accompli. His only recorded comment was, "My secretary turned chickenshit on me."

Brower's fights to save the canyon country had been a flash point in environmental consciousness, signaling that Sinclair Lewis's Babbitt was no longer absolute monarch in America. The outpouring of public sentiment in the Dinosaur Monument and Grand Canyon battles was yet another mark of the receding frontier. The United States had become a technological society where 80 percent of the population dreams of a rural existence but lives in cities. Americans' surroundings had changed but their ideals had not. Jefferson's agrarian model, an individualistic utopia of yeoman farmers in which nature provides the fabric of existence, was still the goal of most Americans. As they felt it slipping away, they clutched even harder. As Reisner writes, ". . . a sea change in public feeling toward the natural world was taking place, one of those epochal shifts that guarantee that things will never be the same."

Edward Abbey was at the crest of this change in consciousness. Having grown up hunting and fishing in the woods of Pennsylvania, he embodied both the new and the old American outdoorsman. Occasionally these impulses were contradictory; but when it came to technology, Abbey was wholehearted. "One should admit at the outset to a certain bias," he wrote in "The Damnation of a Canyon," an essay in the book *Beyond the Wall*. "Indeed I am a 'butterfly chaser, googly eyed bleeding heart and wild conservative.' I take a dim view of dams; I find it hard to learn to love cement; I am poorly impressed by concrete aggregates and statistics in the cubic tons. But in this weakness I am not alone, for I belong to that ever-growing number of Americans, probably a good majority now, who have become aware that a fully industrialized, thoroughly urbanized, elegantly computerized social system is not suitable for human habitation. Great for machines, yes. But unfit for people."

———

Googly-eyed butterfly chaser though he might be, Abbey was clear-eyed enough to know that the environmentalists' victory over the Bureau of Reclamation was hollow. Thanks to Udall's trade-off, the Central Arizona Project was finally a sure thing. What was not so sure was Brower's career at the Sierra Club. He had been behaving in a high-handed fashion for too long. Yes, he had turned the Sierra Club into a war machine, pumping its membership from 7,000 in 1952 to 77,000 in 1969. He had saved Echo Park and the Grand Canyon; he had been responsible for protecting the North Cascades and Redwood National Park. Sales of the nineteen books in the Exhibit Format series that he originated had climbed to $10 million.

But there were problems. The Sierra Club was becoming finan-cially unstable because of Brower's expenditures. And Brower's own personality had changed, his friends said. The white-hot glare of pub-licity burned his shyness into megalomania. He became paranoid at times, usually when someone disagreed with him. Disagreements be-came more frequent as he plunged the publishing program into the red. There were more ambitious projects, new ideas, always new ideas. Good ones, it was true, but they tumbled out too fast and furiously for the creaking democratic machinery of the Sierra Club. As always, Brower took stands that embarrassed the good old boys who liked to pal around with their local Forest Service guys. Maybe he just moved too fast in general. He was an idea man, not a manager. *Visionary* would become the word most commonly associated with him in later years. It was a good one to describe the man who propelled the stodgy conservation movement into the twentieth century. Brower was al-ways running a few steps ahead of history. Like many bright people, he was impatient, not understanding why it took everyone so long to catch up.

By 1969 Brower had figured out that nuclear power was not a gift from the gods. He jiggled the rudder, attempting to bring the Sierra Club into line with his newfound opposition to the proposed nuclear power plant at Diablo Canyon in California. He launched a new ad campaign with Jerry Mander called "Spaceship Earth." He would figure out how to pay for it later.

Brower's abrupt reversal on the nuclear issue was the last straw for the club's directors. After a brutal, convoluted fight, the archdruid was forced out. Many of his former friends and mentors, notably Wallace Stegner, Ansel Adams, and Dick Leonard, believed that Brower had been "bitten by the worm of power," as Stegner wrote.[10] Only Martin Litton and Eliot Porter remained his allies. A *Sunset* magazine editor, pilot, and pioneer navigator of wooden dories through the Grand Canyon, Litton was a crusty individualist. He cared little for what people thought, and his fidelity to wilderness was clear and unwavering. Eliot Porter was a top-notch photographer whose work had found its truest and best home in the Exhibit Format books. But their votes were not enough to protect Brower.

Immediately after leaving the Sierra Club, David Brower founded Friends of the Earth, the first environmental group to view ecology in a social, political, and international context. Fifteen years later, when FOE hit the skids financially and his staff rebelled against him, Brower was ousted once again. Without a pause, he founded Earth Island Institute in 1985. Earth Island was even more innovative. The small groups that functioned under its umbrella were at the cutting edge of the mainstream environmental movement in the 1980s. Some observers, notably journalist Mark Dowie and Public Media Center director Herb Chao Gunther, believe these groups are models for the future of the environmental movement. Using new methods, Earth Island environmentalists tackled issues and institutions that traditional groups shied away from. The Dolphin Project pioneered a consumer boycott against tuna companies whose drift nets caused wholesale dolphin slaughter. Carl Anthony sponsored efforts to bring minorities into the environmental movement, an issue on which the mainstream groups had behaved shabbily. Brower's brilliance had drawn several generations of young environmentalists to him, and he was wise enough to give them their heads. Brower himself remained boyish and buoyantly handsome even into his eighties; there was something in him that would not be quelled even by the inevitable losses of eight decades. But as he grew older, there were occasional signs of humility. Approaching his eightieth birthday, Brower modestly compared himself to the efficient young men whose work he had fostered. "I've had lots of ideas in my time," he said. "I've been rather weak on the follow-up."

The metamorphoses of David Brower took place over decades of alternating triumph, depression, and experimentation. In the meantime, there was a different tradition for the Buckaroos to draw from—a southwestern one. The crackpot romantic tradition in the Southwest went back even further than Black Mesa Defense Fund. In the 1960s, while David Brower was reluctantly sacrificing Glen Canyon in the name of practicality, Ken Sleight was rounding up his fellow river guides to try to sink the whole Colorado River Storage Project. Sleight was a jack Mormon who had found a landscape to match his laconic speech and sharp eyes in the rocks and river inlets of Glen Canyon. Led by Sleight, members of the Western River Guides Association showed up at hearings "sartorially complete in sand-caked sneakers, grease-stained shorts, and straw cowboy hats that had long since begun to crumble."[11] Even combined with a few university town liberals who belonged to the Friends of Glen Canyon, they were no match for the combined power of dam builders and mainstream conservationists. But they tried. They didn't win, but they found a fellow traveler and a poet to tell their story in Ed Abbey. In the 1960s, Sleight and the other guides were grateful just to have a "mouthpiece," as Sleight put it. They had no idea that Abbey would perform a feat of alchemy for them and for other rebels in the desert Southwest, first by turning life into art, and then by helping to transform art back into life in the sloppy, romantic guise of Earth First!

The cracking of Glen Canyon Dam was the public debut of Earth First! Wire services carried the story; photos of the cracked dam appeared like storm warnings across the Rockies. A talented free-lance writer named Stewart McBride wrote an article in *Outside* magazine that permanently cast Earth First!'s public image. Never mind that Earth First! hadn't really done anything yet; McBride's piece was the ultimate cowboy ramble, the *Ur*-journalism that gave Earth First! its

rollicking gait. McBride's article borrowed its sensibility from Ed Abbey's book *The Monkey Wrench Gang*. Dave Foreman was called "Digger," Mike Roselle was Nagasaki Johnson, Ken Sanders was Spurs
Jackson. McBride called Ed Abbey the movement's bard. Other accounts went further, describing Abbey as the movement's icon, its
patron saint. It was an interesting geographical phenomenon that a
writer who was condescended to by the New York literary establishment could be considered a god in the desert Southwest.

A quarter of a century earlier, Abbey had been merely the author
of an extremely bad first novel called *Jonathan Troy*. Sainthood is the
last thing that comes to mind to describe the author of *Jonathan Troy*.
Later in life Abbey categorically refused to allow anyone to republish
it. But this only fanned the desires of the faithful. By then the book
had become a collector's item. Copies of its first and only edition sold
for up to $2,500. The aficionados who laid their hands on it had the
dubious privilege of reading the maunderings of a painfully raw first-
time novelist. He is determined to show you just how goddamn intellectual he is in every labored stream-of-consciousness paragraph.
Jonathan, the main character, is rebelling against his hickory-tough
Wobbly anarchist father. The father is an admirable card sharp; his
character is intriguing. But he is shortchanged and so is the reader.
Jonathan is the novel's only real focus, every sneeze and pimple and
gas attack and bout of adolescent drunkenness. He is obsessed with
sex and unprincipled about how he gets it—or tries to get it. And he
is desperate for the culture that lies outside his small Appalachian coal
town.

It is an awful book and embarrassingly autobiographical. The writer's prose only transcends its self-conscious tone when he is describing
nature. In these supernaturally fine passages there are traces of an older
Ed Abbey, a writer who inspired at least one generation of equally
sex-crazed, nature-worshiping misfits to toss out conventionality and
good sense and follow him into the Great American Desert.

In the fourteen-year gap between *Jonathan Troy* and the publication in 1968 of *Desert Solitaire,* the book many believe to be Abbey's
best work, there were no drastic changes in Ed Abbey's life. Or per-

haps there was one. He changed location. Like Georgia O'Keeffe, whose work was promising but not particularly significant until she found the right landscape, Abbey's work fed on a sense of place.

It was a place Abbey had to find for himself. Born in Home, Pennsylvania, on January 29, 1927, he was the oldest of Mildred and Paul Revere Abbey's five children. His father, like Jonathan Troy's, was a Wobbly and an anarchist. Paul Revere Abbey consistently beat his sons at cards, liked his deer poached, and cut trees for firewood well into his eighties. In later years, Abbey waxed nostalgic about his childhood. But when he was young, he couldn't wait to get out. In "Hallelujah on the Bum," an essay in *The Journey Home,* Abbey writes movingly of his first trip west at the age of seventeen. It was 1944. Tough but naive, Abbey was out to see the country before he risked dying for it in World War II. It wasn't until he was hitchhiking his way home out of Needles, California, truly one of the most godforsaken towns in America, that Abbey saw "a land that filled me with strange excitement; crags and pinnacles of naked rock, the dark cores of ancient volcanoes, a vast and silent emptiness smoldering with heat, color, and indecipherable significance, above which floated a small number of pure, clear, hard-edged clouds. For the first time I felt I was getting close to the West of my deepest imaginings—the place where the tangible and the mythical become the same."

It was love at first sight, he tells you in the next essay, "The Great American Desert." "This desert, all deserts, any desert. No matter where my head and feet may go, my heart and my entrails stay behind, here on the clean, true, comfortable rock, under the black sun of god's forsaken country. When I take on my next incarnation, my bones will remain bleaching nicely in a stone gulch under the rim of some faraway plateau way out there in the back of beyond."

Once he received an honorable discharge from the Army in 1946, it took Abbey some time to lodge himself safely west of the hundredth meridian. He finished college at the University of New Mexico in 1951 and took off for Edinburgh on a Fulbright scholarship. Within a few years he was back in New Mexico. In 1956, he earned a master's degree in philosophy at UNM, producing a thesis that must have made his father proud. It was called "Anarchism and the Morality of Violence." The thesis is a workmanlike survey of anarchist thought which indicates that Abbey hadn't really made up his mind if bomb-throwing Bakunin had more on the ball than gentle Prince Peter Kropotkin. In 1957, he received a writing fellowship to Stanford University.

While he was still an undergraduate, Abbey married Jean Schmechel, the first of his five wives. They were already having problems in 1950 when he met Rita Deanin, a twenty-year-old art student. Jean went with him to the University of Edinburgh, but by 1952 the marriage was over. That same year, Abbey and Deanin were married in a small ceremony at an adobe house in Albuquerque owned by Rita's mentor, the head of the university art department. They stayed married until 1965, living a nomadic existence as Abbey worked in a succession of national parks and monuments in the desert Southwest: Arches, Sunset Crater, Casa Grande. "His limit seemed to be about six months," said Rita. "Sometimes his job was over, sometimes he was restless. He was a runner."

Rita was with Abbey during the stint at Arches National Monument, which he described in *Desert Solitaire*.* She never appears in the book, which makes it seem that Abbey was alone, lost in solitary contemplation as he stared out at the blue desert sky through enormous sandstone arches. To give him credit, the book's original title was not solitaire. It was *Desert Solecism,* meaning a violation of correct language, a breach of good manners, a nasty, brutish barbaric remnant. His publisher insisted on *solitaire.* In any case, according to Rita, Abbey actually was alone much of the time. He would disappear for days, leaving her with their young son, Joshua, who was born in 1956. Sometimes he would go off camping. At other times, she had no idea where he was. When Abbey vanished, his boss, park superintendant Bates Wilson, would check on Rita and Joshua. Wilson was rapidly becoming a legend in the park service. Not only had he persuaded Stewart Udall to protect a 337,000-acre stretch of hoodoo sandstone

---

* When *Desert Solitaire* was written, Arches was still a national monument. It was designated a national park on November 12, 1971.

country as Canyonlands National Park, but he was a kind man, well liked by nearly everyone who knew him. Abbey repaid many debts to Wilson in the introduction to *Desert Solitaire*. Rita remembers Wilson fondly, too. She used to hike in remote spots, searching for newly created arches. Once she showed Wilson an arch she had found, just barely born out of wind and rain. There were, after all, compensations for her unconventional life.

"Ed was pretty defiant. I was pretty much of a rebel myself at the time," Rita said. But Abbey's rebellion ultimately went deeper than hers. He drank alcoholically, fell into too many affairs. The intense feelings they shared about nature and art didn't outweigh his constant abandonment. A second son, Aaron, was born in 1959, after a stint at Casa Grande National Monument, north of Tucson. But nothing changed. In 1962, Rita moved to Hoboken, New Jersey, to nurse her father, who was dying of cancer. Between 1962 and 1964, Abbey commuted between Hoboken and the Southwest. In New Jersey, he became involved with a woman in her twenties named Judy, whom he promised to marry. Rita knew nothing of the relationship. After her father died, Abbey asked Rita to take the boys and meet him in Las Vegas. He lived with her for several weeks, then left to meet Judy. Even after moving in with Judy, he tried to keep his relationship with Rita going by telephone. When she told him that she had instituted divorce proceedings, she says he was incredulous. Later, he avoided paying court-ordered child support, even going so far as to put false return addresses on postcards to Rita and the boys. He seemed oblivious to the pain he caused.

"Ed wasn't very introspective," said Rita. "Even though he had so many women, it always occurred to me that his relationships with men were more important to him. He liked to drink with them, be in the desert with them. Those were the things he liked to do."

In different words, Abbey's best friend Jack Loeffler said something similar. "Ed never quite totally gave of himself utterly to anybody. Clarke (Abbey's fifth and last wife) has told me sometimes that he was closer to me than anybody. I can understand that. But his and my friendship extended longer than I had ever been married. Or he had ever been married. Believe me, he and I were both red-blooded American boys, heterosexually speaking, but we had an intellectual sense of brotherhood.''

Abbey was also intensely ambitious. In 1956, he published his second novel, *The Brave Cowboy*. It was a classic Western, but with a postmodern twist. The cowboy, Jack Burns, is an anarchist. In the culture of the American West, that translates into being a fence cutter, a throwback to the days of the open range. While attending classes at the University of New Mexico, Burns becomes friends with a graduate student named Paul Bondi. Like Burns, Bondi is an anarchist whose beliefs lead him to oppose the military draft. But he is an intellectual. The cowboy does things, while Bondi only reads about them. Being an intellectual rather than a man of action was something Abbey often castigated himself for.

Although he keeps quiet about it, Jack Burns had served with distinction in the military. His resistance to Big Brother is more visceral than Bondi's. When Bondi goes to jail for refusing to be drafted, Burns gets arrested in order to break him out. Bondi, who leans toward civil disobedience both by temperament and by the knowledge that he has a wife and child waiting for him, decides to serve his time. Burns breaks out and flees to the mountains.

In *The Brave Cowboy*, Abbey makes his political point—that industrial society leaves no room for the individual—but keeps a firm grasp on the conventions of the Western. The trampling march of industrial society over the frontier is, after all, the Western's subtext. The character of Jack Burns fits the criteria lined up by Larry McMurtry, the other master practitioner of the postmodern horse opera, in his 1968 book, *In a Narrow Grave: Essays on Texas*. Like all cowboys, Burns exists outside the realm of middle-class values. He is deeply connected to animals, especially his mare, Whisky. And he is a man out of time, a twentieth-century cowboy inevitably being a person whose capacities no longer fit his situation. The cowboy rides his mare across a superhighway, insisting on freedom even in the shadow of the glass-walled city of Albuquerque. The book ends in a wail of sirens and blood as a semi truck maims and kills the cowboy and his mare. In his critique of Western films, McMurtry calls *Hud* (adapted from his early novel *Horseman, Pass By*) and *Lonely Are the Brave*, based on *The Brave Cowboy*, the "two best movies about the mid-twentieth century cowboy." He points out that both films end with the death of animals. "Whisky," he writes, "most appropriately, is run over by a truck: it is trucks, not horses, that move cattle from Texas to Kansas these days."[12]

The trucks might have been new, but the sense of loss was as old as the Western itself. Nostalgia is the blowing topsoil of the western literary landscape. Even *The Virginian*, written in 1902, begins with a nostalgic evocation of a lost frontier. But Abbey takes nostalgia to another dimension. The dust caked into his jeans and boot leather is real, but *The Brave Cowboy*'s protagonist, Jack Burns, is a ghostly presence evoked by the faint notes of a cowboy song. Burns's death on the highway is grisly and believable. Yet the reader barely blinks when Burns, old, ugly, and missing an eye, comes back to life in *Good News* and *Hayduke Lives!*

When Abbey moved into the Western genre, he gained a sure grasp of his material. *The Brave Cowboy* was moderately successful and Abbey made a chunk of money when the film rights were purchased. But Hollywood choked on Abbey's anarchist politics. Even though *Lonely Are the Brave* was written by the blacklisted screenwriter Dalton Trumbo (who later wrote and directed the stunning antiwar movie *Johnny Got His Gun*), the film's politics had been gutted by the time it reached the screen. In the movie version, which stars Kirk Douglas, Gena Rowlands, and Walter Matthau (with Carroll O'Connor as the unwittingly murderous truck driver, Hinton), Bondi is imprisoned for helping illegal aliens, rather than for draft resistance. This change makes the plot a little thin. Without the explanation of anarchist resistance to nationalism and the state, Burns's and Bondi's motivation is obscure. Fortunately, Whisky's death gives the movie a two-hankie ending.

The Hollywood bucks were welcome, but Abbey's crotchety comments about turning illegal aliens back at the border (arming them with machine guns so they could stand their ground on their native soil) sound suspiciously like the long-held grudge of a writer infuriated by namby-pamby editing.

The experience didn't make Abbey shy away from politics. In 1962's *Fire on the Mountain* he stays in the Western genre, but his political agenda is even more overt. Once again, the enemy is the military. His next novel, *Black Sun,* published in 1971, was his most vulnerable piece of writing. The book was written very quickly, after his third wife, Judy, died of leukemia at the age of twenty-seven, leaving behind an infant daughter named Susie. *Black Sun* is about a love affair between a randy, intellectual park ranger who is unable to express his emotions and a fresh young girl from a wealthy background who disappears into the desert before he can reassure her of his love. Abbey considered *Black Sun* one of his best books. But readers liked it better when he stuck to the rowdy, irreverent tone he had mastered by the 1970s.

Despite the "regional writer" label pinned on him by New York critics, later books like *Good News* and *The Fool's Progress* transcended region or genre. Even in his earlier books, Abbey bent the tradition of the Western novel. By inserting politics and antiheroes into a genre that had become stiff and dull, he herded the Western sensibility into a new era. Citing a 1962 essay on film by critic Robert Warshow, McMurtry agreed that one of the reasons for the Western's durability is that it offers an acceptable orientation to violence. Nowhere is this more neatly executed than in *The Monkey Wrench Gang,* which gave violence a politically acceptable, post-sixties twist. The aging, gently lecherous surgeon Doc Sarvis; his lover, a ballsy hippie chick from the Bronx named Bonnie Abbzug; the soft-spoken jack Mormon named Seldom Seen Smith; and a crude, hairy, disgusting, whacked-out but, against all odds, rather lovable Vietnam vet named George Washington Hayduke became the most-wanted monkeywrenchers in the Southwest. Schematic, fun, and fast paced—more like a screenplay than a novel—*The Monkey Wrench Gang* tapped into something big and powerful in the American psyche. If *Desert Solitaire,* a pastiche of journals written in the early sixties, and *Black Sun* were the private Abbey, *Monkey Wrench Gang* was the social Abbey. Although the book was obviously fiction, he cast his friends as characters, alienating some of them in the process and making others into celebrities. Some characters were composites, like Doc Sarvis. For the aforementioned surgeon, Abbey used the name of the New Mexico artist Al Sarvis, his best friend in the 1950s and 1960s. In many ways Sarvis was also a stand-in for Abbey himself. The character of Doc Sarvis also borrowed from novelist Bill Eastlake, whose beautiful novels of the Southwest have become undeservedly obscure in the last twenty years. Like the bald, bespectacled surgeon, Eastlake reportedly corralled the younger Abbey into late-night billboard-burning expeditions fueled by gasoline, alcohol, and a generous measure of righteous indignation. Eastlake wasn't heard to complain. But the real Sarvis, already upset because Abbey had quit several jobs that he had helped him land, was angered and ended their friendship.

Douglas Peacock, the fireplug ex–Green Beret who was the model for Hayduke, had no such compunctions. Peacock, the son of a Michigan Boy Scout leader, had become obsessed with the Rocky Mountains before he left for Vietnam in 1966. When he returned, the solitude and wildness of the Rockies wasn't so much an obsession as a necessity. Peacock wasn't fit for human consumption. Rather than force the issue, he tracked grizzly bears, becoming known for his wildlife footage. Unlike the character Hayduke, Peacock was highly intelligent and well-read. *Sensitive,* even. Not to mention a gourmet cook. There the dissimilarity ends. Peacock remains true to his fictional self, a madman, a drunk, a force of nature, utterly unique, a warrior of the heart. And a little bit of a pig. Eventually Peacock, an inveterate name-dropper, would become one of those people who are famous for being famous.

In *The Monkey Wrench Gang,* hairy Hayduke and the tart-tongued Bonnie Abbzug duke it out verbally for most of the book. Toward the end, suffering from a temporary lapse of taste compounded by incredible lust, Bonnie falls for Hayduke. In some ways, they're the perfect couple. But Hayduke just isn't civilized enough for any woman, even the tough, sexy Abzugg. With the creation of Bonnie Abbzug, the hayseed Ed Abbey put Newark-born Philip Roth to shame, busting the princess stereotype by creating the first Jewish culture heroine/sex symbol in American literature. Who cares that she's a little obnoxious and not too intellectual? Like Hayduke, Bonnie was reportedly a less bookish version of a real person, a woman from New York named Ingrid Eisenstadter, who lived on lower Park Avenue.

Seldom Seen Smith, the lapsed Mormon whose only bow to tradition was his plethora of wives, all of them buxom and satisfied, was based on the river runner Ken Sleight. Sleight and Abbey had a similar appetite for strong-willed—and strong-limbed—young women, preferably in quantity. Even more than women (whom they also occasionally shared), the men shared a belief in holding their ground, the sacred ground of the desert southwest.

If *The Monkey Wrench Gang* was the social Abbey, it also was the political Abbey. But this time he used a light touch. This was fiction, not polemic. True, the monkeywrenchers hit most of the low points of environmental degradation in the Southwest—uranium mines, coal mines, logging, rampant road building. But most of all, *The Monkey Wrench Gang* was fun. Abbey's friend Jack Loeffler was disappointed that it was so much fun. Although the Monkey Wrench Gang attacked the Black Mesa railroad, it wasn't clear to the uninitiated reader exactly why they were doing it or what the issue was all about. Abbey wisely preferred to let the monkeywrenchers' esprit and the backdrop of canyons and mesas speak for themselves. Abbey knew his limits. Faced with the need to include facts and figures in his essay "The Second Rape of the West," Abbey, the least boring of nature writers, became shrill, convoluted, and dull. By contrast, *The Monkey Wrench Gang* was a delightful, picaresque roman à clef.

By the time *The Monkey Wrench Gang* was published, Abbey had changed from the teenager embarrassed by his father's offbeat, angry politics to a writer whose ultimate achievement was as much political as artistic. Perhaps Rita was right when she said that Abbey's lack of introspection prevented him from fulfilling his ambition to write the Great American Novel. The whole idea of the Great American Novel was probably spurious, a simplistic, macho, save-the-world fantasy of the generation of men who fought in World War II. It was predicated on the idea that the nation's redemption lay in the hands of one person, a weedy writer, of all people, who would capture the ultimate myth of a continent and a people. How this translates into salvation is not clear, although it is encouraging to think that people still believe in the power of storytelling. In the last analysis, the Great American Novel was too tall an order for writers like Ernest Hemingway or Norman Mailer. Nobody could reasonably have expected it of Abbey, a man who found the outer world more compelling than the inner. Abbey's talent was undeniable, but his nearly perfect ear for language didn't prevent even his best novels from being flawed. His characters were often "walking ideas," in the words of Charles Bowden, a writer and friend who admired Abbey's work. Too often, Abbey's female characters were not even ideas but merely buxom Vargas girls with word balloons spouting from their lush, curved mouths (although the same could be said for many other male authors, such as Saul Bellow, whose writing received more critical accolades than Abbey's). In any case, a certain independent breed of reader preferred the passion, entertaining honesty, and unequaled passages of nature writing in an Abbey novel to the technically superior work of other writers. He may not have reached the level of maturity attained by many great novelists, but by bringing his resonant and moving ideas about the primacy of nature into American discourse, the rebellious and erudite Abbey did more to change society than his contemporaries who produced better-honed work.

"What I loved about Ed's point of view was that he truthfully saw himself as secondary to the planet; well, to the West, to the landscape, to the land," said Jack Loeffler. "In that sense, he'd made a psychological shift that I don't think our culture is going to be able to pull off in time." Abbey lived with the dichotomy that "there's this incredible landscape that only humans have the ability to be aesthetically moved by," in Loeffler's words. Few could live with the conflict between aesthetics and a biocentric worldview, least of all the academic theorists and humorless Birkenstock-clad, tofu-eating "activists" who took over the concept of deep ecology in Abbey's wake.

All that was philosophy. The Great American Novel was Art. And the Great American Novel was the book that his fans and friends expected from Abbey and that he expected from himself. His next-to-last book was supposed to be it. He called it "The Fat Masterpiece" and told people he was writing an "Eastern." The real title was *The Fool's Progress* and it was the autobiographical antidote to *Jonathan Troy*. His friend, the writer Charles Bowden, believes that Abbey finally fulfilled his promise with *The Fool's Progress*. But few agreed. The book was good, revealing a more mature talent. But it was not great. Abbey seemed stuck.

But stuck where? Like Foreman, Abbey's bottom line was freedom. It was the yardstick he used to measure everything. In Abbey's case, there were two sides to this romantic and thoroughgoing attachment to personal liberty. The adult side cast nature—including people who were gutsy, free, and in tune with their surroundings—against the brutal, dehumanizing technological megamachine. Abbey unwound on this subject in great detail in his many essays and dealt with it in a direct and moving fashion in his fine post-nuclear novel *Good News*. But at least one sympathetic literary critic, Jack Brenner at the University of Washington, believes that Abbey's work also reveals a blind nostalgia for the kind of freedom that is possible only in childhood. Second-guessing the connections between a writer's personal life and his work is a dangerous pastime. But an essay in *The Journey Home* echoes with a telling sense of loss. In "Shadows From the Big Woods" Abbey describes his childhood as a brush with pre-frontier Eden. His contention that we have cut ourselves off from our roots—the physical world of nature—is convincing. But the passage contains something more, a sense of perfect freedom that even in the harsh paradise of preindustrial society may have been the exclusive province of children.

"My brother Howard could talk to trees," he wrote. "Johnny knew how to start a fire without matches, skin a squirrel, and spot the eye of a sitting rabbit. . . . That was good country then, the country of boyhood, and the woods, the forest, that sultry massed deepness of transpiring green, formed the theater of our play. We invented our boyhood as we grew along; but the forest—in which it was possible to get authentically lost—sustained our sense of awe and terror in ways that fantasy cannot.

"Something like a shadow has fallen between present and past, an abyss wide as war that cannot be bridged by any tangible connection, so that memory is undermined and the image of our beginnings betrayed, dissolved, rendered not mythical but illusory. We have connived in the murder of our own origins," Abbey wrote.

Ken Sleight saw this side of Abbey better than most, because he identified so strongly with Abbey's sense of loss. "Both of us tried to resurrect some of those old feelings we had as farm boys," said Sleight. "It was hard to go back again. You know, to try to resurrect that feeling. See, Ed, everywhere he went, he bought a little piece of property here, a little piece of property there . . . the idea is it's a place of home, a farm place. [But] it's still in the past. You can't bring it back, because you know too much, or you've experienced . . . you've had new experiences and you're not content doing what you once wanted to do. There's so much grieving. That's what I found out."

Abbey didn't grieve so much as rage. The romanticism of Abbey's writing—childish, maybe—makes it beautiful and true. It also makes it frustrating. Because Abbey and his followers in Earth First! were asking the impossible. They were asking someone—you? me? the power structure?—to go back and make it right. All of it. Romantics from Rousseau to Saul Bellow's Henderson the Rain King had made the same demand, with the same passion. ("I want . . ." begins crazy Henderson's expansive roar.) In *The Fool's Progress,* protagonist Henry Lightcap parks in the handicapped spaces. Why? Because he *wants* . . . to park. Right now. Anywhere he goddamn well feels like it. Lightcap never changes, although he does make peace with the people who are most important to him. He is released from his struggle only by death.

In real life, Abbey did change from the irresponsible husband that Rita Abbey knew, and even from the emotionally strangled park ranger of *Black Sun.* In 1982, he married his fifth wife, Clarke Cartwright. She was still in her twenties, but in a variation on the Abbie Hoffman line about never trusting anyone over thirty, Abbey never married anyone over thirty. (When asked the age of Abbey's fourth wife, Renee, Ken Sleight jokingly replied, "Eight.") But Clarke was different. Or maybe this time Ed was. At fifty-five, he was finally ready to settle down. He settled into writing the Fat Masterpiece, living for months in the airy mountain house that Clarke's parents had built on Ken Sleight's ranch near Moab. The couple had two children, Becky and Ben. The bearded curmudgeon changed diapers and spooned baby food. His innate gentleness, the flip side of the anger he had inherited from his father, surfaced with strangers. He was kind to fellow writers, generous with journalists who pursued him, intensely loyal to his friends. "I've suffered from my share of personal disasters," Abbey told a journalist in 1985. "The loss of love, the death of a wife, the failure to realize in my writing the aspiration of my intentions. But those misfortunes can be borne. There is a certain animal vitality in most of us which carries us through any trouble but the absolutely overwhelming. Only a fool has no sorrow, only an idiot has no grief—but then only a fool and an idiot will let grief and sorrow ride him down into the grave. So. I've been lucky, as most people are lucky; the animal in each of us has a lot more sense than our brains."[13]

Philosophically, Abbey also seemed to be easing up. For many years, he had believed that the natural world was the closest thing to divinity. After his trip through Glen Canyon he defined wilderness as paradise in Desert Solitaire. He was careful to distinguish this earthly paradise of tarantulas, scorpions, flash floods, and quicksand from "the banal heaven of the saints."

". . . the love of wilderness is more than a hunger for what is always beyond reach," he wrote. "It is also an expression of loyalty to the earth, the earth which bore us and sustains us, the only home we shall ever know, the only paradise we ever need—if only we had the eyes to see."

This passage in the essay "Down the River" in Desert Solitaire was the closest Abbey came to transcendence—or peace—in thirty-five years of writing. It echoed the words of a very different kind of thinker, Joseph Campbell. After decades of studying the world's religions, Campbell also concluded that the afterlife was probably an allegory; it was the short stretch of a human life that encompassed both heaven and hell. The individual's task was to experience the full range of existence.

By the late 1980s, Abbey seemed to have expanded his vision to include human beings and some form of otherworldliness in the lexicon of paradise. In 1986, he told me that while wilderness was valuable for its own sake, it also had "symbolic value from a human point of view."

"It can mean freedom, liberty, spontaneity, the unplanned, unplannable progress of life," he said. "Wilderness also symbolizes—in my mind—the world that lies under the human world and encloses it."

Abbey may have mellowed in private, but on paper he was crankier than ever. Letters to the editor flew faster and with greater political incorrectness from his typewriter. Polemics blasting everything from feminism to illegal border crossings made him a whole new generation of enemies.

And still he disappeared. "He was older and more settled," said Clarke. "But there was always the real complex issue of wanting to be married and have a family and wanting to be totally on his own and doing what he wanted." He spent three months living alone in an empty mansion with a grand piano at the Amerind Foundation in Dragoon, Arizona, sweating it out with the Fat Masterpiece while Clarke stayed in Tucson with the children. The habit of solitude had always competed with sexual adventure; now that he was famous, finding solitude was more of a challenge. Abbey had experienced it most thoroughly while working for the U.S. Park Service, a gravy-train gig for a starving artist, even a self-proclaimed anarchist opposed to government. Other writers with a similar anarchist bent, notably the Beat poets Gary Snyder and Philip Whalen, also accepted Big Brother's offer of free room and board, unlimited fresh air, and horrifying, soul-deepening solitude. Living in a place like that day in, day out, changed a person; it humbled you. It turned you from the author of *Jonathan Troy* into the author of *Desert Solitaire*. Afterward you felt a hole in your heart when you went to live in the city, even if it was a city like Tucson, surrounded by mountains, the desert as close as your skin. Though you ventured out into the country again frequently, it wasn't quite the same; it was stolen time.

In 1987, just two and a half weeks shy of his sixtieth birthday, Edward Abbey, the author of more than a dozen books, father of two young children, in the midst of writing his Fat Masterpiece, *The Fool's Progress*, gave in to nostalgia. He wrote to the superintendant at Organ Pipe Cactus National Monument. This is what he said:

"While cruising about through Organ Pipe and the Cabeza Prieta recently I saw evidence of illegal border crossings and the cutting and removal of ironwood in the vicinity of Quitobaquito and Papago Well. Are you people aware of these incursions?"

Then he got to the point.

"I hear rumors that you may soon need a new caretaker at the old Bates Well cowboy camp near Kino Peak. If true, I would like to apply for the job. I worked as a seasonal patrol ranger at Organ Pipe for three winters in the late Sixties and am familar with and extremely fond of the area."

As it turned out, Park Superintendent Harold Smith decided to close Bates Well to visitors rather than hire a park ranger. Ed Abbey stayed in Tucson. He contented himself with periodic excursions across the brutal desert of the Cabeza Prieta and the occasional benefit speech for Earth First!, the Monkey Wrench Gang that had been born out of the tanned, bony forehead of a renegade Appalachian intellectual.

The
Road
Show

I went down in September on the Grand Canyon Colorado River and the test, of course, as all of you are familiar, is whether we ought to keep the motors on those rafts or not. The first day was spectacular. . . . The second day started to get a little tedious, but the third day I wanted bigger motors to move that raft out. There is no way you could get me on an oar-powered raft on that river—I'll guarantee you that. On the fourth day we were praying for helicopters and they came.

—James G. Watt, speaking to the
Mountain States Legal Foundation
February 27, 1980

I've heard an Englishman say this: the black man is indolent, lazy by nature. He drinks his beer at sunrise and sleeps all day. Well, perhaps. It can be 120 degrees at the equator. That man is consumed with the same daily task; let's say, gathering food. Gathering wood. He does it with primitive tools and he does it at sundown. And then he dances. He tells stories. What does he accomplish? asks the Englishman.

What does the Englishman accomplish? If he mines coal all day, sips his beer at night, and then succumbs to fatigue, failing to make love and then forgets how. . . .

—Sir Richard Francis Burton, nineteenth-century explorer
Dialogue by William Harrison and Bob Rafelson
from the film *Mountains of the Moon*

1982 – New Mexico

THE BISTI BADLANDS are an eroded wasteland so bleached by heat and sun that the whole twenty miles or so merges into one giant, overexposed photo. Ghost-white hoodoos bubble across the horizon. They clump together like Easter Island statues, oddly pale, marked by vague striations of pink and gray; layer upon layer of shale and sandstone. The sandstone erodes first, thinning into narrow stems. At the top of these stems are mushroom caps of shale. Some are large and heavy enough to make the hoodoo topple in a high wind like a candlestick knocked over at a dinner party.

The Bisti's smooth, mounded hills are looser diagrams of the same mechanism of erosion. The hills are separated by deep, sudden rifts. A ranger once left his truck in a low spot between two hills. It started raining. When he returned a few hours later, the truck was buried up to its windows in quicksand. By the time the tow truck got there, only the roofline was visible.

Hidden in the hollows of the badlands, there are caves big enough to sit in. Even when the Bisti is unimaginably hot and dry—not just hot, but *hard* hot—you can dig down into the cave floors and find water. Pressing your hand against wet-packed clay, you can forget the glare of 113-degree heat outside. If you drink the water, its high mineral content will make you sick, but it makes you feel better to touch it. If you don't know about the caves and their hidden caches, you might feel lost on an inland sea of rock, impaled by the painful staring light of the sun, with nowhere, nowhere at all, to escape to.

Tangled in the Bisti's white sedimentary sea are waves of another kind of rock. Long-dead ferns and prehistoric lawn clippings. Black coal. It seeps out of the cracks between sandstone and shale like chocolate layer-cake filling, cheap and easy to mine because it is so close to the surface. In the early 1980s James Watt was trying to make the coal industry's job even easier. His method was to eliminate all Bureau of Land Management roadless areas of fewer than 5,000 acres from wilderness consideration. If he succeeded, it was sayonara to a particular 3,946-acre stretch of desiccated rock in the middle of the badlands called simply "the Bisti." Not to mention a handful of other "wilderness study areas" that had valuable commodities piled up under their desert and forest skins.

Even without Watt's help, the Bisti's edges were fraying. In 1982, the Gateway Mine, operated by Sunbelt, a Public Service Company of New Mexico subsidiary, was sinking its earth-moving equipment into the mouth of the Bisti Wilderness Study Area. The mine was not actually in the study area, but it was just outside the gate. The utility told everyone that the mine was being located there to supply coal to the San Juan Generating Station, forty-five miles away. But Foreman and the other Earth First!ers knew the real reason. Yet another dirty, coal-fired power plant was being planned for the Four Corners region, this one just three miles south of the Bisti wilderness.

New Mexico Earth First!ers had hiked into the Bisti months before. Their wilderness experience, like other people's, started with a mile-long tour of the Gateway strip mine. It took a long time to walk the mile, and it took even longer to get out of sight of the mine once you were past it. But that fall they weren't trying to get away from the mine. Along with a couple of dozen other Earth First!ers, they were trying to get arrested.

Around noon, demonstrators started lining up at the mine's barbed-wire fence. Black armbands were passed around. (Hoodoo Mourners. A new band.) When the crowd got large enough, someone gave the high sign and they hiked over to the rally site, trailed by cameramen from the local TV news. From here they had a view of the dragline, framed by its handiwork: an acre of freshly ripped-open desert. It looked as if someone had taken a fork and knife to a piece of rare steak. In the other direction was the open hoodoo country of the pastel-colored Bisti wilderness, humped and gullied like a miniature basin and range. As the crowd arrived, Bart Koehler—posing as country-and-western singer Johnny Sagebrush, thank you ma'am—rocked out on two sing-along numbers. Koehler was no Eric Clapton, but he had a way of wearing his heart on his sleeve that grabbed you whether he was talking over a beer or shucking and jiving with his guitar.

A local activist named Neil Cobb gave a speech. Then Wes Leonard, the frustrated scion of a New York publishing family, took the stage. When he began to speak, at least a few people held their breath. The night before, while everyone was hanging out around the campfire in a fairly friendly fashion, Leonard had gotten loaded, whipped out a gun, and waved it around until someone stuffed him into the back of his pickup to sleep it off. Either Leonard had spent too many years in the gun-crazy Lone Star State or he was taking Foreman's samurai ecowarrior fantasies a tad seriously. But that morning he seemed to have recovered. Facing the mine boundary, he shouted fairly coherently and sans firearms, "Here's where we draw the line! Sunbelt will go no further!" Leonard was followed by a Navajo named John Redhouse, who impressed the crowd with his more restrained but equally forceful presentation. All the Navajo chapter houses were against coal mining in the Bisti, said Redhouse. He, too, called for direct action.

Sagebrush got up again. He told the crowd to be quiet for a minute. Listen to the wind. It's the same wind that carved these striated statues. The crowd tried to connect the sound in their ears with the feel of stone under their hands. After the silence, Sagebrush riled them up again. He launched into a raucous rendition of "Stand in Front of that Dozer" and "Monkeywrenchin' " before winding up with another sing-along number, this one called, à la Clif Merritt, "You Can Take the Bisti—Over My Dead Body."

Finally it was Foreman's turn. He had spoken in public many times, but never to a crowd this jazzed. Something told him to take the hardest line he could think of.

"I usually tell a joke when I start out—but not today," Foreman twanged. "Today, I'm damned mad at what Sunbelt and Jerry Geist (a Sunbelt executive) have done to the Bisti so far. I am damn mad that James Watt and Garry Carruthers* have chosen to drop the Bisti from Wilderness Study status because it's less than 5,000 acres. If they have their way, this whole country will be destroyed!

"The only way to save this country is to return these public lands to the Navajo—and establish a 100,000-acre Bisti National Park!"

As Foreman spoke, the crowd grew more and more energized, even jumpy. Finally someone shouted, "Enough talk! Let's do something." Foreman thought fast. Then, according to Ken Sanders, he

---

* Carruthers, a Watt appointee at the Department of the Interior, later became governor of New Mexico.

"just kind of told everyone to trespass onto the mine property. People started moving across this secured compound."

About fifty people crossed the fence and marched into the mine. A mine guard tried to hand out trespassing tickets, but nobody would take them. Soon he was swallowed by the crowd, leaving only a fluttering of white papers on the bare ground.

Circling a lone hoodoo inside the mine's perimeter, the Earth First!ers joined hands, sang, and waited for the cops.

None came.

A couple of Earth First!ers dragged out dummies made up to look like Sunbelt honcho Jerry Geist and bullet-headed James Watt. Someone whipped out a Zippo and the dummies went up in flames.

No cops.

Even the mine's security guards hung back. Chanting, joking, and singing, the protesters walked over to the dragline, nearly a mile away. Carrying signs and flags—the Revolutionary War "Don't Tread on Me," along with the forty-eight-state version of the American flag— the Earth First!ers lined up in front of the tall fence protecting the dragline. They sang "America the Beautiful" and "Home on the Range."

After the singing stopped, about a dozen people began shaking the fence, yelling, "Save the Bisti" and "Earth First!" The swirls of razor wire at its upper edge rippled like a nasty Slinky toy.

Someone muttered, "When are we gonna get arrested?"

Still no cops.

The demonstrators were drifting away when a tall figure broke from the crowd. He hurtled over the dragline's high fence, landing flat on his back in front of the big machine. He lay there for a few seconds, a dazed expression on his face. Then he stood up. His body started jerking, the flap of his torn flannel shirt waving like a flag. It was Mike Roselle, doing a crazy war dance with the dragline. Everyone turned and stared. As they figured out what was going on, they started cheering. Roselle made a little bow and disappeared into the dragline's twisted metal guts. He popped up again on its uppermost section, the boom, which was two or three stories up in the air. His big hands unrolled a "Save the Bisti" banner down the dragline's flank.

The crowd went apeshit, hammering on the gates and screaming. The sound of their cheering was everywhere, rushing through wind-torn tunnels in the rock, bouncing off the long expanse of rolling white. It must have been only a few minutes, but it seemed like forever before Roselle, still smiling, rolled himself up into the smallest ball he could manage and skibbled under the wire fence that was being raised for him.

Had it only been a year and a half since Victorio? Something had definitely changed. The Buckaroos were no longer ahead of the wave—they were riding its crest. Soon it might overtake them. Ken Sanders was already watching his back.

"When Roselle went over that fence and up the dragline, those people were under our control," remembered Sanders. "If we had wanted them to push those gates over and burn that dragline, they would have."

Sanders took Foreman aside. "My God, what have we unleashed?" he asked.

Foreman looked at him uncomprehendingly. He was having a blast. Sometimes he even believed his own bullshit. Of course he believed in what he was saying—that was a given—but now he thought it was *possible*. Being surrounded by people who agreed with him was a liberating experience. The previous fall, Foreman had found hundreds of them. He had gone on a grueling road trip with Koehler, putting on an old-fashioned medicine show with a new message. Bart would play ecohits from Johnny Sagebrush's *Li'l Green Songbook*, and Dave would preach the new gospel of radical environmentalism. "He and I had this fantasy that we were going to do the college circuit and he was going to be Ed Abbey and I was going to be like Jerry Jeff Walker," Koehler said nostalgically. "That was our goal in life."

Koehler and Foreman may not have matched their idols, but they made a decent attempt. The Road Show was a great success. Their audiences were mostly college students. But there was a smattering of older, environmentally aware people who lived in small, hip towns like Moab, Utah, and Telluride, Colorado. They were part of what reporter Philip Fradkin calls the "rural renaissance" or what others have termed the back-to-the-land movement. Joined at various points by Ron Kezar and Bart Koehler's girlfriend, Shaaron Netherton, the Buckaroos hit forty stops in less than three months, drinking heavily and, in Foreman's case, getting laid by enthusiastic female wilderness supporters. It was a hell of a way to get over a divorce. And it wasn't a bad way to start a political movement. People all over the United States were starting small, unaffiliated, grass-roots environmental groups. By starting their own groups, they avoided the internal politics and bureaucracy of the big organizations and got things done faster. This also meant that environmental issues were reaching beyond their traditional constituencies. Some of the highest-profile groups formed around pollution issues. Housewife Lois Gibbs, the heroine of Love Canal, got a divorce and moved to Washington, D.C., where she began the Citizens' Clearinghouse for Hazardous Waste to help members of these small groups develop their political skills. Many of the new environmentalists were black, Latino, and Native American. Environmental concern was rising in minority neighborhoods, where two thirds of the country's toxic-waste sites were located.

Wilderness freaks were also losing interest in working through the big national groups. They shared the frustrations that had driven the Buckaroos out of the Wilderness Society. The big groups seemed to be straying from their roots. Passion, philosophical clarity, and scientific curiosity had drained away as the movement's founders were replaced by a managerial class, an inevitable succession in an organization's middle years. On a substantive level, many grass-roots activists felt that although the big groups were great at mobilizing on national issues like Alaska wilderness, they simply weren't doing enough on local issues. Mike McCloskey is one of the few career environmentalists to examine seriously the reasons for this cleavage in the movement. McCloskey is the Sierra Club's intellectual elder statesman. After working as the club's first Northwest representative, he succeeded David Brower as executive director in the late 1960s, stabilizing the club after Brower's difficult departure. McCloskey readily admits that complacency had set in after the 1960s and 1970s, leaving the movement vulnerable in the Reagan years.

"Despite initial skepticism, environmentalists came to accept progress under the Nixon and Ford administrations as normal, and they were elated by the strong commitment they perceived in the Carter administration (though this changed in the end)," McCloskey writes. The movement was stunned by the hostility of the Reagan administration. Expectations became lower and members of the "pragmatic camp" became more cautious. At the same time, the smaller, antiestablishment groups that had also been considered pragmatists— Friends of the Earth, Environmental Policy Institute, and Environmental Action—were flagging financially.

"This lack of utopian vision left the new recruits, who were mobilized by the anti-Watt wars and the seriousness of the new threats, unsure of what flag they were following," according to McCloskey.[1] Except for the Nature Conservancy, which generally could only afford to buy small tracts of land, nobody was using an ecosystem approach to saving wilderness. To the Buckaroos' generation, brought up on the word *ecology,* it didn't make sense.

There might have been other reasons for Earth First!'s popularity in places like Lancaster, New Hampshire, and Missoula, Montana. In *The True Believer: Thoughts on the Nature of Mass Movements,* gadfly philosopher Eric Hoffer gives a biased but insightful analysis of the appeal of mass movements. The kind of people attracted to mass movements include the new poor, who are often children of a ruined middle class, writes Hoffer. Despite the media frenzy over yuppies, this describes most real baby boomers, especially those born at the tail end of the boom. Newly poor is also a good description of the middle-class young people in do-gooder professions who were caught in the squeeze of rising living costs in the 1980s, the so-called thirteeners.

Hoffer believes that the great unifying factor among adherents of a mass movement is frustration, the kind born out of the collapse of the 1960s counterculture, the failed promise of the Carter years, and the reassertion of the military-industrial complex in the Reagan era. Mass movements harness this frustration by holding out visions of a glorious past and the promise of a glorious future, thus robbing the present of reality. This is just fine for the follower, who is generally in flight from himself anyway. "A deprecating attitude toward the present fosters a capacity for prognostication," writes Hoffer. "The well-adjusted make poor prophets." The only one who can harness this kind of discontent is a man of words, writes Hoffer. But not just any man of words. A noncreative man of words is needed. Someone who has great facility for expression, but no particular artistic outlet. Someone like Dave Foreman in the early eighties.

During the Road Show, it was easy for Foreman to harness the frustration he saw all around him. It wasn't just short-term annoyance with the environmental movement. It was the discontent of a generation that had grown up at a time when societal disarray was the norm. The children of the sixties had been having a great time dismantling America; the children of the seventies were left with the more difficult task of putting it back together. Joining Earth First! was one of the ways they found to do it. Especially in the early years, Foreman was less enamored of an apocalyptic vision. He fantasized that the Buckaroos were not just starting a new environmental group, but a new society. He was the one trying to develop the blueprint for the Earth First! tribe. "When we formed Earth First! the basic concept was to have a tribal structure, to try to use music, to try to use humor, passion, to talk about visionary wilderness proposals. I think we're developing culture, myth, and ritual. From my anthropological background, it's a fun thing to watch," he said optimistically in 1986. On the Road Show, Foreman fine-tuned the schtick that writer Ken Brower (David Brower's son) would later dub "The Speech." It was a pastiche of the cutting-edge environmental ideas that the voracious reader Foreman had jammed together into a semi-coherent philosophy over the years. But it was also something deeper.

Years later, an old beatnik friend of Ed Abbey's heard Foreman give a speech. Afterward the actor buttonholed him, telling him that he had once studied with Lee Strasberg at the Actors Studio in New York. "Do you know that what you're doing is The Method?" he asked the former horseshoer. No, the former horseshoer didn't. But once Strasberg's acting philosophy was explained to him, it made sense. Foreman's spiel was a vivid exhumation of self, reaching into the universals of birth, life, and death. He used his own experience, along with cadged stories from literary greats, to grab his audience. One of the funniest was Foreman's tall tale about running into Secretary of the Interior James Watt in the Grand Canyon. He perfected the routine with the help of Ed Abbey and another ornery American writer named Samuel Clemens.

As he tells it, Foreman and his friends were preparing to approach Lava Falls, the Colorado River's biggest rapid, by lightening their load of beer, when a strange apparition entered their field of vision.

"First of all, he had on a three-piece suit and cowboy boots that looked like they were made out of some kind of endangered lizard, looked like they'd never been off a sidewalk before. And he just was not enjoying himself at all, you could tell.

" 'I hate to paddle,' this dude said. 'I hate to walk. When's that helicopter gonna get me out of Grand Canyon Park?'

"He was really gettin' on our nerves," says Foreman. "I finished my beer and I opened another one, took a sip of it, and kept watching, and walked back and forth on the beach and all of a sudden I realized who he was.

" 'You're Jim Watt!' Everybody with me jumped up and I said, 'Sit where you are! Leave him to me. He's my meat!' And I threw my hat off and said, 'You lay there till the sufferin's over with,' and I pulled my life jacket off and threw it over and said, 'You lay there till the chawin' up's done.'

"Hoo-ooo!!!!!"

Foreman leaps into the air like a cattle prod has just landed on his rear end. He rips off his button-down Oxford shirt to expose the Earth First! T-shirt underneath.

"I'm the old original half-grizzly, half-wolf, half-rattlesnake from the wilds of Wyoming. I'm the man they call Summer Thunder and Sudden Avalanche. *Hoo-ooo!!!* Look at me, sired by a hurricane, dammed by an earthquake, half-brother to the cholera, nearly related to the smallpox on my mother's side. Well, I eat nineteen oil executives and a barrel of whiskey for breakfast when I'm in robust health and a dead bulldozer and a bushel of dirt-bikers when I'm ailin'. *Hoo-ooo!!!!!* I crack Glen Canyon Dam with my glance. The blood of timber executives is my natural drink and the wail of dying forest supervisors is music to my ears. So cast your eye on me, you half-human, land-rapin', antienvironmental scumbag, 'cause I'm about to eat you for lunch. Yeah!!!"

Foreman's voice suddenly turns reasonable as he comes back to earth. He explains to the audience, "Well, I figured after that Jim Watt would just fly right out of the Grand Canyon without his helicopter. And so you can imagine how surprised I was when he just looked at me and went: '*Whoo-ooo!!!!* Bow and pray, you environmental extremist, because the kingdom of ecological calamity is upon you! Hold me down to earth, Sweet Jesus, because I feel my powers arisin'. Here, sunglasses for all. Don't attempt to look at me with the naked eye. Why, when I'm in a playful mood, I used the meridians of longitude and the parallels of latitude as a seine and I drag the Pacific Ocean for whales. When I'm cold, I boil San Francisco Bay with radioactive waste and I bathe in it. When I'm hot, I dam the rivers of the West to make electricity and I air-condition the deserts. I suck the Colorado dry when I'm thirsty. The destruction of endangered species is the pastime of my idle moments and the devastation of whole ecosystems the serious business of my life. So bow and pray, you environmental extremists, because the pet child of ecological calamity is about to eat *YOU* for lunch!!' "

Foreman's voice drops off again. He tells the audience what he learned from the encounter with Watt. "Rhetoric is not enough," he tells them. "There comes a time, every now and then, when you have to go beyond rhetoric, when you have to go beyond just talking about things, when you actually have to stand up and actually do something, put yourself on the line."

Well, no one could miss the message in that one, even if they hadn't read "Howling in '06" by Mark Twain. As amusing as the Watt story was, the climax of the speech was Foreman's retelling of an anecdote from Aldo Leopold's book *A Sand County Almanac*. Up until this point Foreman has been jumping around like a bear stepping on campfire coals. Now his voice grows quiet.

Eighty years ago, a young man graduated from the Yale School of Forestry with a master's degree in forestry, one of the first in this country. He caught a train out west that summer for the territories of New Mexico and Arizona to take a job with the newly created Forest Service. His name was Aldo Leopold. His first job with the Forest Service was on the Apache National Forest in eastern Arizona, in the White Mountains. At that time, the White Mountains were this huge wilderness of rolling high country and isolated peaks and streams, deep coniferous forest. The Forest Service had no roads in the White Mountains, no plan to log the timber up there for several decades. But they wanted to know what was there. They wanted to inventory the timber. And so Leopold's job was to take a crew of men on horseback for two weeks at a time and cruise timber. Well, many years later he wrote about one of those trips. They had stopped for lunch on a rimrock overlooking a rushing little stream below. As they ate their lunch, they saw a large animal ford the river. At first they thought it was a doe. But when they saw a bunch of wolf pups run out of the rocks on the other side of the stream they realized it was an old she-wolf.

Well, in those days, before World War I, every wolf you saw was a wolf you shot. So Leopold and his men ran for their horses and pulled their 30-30s from their scabbards, went back and blazed down the hill. If any of you have hunted you know how difficult it is to aim downhill. But Leopold and his men sent enough lead down the hill . . . the old wolf dropped. One of the pups dragged its crippled legs down the talus slope. And Leopold and his men mounted up and rode down the hill to finish their job. He wrote, decades later, "We reached the old wolf in time to watch a fierce green fire dying in her eyes. I realized then, and I've realized ever since, there was something new to me in those eyes, something known only to the wolf and to the mountain. I was young then and full of trigger itch. Because fewer wolves meant more deer, I believed no wolves would mean hunter's paradise, but after watching the green fire die I realized that neither wolf nor mountain agreed with such a view."

What we need to do is remember how to think like a mountain. We need the green fire in the wolf's eyes. We need the green fire in the land. And God, how we need the green fire in our own eyes. Leopold also wrote, "A deep chesty bawl echoes from rimrock to rimrock, rolls down the mountainside and fades into the far blackness of the night. It's a cry of wild, defiant sorrow, of contempt for every adversity in the world." And it is. The wolf's howl is the cry of defiant contempt. But it's also something more. It's the cry of joy, of pleasure in being alive. No matter how bad it gets, it's wonderful to be alive on earth. This beautiful, flowering, blossoming, evolutionary world with over a million species, an incredible complex of ecosystems, beauty all around us, sunsets, goose music, whales off the shore. No matter how bad it gets, there's still beauty out there, there's still meaning. No matter how depressed we get, how angry, we still have to be full of joy, happiness. That's what keeps us going. So, yeah, howl with contempt for adversity. Howl with defiance. But howl with joy, too. *Aaooo!* Robots don't howl. But animals do. Free, wild animals with green fire. So howl with me. We're in a concrete box, but still howl. Remember what it was like. Don't be embarrassed. Remember the greatest thing you can do is howl. *Aaaoooooooooo!*

And everyone did.

Foreman, a man of words with no particular creative outlet, had found his métier. His speech became a land bridge between two continents: the metaphorical and the real. Foreman's confrontation with James Watt in the Grand Canyon was fictional, of course. But in the summer of 1981, spurred on by the felicitous combination of myth, metaphor, and charisma, the scruffy radicals of Earth First! were getting ready to stage a real one. They had done their time in the desert. Now they were on a mission to confront their own bald-headed environmental Satan.

The first shot was fired, appropriately enough, in Washington, D.C., where the Buckaroos' other archenemy, Bill Turnage, was leading the mainstream charge against Watt. Taking advantage of "Big Don Schwarzenegger's" resemblance to the Secretary of Inferior, the Buckaroos duded him up in the appropriate business suit and tie so that he could masquerade as Watt on the Capitol steps. Big Don's drag show, with Johnny Sagebrush singing backup, was the lead-in to a network news segment on the Sierra Club's Dump Watt petition drive, which had gathered one million signatures.

The news report left out the event's most trenchant satirical touches. Like the plaque naming Watt Earth First!'s Honorary Membership Chairperson. And his acceptance speech, in which Watt/Schwarzenegger promised to make the environment "the Vietnam of the eighties." As usual, the Buckaroos were ahead of their time. It wasn't until the late 1980s that veteran *New York Times* columnist Flora Lewis told her readers that the environment had replaced the Cold War as the central issue facing Americans. And like Vietnam, the Cold War's last fling, U.S. environmental policy was turning into a quagmire based on bad decisions and a corrupt worldview. Drawing from the same wellspring of arrogance, environmental policy was looking more and more like a disaster.

The Buckaroos' other jibe also was more than a little serious. In the late 1980s, every conservation group in the United States fattened off the Reagan administration's black hole of an environmental policy. With each new Reagan perfidy, membership in environmental organizations went through the roof. By 1982, newspapers were delivering an almost daily barrage of evidence implicating Environmental Protection Agency head Anne Gorsuch in corporate payoffs. Her affair with Bob Burford, the head of the Bureau of Land Management, had already created a scandal. James Watt provided even better fodder for journalists. He almost seemed to do it on purpose.

"We have tremendous biases," he told one reporter. "We have a bias for private enterprise."

"I make lots of mistakes, 'cause I make a lot of decisions. But we're in a hurry and we're willing to take risks," he announced to another.

These were just a few of Watt's bon mots. His politics were even more off-the-wall. Nothing seemed to deter him from coming out with impossible proposals, like the pitch to open legally designated wilderness to oil and gas development. The environmental movement's rakeoff from these peccadillos was nothing short of astonishing. During the three-year period before Reagan took office, 1977 to 1980, the Sierra Club's membership increased from 178,000 to 181,000, "a giant increase of 3,000" as a club spokesman wryly put it. But in 1981 alone, the very first year of the Reagan-Watt axis, the club gained 63,000 members. Two years later, when Watt finally took a dive, the club had gained another 100,000.

Membership was one thing; effectiveness was another. As long as Reagan held office, environmental groups were mainly confined to holding actions. It was grunt legislative work, not necessarily imaginative, but desperately important. Holding the line wasn't sexy; you couldn't claim big, sweeping victories. You couldn't try out new ideas. This sort of trench warfare formed the political philosophies of many of the mainstream environmentalists who came of age in the 1980s, including people like Doug Scott and Bruce Hamilton.

That left a clear field for Earth First! After all, the cowboy poets didn't really expect to accomplish anything anyway. When the butt of their best jokes foundered on payoff accusations in early 1983, it was almost too good to be true. Emboldened by the scent of blood, Earth First! and its sympathizers intensified their Western offensive. On May 19, 1983, the twentieth anniversary of the construction of Glen Canyon Dam, the Secretary of Inferior arrived at Lake Powell with all the pomp and ceremony of a head of state. Thanks to the largesse of Ken Sanders, so did Earth First! Along with Ed Abbey and a tiny handful of others, Sanders was one of Earth First!'s financial angels. Sanders owned two houses in a funky section of Salt Lake and when ex-newspaperman Pete Dustrud (aka "Prickly Pete") took over as editor of the *Earth First! Journal* in the late fall of 1982, Sanders let Dustrud live and work in one of the houses. For the assault on Lake Foul "by land, by sea, and by air," Sanders estimates he dropped about three thousand dollars.

With that kind of cash, Sanders could produce an entertainment that fairly reeked of his inimitable warlock style. Like a twisted Santa Claus, Sanders was helped by a number of elves. One was Louisa Willcox, who was on her summer break from the master's program at Aldo Leopold's alma mater, Yale School of Forestry. Along with Prickly Pete, Willcox and Sanders decided they would create yet another "art project." The Buckaroos racked their brains for an appropriate greeting for Watt. The Beach Boys would have to be included somehow. Back in April, Watt had banned the aging SoCal rockers from playing on the Washington Mall, saying they would attract "the wrong element." The ban ended when Watt emerged from lunch at the White House carrying a foot with a hole in it to symbolize having shot himself in the foot. Nancy Reagan, as it turned out, was a Beach Boys fan.[2] Eager to rekindle Watt's embarrassment, Sanders snagged a cohort of old mannequins from a defunct Salt Lake City department store and spray-painted surfer shirts on five of them. As the spray-can fumes wreaked havoc on their brain chemistry, Sanders and his elves became even more inspired. They painted a second and then a third series of mannequins—Mutants for Watt (punk hairdos) and Cattle Mutilators for Watt, with surreal black-and-red paint jobs inspired by the mysterious cattle mutilations of the late 1970s. But the best one was the Watt mannequin himself. He was on his knees holding aloft a crushed can of Coors beer. He wore a business suit. The number "666" was painted on his forehead. Like Watt, the mannequin was bald. And he was praying for helicopters.

"Oh, Jesus, I got carried away with this thing," Sanders said. "All of a sudden, the Park Service at Glen Canyon is getting ten phone calls a day from journalists from one coast to another, asking them, 'Well, what are you doing about this gigantic Earth First! invasion that's coming?' What? And they're freaked.

"Well, then the media would call us back up and say, you know, you guys don't have a permit for this, and I'd just laugh at them and say, at this point in time, this is way out of my control. Permit? Give me a break. What are they going to do?"

Eventually Sanders decided it might be best to seek a permit for the funeral. He arranged a meeting with law-enforcement officials at the Glen Canyon National Recreation Area. Bart Koehler—the likeable ace negotiator—agreed to accompany Sanders to the meeting. The Buckaroos weren't quite prepared for the dozen armed men facing them across the table. Because Glen Canyon sat on the border of Utah and Arizona, there were representatives from law-enforcement agencies in both states: sheriff's departments, highway patrols, even the Coast Guard. The Coast Guard? Well, apparently the U.S. Coast Guard held jurisdiction over Lake Powell.

"Hey, Bart. It looks like you and I forgot to bring our uniforms," Sanders whispered.

After everyone settled down, a couple of impassive men in cheap J. C. Penney–style business suits slipped into the back of the room. They were not introduced.

The meeting went on for about two hours, with Bart and Ken answering questions as politely and noncommittally as they could. Finally one of the cops asked, "Is there anything else?"

"Well, you see, we've got this boat," Sanders admitted. Aha, the officers nodded. How big is it? Oh, about sixty feet. Sanders and Koehler filled out yet another sheaf of documents. Sanders could sense that the cops were getting bored. Basically they just wanted an idea of what was coming down. It was obvious that they were going to issue the permit.

"Okay," said the chief law-enforcement officer, impatient to end the meeting. "Anything else?"

"Wellll, there is one more thing," said Sanders.

"What's that?"

"We've got this airplane coming."

At this point, Sanders recalled, one cop elbowed another and said, sotto voce, "I told you they'd have an airplane." Even the chief had to crack a smile at this one. In fact, the only people not stifling laughter were the mysterious men in cheap suits. In the end, aircraft notwithstanding, the permits were duly issued. The Lake Foul invasion was under way.

On May 19, Ken Sanders awoke to a perfect stage set. The weather was warm and sunny, with a sky so sparklingly blue he couldn't have been anywhere but the desert Southwest. As with any good general, Sanders's main job was to delegate authority. Howie Wolke was burning to be captain of the sixty-foot houseboat Sanders had rented from park concessionaire Del Webb. Sanders said okay, not realizing that Howie had never piloted a boat before. Undaunted by his lack of experience, Howie wobbled off in the big pirate ship, somehow managing to chase two big boats loaded with politicians. A Park Service speedboat darted in and out, protecting Arizona Governor Bruce Babbitt and Utah Governor Scott Matheson from Howie's depredations. For most of the afternoon, the speedboat kept Howie and his crew just far enough away to render their chants unintelligible. But signs like "Watt for Ambassador to Uranus" got the point across.

That was just the first stage of the marine assault. Howie's pirate ship carried a rubber raft aboard that held a black coffin. The coffin was hand-painted with the name of every well-known natural feature that had been drowned by the Glen Canyon Dam. Music Temple, of which John Wesley Powell had written: "We are pleased to find that this hollow in the rock is filled with sweet sounds. It was doubtless made for an academy of music by its storm-born architect." Labyrinth Canyon. Dirty Devil Stream. Cataract Canyon. The coffin was covered with lost places, a Vietnam War memorial for a vanished world. Six pallbearers dressed in black hooded robes accompanied it, chanting and keening.

Once the mother ship reached the shoreline stage where Watt and the two governors were going to speak, the raft carrying the coffin and pallbearers would be rowed to shore. The pallbearers would carry the coffin up the banks, where they would join the other demonstrators. For the coup de grace, Sanders's hired plane was supposed to haul a banner overhead at this exact moment.

The Earth First! guerrilla forces ran into problems almost immediately. First, the pilot told Sanders he might not make it. As the ceremony went on and no airplane appeared, Sanders resigned himself to a two-pronged assault. Then, just as the high-school marching band reached its screeching climax, the wind picked up. Howie's pirate ship zigzagged more crazily than ever. Sanders wondered if his invading environmental army might be reduced to a single battle cry. Dark thunderheads shivered and shook. The waves on Lake Powell got rougher.

Howie managed to steer the pirate ship close to shore. As the coffin was unloaded, rain began sheeting down. The pallbearers staggered through the surf, wet and bedraggled, their chants drowned out by wind, thunder, and whipping rain. The marchers—"by land"— met them and together they slogged up the road to the rally site. River guide Ken Sleight was there, waiting to begin his speech. There may have been a handful of others who had known Glen Canyon as well as Sleight, but no one loved it more. His feeling was evident as he clambered onto the truck bed, the wind lifting his gray hair, his middle-aged reading glasses falling down his nose. In his flat Mormon farm-boy twang, Sleight read from his notes, pausing now and then to train his snowy blue eyes on the sky. As he spoke, an astonishing thing happened. The fat, gray clouds moved to the edge of the horizon. The winds blew themselves out. The rain stopped. The sky grew still and blue, coming out from hiding like a horse who had thrown a stranger with hard hands.

One person who was not uplifted by this inspiring scene was the production's godfather, Ken Sanders. Glumly, Sanders sat by himself, worrying that the group's rented airplane wasn't going to show up.

Then he heard a distant engine.

"It's the airplane. It's got this huge sixty-foot banner," recalls Sanders. "They fly over the town of Page and swoop as close over the dam as you're allowed to. They're carrying this banner that says: 'Earth First! Free the Colorado!'"

The reporters loved it. But the Buckaroos' archenemy, James Watt, claimed to have missed the show. Asserting that he had "never heard" of Edward Abbey or *The Monkey Wrench Gang*, he said, "If that's all they can think of doing, concern about something that happened twenty years ago, I'd say, 'My God, it means we must be doing a great job,' and that's a tribute to James Watt."[3]

Arizona Governor Bruce Babbitt, whose career was marked by an effort to tread a fine line between sincere environmental concern and political survival, expressed different sentiments. Privately, he praised Abbey, crediting *The Monkey Wrench Gang* with inspiring the day's amusing counterdemonstration.

That night, the Buckaroos sang around the campfire, blaring out off-key renditions of inspiring environmental ditties by Bo Diddley, Elvis Presley, and the Isley Brothers. Jerry Jeff Walker's "Up Against the Wall, Redneck Mother" was a particular favorite. It was a long night, and a good one, with lots of talk of mining strikes, gossip about other environmentalists' sex lives, and musings on the way canyon walls looked under the swing of the white, sculptured moon.[4]

After the funeral, a few Earth First!ers hiked up Dive of the Buckskin, a sixteen-mile sandstone canyon with "walls four hundred feet high and a width at times that of your shoulders." Tucson *Citizen* reporter Charles Bowden had found his way to the canyon, too. "I found Foreman sitting silently in a tiny grotto and staring blankly like a spent deer that had just barely escaped the hounds. This was after a three-day bout of speech making and demonstrating at Glen Canyon Dam. . . . He was holding a fifth of Bacardi Dark and looked tired, the face puffy, the body slouched. It's not easy being Summer Thunder," Bowden later wrote.[5]

Ken Sanders was relieved. The funeral had come together. Nobody had been arrested. Nobody had drowned. At the last minute, the plane had furrowed the abruptly cleared sky. He was high on his last-minute victory. But Sanders felt a new resolve growing. This was going to be it. His last big production. It wasn't just the money, although he wasn't prepared to be the Mike Todd of the radical environmental movement forever. No, it was something more serious. The political stakes were getting too high. It started when reporters kept asking him why Earth First! hadn't confronted Watt directly. Hell, it was all Sanders could do just to keep the whole thing running. Weren't they ever satisfied? But there was more. The scene at the Bisti had unnerved him. Sanders didn't like crowds. They were dangerous at worst, stupid at best. Earth First! was attracting weirdos. At the funeral, Ken Sanders met a guy who called himself Piton Pete. Piton Pete had shown Sanders the inside of his truck, which was equipped with weird stuff that looked like surveillance equipment. Sanders, frightened, suspected that Pete was a police informer.

Paranoia was only one of the problems surfacing as a result of Earth First!'s radical tactics. Newspaperman Pete Dustrud had already resigned as editor of the *Earth First! Journal* after a dispute about monkeywrenching in 1982. Dustrud, a Vietnam vet, objected to a feature submitted to the "Dear Ned Ludd" column on devices that reminded him of pungee sticks used by the North Vietnamese. It was an exaggeration—Dustrud wasn't nicknamed "Prickly Pete" for nothing—but monkeywrenching was starting to cause divisions in the group. At the Earth First! Rendezvous that year, Louisa Willcox spent a long time discussing it with the poet Gary Snyder. Monkeywrenching ran counter to her Quaker background. What bothered Louisa most was the idea that someone might get hurt by mistake. As a Buddhist, Snyder had problems with it, too. But Snyder's problems with monkeywrenching were as much tactical as moral. Personally, he got a kick out of fantasizing about doing some highly strategic monkeywrenching of his own. But he felt that Dave Foreman was upping the ante without enough in the bank. The group couldn't have it both ways—they couldn't deny endorsing monkeywrenching to cover their asses legally while making a virtual fetish of tree spiking and bulldozer burning. Either you were a kamikaze or you weren't. Even in a casual conversation, Snyder weighed each word. Words were powerful. It was important to take responsibility for them.

Like Snyder, Ken Sanders was mindful of the fact that mobs brought down repression. In fact, he believed that the crackdown was already starting. It might have been paranoia, but he felt sure that he and Bart had been followed before the funeral. A few days later, he thought he saw someone taping with a video camera as he helped Captain Howie get the recalcitrant houseboat out from the dock. Sanders believes that a number of other security measures were taken by the authorities during the funeral, including staking out the Navajo Generating Station with SWAT teams and closing Glen Canyon Dam's public elevators, which the Buckaroos had ridden down after "cracking" the dam in 1981. You couldn't really blame the law-enforcement people. Hadn't Abbey fantasized in print about blowing up the dam? In fact, he had written about it more than once. Sanders could see that Earth First! was going to have trouble remaining an invisible guerrilla army.

Sanders may have backed out from a visible role in Earth First! after the funeral, but his mannequins became stars. After James Watt's appearance at the dam in May, the secretary spent the summer touring the rest of his kingdom. Everywhere he went there was a mannequin waiting for him, or a banner, or an actual demonstration, sometimes with as many as 400 people. An important stop on Watt's itinerary was Canyonlands National Park, outside the town of Moab. It was the same sunlit apricot-and-yellow canyon country that Edward Abbey had described in *Desert Solitaire*. It was the place where Marc

Gaede had reclaimed his life. It was also where the Department of the Interior was planning to site a nuclear-waste dump. Canyonlands Park supervisor Pete Perry was not enthusiastic about the idea. Neither were the folks at nearby Arches National Park, where Ed Abbey had once worked. Abbey's gadfly role at the park was now being played by a young ranger named Jim Stiles. The day after the funeral, Stiles received a visit from Louisa Willcox and Ken Sanders. They showed up around 11:30 at night with leftover mannequins piled into the bed of Alfonso the pickup truck. And they were on a mission.

The Buckaroos knew that Watt was due to show up at the park for a tour the next day. On the drive down, Louisa had talked about hanging the Watt mannequin from the 128-foot slick-rock hoodoo called Balanced Rock. What a photo opportunity! It even had historical significance. Balanced Rock was the first sight that had greeted Ed Abbey every morning when he opened the door of his trailer while he was writing *Desert Solitaire*. But when she arrived, Louisa wisely decided not to carry out her plan. Not because it was illegal—which it was—but because it was too late at night and she had been drinking too much beer. So they came up with an alternative. The next day Salt Lake City television cameras filmed the surprised James Watt stumbling on his effigy planted in the ground, praying to the ubiquitous can of Coors.* By then, Watt presumably knew about Ed Abbey and *The Monkey Wrench Gang*. He certainly knew about Earth First! "We know which environmental group did this, though we don't need to mention any names," the interior secretary prissily re-

---

* True to its purpose of reclaiming western mythology from the right wing, Earth First! featured Coors Brewing Co. in its line of trinkets and memorabilia. A phosphorescent green Earth First! sticker of the era announced:

**Coors is Anti-Earth
Coors is Anti-Women
Coors is Anti-Labor
AND IT TASTES AWFUL!
BOYCOTT COORS**
EARTH FIRST!POB 235, ELY, NV 89301

marked. Watt, of course, blamed Earth First! for the whole thing—he was really starting to hate those dirtballs. But while Louisa, Stiles, and Sanders were out planting the mannequin, they had been shocked to discover the tracks of another monkeywrencher. A whole series of signs had been spray-painted with direct, if not exactly poetic, messages like "Keep Watt out of Arches." They even wondered if the signs were some kind of setup. Later they discovered that Stiles's girl-friend, a park naturalist, had beaten them to the scene.

Anti-Watt protesters tripped over one another all summer. Watt's next whistlestop was Zion National Park, outside Springdale, Utah, where he encountered a banner on a giant rock outcropping called the Great White Throne. "Burn Watt, Not Coal," the banner announced. Louisa was in Alaska teaching a NOLS course when she heard about the incident. "Who's down at Springdale?" she kept wondering. The town near Zion was full of climbers, the so-called Boys' Club of Springdale, and Louisa knew them all. She kept asking around, but all she found out was the name of the guy who had climbed the rock after Watt's visit to take down the banner. He was an old NOLS friend who had gotten a job with the Montana state government by the time Louisa caught up with him. "I said, 'Geo, you fucking asshole, you mercenary son of a bitch, you got three hundred dollars to take it down.' . . . Geo looked at me and said, 'Louisa, you're so stupid. How do you think it got up there?'" Louisa laughed.

"Then he [Watt] went up to Alaska and he got the same shit," she said. "It was like this spontaneous eruption. Starting with the Glen Canyon Dam funeral boat parade and ending up in Juneau, Alaska. I mean, everywhere he went he was just bothered."

One of the most dramatic confrontations between Earth First! and the Environmental Antichrist came when Watt made an appearance in Jackson, Wyoming. Three hundred Earth First!ers showed up for the obligatory demonstration. In the midst of it, Howie Wolke came face-to-face with the secretary. The strains of "Do not forsake me, oh my darling" could barely be heard above the din. The two men cocked their cowboy hats. Wind whistled through the saloon doors.

Children cowered on the long, wooden porch. Horses snorted and stamped their feet. Then Howie clasped Jim Watt's hand in a bone-crunching handshake. "Mr. Secretary, I'm Howie Wolke and I organized this demonstration against you," he managed to get out before Watt's aides hustled the secretary away.

After the summer, Ken Sanders and Louisa wound up at Arches again. They climbed on the roof of Jim Stiles's ranger house in Devil's Garden, the park's main campground, and dangled a noose in front of his door until they finally figured out that he was ignoring them. So they shouted down, "Hey, Stiles, where's the mannequin?" Cracking up, he opened his door and invited them in. Wait until daylight, he told them.

In the morning, Sanders and Louisa went outside and saw a mannequin leg stuck upside down into the ground, foot reaching to the sky. Next to it was a standard-issue Park Service sign. Except instead of Smokey the Bear drivel, it announced: "Watt Looking for Oil and Gas."

"And then Stiles said, 'You know where the head is?' We said no. He said, 'It's down in Denver at the regional office.'

"This mannequin had many lives."

James Watt could have used an extra life or two himself. He was getting nothing but grief about his leasing policies, first from western governors upset about their prerogatives being yanked away, and then from critics who thought they were shortsighted and uneconomic. By spring of 1982, even *The Denver Post* was running editorials that echoed the warnings of Black Mesa defender Terry Moore. One editorial explained that although low-sulfur western coal had gone great guns in the 1970s, the party was over. The nation's energy use was tapering off. Even in the boom state of Colorado, annual growth in energy demands had dropped to 3 percent and it looked as though it would continue to slacken. By auctioning off coal leases at a breakneck pace, Watt was giving a bonanza to coal companies, who would simply sit on the leases until prices went up again.

In the summer Watt appointed a University of Illinois professor named David F. Linowes to head a coal-leasing study group. Linowes then appointed the other committee members. Watt tactfully characterized them as "a black, a woman, two Jews, and a cripple."

This faux pas dwarfed his previous ones. Watt resigned two weeks later. But his troubles weren't over. The coal-leasing oversight committee continued its work. Despite his unforgivable gaffe, the committee initially took it easy on Watt, issuing a report that environmentalists called a whitewash. The outcry was strong enough to send them back to work. The revised report, issued in early 1984, indicated that David Russell and William "Perry" Pendley, two of Watt's top staffers, had fed inside information to Colorado coal developers about the largest coal-lease sale in history, which was about to take place in the Powder River Basin of Wyoming, North Dakota, and Montana. Even worse than the "suspicion of wrongdoing" were the actual numbers. According to Linowes's report, the Powder River leases were being sold to the developers at $100 million below market value. No wonder Perry Pendley's pro-development credentials were considered strong enough for him to be appointed head of the Coors-backed Mountain States Legal Foundation in March 1989. Ironically, the foundation had just been weakened by a scandal in which two of its top officers were accused of misappropriating funds for their private use. Pendley was brought in to clean house.

Watt's record would have been bad enough on its own, but it looked even worse to environmentalists fresh from working with the Carter administration. Even the embittered Foreman, who tends to lump politicians into one slimy, opportunistic mass of undesirable humanity, believes that Carter genuinely attempted to develop a reasonable environmental policy. "I still think he was the most genuine person we've had as president in this century, and certainly on the issues, the best," said Foreman.

Carter's greatest achievement was probably the passage of the Alaska National Interest Lands Act (ANILCA) in 1980. This piece of legislation was Chuck Clusen's baby. With Doug Scott solidifying Congressional support, a staggering 104.3 million acres in Alaska was brought into the federal land conservation system, an area larger than the state of California. More than half of it is protected as wilderness.

But Carter was unable to implement his program in the Lower 48. His attempt to stop the juggernaut of water projects in the West was a disaster. David Brower had been forced to muster every iota of political muscle in the conservation movement just to stop one of the Bureau of Reclamation's schemes. Carter's inept attempt to ax more than half of them firmly established his naiveté in the eyes of Congress.

Carter, of course, was right in principle. Although it was still politically powerful, the Bureau of Reclamation was already becoming obsolete when Carter took office in 1976. For one thing, most of the places that were suitable for big dams had already been taken. For another, many of the Bureau of Reclamation's water projects were funneling unofficial subsidies to the nation's richest agribusinesses at the expense of the environment. The western landscape bore the scars of a century's worth of engineers working with blank checks and big ambitions. Ninety-nine percent of Iowa's wetlands were gone, 90 percent of Nebraska's, 89 percent of Illinois's, and 80 percent of Minnesota's.[6] The Missouri bottomlands had disappeared. Nine tenths of California's wetlands had been eradicated, along with huge numbers of migratory birds. More than 90 percent of the woodlands along rivers and streams in the arid West had been sacrificed to flood control or irrigation. The Colorado Delta had turned into a bare, rubbery-looking wasteland. The cold, clear rivers of the Pacific Northwest had turned silty; salmon were being mauled by dam turbines or giving up in exhaustion after trying to negotiate the unfamiliar shoals of a river turned brown by erosion.

With budget deficits and a recession looming, the construction of additional costly dams made no sense. Yet a staggering number of water projects were still on the boards. For western congressmen, these projects were tantamount to money in the bank: political currency for them, hard cash for their constituents. But Jimmy Carter's tidy engineer's mind recoiled at the waste involved in the Bureau of Reclamation's grandiose schemes. As an easterner, he didn't fully understand that water was the westerner's totem. Backed by his aggressive Secretary of the Interior, Cecil Andrus, and a staff both arrogant and ignorant when it came to the ways of Washington, Carter went for the throat. He tried to enforce the 160-acre limit for water subsidies in the agricultural Central Valley of California, a place where the crooked bends in the law had become so entrenched that they were stronger than the law itself. In April 1977, he issued what came to be called the water project "hit list." It recommended dropping eighteen major water projects, modifying five, and continuing only nine. As an example of the waste endemic to the Bureau of Reclamation, Carter's review cited one project that "benefited only two companies" and another that "spent over $1 million per landowner." It called for a more realistic assessment of costs and benefits and for better conservation, noting that "over half of the water delivered through Bureau of Reclamation irrigation systems is completely wasted."

Congress and the Carter staff went around and around on the hit list. Carter and his aggressive lieutenants lost the first round. On the second, they thought they had lined up enough support to stop a bad compromise bill. The so-called compromise was really just a return to the status quo. If it was defeated, the road would be cleared for a reform bill. As the compromise bill fought its way through Congress, Carter pledged that he would veto it if he had to. To stave off the possibility of a congressional override, conservationists cashed in every chip they had, called in every favor. By the time the bill landed on Carter's desk, they felt sure that they could make a veto stick. At the last minute, Carter, without telling anyone, backed off. He signed the bill, squandering not only the environmentalists' political capital, but his own. Worst of all, he gave the impression that he couldn't tough it out in the clinches.

After this fiasco, Carter continued to push energy and water conservation, with varying results. So did Cecil Andrus. Like Carter, Andrus came into office with high ideals: passing a strip-mine reclamation bill, revising the 1872 mining law, and reorganizing the Interior Department to end the era of what he called the Three *R*'s: "Rape, Ruin, and Run." Andrus achieved some of his goals. But he, too, disappointed environmentalists when he agreed to stop trying to scale back the Central Utah water project in order to get the Carter-backed MX missile on line.[7] Despite the uneven results of the Carter years, at least the United States had a president who was trying to grapple with environmental problems, instead of denying them.

Unfortunately, Carter's record suggested that fighting the forces of darkness could sometimes make things worse. "In the end, Carter's reform measures only revitalized the old water lobby, now strengthened by the addition of major energy companies seeking federal water for their new projects," wrote Peter Wiley and Robert Gottlieb in their 1982 book *Empires in the Sun: The Rise of the New American West.*

Whether it was because of political ineptitude or the country's bloated inertia, Carter's sensible energy policy was sadly short-lived. "I was a graduate student and I just interviewed with Exxon as a joke," recalled one staff member at a environmental organization. "But the guy who interviewed me was the most brilliant geologist I had ever met. I agonized over it, but I decided to take the job. It was an exciting time. There was a lot of money around for exploration, for R&D. We saw what was happening; we were buying time for alternative energy sources to be developed. But then we blew it, totally and completely, by going back to a complete reliance on oil." When he saw what was happening, the geologist left Exxon to work at a fraction of his former salary for a nonprofit group associated with Arches National Park.

The backlash of the Reagan years was in full swing by 1982. Deregulation was lifting restrictions on oil and gas developers. They had started buying leases back in the sixties, then revved up in the seventies. In the 1980s, James Watt dispensed rights to federal lands like a low-rent auctioneer selling the cargo of a foundering ship. By 1986, 80 percent of what scientists call the Greater Yellowstone Ecosystem —Yellowstone Park and the eight national forests that surround it— had already been leased for oil and gas development. This was one of the few places in the country where big animals hadn't been kicked off the land. Bear. Elk. Buffalo. But these animals needed lots of space. They didn't pay attention to park boundaries. National forest land leased to oil developers included places where grizzlies mated and eagles hunted. Of course, the oil companies weren't going to drill every place they had leased. But with so much land spoken for, it was more than likely that things were going to be torn up pretty good.

At least that was what Bart Koehler and Dave Foreman were thinking in 1982, when they decided to hold the third Earth First! Rendezvous in the Gros Ventre section of the Bridger-Teton National Forest.

Bart
Rides
Out

I have never questioned the route this journey took: it seems a single trip, the sole option, driven by that same potency that drew me into grizzly country in the beginning.

—Doug Peacock
The Grizzly Years, 1990

1982–Grizzly Country

THE ROUND RIVER RENDEZVOUS in Wyoming was the biggest yet. But even with 500 people milling around, Foreman felt surrounded by the old wilderness tribe. The Buckaroos all came. So did the men Foreman called tribal elders. Ed Abbey. Cecil Garland, the moustachioed ex-ranger who had been Clif Merritt's partner in the Lincoln-Scapegoat Wilderness fight. There was beer and steak and corn on the cob. Nobody brought tofu—or if they did, they kept it quiet. Not a word was spoken about animal rights, hemp farming, or Central America. Bart and his brother twanged away, playing rock and roll under the half-serious name the Lithium Brothers. Ed Abbey even added a few flourishes to his boilerplate speech.

"I'm here today in support of the E.R.A.," said the reformed sexist pig, startling the crowd for a moment. "I mean Equal Rocks Amendment, or equal rights for rocks, and for trees and grass and clouds and flowing streams and bull elk and grizzly and women—yes, ladies, I also support the E.R.A. for women," he wound up grinning. Nobody gave him any shit. The women laughed along with the men.

Cecil Garland won the audience's affection as soon as he climbed onstage. "I'm here on behalf of the Utah Wolf Grower's Association," he announced. Garland said he had been impressed by the Earth First!ers "utter humility before the ecosystem." He even told the radicals that he would be proud to join forces with them. "I raise my fist, also," the former Forest Service employee said with good-hearted awkwardness.

The third Round River Rendezvous was a blending of old and new converts to radical environmentalism. A giant barbecue, drunk-in, and environmental conference, it was deep ecology by total immersion. People wandered in and out of workshops, played hooky to go hiking up in the nearby mountains, and fell in like with other rendezvousers. A few people even had serious business there. One was Sierra Club representative Bruce Hamilton. Of course, Wyoming was Bruce's home turf and the Northern Buckaroos were his friends, so it was natural for him to show up. But Bruce also had a political reason for coming. The Earth First!ers were going to protest oil exploration in the Gros Ventre section of the Bridger-Teton National Forest—an issue already high on his own agenda. In the early 1950s, Olaus Murie had discovered that the Gros Ventre (Big Belly) contained essential calving grounds for the famous Jackson Hole elk herd. Subsequently, the Forest Service dropped its plans to build roads there. But because the Forest Service had already completed its primitive area system in 1939, the area received no formal protection.[1] In the following years, mining and timber claims were established. Now Bruce was pitting as much Sierra Club clout as he could muster against development in the Gros Ventre. It was a tough issue. The claims were valid, even if most of them had been sold before the days of public involvement in the process. Even with these odds, Hamilton believed the issue was worth taking on. It was now or never. Getty Oil would be going into the Gros Ventre in a matter of weeks. Whether or not Getty struck crude at its first site, the head of Little Granite Creek, the company would still be bulldozing a seven-mile road just to sink its exploratory wells. The road would serve a dual purpose, opening the area to loggers as well as to energy development. Already, the Forest Service was making their intentions plain by auctioning off the surrounding timber. Once the road was built, it would blow any chance for preserving what had always been a de facto, but not official, wilderness.

It was always like that. Delaying formal protection always started a race between environmentalists and industry. It was a stupid game, really. It was too easy to get lost in the intricacies and forget why you got started in the first place. But Bruce had no doubt that the Gros Ventre was worth fighting for. The elk were only one consideration. The Gros Ventre was a broken circle of loping, snow-covered peaks higher than 10,000 feet, with bighorn sheep, antelope, moose, grizzly bear, black bear, wolverine, and cougar. Some people claimed that wolves also hid in its tented folds.

As the Rendezvous rolled around that July Fourth weekend, Getty hadn't any gotten further than planting a line of road-survey stakes. But the period for appealing the U.S. Geological Survey's approval of Getty's project was over. In the event that Getty took advantage of this lull to start building the road, Earth First! was prepared for a blockade. On July 3 a few Earth First!ers decided to make a preemptive strike. Very early that morning, five miles of survey stakes mysteriously disappeared. Survey equipment was damaged, enough to make it a felony if someone were caught.

"There were people pointing fingers at me and Dave and Howie, saying that we did it. We didn't do it. Hell, we were doing a rally there the next day," said Bart Koehler. When asked if he knows who pulled the stakes, he smiles and says cutely, "According to legend, it was a daring daylight raid. It was either beavers—beavers are real fond of survey stakes—or ravens. We have learned over the years that ravens really like survey tape. They like to wear it as headbands and they like to fill their nests with it."

On that day, the Earth First! beavers—or ravens—joined a venerable tradition of survey-stake sabotage on the North American continent. In the 1880s, Yukiuma, of the Fire Clan of the Hopi, encouraged his people to pull up survey stakes marking their allotments under the General Allotment Act of 1887, also known as the Dawes Act. As far as Yukiuma was concerned, the land had already been allotted to the clans by Maasa'u, the Spirit of both Death and Life.[2] Maybe Maasa'u had come back as a raven in 1982.

As preparations for the Rendezvous got under way, Bart Koehler found that there was a surprising amount of support in northwestern Wyoming for protecting the Gros Ventre. "There were a lot of people around that did not want that project to go through. Including some of the county sheriffs," recalled Bart. "When we did the rendezvous thing, we had to get legal permits and all that shit, we were talking to them, and they said, 'Yeah, I hope they don't get that road through there.' "

The cops may have not wanted the Gros Ventre split open by a road, but they were not quite prepared for what happened when the Preacher, as Pete Dustrud had taken to calling Foreman in the *Earth First! Journal*, did his thing. After the initial speeches by Garland and Abbey, Foreman went through his usual hooting and hollering routine. He wound up by telling the crowd to form a human chain across Getty's road site. Jumping off the stage, he led several hundred people to the head of the dirt road, where they shouted, "Getty Go Home," and "Earth First!" A local newspaper reporter wrote that it looked like hundreds of people who hadn't seen the inside of a church in years had suddenly been gripped by religious fervor.

But the devil disappointed them. Although a number of reporters showed up, nobody from Getty did. The demonstration was successful, but not particularly dramatic. Still, it made a difference. Instead of its usual rubber stamp approval, on August 10 the Wyoming Oil and Gas Commission voted to deny Getty's application for a state permit to drill at Little Granite Creek. Bart Koehler said that one of the commissioners, who requested anonymity, told him, "The threat of civil disobedience has been a thunderstorm over the entire issue.

We're not sure what those Earth First! folks will do if Getty goes up there." Mass demonstrations just hadn't happened in the wilds of Wyoming before.

Later that summer Getty lost more ground in the Gros Ventre. But Earth First! didn't have much to do with it. Bart Koehler stopped Getty almost singlehandedly, not by chaining himself to a tree or dumping a can of oil on a forest supervisor's desk, but with a piece of paper. A bar napkin, actually. Bart was studying maps of the Gros Ventre when he realized that the company needed a right of way to build a road to the drill site. Because they were already legally allowed into Little Granite Creek, the only way to keep them out was to deny the right of way. Bart drafted an administrative appeal, based on the right-of-way question, as well as alleged NEPA violations, and filed it under the aegis of the Wyoming Wilderness Association. But first he showed it to some guys he knew in the Wyoming attorney general's office and also to a good friend who happened to be Wyoming's director of planning.

About a week later, the state of Wyoming filed its appeal, which was a fleshed-out, more legalistic version of Bart's. On September 22, the chief of the U.S. Forest Service granted a stay on construction of the Little Granite Creek road, based on the appeals by the Wyoming Wilderness Association and the state of Wyoming. Only then did the Sierra Club Legal Defense Fund jump in and file a lawsuit to stop drilling in the Gros Ventre. Most of the Gros Ventre stayed free of roads. Eventually 287,000 acres out of 400,000 were protected by the Wyoming Wilderness Act of 1984.

Tom Turner, a longtime Brower associate who is now an editor at the Sierra Club Legal Defense Fund, was working for Friends of the Earth in those days. According to Turner, the Little Granite Creek incident gave Earth First! a modest dose of credibility, at least with some of the more liberal people in the mainstream movement.

"I always thought Earth First! was a trumped-up excuse to drink beer and go out in the woods and yell 'Fuck!' at the top of your lungs," said Turner. "But I expect if Earth First! hadn't gone into Little Granite Creek, the lawsuit would have been too late."

Although the demonstration had played a role in saving the Gros Ventre, the stunning success of his administrative appeal turned Bart's head around. "I loved playing guitar," he said. "But when we weren't on the road, I kept thinking Earth First! should have a wing that could go into hearings and not be branded as terrorists, and do very well-founded proposals for bigger wilderness areas."

Bart and Howie had always planned to set up a more traditional environmental organization within the Earth First! nonorganization. But the idea always seemed to get shuffled under a pile of papers or beneath a wet beer glass. Only Foreman managed to keep the paperwork flowing. In the mid-1980s, he stopped more than three dozen timber sales on Idaho's national forests, using a simple, one-page administrative appeal form. But as a group, Earth First! was too decentralized to fill the more conventional, nuts-and-bolts role that Bart envisioned.

"We were just too busy," said Bart. "That would have been much more accountable. Earth First!'s lack of structure, I mean, it was fine when there were only a few of us, when it was just a small tribe. But pretty soon it was totally out of hand. There was no accountability and it got pretty crazy."

The second Road Show in early 1983 clinched it for Bart. Son of Road Show was smaller but more grueling than the first one. This time Bart and Dave were booked for sixteen gigs in fifteen days, up and down the West Coast. Even if they hadn't been booked so tightly, this Road Show would have been crazier, busier, louder. This time people were ready for them. Stewart McBride's *Outside* magazine article, the template for Earth First!'s environmental cowboy image, had been published in December 1982. In October 1981, Dave's article, essentially the Earth First! position paper, had appeared in *The Progressive*. The *Progressive* polemic had blown people's minds—well, maybe not everyone's, since the magazine was generally read by people who were already well ensconced on the left. But those were the ones you wanted to reach. They were the committed ones. For the most part, they were the ones who turned out to see Dave and Bart that winter.

When the Road Show hit the central California college town of Chico, a few people turned out who were not classic left-wingers. But they *were* wilderness activists. For instance, a ranger, Rod Mondt, had made it a point to attend Foreman and Koehler's medicine show that night. Mondt was a burly, dark-haired guy who talked slow but thought fast. He was a veteran of both the Park Service and the Forest Service, and he was becoming increasingly disillusioned with them both. His girlfriend, Nancy Zierenberg, stayed home studying that night, but she would later become an even more hard-core Earth First!er than Mondt.

A nursing student named Nancy Morton was yet another disillusioned environmentalist who came to hear the Buckaroos that night. The strong-willed, ambitious daughter of an industrial psychologist, she grew up in Sacramento, where her father worked in the aerospace industry. After the show, the Buckaroos followed the usual practice of asking the locals where they should go for a drink. At the bar, which was called Canal Street, Mondt and Foreman hit it off immediately. Mondt had the same sort of western courtesy as Foreman, the tendency to hide his considerable intelligence behind a reluctance to speak ill of anyone, even his enemies. As cynical and pessimistic as Mondt was about the way things were going politically, there was something homey and reassuring about him. Maybe it was all those years working in Park Service law enforcement. In any case, with his twisted sense of humor, longish brown hair, full beard, and the big frame holding up his beer belly, Mondt was an obvious Buckaroo. As for Nancy Morton, well, you couldn't miss her. She was wearing a white lace dress that set off her long brown hair and dark blue eyes. In those days, Nancy resembled the singer Emmy Lou Harris, cowboy's daydream, rock-and-roll girl of the West.

She also looked remarkably like Debbie Sease.

"I remember being in Chico," said Bart. "Dave and I had this great standing-room-only crowd and Roselle was there, too. He was going under the name Nagasaki Johnson at the time. This is when we were still wearing cowboy hats and Fuck Bechtel T-shirts. Dave had been bemoaning the fact that the only woman he ever loved was Debbie and he was doomed, and all this stuff. . . .

"All of a sudden I see this woman setting over across the way. And I say, Oh, my God. Poor Dave is in deep shit. Here is this woman who looks like Debbie and sounds like Debbie . . . and she looks like she's here to check Dave out. I mean, I really like Nancy. I just took one look at her and I knew Dave was in big trouble."

Trouble like this was just fine with Dave. It was all right with Nancy, too, although she wondered later if the lightning that hit a big tree, causing it to crash in her front yard that night, was an omen. In any case, when the Buckaroos came back for Endangered Species Day in April, Morton took Foreman on a hike in the Ishi wilderness. By the end of the summer the *Earth First! Journal* office had relocated to Chico. Six months later, Ken Sanders got a letter from Nancy about some publishing business he had undertaken for Earth First! "Dear Spurs: How did I get into this? I pick up on Dave thinking 'here's a guy that lives 500 miles away and won't interfere with my life' and now here I am—surrounded by a 2,000-piece mailing that's already 4 days late, working on an accounting system for wholesale merchandise and *not getting laid!!* God damn."

The old gang was breaking up. Koehler lit out for Wyoming one more time, determined to hang up Johnny Sagebrush's cowboy hat for good. During the second Road Show, Koehler had gone into another manic episode. This time a posse of good-natured cops reluctantly handcuffed him on Redondo Beach in Southern California. He hadn't been doing much, just playing a game of baseball—with himself. Naked. At six in the morning. The Road Show had been too much for him, too disorderly, too drunken, too busy. "I discovered how Janis Joplin and Hank Williams died young," said Bart. "Not doing heavy drugs . . . well, it was like you play all night and it just gets wild and you drink beer and tell stories and then you have to get to the next place and so you drink a bunch of beer to get loose again."

Substituting Lone Star for Lithium just wasn't going to cut it.

Koehler knew he was going to have to get some order in his life if he was going to survive. A friend got him a summer job as an interpretive ranger at a Wyoming state park. But soon he was back in the conservation loop. In 1983 he moved to Lander to work with Bruce Hamilton on the Wyoming wilderness bill. One of the most gratifying moments in his life came after he testified at a public hearing on Wyoming wilderness. A colleague who had seen him through the highs and lows of the past few years grabbed him after the hearing, saying, "You're back." It was what Bart had been waiting to hear.

After the Wyoming Wilderness bill passed in 1984, Bruce Hamilton was promoted. He would head the Sierra Club's field program, working out of the national office in San Francisco. It was a high-level job, similar to Foreman's post with the Wilderness Society. Bruce hinted to Bart that he should replace him as the Sierra Club's Northern Plains field representative. With Bruce's wife Joan's voice added to the chorus, Bart agreed to apply for the job. But he had misgivings about working for the Sierra Club. Part of him wanted to get hired to prove that he had the manic stuff licked. But working for the Sierra Club seemed like a step backward.

Just when he was about to find out if he had gotten the job, Bart was called out of town. After completing his business, he rode the train home to Cheyenne. Bruce's answer would be waiting in his mailbox. The train dove through steep valleys, skimming rickety railroad bridges painted with rust. Every so often Bart would catch sight of the nearly full moon. He remembered a conversation with Bill Turnage that took place at the Keystone resort in the Colorado Rockies, which Bart described as "this godawful, dee-luxe ski area with these godawful condos." Turnage had stopped calling Foreman and Koehler his shining stars, Bart recalled. Now he called them "The Untouchables," both accolade and hostility intended. At Keystone, Turnage had humiliated the Buckaroos by forcing them to throw their credit cards in a trash pile. Afterward, he took Koehler aside. This was the gist of their conversation, according to Koehler: " 'You know, I've been looking around the room at the field reps. I see eleven men out there. They're all between the ages of twenty-five and thirty-five.

They all have long hair. They all have some kind of facial hair, either moustache or a beard. They have sideburns. They're either wearing T-shirts and/or flannel shirts, belts with western buckles on them, jeans, and either cowboy boots or running shoes. Some of them are wearing down vests. Some wear baseball hats and stuff. And you all have master's degrees from funky western schools: Montana, Oregon State, University of Wyoming.' He says, 'Now either you guys are clones or you're rugged individualists.'

"I said, 'Bill, we sure as fuck ain't clones.' . . . That was the beginning of the end as far as I was concerned." As the night went on, that incident kept recurring to him. By the time the train pulled into Cheyenne, Bart had that feeling of clarity that sometimes comes when one is returning from a far longer trip. He decided to turn the job down.

As it turned out, he didn't have to. When he checked his mailbox late that night, Bart found a mailgram from Bruce. Bart remembers that Bruce had written something like: "Oh, shit. After agonizing all this time . . ." It ended "Love and kisses, Bruce." At the last minute, Bruce had hired someone without a checkered past. Larry Mehlhaff was not the dynamo that Bart was, but he was an extremely nice guy with solid credentials. Among his other attributes, Mehlhaff was less likely to be perceived as a threat by the sharks who constantly circled at the Sierra Club's headquarters. Without a doubt, Bruce was covering his own ass by hiring Mehlhaff. But he was probably making the right decision for all concerned.

Not long afterward, Bart was hired by the Southeast Alaska Conservation Council. SEACC was little more than a handful of fairly ordinary folks scattered throughout the rainy panhandle. But they had a big issue. They lived at the edge of the Tongass National Forest, the largest temperate rain forest in the world. At seventeen million acres it was also the biggest national forest in the United States. But one fourth of the forest would be clearcut if they didn't succeed in reforming a notorious piece of pork-barrel legislation that artificially inflated its timber program. Because of a deal made to grease the wheels for passage of the 1971 Alaska National Interest Lands Act, the

Forest Service was legally required to spend $40 million a year to prop up logging in the Tongass. According to Sierra Club figures, the Tongass timber program hemorrhaged $360 million between 1977 and 1988. The pork-barrel provision supposedly was inserted to preserve jobs in southeast Alaska, but hadn't even done that. By 1987 the number of Tongass timber jobs had dwindled from 3,500 to 1,800 and a number of small, locally owned mills had closed. Most of the logs from the Tongass were being minimally processed in Alaska before being rushed off to Japan. The only ones profiting from the deal were two corporations, Louisiana Pacific/Ketchikan and the Alaska Pulp Corporation, a consortium of Japanese companies. In exchange for building two mills in southeast Alaska, these corporations had received fifty-year contracts guaranteeing them timber at low prices. For example, according to Catherine Caufield in *The New Yorker*, in one year Alaska Pulp paid $2.26 for a thousand board feet of Sitka spruce valued at $700 on the open market. Louisiana Pacific/Ketchikan paid $49. Even with this advantage, both were cited for significant antitrust violations, including conspiracy and restraint of trade. The Forest Service reported that the corporations had cheated it out of $83 million and brought a claim to the U.S. Department of Justice. Ketchikan Pulp settled out of court, paying a million dollars in damages. Alaska Pulp refused to settle. The company countersued the Forest Service, but by the time the case went to court, the Justice Department announced that the statute of limitations had run out.[3]

The only real way out of this mess was congressional reform. But it wasn't going to be easy. Alaskans have a history of favoring development at all costs. Fortunately for SEACC, a small, patchwork contingent of environmentalists was making inroads into the old frontier mentality. But the group needed a leader who could get down not only with the log-cabin hipsters eager to buck the establishment, but also with the region's influential hunters and commercial fishermen. Most important, they needed someone who could pull these characters together in a way that would play in Washington, D.C.

On Easter Sunday, Bart talked to the SEACC people on the telephone from Nancy Morton's garage in Chico. He was still feeling high from playing his guitar at a gathering along the Tuolomne River in Yosemite the day before. The party had been held to celebrate John Muir's birthday, but April 21 was Koehler's birthday, too. He was thirty-six. It was time to settle down. The match felt right, both to the people in Alaska and to Bart. In May, he spent a deceptively sunny week in Juneau. One day, he rowed a skiff out on Stephens Passage. It reminded him of Yellowstone Lake, but bigger. Everything was bigger. Koehler was overwhelmed by the country that surrounded him, its outlines sharpened and lit by bright sunlight. "I kind of looked around and went, holy shit; I'm in charge of protecting *this*?" But his confidence was returning, in large part because he felt that the members of SEACC had faith in him. The people in southeast Alaska knew Bart's history. They wanted the whole package, the real Bart, not a manicured résumé version.

It wasn't just broadmindedness that made Koehler attractive to SEACC. They were up against the wall. Few grass-roots environmental lobbyists had Bart's national political experience. Even fewer were romantic enough, or desperate enough, to take on a long shot like the Tongass. It was almost as if Bart's mania—he never experienced the depressive aspect of the disease—gave him a psychic frame more all-encompassing than the average person's. Here was a mushhearted idealist who could play hardball in the toughest league of all —and win. One of his first acts as SEACC's executive director was to tape a photo on his office wall of Teddy Roosevelt riding a white horse. Beneath the picture he copied the T.R. quote: "Fighting for the right is the noblest sport the world affords."

The
Oregon
Trail

11

*All the next day Floyd spent in the bathtub, and used the whole new bottle
of Vick's. It was Thursday before he made another attempt to dissuade Hank.
Alone this time, he drove up to Scaler's bridge and parked his car out of
sight up a back road; while the government men were talking with John
Stamper in the little shack, he slipped out on the blind side with a hammer
and a bag of ten-penny spikes. . . .*

—Ken Kesey
Sometimes a Great Notion, 1963

January 1983—Goose, Wyoming

MIKE ROSELLE WAS LOOKING FORWARD to coming home to his
scuzzy first-floor apartment in Goose, Wyoming. Goose wasn't really
a town, although Roselle might try to fool you into thinking it was.
It was Roselle's nickname for a small cluster of buildings and mobile
homes on the outskirts of Jackson. Roselle, who was going by the
name Nagasaki Johnson in those days, and his roommate, Kevin
Everhart, aka Airhead, were on their way home from Mexico. The
Buckaroos had been celebrating the Little Granite Creek victory on
the Seri coast of Sonora, Mexico, just across the Sea of Cortez from
Baja California.

When Airhead and Nagasaki got home, they walked into a little
Hiroshima of their own. One of their friends had visited while they
were gone and left the front door ajar. While the Buckaroos were
lolling on Mexican beaches, twenty-below-zero temperatures had

burst the pipes in Goose. An illegal upstairs apartment and three trailers all ran off the same plumbing, so nobody in Roselle's Little Appalachia had water. Their landlord was incensed. He had been a plaintiff on the environmental side in the Little Granite Creek suit, so he was favorably disposed toward Roselle. But when expensive plumbing problems were involved, political loyalties flew out the window. Or could it have been those divots in the floor from the time Kevin decided to chop firewood without making that chilly, inconvenient walk to the yard? In any case, there was only one thing to do. Have a party. Sell everything to friends and neighbors. (Well, maybe not *those* neighbors.) Pack the rest and hit the road. It was time to join Koehler and Foreman on Son of Road Show.

Nineteen eighty-three's Son of Road Show was booked from one end of the West Coast to the other. The Buckaroos had done a bit of research before leaving for Mexico. There was trouble in the Pacific Northwest, but they couldn't tell which part of the region would blow up first. "We were actually looking for the next big wilderness stand-off. We were trying to look for big areas where the Forest Service was particularly culpable," said Mike Roselle. It wasn't that the Buckaroos had a vendetta against the Forest Service. Not exactly, anyway. Other than Howie Wolke, who had studied forestry, the Buckaroos possessed only the normal environmentalist fixation with an agency that seemed hell-bent on cutting every tree it could get its saws on. Of course, Howie made up for any lack of enthusiasm among the other Buckaroos with his tendency to use the word *Nazi* to refer to respectable employees of the federal timber program. But Howie's pet peeve wasn't the real reason the Buckaroos were targeting the Forest Service. Timber from private lands was running out and loggers were counting on the national forests to fill the gap. As a result, the pace of logging had increased radically, from an annual cut of two billion board feet in 1949 to six times that amount.

Although they didn't know all the details of what was at stake— research that would reveal the importance of old-growth forests was only starting to surface in 1983—the Buckaroos did know that the Forest Service was in danger of wiping out an entire ecosystem. They couldn't have picked a tougher fight. All the Buckaroos really had going for them was the knowledge that there were rebels scattered in the hippie enclaves of northern California and southern Oregon, along the oddly placed horizontal spine of the botanically rich Siskiyou Mountains.

In 1983, two controversies in the Siskiyous were reaching critical mass. In California, in the southern part of the range, the Forest Service was zigzagging a multimillion-dollar road across a mountain trail that was sacred not just to one, but to four Indian tribes. The Gasquet-Orleans Road, or G-O Road, named for the two towns it would connect, was becoming a cause célèbre. Because of the Native American connection, it was a natural issue for Earth First! Foreman was still in his tribal phase, teased by fantasies of starting a new culture made up of equal parts cowboy and Indian.

But in late 1982, another issue cropped up. The *Earth First! Journal* received an anonymous letter from someone claiming to be a veteran Forest Service employee. The employee wrote that he was nearing retirement and didn't want to risk losing his pension. But he was worried that if something wasn't done to stop the road that was planned for Bald Mountain, a 3,811-foot peak in the northern Siskiyous, the whole place would be ruined.

The author of the letter wasn't really an old geezer. In fact, two people eventually claimed credit for writing the letter. One was a Forest Service scientist who got drunk one night and admitted the deed. The other was a terminally hip timber road surveyor named Charles Thomas, who sometimes used the pseudonyms Chant Trillium, or Chant Thomas. Thomas claims that he met an old ranger who told him about Bald Mountain. When Thomas suggested that the ranger write to the *Earth First! Journal,* the ranger refused. Thomas got the impression that it wasn't so much that the ranger *wouldn't* write as that he *couldn't.* After deliberating for about a year, Chant says that he wrote the letter himself, adopting a corny backwoodsy style.

Most of the Buckaroos think it was the scientist who alerted them to the Bald Mountain issue. But whoever it was, the anonymous scribe introduced Earth First! to a region whose political history was as pitted and convoluted as its geology. Bald Mountain was located in a million-acre section of the Siskiyou National Forest called the North Kalmiopsis. Kalmiopsis might sound like a species of dromedary, or a relative of Dr. Doolittle's Push-Me Pull-You. But it was actually the name of a rare flower, *Kalmiopsis leachiana*, a blood-red representative of the heath family. It was fitting that the area was named after a plant, and a rare one at that. The low, dark Siskiyou mountains are an extremely unusual place, if largely unknown. Part of the reason for their obscurity is that they are neither high nor dramatic, like the nearby Sierra and Cascade ranges. Writer and naturalist David Rains Wallace used the word *wizened* to describe them, making them sound like a chorus line of Rumpelstiltskins. But these modest, overgrown hills hold one of the greatest concentrations of botanical diversity in the United States, second only to the Great Smoky Mountains of Tennessee. The Siskiyous were originally an arc of volcanic islands whose isolation fostered the development of unique plant species. As the islands uplifted and eroded, they linked up to the mainland, becoming a peninsula. Eventually the peninsula became a landlocked mountain range. This unusual geologic history caused the Siskiyous to run in an east-west orientation, unlike most mountain ranges, which run north-south. The Siskiyous' strange angle formed the crossbar of an H. On one side of the H are the Sierra and the Cascades. On the other are the Coast ranges of Oregon and Washington. The entire region, which stretches across three states, is called the Klamath geologic province. Wallace has a more lyrical name for it: the Klamath Knot. Wallace's name, which is also the title of his 1983 book about the region, reflects the Siskiyous' diversity. It also hints at the Klamath's tangle of evolutionary influences, many of which remain mysterious. The Siskiyous—the crossbar of the H—are the knot's center, the place where everything meets before taking off in a new direction. When the Siskiyou peninsula joined up with the other mountains, it became both a sink and a source for genetic material. Later on, there were a lot of changes in the weather. Glaciers seeped in and out at either end of the Ice Age. Then, in the xerothermic period, which lasted from

8000 B.C. to 4000 B.C., average temperatures jumped about four degrees. This is roughly equivalent to the increase expected from global warming. As these changes occurred, species floated back and forth across the Siskiyous.[1]

Wilderness Society founder Bob Marshall knew the Kalmiopsis was a storehouse of genetic diversity. In 1938, when he was the Forest Service's recreation director, Marshall had recommended the establishment of a Kalmiopsis Wilderness of more than one million acres. In 1946 the Forest Service followed his advice—more or less—and designated a 77,000-acre wild area in the Kalmiopsis. The Kalmiopsis wild area became official wilderness with the passage of the Wilderness Act in 1964.

Even as late as 1964, Bob Marshall's million acres of wilderness still existed in a de facto sense, although less than one tenth of it was protected on paper. Environmentalists and loggers were already vying for the other nine tenths. In the late 1960s, logging roads appeared in the Kalmiopsis, fissures that threatened to spread through the forest. The same cracks were appearing on mid-elevation mountain slopes all over Oregon. The high peaks had been protected by the Wilderness Act, which was based on scenic rather than ecological considerations. Mountain slopes, where wildlife found forage and shelter during the winter, were left unprotected. The Kalmiopsis became a symbol of how biodiversity had been left out of the political equation.

When logging roads started appearing on the steep, rainy mountainsides in the 1960s, there was less than a handful of professional environmentalists in the Pacific Northwest. Brock Evans, who worked for the Sierra Club in Seattle, was a member of this small fraternity. Evans often felt as if he were in a remote, hostile outpost of the French Foreign Legion. He remembers a newspaper columnist in Mormon-dominated Lemhi, Idaho, who called Sierra Clubbers "green niggers." Evans was careful not to trumpet his affiliation with the Sierra Club in such places. As a part-time representative for the Federation of Western Outdoor Clubs, he availed himself of the opportunity to pass himself off as one of the hook-and-bullet boys when it seemed more politic.

The environmental movement was stronger by 1973, when Doug Scott succeeded Evans as the Sierra Club's Northwest Representative. Not content to finesse his way out of awkward situations—and perhaps not possessing quite as much finesse—Scott brainstormed with fellow Legionnaires, Wilderness Society representative Joe Walicki and Sierra Club activist Holly Jones. In early 1974, they decided that the solution was to start a statewide front group called the Oregon Wilderness Coalition. Veteran activists, mostly Sierra Club people, would sit on the board. But the group's more visible members would be Oregonians, many of them new to the environmental wars. That way, nobody could say that environmentalists were outsiders bent on taking jobs away from loggers.

The OWC might have ended up as just another state wilderness group. But in the fall of 1974, its executive board hired a soft-spoken wildlife biologist named Jim Monteith. Monteith replaced the group's recreation-oriented approach to wilderness with an ecological one. But there was more to Monteith than science. There was passion, intelligence, and a healthy dose of eccentricity—almost enough to make him an honorary Earth First!er. From the beginning, Monteith made it clear that he was willing to go to the mat for his beliefs. He informed OWC's board of directors that he would accept the coordinator's job only if they would back his position on wilderness. His position was this: Save it all. Monteith's stance stopped just short of Earth First!'s. He wasn't pledging to roll back the frontier by reintroducing grizzly bears and tearing down dams along the Columbia River. But his beliefs went beyond anything OWC had previously endorsed. Fred Swanson, a Sierra Club activist who was the outgoing coordinator, agreed to Monteith's terms.

"That is not a commitment I made to you, or even to Fred, so much as it is made to myself," wrote Monteith to the OWC board a few years later. "This wilderness resource we deal with every day is part of us. No OWC staff person has ever felt that less than 100 percent of the roadless land base should be retained. Regardless of so-called realities, it is this goal which will enable us to save maximum Wilderness acreage."[2]

When Nagasaki Johnson and Airhead arrived in Oregon, Monteith was one of the few local environmentalists who welcomed them. But it was another OWC staff member, Andy Kerr, who saw the true significance of Earth First!'s local debut. Although Kerr worked within the system, his style was as bold as Earth First!'s. Ultimately it would fall to bare-knuckled rebels like Andy Kerr and the Buckaroos to create a new mythology for the forest. Kerr, in particular, was well suited to the task. He had grown up as a scrappy mill-town kid steeped in the old myth of inexhaustible resources.

"I had a choice in high school," he said. "I could have dropped out and worked in the mill or in the woods. I could have made a lot of money, got my pickup, got married, had kids, all that stuff."

Most of the guys in his high-school class did exactly that. But Kerr was different. For one thing, he was smarter. And he knew pretty early on that he didn't want to work in the woods. "It was a dangerous, cold, miserable occupation. I guess it was all the old guys walkin' around town that were crippled and missing fingers," he said wryly.

Like the Earth First! founders, Kerr was not a product of Earth Day or the antiwar movement. He remembered Earth Day, of course. He was still a teenager, living with his parents in Creswell, Oregon. His high-school class got half the day off. They were supposed to do something for the environment. Most of them picked up trash. "I screwed off," said Kerr.

But a demonstration on the TV news the previous year had made an impression on Kerr. That time, protesters hadn't been marching against the Vietnam War, but against logging French Pete Valley in the Willamette National Forest. This was a far more radical stance, at least in Creswell, a typical Oregon town where timber had been a way of life for more than a century. Many of Kerr's classmates would grow up to be the third or fourth generation of loggers their families had produced. But things were changing. There were only three large valleys in Oregon that hadn't been cut; French Pete was one of them. The battle over French Pete signaled a turning point in the Pacific Northwest. Like the birth of the wilderness movement at the end of the nineteenth century, it was yet another moraine left by the receding frontier.

In the late 1960s, Brock Evans and Mike McCloskey had made protecting French Pete a top priority. Before he replaced David Brower as the Sierra Club's executive director in 1965, McCloskey had preceded Evans as the club's first representative in the Pacific Northwest. He knew about the region's reliance on the timber industry firsthand. If environmentalists can win on French Pete, they can win anywhere, McCloskey told reporters. Instinctively, Andy Kerr, a kid who had grown up in a town of 1,000 people and three lumber mills, grasped the significance of the French Pete fight. The sight of 1,500 antilogging protesters massed outside the Eugene federal building in 1969 was a revelation, tantamount to the storming of the Bastille. "I remember watching TV and thinking, 'What a novel idea—a national forest that you don't log,'" said Kerr.

No blinding flash turned Kerr into an environmentalist. It was more like burnout. In the spring of his junior year at Oregon State he made the dean's list and came down with mononucleosis. That summer, he spent six days pounding nails for his contractor father. His dad was on vacation for five of those days. On the sixth, Kerr quit. It was time to grow up.

Since his freshman year, Kerr had been hanging around the Oregon Wilderness Coalition, which was based in Eugene. In September 1977, Monteith and another staff member, who already were sharing a single salary of $750 a month, each offered to donate $50 a month to hire Kerr and another young organizer, Tim Lillebo. It was enough to convince Kerr to drop out of college right before his senior year. "One could go to school anytime," said Kerr. "The forest was being cut down. The war needed to start." A war was indeed starting. And in the ranks of professional fighters, Kerr and Lillebo were the leanest, meanest guerrillas. Few people could boast that their wages were lower than the $300 a month Bart Koehler had been paid by the Wilderness Society in 1973. Kerr recalls that in 1977 his $50 salary didn't quite cover the cost of gassing up his VW bug to make the daily commute from Creswell, where he still lived with his parents because he couldn't afford to pay rent. Three months later Kerr got a 400 percent raise—to $200 a month. "I call it operating costs, but no maintenance," Kerr says. "You're using up your clothes, you're using up your car, you're using up your teeth."

But it was worth it. When he took the job with the Oregon Wilderness Coalition, Kerr walked into a firefight. That year, Monteith began pushing for a national lawsuit to challenge development in de facto wilderness areas. The Sierra Club's reaction to Monteith's idea was much the same as it would be two years later when California's commissioner of natural resources, Huey Johnson, came up with a similar plan. They told Monteith they feared a backlash, especially if the suit was successful. In the years since the Alaska pipeline's narrow victory, Congress had become adept at creating exceptions to environmental laws. Oregon's congressional delegation wouldn't hesitate to use their power to protect the state's timber interests. As things got rougher, the Sierra Club tried to oust Monteith in 1978. But Monteith prevailed, winning a two-to-one victory that cemented the Oregon Wilderness Coalition's commitment to hard bargaining. Animosity between the Sierra Club and Monteith's group, which is now called the Oregon Natural Resources Council, remains to this day.

"The Sierra Club leadership in Oregon thought the OWC was politically naive while the OWC prided itself on its Indian and sportsmen constituency and felt that the Sierra Club was an 'elitist western Oregon recreation group' populated by the 'wine and brie set,'" wrote Forest Service historian Dennis Roth.[3]

Although Roth relegates the attribution to a footnote, the "wine and brie" remark, not surprisingly, was Andy Kerr's.

Because of their frustration with the Sierra Club's wimpiness, Jim Monteith and Andy Kerr thought it was just great when the Buckaroos showed their unshaven faces in Oregon. When Foreman's infamous VW bus slid into Oregon in January 1983, the Buckaroos were rested, tanned, and ready to rock and roll. Their first stop was La Grande, where they had arranged to pick up a dark-haired folksinger named Cecelia Ostrow. Foreman had assumed Ostrow would be a weedy vegetarian hippie. At least she could keep Roselle company when he smoked pot, he figured. But his stereotype was blown when Ostrow ordered a chili cheeseburger at the first truck stop they reached. Later she matched the Buckaroos beer for beer, quite a feat in those days. If you could stop her from telling people about how the trees talked to her, Ostrow made a dandy Buckaroo.

The Earth First! caravan worked its way south to Grant's Pass, where Chant Thomas lived. Even though Foreman didn't know about Thomas's claim to be the author of the geezer letter, his name (or names) was on file at the *Earth First! Journal* office. Thomas was one of a grand total of two *Journal* subscribers in southern Oregon at the time, recalled Mike Roselle. Thomas invited the Buckaroos to his ranch, a commune called Trillium, or more familiarly, the Trillium Trout Farm, which lay on the banks of the Applegate River. He told the Buckaroos to consider their stay at Trillium a vacation. They wouldn't even have to entertain anyone. Instead Thomas's "eco-folk-rock" band would play for them.

Trillium turned out to be a gold mine for the Buckaroos. Thomas, a big, blond paterfamilias, invited every disgruntled government employee he had ever met. To the Buckaroos' surprise, the green uniforms of Thomas's Forest Service and Bureau of Land Management buddies had very deep pockets. Bumper stickers and T-shirts practically flew out of their hands. Donations flowed like beer. These folks were *pissed*. Bald Mountain, which was right in their backyard, inched higher on the Earth First! list of windmills to tilt at.

Not long afterward, the Buckaroos checked in with Ogden Kellogg, Jr., a Sierra Club volunteer from Gold Hill who had worked on an unsuccessful lawsuit to save Bald Mountain. Kellogg explained that his wife had just had a baby, and he was devoting less time to environmental work. "They tracked me down at work," recalls Kellogg. "We sat in the coffee room and I basically handed it over to them."

The Buckaroos wouldn't have much competition on the Bald Mountain issue from the Sierra Club—or much help. Local Sierra Club volunteers were simply burned out. Since the 1960s, when the loggers started hacking away at the Kalmiopsis, club members had been pressuring Senator Mark Hatfield, the state's powerhouse Republican, to preserve a significant portion of the forest. After all, the Kalmiopsis was not only a storehouse of biological diversity, but also the largest temperate rain forest outside of Alaska. At one point, Hatfield had even proposed a 134,000-acre wilderness addition. But like many good old boys in the West, Hatfield had philosophical problems with "locking up" land. His major campaign donors were even more uncomfortable with the idea. Under timber-industry pressure, Hatfield reduced the Kalmiopsis wilderness proposal to 86,000 acres. In 1978, he backtracked even further, fighting the inclusion of the North Kalmiopsis in the Endangered American Wilderness Act. Hatfield's doggedness held up the entire bill for more than two months. Finally, over Monteith's and Kerr's protests, Doug Scott redrafted it. He cut back the OWC's 325,000-acre wilderness proposal to 102,950 acres. The new wilderness included the south slope of Bald Mountain, but not the north slope. The south-facing slope wasn't worth much; there were a few big trees, heavy brush, and hardwood groves. But the mountain's north slope was valuable old-growth timber.

By coincidence, Dave Foreman happened to have been sitting in on a Senate-House conference, waiting for New Mexico to come up on the agenda, when Mark Hatfield killed Oregon Congressman Jim Weaver's bid for protection of the Kalmiopsis in the Endangered American Wilderness bill. Not long afterward, Hatfield slipped through one of his infamous "Riders from Hell." These were not stars of a spaghetti Western, but fine-print amendments tacked onto important legislation. Often riders had absolutely nothing to do with the bill they were "riding" on. Hatfield, because he served on the Senate Appropriations Committee, had access to indispensable budget bills. It was a simple matter for him to attach a rider that would escape most people's notice but cause environmentalists in his home state to writhe in agony.

Foreman was aghast when Hatfield changed the Bald Mountain wilderness boundary, reducing the American wilderness system by a minuscule, but crucial, percentage. The wilderness boundary originally had been drawn slightly north of the mountain's summit, making it difficult and expensive to build a logging road there. Now the line between wilderness and nonwilderness ran right across the top of the mountain, where bulldozing a road would be a simple matter. Brown bears still circled Bald Mountain in the spring. In winter they returned to their dens, whether the dens were in wilderness or nonwilderness land. Yet half of their habitat had been opened to logging. Bald Mountain's fate was a textbook example of politics imposing its map over the ecological map of wilderness. Bald Mountain was not the most unique ecological spot in the Klamath. It wasn't the tallest mountain, or the steepest, or the most densely forested. But when bureaucratic hubris so blatantly imposed its badly tailored laws on nature, the mountain's importance grew.

In 1982, the Sierra Club tried one last time to save the Kalmiopsis. Despite the difficulties between the two groups, the club backed Kerr and Monteith in a suit to stop the Forest Service from building the Bald Mountain Road. The Sierra Club lawyers argued that under NEPA the Forest Service should conduct an environmental-impact statement for the region, instead of merely an environmental assessment. (An environmental-impact statement is more rigorous than an environmental assessment.) But once again, the Sierra Club didn't allow OWC to mount a NEPA challenge to RARE II. In the meantime, of course, Huey Johnson had done just that and won. In the Johnson case, the court had blown away RARE II by ruling that it had not adequately examined the environmental consequences of logging. This forced the Forest Service to write more specific and comprehensive environmental-impact statements. (The exception was in cases where a state wilderness bill had passed with "soft" release language that declared RARE II sufficient for all land not included in the bill.) But Huey Johnson had sued only on behalf of *California's* forests. The California delegation, which included the powerful congressman Phil Burton and California desert advocate Senator Alan

Cranston, was friendly to the environment. Doug Scott was still concerned about a backlash if Johnson's suit cloned itself in less friendly states across the nation.

This time ONRC knuckled under to the Sierra Club, omitting RARE II from their case—and lost. "We made a good argument," said Andy Kerr. "We didn't make the *great* argument."

The bulldozers were on their way to Bald Mountain.

But as the Caterpillars crawled toward the forest, there were other changes occurring, mostly in people's attitudes about the big trees that they had always taken for granted. True, the Forest Service budget was not about to replace *Dynasty* as the top entertainment of the early 1980s. But people couldn't help noticing that the trees were disappearing. The problem was particularly severe in the Northwest, which was the cash cow for the entire Forest Service timber program. Two billion board feet were being cut annually from the forests in California alone. This equaled the total cut from all the nation's forests in 1949. The equivalent of 120 football fields a day was disappearing from the forests on the west side of the Cascade range in Oregon and Washington.

One of the first people to get curious about the consequences of these actions was a scientist named Jerry Franklin, a mill worker's son who had played in Douglas fir forests as a boy. "I was thinking, My God, here are these incredible forests, and nobody really knows a damn thing about them," Franklin recalled in a conversation with *New Yorker* writer Catherine Caufield.

Once Franklin began to study it, he discovered that the Pacific Northwest forest is the most densely green place on earth. One acre of old-growth Douglas fir forest contains more than twice the living matter of an acre of tropical rain forest. Some stands of trees harbor as many as 1,500 species of plants and animals. "If human beings were as efficient in supporting themselves as these forests are, one square mile would be enough land to sustain nearly three million people," wrote Caufield.[4] But as unique as its green, tumbling plants is the forest's *smell*. The mixture of moss, wet bark, and pine needles is like a half-remembered childhood walk in the woods. The odor of the newly born combines with the sweet, familiar smell of decay. It is air that has passed through a cleansing filter, transpired mistily in an alchemist's retort. Even the reserved Caufield, whose earlier book, *In the Rainforest,* brought her to the most spectacular of Brazil's tropical forests, sounds a note of excitement in the Pacific Northwest. "As one walks through these forests, one is struck by the sheer volume of green stuff and by the exuberance with which it strives to live," she writes. "Things grow in the oddest places. Every tree is hung with epiphytes and ferns. More than a hundred species of mosses and lichens grow high in the canopy. Fifty or a hundred feet above the ground, large trees sprout from the trunks of even larger trees."

Wandering through the bare-floored cathedral of the old-growth forest, early conservationists like Robert Sterling Yard and Bob Marshall could understand it instinctively. If you were sensitive enough, you could feel it, too. The Douglas fir forest was some kind of mysterious science experiment, a perpetually-in-overdrive, hydraulic, pneumatic, and aesthetic engine. In 1969, Jerry Franklin set out to prove this, with the help of a grant to study the forest's ecology. It may have been the first time that anyone had looked at these giant trees with the broken-off tops as anything but potential Pampers since Yard's impassioned 1936 article called "The Third Greatest American Tree." Comparing the Douglas fir favorably to the redwood and sequoia, Yard wrote in *The Living Wilderness*: "Seen from below, the high plumed ceiling of many hues of green, light-shot in places and often swaying gently from the winds above, these forest scenes are very different indeed from the vast dim cathedrals of the Redwood. Here we have variety and color, spread magically over a canvas of size."

In the 1970s, Franklin and his interagency team of scientists started the long process of laying bare the skeletal framework of this moss-laden honeycomb. Douglas fir trees, which reach as high as 300 feet into the air and measure more than 5 feet across, were the forest's most spectacular sight. But Franklin found that the big trees are only one lever in an intricate mechanism that includes birds of prey, rodents, yeasts, and fungi. In fact, it was Franklin and his team of scientists who made mycorrhizal fungi a household word in the 1980s —if you happened to live with an environmentalist. What Franklin discovered was that mycorrhizal fungi (truffles, for instance) bind together the forest's fragile soil. Small mammals like the red-backed vole eat and disperse the mycorrhizal fungi. Spotted owls eat voles, which tend to live in fallen trees. So when trees aren't allowed to fall down and decay naturally because they are being clearcut, voles disappear. Then the owls die out. It isn't a good sign for the fungi—or the forest.

It took many years for Franklin's 1981 report "Ecological Characteristics of Old-Growth Douglas-Fir Forests" to reach a wide audience. Eventually it would play an indirect role in changing the public's perception of a forest from a tree farm to an ecosystem. From this new evidence for John Muir's idea that everything was hitched to everything else in the universe, some environmentalists would extrapolate that the forest had spiritual significance and make common cause with Native Americans who felt the same way.

But even people who had never heard of John Muir had a gut feeling that something was wrong. With clearcut patches bleeding into one another, the national forests looked like big, harmless victims of a psychotic barber. Foresters kept telling people that clearcuts just *looked* bad. But the research of Franklin and other biologists indicated that the soil's architecture was breaking down under the constant barrage of "management." Of course, if you never left your car, you could drive through national forests for months without getting a clue. The Forest Service nearly always left narrow strips of trees lining the roads.

But as nature became fashionable, more people were leaving their cars. Someone who had been slamming car doors long before it was chic was the writer Peter Matthiessen. In the 1960s Matthiessen had written about endangered mountain gorillas in East Africa. In the 1970s, he trekked the Himalayas in search of rare snow leopards. In the 1980s, his attention was caught by vanishing pieces of the American landscape. Twenty years before, he had written *Wildlife in Amer-*

ica, a depressing but impressive compendium of extinct and extirpated species. Now he turned his attention to American Indians, and, inadvertently, to the old-growth forest. When he visited the Klamath region, he learned that in many places where the soil is particularly unstable, logging is not just destructive: it is catastrophic. While researching the 1984 book *Indian Country,* Matthiessen visited the southern Siskiyous. He saw the disintegration of the landscape that Jerry Franklin's research had been predicting:

> Natural landslides are common in this region, where the most recent uplifting of two million years ago did not turn the old rivers from their courses but only deepened them, so that the steep mountainsides may fall away even without excessive rain or snow. The soil itself, shot through with intrusions of the beautiful weak slaty jade called serpentine, is poor and shallow, and those slopes that are marginally stable when bound up by forest roots collapse quickly in the first rainfall and erosion that follows road-building and the removal of trees.[5]

Land is not the only thing lost to logging erosion. Rivers are transformed from vodka clear into a substance resembling café au lait. Sometimes they disappear altogether, leaving a channel of drying mud. Even when the rivers remain, they can easily become barren. When rivers silt up from logging, salmon and steelhead, an anadromous rainbow trout, can no longer reach the clean gravel beds that they need to lay eggs. Fish that must return to the same section of river where they were born in order to reproduce are blocked by logjams and erosion slides. Clearing land also causes higher temperatures, which can kill young fish. Almost all of northern California's rivers have been affected by logging in one way or another. More than a thousand summer steelhead used to run in the south fork of the Trinity River in northwestern California. Now fewer than fifty fish return each year.

The Siskiyou high country contained one of the region's few undamaged watersheds. While he was there in the 1970s, Matthiessen visited a network of trails that Native Americans called the ladder to the "sky world." The ancient paths had been cleared by the Yurok, Karuk, Tolowa, and Hupa people, who used them in their vision quests and medicine training. Along the trails lay a series of stone outcroppings, all with religious significance. The largest was a one-hundred-foot-tall boulder, which in the nineteenth century had been called the Medicine Rock. Matthiessen's guide, a young Yurok, called it "Doctor Rock" and made no bones about the fact that "nine tenths of the people have never been to Doctor Rock and the rest of 'em went up most of the way by truck." But when Matthiessen traveled to the high country in the 1970s, native people were trying to resurrect the old ways. Into this effort walked the U.S. Forest Service, which was determined to add yet another fifty-five miles of road to the hundreds of thousands of miles it had already built. The Gasquet-Orleans road would be a two-lane highway. Once it was built, loggers could get into a big stretch of wild country lined by one of the region's clearest streams. In return, the Forest Service promised to protect the sacred rocks with a chain-link fence. Maybe the medicine men could wave feathers over it or something.

In February, the Road Show was booked in Arcata, California, not far from the Siskiyous and the proposed Gasquet-Orleans road. Arcata is a Victorian college town on the rugged northern California coast and the home of perhaps the best food co-op in the state. (Because the state is California, it may be the best food co-op in the world.) One of the *Earth First! Journal*'s more vocal subscribers happened to live in Arcata. He was a Humboldt State University sociology professor named Bill Devall. Devall was one of the American popularizers of deep ecology, a not-quite-philosophy invented by Arne Naess, a Norwegian professor, mountain climber, and Buddhist. In their 1985 book, *Deep Ecology: Living As If Nature Mattered,*[6] Devall and George Sessions provide a valuable service by tracing the intellectual lineage of deep ecological thought, which has probably been around since the days of the cavemen. They characterize the underlying worldview of Western civilization as dominance over nature, while deep ecology is based on the idea of harmony with nature. All nature has intrinsic worth, Devall and Sessions wrote. It wasn't a very controversial point or a very new one. But one of its corollaries pushed Aldo Leopold's ideas one step beyond the old game manager's well-trodden intellectual path. In their deep ecology commandments, they included the idea that all species are equal. The message had been hinted at by the Endangered Species Act, which gave legal protection to other species. But by saying that other species not only had a right to live and thrive, but a right *equal* to humanity's, deep ecology became truly radical.

Still, this assertion was not enough to transform deep ecology into a philosophy. As Bron Taylor, a religion and social ethics professor at the University of Wisconsin wrote in *The Ecologist*, referring to the explanation of deep ecology offered by *Earth First! Journal* associate editor Christopher Manes: "Manes' argument displacing humans from the centre of moral concern does not adequately explain where *value* actually resides."[7] At its worst, deep ecology is fuzzy-headed, anti-intellectual, pie-in-the-sky, pseudo-spiritual gobbledygook. Deep ecologists have an unfortunate propensity for using the intellectual tools they are bashing—obscure, academic philosophical constructs—to wend their way back to the basic ideas expounded by Aldo Leopold in *A Sand County Almanac*. "A thing is right when it tends to preserve the integrity, stability, and beauty of the biotic community. It is wrong when it tends otherwise," wrote Leopold in the 1940s. At its best, deep ecology offers a blueprint for putting Leopold's ideas into practice.

The confusion engendered by deep ecology could be explosive when it was injected into the political test tube of logging communities, particularly in places where a cyclical economy was already putting the squeeze on blue-collar workers. Even in the early eighties, environmental issues in northern California had a violent tinge, as the Buckaroos discovered when they blew through town in February. Devall had rounded up their biggest audience yet. Almost three hundred people showed up to listen to their kick-out-the-jams environmental proselytizing. After the professor briefed them on the G-O

Road controversy, Mike Roselle and Dave Foreman decided they would return to Arcata. A few weeks later they drove through a blizzard to attend a strategy session on the road.

At the meeting, the Buckaroos encountered a fractious group of counterculture homesteaders. There were refugees from the peace movement, lesbians from sheep-farming communes, and Native Americans with ties to the American Indian Movement. This was the first of many informal alliances that Earth First! made with AIM, which by the late 1970s had been forced underground and practically destroyed by the FBI. Although it remained a presence on reservations, AIM kept a low profile for a decade or so, often operating through its United Nations entity, the Native Treaty Council. Later the organization emerged as a public presence called AIM once again, with more of a focus on working within the system. At the time, though, AIM was still in its radical phase. "The Indians were really militant," said Foreman. "The peace and love types were appalled. Roselle and I got along better with the Indians. We were dressed like them, in cowboy boots and sunglasses."

It wasn't just sartorial style that caused tension among the various groups. The "peace and love people" were taken aback when the Indians talked about violence, Foreman said. At one point, the meeting got so contentious that each faction wandered off to meet separately before reconvening to negotiate an overall strategy. "Eventually everyone agreed the honkies would do their wimpy Gandhi CD stuff at the lower elevation, get arrested," and then the Indians would stage their demonstrations up in the sacred land near Doctor Rock, said Foreman. The Indians thought the lesbian separatists should stay in camp and cook. The lesbians, torn between feminism and Native American cultural sovereignty, were in a quandary.

Fortunately, they never had to choose. On May 25, a federal court blocked construction of the G-O Road. It was the first time that Indian territory had been protected under the freedom-of-religion provision of the First Amendment. Years later the Supreme Court reversed the decision, setting a damaging precedent for Native American cultural rights. But by the time the Supreme Court got around to hearing the case, the G-O Road was a dead issue. Half of it had been constructed, but the second half would remain nothing more than a ghostly white line on an old surveyor's map. The action moved north to Bald Mountain, and so did Mike Roselle.

In April, Mike Roselle and Kevin Everhart parked the Lumbago, a 1962 GMC motor home Roselle and Foreman had bought to use as a mobile office, just outside Grant's Pass, Oregon. Shortly after their arrival, Nagasaki and Airhead made an executive decision. They would blockade the Bald Mountain Road. Since the Gros Ventre rendezvous, the Buckaroos had been itching to mount a civil-disobedience action, but all those successful injunctions and administrative appeals kept getting in their way. Direct action was the hot new thing in the environmental movement. It had started in the early 1970s, when a boom-and-bust real estate developer and Canadian badminton champion named David McTaggert was beaten up by French sailors for trying to stop nuclear testing on a South Pacific atoll. The organization that McTaggert had recently joined, Greenpeace, would become the best-funded environmental group in the world. Direct action was the group's raison d'être. They left almost everything else, including philosophy, lobbying, and sabotage, to others. The Greenpeace image was brilliantly molded in a campaign orchestrated by direct-mail expert Richard Parker and a young man named Herb Chao Gunther, who was later joined by eco-advertising veteran Jerry Mander at the Public Media Center in San Francisco. In their Greenpeace campaign, Gunther made the astounding discovery that cute, furry baby seals opened wallets even more effectively while they were actually in the process of being clubbed to death than when they were on a coatrack.

Although it began with individual acts of heroism, Greenpeace soon became bloated beyond recognition. But some direct-action heroes turned down the chance to go big-time. One was Mark Dubois, a Friends of the River founder who chained himself to a cliff along California's Stanislaus River in 1979 to stop construction of the New Melones Dam. Dubois's passion grew out of a sense of place. He grew up in prosaic Sacramento, the son of a secretary and a Mobil Oil executive. But after he got his driver's license at sixteen, he began caving in the canyons of the Stanislaus. Eventually he turned to river running.

"I had never been very good with people," he said. But like David Brower, the tall, boyishly direct Dubois felt at ease in the outdoors. Eventually, that ease communicated itself to others. Dubois lived the next decade of his life in the company of people who loved the river almost as much as he did. "I realized in a way the river had become every relationship I had ever had: spiritual teacher, guru, almost lover. For me, there weren't too many choices. Once you fall in love with something, you can't walk away."

Like the funky grass-roots appeal of Earth First!, Dubois's approach was a sign that the wilderness movement was changing. It came after Friends of the River literally tried everything else, including a referendum, to stop the New Melones dam. When authorities were unable to locate Dubois, Governor Jerry Brown asked the U.S. Army Corps of Engineers to reconsider filling the dam. The Corps agreed to stop the water from rising beyond 808 feet of altitude until Friends of the River could negotiate a deal with Congressman Phil Burton. Mark Dubois had been hidden for a full week before the 808 agreement flushed him out. When he emerged from the canyon, he was shrouded in an aura that approached myth.

Despite Dubois's willingness to be a martyr, the Stanislaus was cut from the 1980 Wild and Scenic Rivers Act when Burton found himself one measly vote short in committee. The members of Friends of the River, who had worked eighteen-hour days and lived on tiny salaries through the whole campaign, were bereft. "I remember sitting there and thinking, this group of goddamn *men* had just destroyed the river," said Catherine Fox, a blond, gentle-voiced woman who was a stalwart of the group. "I remember bursting into tears in the halls of Congress. Phil Burton called a few of us into his office. Phil offered us all a drink and said he was sorry. This hadn't happened to him in a long time. 'Sorry, kids.' "

Despite the defeat, Friends of the River survived. They hadn't intended to. The group had formed for the express purpose of saving the Stanislaus. Its founders had even called David Brower to ask permission to "borrow" the name from Friends of the Earth, because Friends of the River was meant to be an ad hoc, temporary outfit. But its members found that there were more than enough issues related to western rivers to keep them busy for years to come. Dubois, who could have parlayed his bravery into a political career, didn't do so. He remained active on river issues, but worked for small groups. He married Sharon Negri, the founder of the Mountain Lion Foundation. They continued to live in the funky Sacramento house that had been the Friends of the River group house during the Stanislaus fight. Despite his shyness—or maybe because of it—Dubois remained a symbol to other environmentalists, including Earth First! founder Mike Roselle.[8]

In America, the environmental movement was becoming more confrontational. But in other countries things were happening even faster. While "the decade of environmental legislation" had given U.S. environmentalists leverage through the court system, environmentalists in other countries did not have the same degree of recourse through official channels. They were forced to rely on moral pressure. When that failed, they got physical. Often, civil disobedience attracted respectable members of society who probably would have confined themselves to acting within the law if they had the choice. In Australia, things were positively raucous. Logging blockades in Australian rain forests began in 1979. In 1982, John Seed, a diminutive, fine-featured back-to-the-lander of a somewhat less recent vintage than some of his hippie compatriots, allied the Australian movement with Earth First! The Australians staged protests far larger than U.S. Earth First!ers could even dream about. In 1983, for instance, 1,500 people demonstrated to save a wild river in Tasmania. In New South Wales, 300 people blocked a logging road being cut into a rain forest called The Big Scrub. The protesters lay down in front of equipment, climbed trees to prevent them from being felled, and tied the trees together with cables, wrote former *Earth First! Journal* associate editor Christopher Manes in his lively, if somewhat pompous, Earth First!

manifesto, *Green Rage*. "The scene had a surrealistic air about it as a squad of police one hundred strong escorted the rumbling road-building machinery through the primeval forest half-light, harassed at every turn by protesters," wrote Manes. Eventually half a million acres of The Big Scrub became parkland.

Mike Roselle thought it would be a piece of cake to pull off a similar demonstration in Oregon. The Pacific Northwest was full of old antiwar activists trained in nonviolent civil disobedience, including Roselle himself. But for some strange reason, Roselle found that there was a shortage of people willing to get arrested. "Everyone always wants to save themselves for later," Roselle said crabbily. "They think if they get arrested they'll never get out."

On April 26, four people strode up to the clearing where a crew would be bulldozing the Bald Mountain Road the next day. At the last minute, Mike Roselle and Kevin Everhart had been joined by two locals, Steve Marsden, a former logging road engineer, and Pedro Tama, the editor of a bioregional newspaper called *Siskiyou Country*. When the road crew arrived, the two sides parleyed. Roselle told the crew flat out that the protesters were going to stop the road. Period. End of story. One of the bulldozer operators was a particularly aggressive fellow named Les Moore. Moore and the rest of the road crew didn't seem to be taking the protesters very seriously. They suggested that the Earth First!ers wouldn't have the balls to be there the next day, when construction was scheduled to begin. But when Moore & Co. arrived the next morning to start bulldozing the road, the suckers were there again. This time they were standing right in the middle of the road, holding a goddamn banner.

Nothing like this had ever happened in Oregon's timber country. These tall hippies were spitting on Mom, apple pie, and Les Moore's paycheck. Moore cursed and shouted, but his theatrics had little effect on the demonstrators. Then he jumped off his bulldozer, a big D-8K Cat. He shouted at the blockaders, who stood there silently, in good civil-disobedience fashion.

Finally Moore ran out of words and clambered back on the bull-dozer. He backed down the road scar about fifty feet, lowered the blade and prepared to charge. The big Cat moved forward, its thirteen-foot blade scraping a wall of dirt up against the protesters' feet. Raising the blade, Moore swung it around, expertly dislodging rocks from the high side of the road onto the pile of dirt. Nobody moved. Visibly frustrated, Moore backed up the bulldozer about ten yards. The protesters jumped over the dirt pile, hustled up to where Moore was, and faced off against the blade again.

"First down!" someone shouted.

Now Moore was really disgusted. He backed the bulldozer up another ten yards or so, grabbed his thermos, and took off for the nearest pay phone, spitting over his shoulder, "Bunch of communist bastards! Who funds you, anyway? The Rockefellers?"

"Touchdown!" barked the Earth First! announcer.

In the meantime, Dave Foreman was slogging through the mud, a mewling passel of out-of-shape reporters dogging his heels. Foreman and the press arrived about half an hour after Les Moore had stomped off in frustration. Fortunately, the sheriff's department took even longer to arrive, so the reporters had plenty of time to interview everyone. When the cops finally got there, they duly arrested the blockaders. Chant Thomas watched them being carted off, shaking his head as he saw Mike Roselle ignore his advice.

"Mike, don't go limp," Thomas said he had warned Roselle. "You and other people who come in from other parts of the country . . . it's the same cops we deal with all the time. They resent driving three hours and they get skinned knuckles and stuff because they're trying to lift a two-hundred-pound oaf."

Despite Roselle's limpness, the blockade was deemed a success. Roselle even wrote his own account for the *Earth First! Journal*. "The blockade of the Bald Mountain Road had begun, after months of planning and preparations; so too, began the nonviolent struggle to save all wilderness," ran his modest pledge in the June 21, 1983, edition. The charm of his hyperbole lay in the fact that the blockaders were literally possessed by their own breakneck idealism. The mood was incredibly optimistic, especially among the native Oregonians. The blockade confirmed their long-buried perceptions about the closed-off, provincial society in which they had grown up. It was as if an evil empire were toppling before their eyes, the victim of a freak gust of fresh air.

It was a great time for Mike Roselle, too. The hillbilly mongrel from Kentucky via Los Angeles had found a home on the Pacific coast, at least as much of a home as he would ever have. He felt comfortable with the hippies and back-to-the-landers; he could speak their language, and they respected him in a way that nobody else ever had. Cowboy hat notwithstanding, he was one of them. Unlike the other Buckaroos, he had a social conscience that extended beyond wilderness issues. It was easy for him to see the big picture: the links between technology's oppression of people and its destruction of nature. Somewhere in between the Yippie period and the Kalmiopsis blockade Roselle had become an autodidact. Abbie Hoffman's *Revolution for the Hell of It* was still his bible, but he had also read Thoreau and Abbey and Leopold. Once he got to Oregon, he read up on the peace movement and studied the lives of Gandhi and Martin Luther King. "Roselle and I were both having fantasies of being the Mahatma Gandhi of the environmental movement," recalled Foreman.

Roselle versed himself in forest legislation, parks legislation, the history of the wilderness movement. Not only that, he learned about art, music, food. He developed the ability to analyze politics from a variety of perspectives. This protean quality was his greatest strength as an organizer. Dave Foreman and the other Buckaroos kept saying they welcomed diversity, that anyone could join Earth First! But they felt most comfortable with people like themselves: traditional wilderness activists. They might be narrow-minded, but they knew how the game was played. If they broke the rules, the way Earth First! was designed to do, they did it consciously, strategically. At least they knew the rules they were breaking. The people in Oregon were different, and the Buckaroos didn't know what to make of them.

"Most of the people in the blockades weren't environmentalists," said blockader Steve Marsden. "They had a feeling for the land, the place. There was a spiritual connection. But they were mostly back-to-the-landers and liberal arts college majors who had moved to the boondocks. Environmental groups had never catalyzed that energy because these people weren't environmentalists."

Roselle didn't care if they were Sufi dancers or hog callers. When he said anyone was welcome, he meant it. Besides, Roselle wasn't allergic to crowds. Foreman only liked large groups of people when he was separated from them by a stage. Bart Koehler, for all his warmth, tended to be the same way. Howie Wolke was happiest rooting around the forest by himself. Ron Kezar was even more allergic to Homo sapiens. His brand of misanthropy took the form of living in Ely, Nevada, located smack on Route 50, "the loneliest road in America." If the Buckaroos hadn't created their own mass movement, they wouldn't have come within a mile of one.

Roselle was different. If he had been a teenager instead of an experienced old pro of twenty-seven, he probably would have been among the gaggle of fresh-faced, long-haired freaks coming out to blockade the Kalmiopsis. He was attracted to the frenzy of political movements. He liked living outside the mainstream. Even years later he would say, "I'm not a workaholic like Foreman. If there wasn't so goddamn much to do, I'd sit around and smoke dope all day."

But between April and July of 1983, there was a lot to do, not just for Roselle, but for everyone. During this four-month period Earth First! staged seven blockades in the Kalmiopsis. Students from the University of Oregon started showing up, people like Mary Beth Nearing, Marcy Willow, and Doug Norlen. Mary Beth Nearing was the daughter of Catholic social workers in the Dorothy Day mode; political activism came naturally to her. So did physical guts. Geared more to action than reflection, Nearing became an ace tree climber and the best civil-disobedience trainer in Earth First!

Marcy Willow was one of Dave's myriad ex-girlfriends and a liberal-arts student at University of Oregon. Along with a couple of other blockaders, she introduced a new tone to Earth First! Later it would be disparagingly called "woo-woo," a euphemism for ecological maunderings in a vaguely New Age spiritual vein. When Willow wrote about "ancient new-born hills" [sic] and "passionate misfit[s] in

the selfish world of moderation and compromise" it was a far cry from
the usual nose-picking gnarliness of the *Earth First! Journal*. Other
Oregon blockaders wrote rhapsodies like this one, after an out-of-
control bulldozer driver tried to bury them alive: "Our blockade
taught me that there are greater forces than us working on this. When
the dozer was coming on the final run that plowed us under, my fear
was taken away and I was given a feeling of peaceful acceptance of
whatever was coming. I felt a unity with the earth and the spirits that
I can't describe and I knew that that time I wasn't going to move."
This was the sort of account that caused cowboy Earth First!ers to gag
and mutter, "CD junkie!!!" Civil disobedience did seem to produce
a weird, passive-aggressive sort of high. It was pretty wimpy compared
to the terminal Rocky Mountain weirdness that *Journal* contributor
Jim Stiles, the Arches National Park ranger, exhibited in his column,
"Sleaze from the Slickrock." "I am the head of Joaquim. I live in the
slickrock desert of Southeastern Utah and watch the many imbeciles
who have no heads attempt to destroy this sacred place. Let me tell
you but a few of the stories . . . ," wrote Stiles. "I was perched in
the Westerner Grill only yesterday watching my friend eat lard. (I do
not eat-it just comes out of my neck) when Moabite M.H., average
I.Q. known to exceed certain specimens of Entrada sandstone says to
no one in particular, 'any envir'nmentalist pukes in here?' I mention
this incident, so as to set the tone for all that is to follow. Southeast Utah, land of red rock splendor and dreamlike skies, home of
M. H. . . . let us pray." Eventually Stiles would leave the park service
and start his own newspaper in Moab, *The Canyon Country Zephyr*,
causing intestinal distress closer to home.

Not everyone fell into the two extremes of woo-woo or Hunter
S. Thompson–derived hallucinations. There were a few blockaders—
and the occasional *Earth First! Journal* writer—who fit neither mold.
Doug Norlen was a bright, unassuming Mayberry RFD–type kid who
had been a business major before becoming a blockader. He ended
up taking the usual vow of poverty by becoming a professional
environmentalist.

The Bald Mountain blockades also changed Lou Gold's life. Gold, a chain-smoking former political-science professor who had taught at Oberlin and the University of Illinois, was visiting friends in southern Oregon when he heard about the action at Bald Mountain. He had never seen the mountain but decided to take part in a blockade. Afterward, Gold started spending four months each year on Bald Mountain, becoming a Jewish hippie mystic who made his wisdom and herb tea available to youthful tie-dyed pilgrims. He also provided a practical service by cleaning up the mess left behind by fire-lookout stations. The rest of the year, Gold toured the United States, giving a bang-up slide show on old-growth forests. Forest Service officials would later say they could trace Gold's route from the postmarks on letters they received from citizens complaining about logging in the Siskiyous.[9]

The Bald Mountain blockade also drew a young woman named Karen Pickett. Pickett was pure Yankee. She had even grown up right next to Plymouth Rock. When she moved to the forested hippie enclave of Canyon, California, just west of Berkeley, she brought with her the sensibility of her Puritan forebears. Yankee frugality motivated her to co-found Berkeley's recycling program. Her Puritan moral sense led her to Earth First! Pickett was converted to the Earth First! philosophy after Dave Foreman walked into the Berkeley Ecology Center armed with newsletters, T-shirts, and ideology. "He said, 'There's this group of people and we're trying to do things a little differently,'" Pickett said. "He caught my interest, and when he left a *Progressive* article he had written, I read it. Not to sound corny, but it was like a religious experience, it caught me so hard and so fast."

Although she admired Foreman, Pickett became closer friends with Mike Roselle. His good-time hillbilly looseness appealed to her; it was so different from her own brand of intensity. But his political commitment went as deep as hers. Pickett, along with almost everybody else in Oregon, was impressed with how Roselle could support and motivate people.

With Mike Roselle hitting his stride, and forceful figures like Pickett, Nearing, and Gold entering the scene, Dave Foreman was receding from the central role that he had played since 1980. Although he had good memories of a childhood stint in Blaine, Washington, he felt uncomfortable with the peace-and-granola people who were joining Earth First! in the Pacific Northwest. Foreman left the hands-on organizing to others and went back to concentrating on the Southwest and the Rocky Mountains. To Mary Beth Nearing, Dave Foreman was "just some guy named Digger that we used to call when we needed money." But Foreman did his stint as a road blockader. Although forty-four people were arrested in road blockades, Foreman's was the only civil-disobedience action to become enshrined in Earth First! mythology. Maybe it was his karma. In any case, Foreman's blockade turned out to be the most violent.

By the time Foreman arrived, things were already getting weird. On May 10, five blockaders, including Doug Norlen, had been attacked by a bulldozer operator. First the driver tried to back over them. When that didn't work, he tried to bury them, stopping only after one woman had been covered with dirt up to her neck. When the cops arrived, they refused to make an arrest.

Foreman and Roselle went to the office of the Siskiyou National Forest supervisor and demanded that he revoke the road construction company's contract. The supervisor denied that violence had occurred. Later, the sheriff's department backed him up.

Two days later, Foreman and Dave Willis set up a blockade on an access road ten miles from the construction site. Willis, a mountaineer who had lost his hands and feet to frostbite, was in a wheelchair. A support team, which included Chant Thomas and a few other regulars, dragged a felled tree across the road. Not long afterward, a sheriff's deputy arrived. It was 6 A.M. The deputy asked Foreman and Willis to move. When they refused, he had the log winched out of the way. Fifteen minutes later, Les Moore drove up in a truck carrying five workers. Moore decided to run the blockade. Avoiding Foreman, he whipped the truck around Willis, almost knocking his wheelchair over. Foreman ran over to block the truck. When Moore swerved again, Foreman ran back to his original position.

For a very long minute, there was stasis. Truck and man faced each other in the cold gray mist of the early morning. The quiet evaporated when the truck shot forward, hitting Foreman in the chest and knocking him backward. He righted himself, leaning onto the hood with his hands. Moore drove the truck forward again, digging its grill into Foreman's chest. Foreman pushed back, but the truck kept going. Foreman found himself running backward, uphill, holding on to the truck. The truck speeded up. Foreman ran faster. Everything kept getting faster, Foreman running backward, the truck surging forward. But to the people watching, it was almost as if things were moving in slow motion. Every detail became clear, the way things do when there is going to be blood or pain and it is going to happen and there is absolutely nothing you can do about it. Then it happened. Foreman's foot caught a rock and he went down. He grabbed the truck's bumper and it dragged him like Indiana Jones, except he felt more like a road-killed raccoon. It dragged him and dragged him until Les Moore finally slammed on the brakes. Winded, Foreman lay under the truck for a few seconds, while Moore screamed down at him. "You dirty communist bastard! Why don't you go back to Russia!"

"But, Les," Foreman replied. "I'm a registered Republican."

It was the only documented case of one-upmanship by an environmentalist lying on his back in the mud, a fat rubber tire inches from his face.

Being a smartass didn't do Foreman much good. The deputy handcuffed him and led him away to Grant's Pass, where Foreman unsuccessfully tried to file assault charges against the construction company's employees. Instead he was charged with Blocking a Public Thoroughfare. Nancy Morton sent the money to bail him out. When he was released that afternoon, Foreman mounted the Josephine County courthouse steps to accuse Les Moore of attempted murder. Later that evening, two local television news programs ran his accusation, along with footage of Foreman being run over by Moore's truck. On Friday, May 13, Moore's employer tacitly admitted guilt when he ordered employees to refrain from further violence. Foreman was arraigned the same day. He pleaded not guilty and was released on his own recognizance. Unmoved by Foreman's explanation of civil disobedience and equally unimpressed by his disquisition on wilderness, the judge told him to stay out of national forests.

The incident was reported in the *Earth First! Journal* of June 21, 1983. Tucked down at the bottom of the article was a one-paragraph, one-column-wide story. "Sue the Bastards," read the headline. Lawsuit? Earth First!? Things were happening pretty fast. By the next issue of the *Journal*, everything became clear. The real story was that Andy Kerr had gotten hip to the true potential of the Buckaroos' migration to the Pacific Northwest.

Once Earth First! had gotten publicity for Bald Mountain, Kerr discovered that he was suddenly able to raise money for ONRC's long-awaited RARE II lawsuit. Now the local boys could finally mount their own battle, without depending on the chickenshit Sierra Club for funding. As it turned out, the lawsuit came just in time to put additional pressure on Hatfield et al. to pass the Oregon Wilderness bill. "Earth First!, literally like the cavalry, came to the rescue in two ways," said Kerr. "One way, they came and brought attention to the issues by their demonstrations. And eventually they slowed down the bulldozers. People got upset. 'Save Bald Mountain' became the rallying cry. So we said, send us a check." Kerr and Monteith not only found money, they found a lawyer. Neil Kagan, a refugee from suburban Long Island, New York, with a background in biology, had just graduated from the University of Oregon law school. Unlike the Sierra Club, Kagan had no reservations about using the Huey Johnson case as his main argument against the road, which he claimed violated NEPA because of RARE II's inadequate evaluation of the roadless area. He even made Earth First! the lead plaintiff in the suit, reasoning that ONRC had already sued once. It was the first time Earth First! participated in a lawsuit, and probably will be the last. By early July, when the Round River Rendezvous rolled around, Kagan had made headway. A judge had issued a preliminary injunction, stopping construction of the Bald Mountain Road. The Rendezvous, which Earth First!ers had expected to be a war, turned into a victory party. Marcy Willow presented Dave Foreman with a T-shirt with a big bulldozer track silk-screened onto it. There were speeches, dancing, and music. The hippies and the rednecks partied happily together.

Things were not so simple once the case actually went to court. The government argued that Earth First! did not have standing to sue, under the doctrine of "unclean hands," which meant that people who do illegal things can't fight their battles in court, too. Federal attorneys also attacked the legal standing of the Oregon Natural Resources Council, saying that ONRC had already sued unsuccessfully. Of the seven individuals named as plaintiffs, almost all of them were members of Earth First! or ONRC. Some of them had been arrested, too, making their "hands" unclean. But the environmentalists lucked out. One woman had just moved to town. She had no track record as an environmentalist. She hadn't even been arrested yet. As a citizen, she had legal standing to sue. The road was stopped, at least until a state-wide wilderness bill could deal with the issue.★

After the Bald Mountain blockades, Earth First! became a prominent feature in the political landscape of the Northwest. A few months later, it became notorious. That was when a stand of trees in the Willamette National Forest was spiked by monkeywrenchers calling themselves the Bonnie Abbzug Feminist Garden Club. Tree spiking was a time-honored ruffian's tactic. A sawblade hitting a spike blade could shatter into shrapnel, costing time and money, and possibly injuring a logger. The "official" Earth First! policy was to notify newspapers, radio, and TV stations after trees had been spiked. Publicity forced the timber companies to comb the woods with metal detectors to show that they were concerned about the safety of their workers.

Tree spiking certainly had potential to be dangerous. But Mike

---

★ Subsequently, Bald Mountain was left out of the 1984 Oregon Wilderness Bill and remained open to development. Earth First! protests resumed in 1986 and 1987, with demonstrators camping out in trees to stop logging. Another series of blockades took place in 1988. In 1992, Earth First!ers in southern Oregon, including Steve Marsden, who never rejoined the U.S. Forest Service, were still trying to protect roadless areas in the Kalmiopsis.

Roselle liked to downplay the ethical questions. Even loggers admitted that they had been hitting everything from bullets to tin cups since their granddads started whaling away on big trees in the late nineteenth century. Few, if any, had been killed. If the modus operandi subscribed to by Earth First! was followed, nobody would even get hurt. After timber cruisers went over the woods with detectors, the whole timber operation actually became safer than it would have been otherwise. It also became more expensive. That was the point. Spiking was calculated to infuriate, not to wound. "At Hardesty Mountain, we flagged the trees with survey tape," said Mike Roselle. "In the Middle Santiam, we spray-painted them. All they had to do was locate and remove the nails. The big deal is that it's a very marginal business, harvesting on public land, and spiking threatens its economic viability."

Roselle was going around taking credit for the actions of the Bonnie Abbzug Feminist Garden Club. Of course, Mike sometimes acted like one of those loonies who rush to the cop shop to confess every time there's an all-points bulletin. He seemed to want to reassure others that you could be radical and get away with it. While sources have confirmed that Roselle was hammering away somewhere in the grove of giant trees, they also believe that Bonnie Abbzug's name was not taken in vain—there was a woman or two sneaking around the woods, too.

Not long after Bonnie Abbzug's acolytes hit, a young, slightly crazed mountaineer named Mike Jakubal was sitting around the proverbial Earth First! campfire when he had a brainstorm. Jakubal had brainstorms frequently, but this one had some real heft to it. Jakubal had been blockading timber sales, but was frustrated that he was only able to delay them a day or two. He had heard about Australians who climbed trees to stop logging. In typical American fashion, he resolved to do it bigger, better, and longer—and to get as much publicity as possible. Using mountain-climbing techniques, Jakubal ascended a big tree that was about to be cut in the Middle Santiam wilderness. Unfortunately, he had been camped out in the treetop for only a day when, mistakenly thinking he was alone, he descended to urinate and was nabbed by authorities.

By the time of the next protest Jakubal had fine-tuned his technique in such a way that obviated the need to descend. A month later, half a dozen protesters joined him in the branches of Douglas firs large enough to house the whole Swiss family Robinson. Each protester used pitons and climbing ropes to ascend the thousand-year-old trees. The trees, thought to be among the oldest in Oregon, were located in a section of the Willamette National Forest that environmentalists took to calling Millenium Grove. Jakubal stayed up for a week; another protester named Ron Huber persevered for a month. Their trees began to feel like home. When Jakubal revisited the grove after the trees had been cut, he seemed gripped by nostalgia, the kind people feel for any inanimate object that they invest with emotion and time. But the tree sitters might have argued that they had experienced something else, the essence of each individual tree. It certainly didn't take Jakubal long to spot "his" tree. Immediately upon entering the grove, he made a beeline for the enormous stump and sat on its flat, round surface for a while, his long legs splayed but still not reaching over its sides.

After the initial bathroom glitch, Mike Jakubal had managed to invent tree sitting, which would become standard Earth First! protest fare, although after Ron Huber's stint, no Earth First!er would be crazy enough to spend a whole month living on a platform the size of a closet again.

In 1984, at the height of Earth First!'s guerrilla war, Kerr and Monteith made a tactical decision to go national. Former Buckaroo Tim Mahoney, who was working for the Sierra Club, had just managed to ram through the Oregon Wilderness Act. If Doug Scott was the hero of the 1970s, Tim was the mainstream star of the 1980s. "Tim was a genius," Scott said. "We passed twenty-two state wilderness bills in 1984 for a total of 8.9 million acres. That's a high-water mark. It was a tour de force."

Or a debacle. Even though Dave Foreman's relationship with Tim Mahoney was still one of mutual respect, Foreman noted unhappily that Tim's victory had resulted in the release of almost twenty million acres from wilderness consideration. Much of this land was even more valuable ecologically than the high-elevation "rocks and ice" that were preserved as official wilderness.

Certainly, at 950,000 acres, the Oregon Wilderness Act was a far cry from the 3.4 million acres of roadless land that ONRC and Earth First! had wanted to preserve. Even the Sierra Club and the Wilderness Society had proposed 1.2 million acres. The environmentalists got what they could. Normally, they would have simply resolved to go after the rest later.

But this time Mark Hatfield was pledging to hold the line on wilderness. There was reason to believe that Hatfield would change his mind. Every previous election year, Hatfield had caved in to environmentalist pressure and shepherded a wilderness bill through Congress. Today, Kerr thinks that Hatfield might have let another bill pass when he came up for reelection in 1990. But ONRC was not content to depend on Hatfield's reelection blues. Earth First!'s effect on legislation may have been negligible, but the group was influencing the political climate. With the increased publicity from Earth First!'s actions, the ONRC staff decided to take on their mortal enemy. After the 1984 bill passed, they began lobbying the lobbyists, trying to convince the national groups that old-growth forests were an issue of importance to all Americans, a green, leafy version of the Grand Canyon, a wonder of the world, a Sistine Chapel you didn't want to flood. They were attempting the impossible, an end run around their own state's delegation.

It took the Oregonians several years to pull the big national groups into line. Brock Evans, who had joined the staff of the National Audubon Society in 1981, was one of the first to support their cause. He didn't regard Kerr and Monteith as upstarts. He even said Andy Kerr was as good a strategist as Doug Scott, albeit with a different philosophy. Nationally, Evans became known as "the savior of the ancient forests." Between 1982 and 1988, he served on the Sierra Club board, where he lobbied to make old-growth forests a national priority. But he couldn't buck the staff, which persisted in the belief that the way to win on old growth was through working with Hatfield and Les AuCoin. (AuCoin had been a valuable ally to Doug Scott when the Sierra Club was trying to convince Congress to pass the Alaska National Interest Land Conservation Act in 1980.) To critics, the Sierra Club's failure to take a stand on old growth was a tragic repudiation of John Muir's legacy. "John Muir is back and, boy, is he pissed," wrote a columnist in the environmental magazine *Buzzworm* in 1992.

But other environmental groups not geared so exclusively to pummeling legislation through Congress were working on saving old growth. The National Wildlife Federation fought Forest Service policies by filing a series of administrative appeals in the early 1980s. These appeals later became the basis for a succession of lawsuits, mostly focusing on the spotted owl. It soon became clear that the owl was going to be the snail darter of the 1980s. In the Pacific Northwest, the owl became such political football that everyone became heartily sick of the whole subject. By the end of the 1980s even environmentalists were throwing darts at photos of the shy, small raptor—when no one was looking, of course.

The timber industry's charge that environmentalists were just using the owl as a way to save the habitat were well-founded. The problem was that no "Endangered Habitat" law existed yet. But increasing numbers of people were becoming sophisticated about ecology. They understood the relationship between the owl, an indicator species, and the old-growth ecosystem. John Muir's intuitive maxim, "all things are hitched to each other," was vividly brought home by the discovery that the Pacific yew, an old-growth forest species, contained a chemical that helped fight cancer.

Nationally, Forest Service policies were drawing public concern. The Forest Service was a road junkie with a habit that kept growing. By the end of the 1980s there were 340,000 miles of forest roads—eight times the size of the federal highway system. And the agency kept building. Major logging roads cost $45,000 a mile and secondary ones $15,000 a mile, on average.[10] Timber sales were supposed to pay for the roads, but the federal government found itself making up the shortfall each year to the tune of almost $200 million. In effect, the government was giving an unofficial subsidy to the timber industry, just like its unofficial subsidy to cattle ranchers. To justify these outlays, the timber program had to produce high revenues. The pressure to cut timber beyond sustainable yield (a forestry buzzword that means cutting trees no faster than they can be grown) eventually led the timber beasts themselves to start a reform group called the Association of Forest Service Employees for Environmental Ethics, which began in 1989.

In terms of national strategy, everybody knew that the best way to uncover the timber program's disastrous financial picture was to get at the Pacific Northwest. The majority of Forest Service timber sales actually lost money. But revenues from the Northwest kept the program afloat. In 1987, for instance, 90 percent of the program's net receipts came from the twelve old-growth forests in California, Oregon, and Washington, even though two thirds of the timber came from the other 144 forests.[11] If the carnage in the Northwest stopped, the bad economics behind the program would be exposed.

Slowly, the majors fell into line. Around 1986, the new, improved Wilderness Society began to wake up. By this time, the society had changed radically from the grass-roots-oriented group it had been in the 1970s, becoming an environmental think tank without a real presence in the boondocks. But think tanks could be valuable, too. The new, streamlined Wilderness Society funded aerial surveys and photography by Project Lighthawk, a Santa Fe–based group of volunteer pilots who called themselves "the Environmental Air Force." According to Catherine Caufield's account, Lighthawk discovered that the U.S. Forest Service had grossly miscalculated the amount of old-growth forest. Peter Morrison, a forest ecologist, compared the Lighthawk photographs with Forest Service data for six national forests in the Pacific Northwest. Morrison's estimates cut the agency's in half. When his information was presented to the Forest Service, they lowered their own estimates.

The first significant lawsuit was filed in 1987 by the Sierra Club Legal Defense Fund on behalf of the Audubon Society. The Sierra Club Legal Defense Fund had formed in 1971, at the height of the controversy that ended in David Brower's dismissal. The original funders of SCLDF, particularly the Ford Foundation, felt more comfortable with the new organization being legally independent of the Sierra Club, which appeared to be somewhat unstable at the time. Nevertheless, the Sierra Club was SCLDF's most frequent client. In this case, though, SCLDF's strategy was at odds with the Sierra Club's political game plan. Although the Sierra Club later joined lawsuits over the spotted owl, the club's participation was grudging, especially at first.[12]

The National Wildlife Federation. Audubon. Even the Wilderness Society was getting in on it. The one group still dragging its feet was the Sierra Club. Doug Scott had vociferously opposed the spotted owl lawsuits, which he called "incredibly counterproductive." His argument appeared at least partially valid. It seemed as though every time a lawsuit threatened to stop logging, Hatfield nuked it with another "Rider from Hell."

"You're not going to win that fight on biology. Biology is important, the PR those groups have done is excellent, the movies, all that stuff," Scott said. "But in the final analysis, if you want to pass a law in Congress and get a stick of timber saved, you still gotta contend with some realities.

"And the realities start like this. The ranking minority member of the Senate Appropriations Committee is Mark Hatfield. The Speaker of the House of Representatives is Tom Foley. Before he was Speaker of the House of Representatives and majority leader, Tom Foley was the chairman of the Agriculture Committee. In many ways, he still is. No piece of legislation involving old-growth forests in Oregon and Washington can be passed if it is not with the compliance of Mark Hatfield and Tom Foley."

Scott believed it was possible to get Hatfield, AuCoin, and Foley to play ball. After all, he had done it with French Pete, which he had been able to include in the Endangered American Wilderness Act of

1978. Of course, it had taken twenty years to save French Pete. The old-growth forests would be gone by then.

To be fair, Scott was not the sole architect of the Sierra Club's policy on old growth. The Sierra Club's approach to the old-growth issue had also been fashioned by Jim Blomquist, who succeeded Scott as the Northwest regional representative. But Scott took most of the heat, both out of staff loyalty and a sense of integrity so stubborn it verged on contrariness. Besides, he agreed with Blomquist's reading of the mood in the Pacific Northwest. Blomquist, Scott, and even Bruce Hamilton argued that preserving Douglas fir forests was a regional issue, not a national one. Local volunteer leaders should be allowed to decide how to handle it and they had insisted on a measured, less confrontational style. It was easy to see why Scott, who liked to call himself "a democrat with a small d," would be swayed by this argument. Yet despite his assessment, a significant number of rank-and-file Sierra Club members felt the logging situation was dire enough to warrant confrontation. They were outraged at what they viewed as the club's policy of appeasement. Some let their membership lapse; others simply became active in other groups. One by one, they realized that the Sierra Club's legislative machinery was not going to power old-growth reform through Congress.

In any case, Congress was nearly paralyzed. Environmentalists were finding new ways to circumvent recalcitrant legislators. Some devised innovative legislative strategies; others bypassed the Congress entirely. Up in Alaska, Bart Koehler was putting together his coalition of old-time Alaskans, fishermen, and environmentally conscious post-sixties transplants. His staff was traveling around the country, trying to generate enough support in the Lower 48 to force the Alaska delegation to make a deal. Brock Evans was interested in Bart's strategy. He had even loaned Bart a windowless cubbyhole in the Washington, D.C., offices of the Audubon Society. When he saw the results of the Tongass campaign, he came to believe something similar could work with the forests of the Pacific Northwest.

Once again, Doug Scott vehemently disagreed. He repeated the conventional wisdom. Alaska is the only state with a delegation you can steamroll. Only Alaska, the last frontier, is icon enough to gal-vanize voters all over the country. Alienating Mark Hatfield isn't going to save the forests.

"It's not easy. It's not glamorous. It requires being in the temple of the enemy," Scott admonishes. "If you're going to have a fight with Mark Hatfield . . . I want to be in the room talking in his ear. He may not vote the way I want but at least I'm talking to him. Because I'm sure he won't vote the way I want if I'm in the street with a torch."

Scott said these words—or words very much like them—to people like Andy Kerr, Jim Monteith, and Brock Evans many times. But by the late 1980s, they were not doing a whole lot of talking. There had never been love lost between Doug Scott and Brock Evans, who had been forced out of the Sierra Club by Scott and Chuck Clusen in the early eighties. Now their dispute over strategy was spilling over into nastiness at public meetings. In 1988 the Wilderness Society held a major old-growth conference in Portland. At the conference, Evans was offended by Scott's behavior. "After three or four years of failure and defeat doing the traditional thing on the ancient forests campaign, trying to deal with the Northwest delega-tion, which was nutty—Mark Hatfield's the most . . . no human being's done more damage to the state than that man—finally we had called the battalion leaders together from all over, including the Sierra Club.

"The Sierra Club cadre were all in the back of the room with their arms folded. They'd be talking when other people were talking, there'd be whispering, snorting, all the body language. Doug is a mas-ter of the rolling eyeballs. All the snorts of contempt. They were just barely participating. But they had to be there, because everybody else was there."

Evans gave a speech in the morning, telling the crowd that they had to "wrench" the old-growth issue out of the Pacific Northwest. "We have to make it a national issue," he thundered. "That's the only thing that's going to save it."

Doug Scott was scheduled to speak at lunch that day. According to Evans, Scott "trashed the whole thing," reiterating his commitment to working with Hatfield and AuCoin. In Evans's view, Doug was slavishly following the tradition of his mentor, the Wilderness Society's Howard Zahniser. Tim Mahoney agreed. "Scott might not have assessed it accurately for the long term," commented Tim Mahoney. "But he was true to Zahnie."

Although both Evans and Scott had defensible points of view, the 1989 conference made it clear that blood would be spilled in the coming battle—and some of it would be environmentalist blood spilled by environmentalists. Ultimately the 150 environmental leaders who attended the Portland meeting adopted Evans's three goals: to form a united front, to support old-growth legislation in Congress, and to "wrench this thing out of the Northwest."

"Brock successfully bridged the ONRC–Sierra Club gap," Tim Mahoney said in 1992. "The ONRC ancient forest strategy—if it was thought out—was to leverage the national groups. The Sierra Club's was to work with the Northwest delegation. Brock combined the two into a national lobbying effort to roll the Northwest delegation. It hasn't happened yet, but he correctly realized—more than the Sierra Club—the national power of the issue."

Needless to say, Doug Scott was not happy. He distanced himself from the old-growth fight, which helped Evans assume a greater leadership role. Not long after this gathering of the clans, there was a smaller discussion among Evans, Monteith, Kerr, and several other environmentalists that helped change the course of the campaign. It was a simple matter, really. The environmentalists were looking for a catchy phrase to describe what they were fighting for. For hours, they talked about how they should describe the forest of big trees and giant ferns, a forest so rich it actually seemed to *breathe*—even if you hadn't been sampling some of the more questionable specimens of the region's fungi. Andy Kerr kept pitching the word "primeval." "This is the forest primeval. The murmuring pines and the hemlocks . . . / Stand like Druids of old," said the thirty-four-year-old college dropout, quoting Longfellow. But this was a strategy session, not a literature seminar. The environmentalists meeting that day in the Portland office of the National Wildlife Federation couldn't afford to consider anything but results.

Brock Evans, talking to them on a conference call from Audubon Society headquarters in Washington, D.C., voted for ancient forests. Primeval was too clunky. Ancient was actually more poetic, Evans thought. "It has that connotation of antiquity."

But it was the scientist who made the decisive argument. *Primeval* has three syllables, Jim Monteith pointed out. *Ancient* has two. Pure marketing. Evans and Monteith turned out to be right. Within weeks, the campaign's effect was being felt. Newspaper headlines were bannering out "THE FIGHT TO SAVE THE ANCIENT FORESTS." Not only did the word *ancient* bring to mind the romance of prehistoric pyramids in the jungles of the Yucatán, but it also was clipped enough to catch a journalist's ear. "When we heard that phrase, 'ancient forests,' we knew we were dead," a Forest Service public-relations man later confided to Evans. It was a gratifying moment.

Despite support from Evans, the rest of the movement was feeling the Sierra Club's absence on the old-growth issue. Each environmental group filled a niche, and the Sierra Club's clout with Congress was one of the strongest cards the movement could play. In 1989, the SCLDF attorneys became so frustrated by the Sierra Club's inaction on old growth that they hired their own lobbyist. The Sierra Club remained unmoved. Not until 1991, after Doug Scott had resigned, did club policy begin to change. By then, even the board of directors felt uncomfortable with the Sierra Club's failure to take action. Privately, a group of them approached Evans. Evans suggested that they talk to the Sierra Club's elder statesman, Dr. Edgar Wayburn. Wayburn was an elegant and canny old gentleman who had twice served as the club's president and steered it to several of its most important victories. With Wayburn's support, the issue of old growth was officially declared one of the club's national priorities. But the Sierra Club still did not take the active role that other environmentalists expected of it. No other environmental group had the Sierra Club's clout with

Congress. As the arguments over old growth grew in volume and intensity, the Sierra Club remained on the sidelines.

In any case, it was beginning to look as if lawsuits would play a larger role than legislation in saving the tiny percentage of old growth that remained. Sensing which way the wind was blowing, Andy Stahl, a forester turned environmentalist, had moved over to the Sierra Club Legal Defense Fund from the National Wildlife Federation. By 1992, Stahl was saying that any compromise bill that could struggle through Congress would be a step backward. There had been a string of courtroom victories—and there promised to be more. Just as Doug Scott predicted, Mark Hatfield had neutralized most of them as easily as a trigger-happy teenager playing Donkey Kong. But environmentalists didn't have to convince Hatfield to *support* a bill, said Stahl. They had to stop him from writing more "Riders from Hell." If enviromentalists took the right approach, the delegation could be rolled.

In the face of congressional atrophy and fragmentation in the environmental community, the strategy on old growth was changing. Environmentalists like Stahl and Kerr were figuring things out, breaking the monumental job of saving an entire ecosystem into more manageable tasks. To stop the decimation of old-growth forests, the short-term answer did seem to be lawsuits, backed by strategic lobbying efforts against the Riders from Hell. After the election of Bill Clinton and Al Gore in 1992, Tim Mahoney predicted that an old-growth bill would finally make headway in Congress. But even successful legislation was likely to continue the polarization between the no-compromise ONRC and the rest of the movement. In the meantime, local environmentalists were still doing the nuts-and-bolts work, racing around appealing all the timber sales they could before every big tree on Forest Service land became a toothpick or a matchbook cover.

Science meant something, too, despite Doug Scott's words. A committee of scientists led by high-level Forest Service biologist Jack Ward Thomas in 1990 issued what is informally called the Thomas Report. The report confirmed what environmentalists had been saying all along. If you wanted to save the spotted owl—an indicator species for the health of the forest—then you had to save most, if not all, of the remaining old-growth forest.

After ten years of work, hundreds of arrests, anger, broken alliances, and new strategies, the old-growth issue moved closer to resolution in 1992 when a Reagan-appointed judge stopped logging until a bona fide plan to save the spotted owl could be developed. The half-baked compromises reached by the Forest Service and mainstream environmentalists just didn't make it.

A compromise brokered by the Clinton administration in the spring of 1994 didn't solve things either. That summer, ONRC and other groups sued to stop the Clinton deal, which was called Option 9 because it was the ninth alternative to be considered. They argued that it failed to take into account that the old growth forests were worth more dead than alive; also by allowing one-third of the remaining old growth to be logged, the government was endangering the Northern spotted owl and Pacific salmon.

Things were changing, not only in the Pacific Northwest, but around the country as well. Montana logging disputes were hitting the pages of *The New York Times*. Forest supervisors themselves were publicly protesting overcutting. The Forest Service was slowly reforming its logging practices, leaving wider stream buffer zones and haltingly agreeing to more selective logging practices.

As for the Northwest, fifty years after Robert Sterling Yard's article on the Douglas fir forest, the "Third Greatest American Tree" was entering the country's mythology. It was happening slowly and angrily. In large part, it was happening because Earth First! acted without considering so-called political realities. They just fought for the old-growth forests because it was right.

"All of these things, people sitting in the trees and getting arrested, in my view were very beneficial to the cause," said Kerr. "Because they got the attention of the assignment editor in New York, of NBC News. They [the journalists] knew there was more to the story than just these fringe dwellers—and I say this affectionately—these people who live on the edge of society sitting in trees. But nonetheless that's what got the attention. It wasn't administrative appeals, it wasn't rational discourse. It was somebody getting busted."

It wasn't enough to get busted. Somebody had to call the newspapers to tell them why it was worth getting busted for a couple of trees, or an endangered cave bug, or a river. "Any publicity is good publicity" became the motto of Earth First!

There was more than a tinge of self-mockery, if not self-disgust, as people recognized the central role that publicity occupied in their work. At the Round River Rendezvous, Earth First!ers began handing out awards for "Media Slut of the Year." As commendable as these stirrings of conscience and self-mockery were, a crucial perspective was missing. What most Earth First!ers didn't realize was that any publicity is bad publicity if there is too much of it.

The
Crackdown

1985–Pinedale, Wyoming

IT WAS A SUMMER DAY in the Rockies. Ice was melting and the marmots were coming out of hiding. Blue harebells dangled from granite crevices. Howie Wolke was enjoying a Sunday stroll on Greyback Ridge. Coincidentally, he and his female companion had chosen the exact spot where men from the Chevron corporation were building a road. The road was supposed to lead to oil. If it did, there would be more men and more roads.

Somebody had already "de-surveyed" the four-and-a-half-mile roadbed twice. Now Howie was doing it a third time. Bending over, he strained to yank up a stubborn stake. Howie was so intent on his work that he didn't notice the survey company owner until the guy was practically on top of him. "Someone's gonna die!" the surveyor yelled.

It was one of those fight or flight situations. Wisely, Wolke's female friend chose flight. But Howie had nowhere to run when the surveyor went apeshit. "He swung the hatchet at me a couple of times," said the big, rawboned environmentalist. "It seemed like he was trying to split my head down the middle. I ducked both times. Then he seemed to calm down a little."

It was lucky for him that he did. Pounding the surveyor into coyote bait wouldn't have been out of character for Howie. In the early eighties, he had worked as a bouncer at The Cowboy Bar in Jackson, Wyoming. The Cowboy Bar was the hippest place in town, even if it was kind of touristy. The whole town was getting that way, tamed and commercialized. But Howie was still living on the wild frontier. Once he lost his temper, Howie couldn't seem to get it back. More than a few times he had to be pried off a bloodied bar patron.

Slowly, though, Howie was getting civilized. Having a girlfriend probably helped. In the old days, Howie had never had much success with women, despite his good looks. Figuring that sexual frustration was adding to his orneriness, his friends got inspired to help Howie over his little problem. Their prescription was a pair of pretty twin sisters with a mercantile bent who worked at a certain now-defunct Wyoming institution. Whatever the twins did, it worked. Bart noted with amusement that Howie suddenly had more women than he could handle. He correctly predicted that Howie might even find a regular girlfriend. "I told him sooner or later he was going to find a woman who would put up with him no matter what, that'll love him no matter what, and I said once that happens, you're in deep trouble, pal. You're finally going to settle down. And he goes, naah, it'll never happen."

His prediction might have sounded like a bad Willie Nelson song, but Bart knew his friends. A gorgeous, busty, Nordic-looking nurse named Marilyn decided that Howie was a Viking god and his fate was sealed. Howie was domesticated. Sort of. In fact, he reportedly told his friends that if Marilyn hadn't been with him on Greyback Ridge, his exchange with the surveyor would have been significantly different. "One of us would have gotten killed," he remarked to someone.

The big Jewish cowboy might not have become entirely domesticated, but he would be living indoors for a while. After being
marched off to the authorities at hatchet point, Howie was hit with
an even bigger shock—a felony property-destruction charge that carried a maximum $100,000 fine and ten years in jail. Wisely he decided
to pursue a plea bargain, which resulted in his felony being reduced
to a misdemeanor. Great. Howie had no problem pleading guilty to
Removing a Landmark. Hell, it even *sounded* trivial. This way he got
to keep his pride—not to mention his all-important sense of moral
superiority—and save his ass at the same time. "The plea bargain
allows me to admit to doing something I'm not at all ashamed of
doing," he said. "I would have been very uncomfortable denying the
charge to avoid a felony conviction."

In fact, things had gone so smoothly that Wolke was totally floored
when Sublette County Justice of the Peace William Cramer gave him
the maximum sentence for Removing a Landmark. Pack your duds,
said Cramer. Six months in the slammer.

Cramer's decision wasn't entirely motivated by Wolke's lack of
remorse. ("I did it and I'm damn proud of it," Howie told reporters,
shaking his fist and grinning.) The judge, a transplanted easterner, said
he had been influenced by local people who explained the area's economic dependence on national forests. "Most times I try not to let
people influence me," said the judge. But, he added, "people's comments do have an effect on me in a case like this."

As the judge blathered on, Howie couldn't help thinking that the
plea bargain had saved a lot more than his pride. His ass had been on
the line here. "If the original felony charge had been pursued . . ."
Cramer told him, "you would indeed have gone to the penitentiary.
If the jurisdiction of this court had been higher, I would have imposed
a higher fine and a higher sentence."

Whew. Six months in jail was bad enough. Howie could tell the
judge was yet another victim of a disease that afflicts easterners during
their first few years in the West. You could call it cowboyitis or
wingtip-in-mouth disease. Even the grizzled old radical Ed Abbey had

been prey to it in his tender youth. Abbey told the story of his own metamorphosis in "The Cowboy and His Cow," a speech he gave at the University of Montana in 1985.

"When I first came West in 1948, a student at the University of New Mexico, I was only twenty years old and just out of the Army. I thought, like most simple-minded Easterners, that a cowboy was a kind of mythic hero. I idolized those scrawny little red-nosed hired hands in their tight jeans, funny boots, and comical hats," said Abbey.

He proceeded to ramble on at great length about a college friend he called Mac. Mac was a cowboy, a bronc-ridin', gun-totin' maniac whose parents had left him enough money to buy a forty-acre spread in the Sandia Mountains where he raised tumbleweed and committed genocide on rabbits. Mac was so disgusting that after a while even the young, impressionable Abbey couldn't stand him. But Abbey didn't get grossed out enough to end his hero-worshiping until Mac had led him on a series of alcoholic, gun-crazy gambling adventures that ol' Cactus Ed probably lifted wholesale from Bret Harte's "The Luck of Roaring Camp" and exhumed from memory expressly for the sake of several hundred credulous University of Montana students. (When he included the speech in his 1987 book of essays, *One Life at a Time, Please*, Abbey pruned its long, digressive gambling stories considerably.) Somewhere in between the rigged poker games and exploding pistols the students got a damn convincing fact-riddled diatribe about the deleterious effect of cattle grazing on the public lands. Then they got the ranting. Shoot the cattle and stock the West with elk, said Abbey. Bring back pronghorn antelope, bighorn sheep, moose, and eagles. Especially eagles. "Real animals, real game, real protein." In other words, restore the prehuman West. In Abbey's imagination, if nowhere else, the frontier had been rolled back. Way back. "Down in the desert, I would stock every water tank, every water hole, every stock pond, with alligators," Abbey wound up, quite correctly casting his lot with the artist's imagination instead of realpolitik.

Fancies aside, by the end of the speech a transformation had occurred in the character of Ed Abbey, Narrator. The greenhorn or dude, sketched in the tradition of Mark Twain in *Roughing It*, had become a bona fide westerner. In the classic western tradition, Ed Abbey could now poke fun at the people he considered dudes, "Especially critical of my [antigrazing] attitude will be the Easterners and Midwesterners newly arrived here from their Upper West Side apartments, their rustic lodges in upper Michigan," wrote Abbey. "Our nouveau Westerners with their toy ranches, their pickup trucks with the gun racks, their pointy-toed boots with the undershot heels, their gigantic hats. And, of course, their pet horses. The *instant rednecks . . .* I'm going to say good-bye to all you cowboys and cowgirls. I love the legend, too—but keep your sacred cows and your dead horses out of my elk pastures."

Even in homespun, hippie Missoula, Abbey writes that his speech was greeted with a "sitting" ovation and gunfire in the parking lot. When it was published in *Harper's* magazine, Abbey reported that it was "rewarded by the usual blizzard of abuse, some seventy-five letters from outraged cattlepersons, including one Gretel Ehrlich of Shell, Wyoming (another instant redneck)." Ehrlich, a Californian who had moved to Wyoming and helped support herself with ranch work, is the author of several books. Her letter denounced Abbey as "arrogant, incoherent, flippant, nonsensical, nasty, and unconstructive . . ."

It was a typical reaction to Abbey, who had indeed verged on incoherence that alcoholic night in Montana and was flippant at the best of times. His style was just a little too, well, a little too *human* for certain kinds of people. Funny when you looked at the people he offended. It was never someone like Katie Lee, one of Abbey's oldest friends, a river rat and cowgirl poet extraordinaire, who qualified as one of the toughest broads in the West.

Of course, there weren't too many Katie Lees around. The pool of readers offended by Abbey's views was broad and diverse. For instance, the editors of *The New York Times* Op-Ed page rejected an article that he wrote on illegal immigration. After unsuccessfully making the rounds of national publications, the column was finally accepted by the Phoenix-based alternative weekly *New Times*. Even the weekly's owner, a feisty Irishman from Jersey City named Mike Lacey, took the precaution of publishing it alongside a rebuttal piece. "Stop every campesino at our southern border, give him a handgun, a good rifle, and a case of ammunition, and send him home. He will know what to do with our gifts and good wishes," Abbey had written somewhat naively. Protest letters streamed in to *New Times* after the piece ran—all from Anglos.

Criticism from the politically correct only provoked Cactus Ed to greater orneriness. For instance, Abbey's reply to Ehrlich and other defenders of the cowboy was positively gleeful. "Our cowgirls and beef ranchers are such *sensitive* people—touchier than lesbians, thin-skinned and high-strung as prima ballerinas. ('Nasty and unconstructive'—I love that)," he wrote in the unregenerate introduction to *One Life at a Time, Please.*

Like Abbey, Howie Wolke had gone through a prickly transformation from dude to real live westerner. He had been working on ranches since arriving in Wyoming in the mid-1970s. In 1978, he started an outdoor guide service called Wild Horizons, but for about ten years he kept taking outside work while he built the business. Usually he worked as a cowhand or an irrigator, often at the Parker Ranch outside Dubois. Howie couldn't be as articulate about it as Ed Abbey (even when he was just as loaded) but his philosophical transformation had followed the same curve. Until he saw the depressing effects of overgrazing in the West, he had viewed cowboys as romantic figures. He couldn't help feeling contemptuous of the little nerd, Judge Cramer, the "preppie transplant" who had sentenced him. It was like getting screwed by your own ignorant younger self.

It was especially ironic because Wolke felt that he had been reasonable about this Greyback Ridge thing. Maybe too reasonable. Wolke, along with the Jackson Hole Alliance for Responsible Planning, had actually helped cut a deal with Chevron. If their test well came up sucking air, Chevron had agreed to reclaim the road. The company also agreed to pay a hunting guide $10,000 because his hunting camp would be off-limits to the public while they searched for oil.

All this good behavior was conditional on the environmentalists' promise not to sue. It was a classic trade-off, a RARE II situation in miniature, but it seemed unavoidable. Howie and the others weren't thrilled with the idea of a road in a steep, easily eroded section of a big roadless area, but the mineral rights had been sold years before. Howie had already agreed to the deal with Chevron when the Bridger-Teton forest supervisor startled everyone by insisting that the road be kept open after the oil company left. Wolke and the other environmentalists knew what that meant—an ugly snowball effect. Give these land rapers an inch, and they'll take a mile. As soon as Chevron was out of the way, Greyback Ridge would be clearcut.

"That's when we decided you just can't reason with this agency," Howie told a sympathetic female reporter from the Casper *Star-Tribune*. But these nuances were lost on Justice of the Peace Cramer, who even called Howie a "coward" for monkeywrenching. Howie replied that it hadn't been cowardice that got him caught, but foolhardiness. Howie had seen the surveyor in the distance that morning. But he decided to go ahead with his Sunday-afternoon stroll anyway. "I spotted him before he spotted me and, at that point, should immediately have said, this is not the time. But I had set that day aside and being a compulsive Type A type of guy I decided to go ahead," Howie recalled. "I was thirty-three years old and afflicted with the nothing-can-happen-to-me syndrome."

Howie wasn't the only one with that syndrome. It was racing through Earth First! like a bad case of flu. The old saw about safety in numbers was particularly untrue when it came to thousands of people thumbing their noses at the federal government. But the psychological effect of being in the tribe defied reality, even if Earth First! was really nothing more than a patched-together, hyped-up conglomeration of rednecks, hippies, and general misfits. (When asked in 1991 if Earth First! was a "tribe," Mike Roselle snorted. "Not as much as the Grateful Dead," he said.) But in 1986, when Howie Wolke was sentenced, many people, Foreman included, still believed that Earth First! might coalesce into a less schizophrenic version of the American dream. Foreman could sense the slow fracturing of the nation-state. The global economy was literally taking places apart, not just in the United States, but around the globe. Indigenous people who had lived in Malaysian rain forests for thousands of years were being torn from their way of life because Japan needed timber. In the United States, company towns were turning into ghost towns as timber giants like Louisisana-Pacific closed mills in the Pacific Northwest and opened operations in Mexico, where labor was cheaper. The big national groups could not seem to respond adequately to a growing sense that communities were under siege. The United States and other enlightened First World countries could pass all the environmental laws they wanted. But on the international level, there was virtually no regulation of industry.

By the late 1980s, two new models for environmental organizations emerged. Sophisticated environmentalists set up international networks, such as the Rainforest Action Network and the Dolphin Project. Fax machines and electronic mail—high-tech, low-cost communications gear used by multinational corporations to hasten their hegemony—also made it possible for protests to start almost instantly. For instance, when more than thirty people were arrested for blockading a logging road being bulldozed into the Malaysian rain forest in 1987, the computer bulletin board Econet broadcast the news to environmentalists around the world. The protesters were released in a few weeks, which many environmentalists attributed to the international letter-writing campaign made possible by Econet.

But most people were not sophisticated or technologically adept enough to tap into global communications. They reacted in a more visceral way to being buffeted by the tides of international commerce. In the 1980s, literally hundreds of small, grass-roots environmental groups were formed around the United States by frustrated, disenfranchised citizens working outside established channels. Foreman tapped into this phenomenon with his inspirational public appearances. As globalization increased, so did Earth First!'s membership. By 1986 the number of Buckaroos—and wanna-be Buckaroos—had already exceeded anyone's expectations. A startling number of them shared Foreman's rootless background, either because they were military brats or because their families had moved around frequently for other reasons. In a sense, they *were* a tribe, unified by their desire to build cohesiveness out of the ruins of a social structure resembling the gray, smoking landscape of postwar Berlin. Hope had become a scarce commodity for everyone, but particularly for environmentalists. It was seductive to believe that Earth First! might go the distance, set a new paradigm, build a new society. Foreman, in particular, was riding high on the movement's success.

"It was only a couple of years ago when there were four or five of us in a car and someone came up with the thought that if we got squashed by a semi truck there would be no Earth First! movement," he said in May 1986. "We're at the point now where it would take a much larger vehicle," he laughed.

There was no way to tell precisely how many Earth First!ers there were. In the second half of the 1980s, the number of subscribers to the *Earth First! Journal* was about 5,000. It was an impressive number, considering the publication's strange combination of dry scientific writing and gonzo politics. For instance, an article with the headline "DENVER BEARS PROTEST YELLOWSTONE" written by someone called "Gainesburger" began this way: "Dogmeat the Berserker had spoken and Colorado Earth First! apeared [*sic*] at the National Park Service Regional Headquarters in Denver to answer the call. At the Park Service sign in a landscaped decorator 'environment,' complete with token pines, we unfurled Brush Wolf's banner, 'U.S. PARK SERVICE: GRIZZLY KILLERS.' " In the same issue, ethnobotanist, author, and MacArthur fellow Gary Paul Nabhan would exhibit some of his least user-friendly prose. "Whereas the tropical agroforester has few growthforms, but many tree species from which to choose, desert agroecologists are actively investigating the genetic resources of water-efficient cacti, drought-evading annuals, drought-escaping perennial tubers and salt-tolerant shrubs," wrote Nabhan.

What made the *Journal*'s growth even more amazing was its relatively high price, which by 1986 had crept up from 0 cents to two dollars a copy and later reached three dollars. Despite its unevenness, the *Journal* clearly was serving a purpose for western environmentalists who wanted the straight poop, unencumbered by the internal politics that weighed down other conservation magazines. Reading the *Journal* was like listening to a friend talk to you on the phone, assuming that your friend was either a scientist or an overly committed maniac with idiosyncratic spelling.

There seemed to be a sizeable number of both breeds running around the hinterland, although the *Journal*'s figures didn't tell the whole story. Like every other environmental group, the number of active members in Earth First! was much smaller than the number of folks willing to ante up a few bucks and receive a publication. Many people who considered themselves Earth First!ers didn't subscribe to the *Journal*. The inner circle, people who were dressing up as bears and getting arrested, was usually a couple of hundred people. But that was enough to grab headlines in publications ranging from *The Wall Street Journal* to the *Corvallis Gazette-Times*. Earth First! was fast becoming a highly charged electrode stuck to the body politic—the shock it delivered was based on intensity, not size.

In 1984, Dave Foreman and Nancy Morton moved the *Earth First! Journal* to Tucson, where Nancy was entering the graduate program in nursing at the University of Arizona. Soon after the move, Dave flew home to New Mexico for a quick visit. Over the years, Foreman and his father had established a friendly relationship. Skip had mellowed and so had Dave. They never talked about it, just gradually let the conflict fall away. Maybe it had helped when the other kids had problems. Roxanne, the baby of the family, was going a little wild in high school, and Steve had gotten into real trouble with drugs. Somehow these days everyone was staying on speaking terms, even though they weren't always on *polite* speaking terms. In fact, when Dave went home that time, Steve came over to see him. The family was sitting down to dinner when Skip clutched his chest. It was a heart attack. He was dead within minutes.

Two years later, Steve died of an overdose. It had been a long time since Steve was the golden-haired boy Lorane Foreman liked to remember. He had been a heroin addict and a drug dealer since college. His habit had bankrupted Lorane both financially and psychologically. When he died, Dave was numb. He was relieved that his mother's ordeal was over, but he couldn't bring himself to feel much of anything for Steve. Roxanne was the one who grieved. She had been closer to Steve, but it was more than that. She was the one in the family who felt things. Dave buried his regrets and moved on.

Within a year or two after Dave and Nancy arrived in Tucson, a cadre of Earth First! supporters had grown up around the couple. Ron Kezar began spending winters in Tucson, living at Dave and Nancy's house and working on the *Earth First! Journal*. Soon an eccentric back-to-the-lander named Lynn Jacobs migrated down from Northern Arizona with his wife and two kids. Jacobs, who had grown up in an affluent Republican family in southern California and resembled an off-kilter Clint Eastwood, had an interest in cattle grazing that bordered on the obsessional. Earth First! was the only environmental group that met his criteria for antigrazing fervor. Jacobs spent the next three years hunched over a word processor, grinding out a self-published tome called *Waste of the West*, a lively and encyclopedic, if spottily referenced, "Everything You Always Wanted to Know About Grazing—Even If You Didn't *Know* You Wanted to Know It."[1]

In February 1985, a skinny kid named John Davis showed up at the door of the suburban tract house that Morton had bought in the foothills of the Tucson Mountains. Davis had graduated from college a few weeks before, but he looked no older than fourteen. He had written a letter to the *Earth First! Journal*, but Foreman had merely filed it with the usual mail. When Foreman answered the doorbell, Davis offered up his services to Earth First! He had majored in environmental ethics at a well-respected school in Minnesota that nonetheless sounded like a sitcom joke—St. Olaf's—and didn't know how to do anything particularly useful. But free labor was free labor. John Davis became the *Earth First! Journal*'s junior staff member.

Davis might have resembled a baby stork, but he actually was fairly competent for a twenty-two-year-old fresh out of college. He made himself useful at the *Journal* and eventually was made managing editor. By summer he had also managed to move in with Dave and Nancy, who appreciated the free ice cream he brought home after strenuous evenings of ecological dumpster diving.

By then Roger Featherstone had arrived, too. Featherstone was a farm boy from Wisconsin who had been radicalized by the antinuclear movement of the 1970s. His dour upbringing made him sound like a twentieth-century John Muir: hard work at an early age, low cash flow, strict but honorable parents.

By the time he dropped out of an electrical engineering program at a state college, the plodding farm boy had become a rebel. In 1975, he started working with Northern Thunder, an antinuke outfit in Wisconsin. A few years later, he got involved with a group of farmers called the Bolt Weevils, who were fighting plans to run a high-voltage power line across their land. Back in 1972, two Minnesota power companies had hatched a plan to build a giant coal-burning power plant next to a North Dakota strip mine. The plant's electricity would run across a 430-mile power line through North Dakota and Minnesota to just outside the suburbs of Minneapolis. It would be the largest direct-current line in the United States, carrying 800,000 volts of electricity.

In two Minnesota counties, farmers took the unusual step of organizing to fight the power line. They had a gut feeling that living under high-voltage lines was dangerous, and this would be the highest-voltage power line ever built. In 1975, the farmers succeeded in getting the county supervisors to deny the right of eminent domain to the power company.

The local authorities were quickly overruled. Eventually the case went all the way up to the Minnesota Supreme Court, where they were overruled again. The power line was going through. In June 1976, power company surveyors were met by sixty angry farmers blocking their path. Over the next several weeks the blockade grew in strength until it reached several hundred people. There was not much violence, just a bunch of obdurate farmers refusing to move.

But the power companies had just gotten the biggest loan ever made by the Rural Electrification Administration. They had plenty of money and plenty of clout. Out of a total of 500 Minnesota state troopers, 200 were assigned to patrol the power line. The companies hired 300 of their own security guards. By 1978, the survey was complete. The 1,685 steel towers began rising out of the wheat fields.

On the night of August 2, 1978, the first tower crashed. The Bolt Weevils had struck. In the next week, three more towers went down. Over the next year, ten more towers toppled. The companies offered $50,000, then $100,000, as a reward for information. Eventually they gave technical ownership of the line to the federal government, so that the FBI could come in. Still, nobody was arrested.

In the end, neither civil disobedience nor Luddism could stop the power line. But token resistance continued even after it was energized. A few more towers fell—the last one on August 2, 1983, the fifth anniversary of the first. To most people, these acts seemed merely symbolic. But others, including the writer Noel Perrin, from whose *Harrowsmith* article much of this information is taken, say the $6 million in damage helped kill the same companies' plans for a 78-mile line called the Wilmarth Extension. Perrin also says that doubts raised by the Minnesota farmers helped stop a similar power line in Texas.

For Roger Featherstone, the farmers' resistance had personal as well as political significance. Although he often felt angry at the rigidity of his upbringing, he understood the farmers' stubbornness. He was struck by the lengths to which these traditional-minded, politically conservative people would go when they felt their rights had been violated. "One of my theories is that when push comes to shove conservative people are a lot more likely to do what they think is right," said Featherstone. "A lot of it there had to do with the fact that the people up there had been kicked around by lots and lots of things."

Featherstone also understood that the Bolt Weevils were a Populist phenomenon, a homegrown variation on the Luddite theme. The Populist movement of the late 1800s began as a reaction to the crop-lien system—a sort of company store setup—that existed in the South. The first Populist organization, the Farmers Alliance, formed in 1877 to bypass the crop-lien system by buying and selling goods cooperatively. But the lawful alternatives offered by the Farmers Alliance were not the only response to a system that was one step away from indentured servitude. In Delhi, Louisiana, the crop-lien system was so crushing that a band of small farmers rode into town in 1889 and demolished the stores of merchants "to cancel their indebtedness," in

a rebellion very much like the English food riots. Before it was sub-
sumed into the Democratic party shortly before the turn of the century, Populism had moved northward to Featherstone's territory, the
upper Midwest.[2]

Although Populism eventually died out as a political movement,
many of its beliefs and mores persisted in rural American culture.
These included a tendency to close ranks against big banks and big
business. For instance, Roger's father refused to buy anything on
credit. Roger himself had even attended a few penny sales—foreclo-
sures where local farmers pushed aside other bidders to buy the farm
and its machinery for pennies and sell it back to its original owner.

During the Bolt Weevil days, Roger lived in northern Minnesota
for six months, working with farmers who were just as strongly
united—this time to fight the power line. It didn't take him long to
realize that the Bolt Weevils were following Edward Abbey's prescription for ethical sabotage. They had exhausted all the legal reme-
dies before taking out their monkeywrenches. "I think it's important
that everybody went through the [legal] process many, many times
and the process was really, really slanted. After that, they decided they
might as well go for it," said Featherstone.

Featherstone was the kind of person who went for it, too. He
threw himself into politics, almost deliberately losing track of everything else in his life. In the early 1980s, Featherstone burned out. He
took the profits from a few seasons of construction work and bought
a house in South Dakota. "I retired," he says. "Raised peaches,
growed chickens, threw out my TV." He lasted a year or two. A
friend had given him a subscription to the *Earth First! Journal*. In late
1983, he read that a guy he knew in Ashland, Wisconsin, was hosting
an Earth First! Road Show. Featherstone packed his dog in the pickup
and headed down to Eau Claire, where he remembers staying up all
night drinking cheap Wisconsin beer with Foreman, Cecelia Ostrow,
and John Seed, who had flown in from Australia to join the band. By
spring Featherstone was in Tucson, stranded at his aunt's house after
a construction firm's check bounced. He looked up Foreman et al.
Mike Roselle was living at the house with Nancy and Dave. Roger

got to know Roselle, who invited him on a trip to Organ Pipe Cactus National Monument to celebrate the five-year anniversary of the founding of Earth First! After a lonely farm childhood and his long stretch of solitude in South Dakota, being welcomed into the unpretentious communal society of Earth First! was deeply gratifying to Featherstone. His whole tone of voice changes when he talks about the trip.

"I got kidnapped to go with them on the famous Organ Pipe trip. I went over to see if Roselle wanted to go for a couple of beers, there were all these people milling around, and he asked if I wanted to go. I think I had a tent and a sleeping bag still in the car. I borrowed a few clothes from him and that was it. There was the night when we went out drinking in Mexico, ten or eleven of us in Kezar's truck. We had a case of beer which we knew we couldn't get across the border. So he dropped us off and we crossed the fence illegally. That's when we became illegal aliens. By the time he picked us up we drank most of the beer. We set the empties out along the road to tell him where we were."

After the trip, Roselle took off for Grants Pass and Roger moved into Nancy's brick house on Calle Carapan. John Davis's possessions were already ensconced, and Davis himself would be moving in when he got back from a family trip to France. After a couple of months Roger stopped working in construction and went to work full-time for Earth First! This unlikely commune—Dave, Nancy, John, and Roger—became the Earth First! office support staff for the next few years.

Like most communal situations, the Calle Carapan household had its problems. Roger and Dave were not a great match. Foreman woke up early, like most desert-rats. He wanted everybody else around him to be on the same schedule. Roger would sit around all morning, then get energized around two in the afternoon and work until the middle of the night. Since Roger was the only handy one in the house, he often promised to fix things. Sometimes they got fixed, sometimes they didn't. But the living arrangement hung together, at least for a while. It helped that Foreman was on the road a lot of the time. He was becoming a hot property on college campuses, where he could get paid as much as $1,500 for a speech. After the speech, there would usually be a potluck at someone's house. Local Earth First!ers would show up, and for a few minutes Foreman would slip away to talk quietly with them at the edge of the yard. It was a remarkably efficient system, with Foreman's speaking engagements providing a hefty chunk of Earth First!'s organizing budget. It might also have been considered a bit of a scam, if the left-leaning professors who booked the bearded, rafter-shaking radical hadn't been in on it. Besides, Foreman's speech was worth every penny. It was mind-bending, the things people said to him afterward. They acted as if he were some kind of a saint, even though he made sure to throw in a little self-deprecating humor whenever he could.

Flattering as all this attention was, it wasn't enough to make Foreman entirely complacent. In 1985, another patron saint of the environmental movement, the legendary David Brower, was ousted by Friends of the Earth. This was the second time that Brower had been overthrown; FOE was the group that he had founded after having been dismissed as the Sierra Club's executive director in 1969. Foreman rushed to Brower's defense, saying that if there were a Mount Rushmore for environmentalists, David Brower's face would be carved on it. But Brower's ouster caused Foreman tentatively to question his own role in Earth First! In early 1986, *New York Times* reporter Daniel Goleman wrote a revealing piece on the psychology of entrepreneurs. Foreman recognized himself in Goleman's article. For one thing, the experts called entrepreneurs "wild men," echoing Bernard De Voto, who, in the 1930s, had called the westerner "the national wildman, the thunder-bringer, disciple of madness, begetter of economic heresy, immoral nincompoop deluded by maniac visions, forever clamoring, forever threatening the nation's treasury, forever scuttling the ship of state."[3] Foreman was all those things, and he reveled in them. But Goleman's article contained a more somber prediction for the man one writer dubbed Summer Thunder.

"To understand the entrepreneur, you first have to understand the psychology of the juvenile delinquent," joked Harvard Business School psychoanalyst Abraham Zaleznik in Goleman's article. A desire for autonomy, which characterizes entrepreneurs, is also a hallmark of the adolescent, Zaleznik said. But the entrepreneur's sense of autonomy is neither simple, immature, nor easily dismissed.

Zaleznik and other analytical psychologists believe that visionary entrepreneurs—David Brower, Steve Jobs of Apple computers, and Dave Foreman are just a few examples—are striving to create the world they craved as children. It is "a world with him as star," where the entrepreneur can outdo even his main rival—his father.

"The tale of childhood that emerged most often was of a young boy who felt close to his mother and disappointed by his father," writes Goleman. Clinical psychologist Harry Levinson concurred, saying, "In some subtle, or not-so-subtle, ways the mother lets the son believe at an early stage that he has a chance to win out in the rivalry with his father."

If Levinson's perception is true, it doesn't require much of a leap to see how the combination of Skip Foreman's absences and his mother's rapt attention could have helped Foreman to grow into the "wild man" at the Wilderness Society. Levinson points out that there may be nothing horribly wrong with an entrepreneur's family. In fact, having a child who grows up to be an entrepreneur may be a sign that a mother has done her job right, by giving her offspring increasingly complex tasks that he succeeds in mastering.

But when there is a strong rivalry between father and son, it almost invariably gets enacted in the workplace. In the case of the entrepreneur it is enacted in a particular way, Levinson believes. "The entrepreneur handles these ghosts of childhood past by rebellion. The final act in this inner drama comes when the entrepreneur frees himself from tyranny by creating his own world," Levinson asserted.

A sense of tyranny also may be evidence of what psychoanalysts call "splitting," said John J. Kao, a psychiatrist who teaches a course on entrepreneurs at Harvard Business School. "For the entrepreneur this takes the form of a mental split in how he sees the world: one domain is full of blocks and frustrations, and the other is an ideal of freedom. He is compelled to seek his freedom by building his own business rather than staying trapped in someone else's," said Kao.

Certainly Foreman's rhetoric was riddled with the extremes of freedom and tyranny. His favorite analogy linked Earth First!ers to the rowdies of the Boston Tea Party, who dumped stores of tea overboard to protest taxation without representation. His aim was to construct Earth First! to embody a similar spirit of responsible rebellion. For instance, some accounts mention that the Tea Party rebels replaced a lock that was broken during their spree. Boston was a small town in those days, and everyone knew one another, including the rebels and the merchants who owned the boats. It wasn't that different from Earth First!'s habit of notifying timber companies after spiking their trees. In both cases, there was a tacit understanding that this was not pure vandalism, but an attempt to overcome a block to negotiations by reducing the disparity between the two sides. There also seemed to be a psychological denial of the act's warlike overtones—and the response they were likely to provoke.

This "act now, think later" approach is common to entrepreneurs. Goleman called it "goalless planning." It also has been described as "a flexible and action-oriented strategy" rather than the rational goal-setting that is supposedly common to large organizations. In other words, entrepreneurs tend to be intuitive, charming risk-takers. They set things in motion without knowing exactly in which direction they will go. "Let action set the finer points of our philosophy," Foreman often admonished people. So Earth First! became a mishmash of deep ecology and spontaneous, kick-out-the-jams, in-your-face blockading. Whatever worked.

In 1986 it seemed to be working better than anyone could have reasonably expected. But according to Goleman's article, all the guts in the world couldn't help the entrepreneur who failed to adjust to the managers he had hired. Steve Jobs, who was bounced from Apple after hiring manager John Sculley, was the perfect case in point. "The great entrepreneur accomplishes his act of conception at the price of his own extinction," John Kenneth Galbraith once said. Goleman concurred. "An entrepreneur's gifts and drives—such as goalless planning and the maverick's thirst for autonomy—do not necessarily serve him well as the leader of a major corporation," he wrote. When he read this, Foreman wondered if he, too, might become a victim of built-in obsolescence. The writer and editor Angela Gennino, who had worked with David Brower at Friends of the Earth, called it "founder syndrome."

At least if Foreman went down in flames it would be for a good cause. Goleman ended his article by talking about the appeal that entrepreneurs have for young people. "The answer may lie, in part, in the hopeful lesson he teaches," Goleman wrote, "a lesson of increasing import as huge corporations dominate work life more and more, and as economic horizons appear dimmer for each coming generation. By virtue of his tenaciously solitary course, the entrepreneur holds out a hopeful message that life is not a trap but a promise."

"We have become a force greater than geology in determining the future of evolution," Foreman admonished college students all over the country. "It's our decision whether the charismatic megafauna in the future will still have grizzly bears and great blue whales in it, or whether there will be cockroaches or Norway rats. It gets depressing after a while. That's why I drink as much beer as I do. If I thought about it all the time I'd go stark, raving mad. That's why I take Ed Abbey's advice a lot and get out in the wilderness and enjoy it. But we've got to encounter the problem, we've got to encounter the magnitude, the enormity of what our generation is doing to the planet. If we confront that I think then we've got to ask what can we do about it, how can we begin to deal with it? I mean, do we just give up, go home, stick something in the VCR and run out a line of coke, sit back, and forget?

"If we can see that grizzly bears and mosquitoes and redwoods and algae have value in and of themselves and are important just like we are, then I think we start making the first step. And after you begin to think of other things as having intrinsic value, I think the next step is emotion; to be passionate, to feel." This was what his audience had been waiting to hear. All their lives, they had been waiting for permission to do the precise thing that their society was telling them not to do—feel.

You know, when I went back to Washington, D.C., to be a lobbyist in the mid-seventies, a U.S. senator put his arm around my shoulders and said, "You know, Dave, we can work with you. You're reasonable. You know how to compromise and consider other interest groups." I was told to put my heart in a safe deposit box and replace my brain with a pocket calculator, to not get emotional. That would harm my argument. I'd ruin my credibility. . . .

But, goddammit, I *am* emotional! I am passionate. I'm angry. I feel something. I'm not some New Age automaton, some goddamn computer, a pocket calculator. I don't have silicon chips up here. I'm flesh and blood. The winds fill my lungs, the mountains make my bones, the oceans run through my veins. I'm an animal and I'll never be anything but an animal. When a chain saw rips into a two-thousand-year-old redwood tree, it's ripping into my guts. When a bulldozer plows through a virgin hillside, it's plowing through my side, and when a bullet knocks down a grizzly bear or a wolf, it's going through my heart. . . . We think with the whole world, we're alive with the whole world. We're not blocked off, just these robots, these unfeeling things. But that's how we've become. We're afraid to love somebody else, to love a place, to feel something because we might get hurt. We don't want to get hurt. Don't care about anything, just cut yourself off, be a happy yuppie robot. That's the way George Bush wants you to be. That's the way Exxon wants you to be. . . .

About twenty years ago, there was a wonderful little case in northern New Mexico that made all the supermarket checkout stand tabloids. The cattle mutilations. I don't know if any of you remember that, but dead cows were being found and there were no external wounds on them at all, but their livers were gone. Cut out with surgical precision. And I mean, the ranchers just freaked out. I mean, obviously there were some Satan-worshiping hippies out there with laser beams doing weird rituals with their dead cows. There were little green men with flying saucers doing something. I mean, it got really freaky in northern New Mexico. The governor nearly had to call out the National Guard to quiet things down. But the New Mexico Cattle Growers Association decided to get to the bottom of this. So they hired a retired FBI agent. He took the latest Vietnam War technology, starlight scopes and all this neat stuff, and staked out a dead cow. Every night for a week he watched the dead cow. And you know what he found? I mean, it wasn't hippies. No Satanists, no laser beams, not a single flying saucer. You know who was doing it? Weasels! Weasels. Little carnivores about this big. Weasels are real smart little critters but they're also really hungry and they have a real high metabolism. They have to eat their own body weight every day or something like that, or they starve to death. And weasels know dead cow liver is really good. It's tasty, highly nutritious, easy to chew up. There's only one problem. If you're a little weasel this size, there's a lot of hair, hide, muscle, bone, and fat between you and that cow liver in the dead cow.

But weasels are smart. They know if they walk around the hind legs of that dead cow there's a perfect pathway in there to the liver. Eat the liver, go home for the day, come back the next night, eat the pancreas.

And when I die I want a weasel to crawl up inside of me and eat my liver. I want buzzards to peck my eyeballs out. I want mountain lions to crunch my bones. Because I want to live forever. I don't want to be pickled and stuck in a lead box. That's how you *die*. I want to be recycled. I want to run around the forest on little weasel feet. I want to go back into the flow, I want to be part of the food chain.

When death comes, I want to enjoy it. I want to embrace it. Let's not be afraid of dying. Let's not kill ourselves. Let's not pretend that we're immortal. We're all gonna die. There's nothing to be afraid of, nothing to avoid. If you aren't afraid to die, then you can be happy to live; you aren't afraid to live, you can open up, you can love somebody else and not be afraid of getting hurt. You can love a place and not worry about losing it, because you have the courage to go out and fight for it.

Foreman's words gave purpose to a whole generation of college students. To disillusioned middle-class environmentalists, he handed their dreams back. To back-to-the-land dropouts, he gave a sense of community. But even in heartfelt, do-gooding entrepreneurs like Foreman there is an element of hucksterism. Despite his attempts at self-restraint, Foreman was just too damn good at creating a legend. Not only did he pander to college audiences by larding his inspirational talk with incessant references to beer drinking; he also milked his hick horseshoer image for all it was worth. Here he was, a buckskinned Daniel Boone who had wandered into history—or better yet, the Andrew Jackson of the environmental movement. Hell, Foreman's encounter with the Antichrist James Watt in the Grand Canyon even *was* a myth. Doctoring up myth was, of course, a venerable tradition of the American West. As *New Yorker* writer Jane Kramer noted in her 1977 book, *The Last Cowboy*, the real cowboys were "range bums and drifters and failed outlaws, freed slaves and impoverished half-breeds, ruined farmers from the Reconstruction South and the tough, wild boys from all over who were the frontier's dropouts." The restorative power of myth transformed these "boys who had no appetite for the ties of land or family, who could make a four-month cattle drive across a thousand miles and not be missed by anyone." Eventually, "the myth, with its code and its solemn rhetoric, caught up with most of them, and if it left them still outside the law, at least it took the edge off their frightful lawlessness and made a virtue of their old failures."[4]

Not everyone came to the frontier from hovels in the New World. John James Audubon, another heroic figure who created his persona

out of the western myth, came from a hovel in the Third World—
Haiti, to be exact. After studying art in Paris, he pursued unsuccessful
get-rich-quick schemes for seventeen years, forcing his wife and family
to live in penury until he was seized by what he later called his "Great
Idea." For the next three decades, he raced around the continent,
drawing every American bird and beast. In a brilliant 1991 *New Yorker*
article, Adam Gopnik puts Audubon, whose real name was Jean Ra-
bin, in perspective.

> . . . Audubon's strange origins, his slow start, and the long
> period of shaky struggle in his middle years add to the clear,
> eighteenth-century glow of his legend a more peculiarly
> nineteenth-century American touch—of frontier purification
> and renewal and reform. Audubon's self-transformation from the
> dilettante in a ruffled shirt arriving in America into the Amer-
> ican woodsman eventually returning to France is one of the
> great awakenings in American biography. In his poem "Au-
> dubon: A Vision and a Question for You," Robert Penn War-
> ren called this transformation a "passion," lending a Christian
> overtone to the story of Audubon's rebirth in the wilderness.

Like Audubon, Foreman became the central character in his own
story of frontier rebirth. Surrounded by beautiful wild animals, the
"charismatic megafauna" that gave his speech its soundtrack of goose
music and wolf howls, Foreman left the East to become the source of
his own myth, a prime example of charismatic megafauna himself. Of
course, he was a native westerner. But as Mike Roselle later said,
Foreman was as much a military brat who wanted to be a redneck as
a real redneck. In fact, Foreman was more of an artist than anything
else. His speech was the canvas he repainted over and over again,
making minor changes to an eternal landscape. It was easy to mistake
the artist for his art. As Earth First! grew, Foreman found himself
battling to retain some degree of humility. But he also acted as the
Earth First! PR man. These two tasks were contradictory, to say the

least. The contradiction surfaced in Foreman's own comments on the subject in 1986.

"I think personality cults are by definition dangerous," he said, explaining that he went out of his way not to publish photos of himself in the *Earth First! Journal*. "It scares me when I think Earth First! has the potential to become one. You have to keep reminding yourself that it's not because of you, it's because you're expressing something.

"But I think there's a definite need in this drab environmental movement for people who can cause some kind of excitement," he added in a lighter tone. "There have always been shamans in society."

Doug Scott was less charitable toward the charismatic megafauna phenomenon. He lumped Foreman together with two of his main adversaries in the environmental movement, Brock Evans and David Brower. These white boys with their sensible running shoes made unlikely Savonarolas. But within their own arena they used the power of speech to unleash the collective unconscious. Since the death of Franklin D. Roosevelt—not to mention Adolf Hitler and Benito Mussolini—black preachers had cornered the market on the oral tradition. It required bravery to take on this role in the white-bread environmental movement. To be a powerful speaker wasn't seemly. It didn't fit the WASP mold. It meant you weren't serious enough. It might even be dangerous. Certainly Doug Scott felt a deep distrust of mob psychology. He despised the effects of mass adulation on his fellow environmental leaders. "When you start getting a standing ovation *before* you speak, you should retire," Scott usually responded when the name David Brower came up. Scott gave Foreman a little more credit. He seemed to believe that Foreman's own ideals had led him astray.

"If you scratch Dave very deep, what you've got is an old wilderness activist who believed his own rhetoric a little too strongly," said Scott.

I'm no mean public speaker myself. Dave Brower only gives one speech. I know two people who are *mesmerizing* public performers. One is Brock Evans. And the other is Dave Foreman. And I know both of them well enough and have talked to them candidly well enough to understand, I believe I understand, that they don't fully understand what that power that they have is. And Brock has said the same to me.

It is possible to have that kind of power and to be very self-indulgent with it. Self-indulgence, that's the word I attach to the Earth First! phenomenon more than anything. . . . Now, you get this whole horseshit history of Earth First! about how Dave went to Washington and was a Washington lobbyist par excellence and then walked away from that because it didn't work.

Dave was not very good at it. He gave it about a year's time . . . He had no mentor. . . . Dave went and tried being a lobbyist, wasn't very good at it, didn't think deeply about it. Doesn't have a strategic mind that matches the parliamentary procedures of the Congress. Dave and Tim Mahoney and Debbie were housemates for a long time. Fascinating to think about that. Tim has the best strategic mind I ever saw. Dave doesn't . . . Dave has this magic. The magic is not backed up by a very strong background in that particular kind of politics.

What I've always thought was kind of tragic was that we didn't have one creature who had a little bit of Tim and Doug and a little bit of Dave and Brock all in the same thing, who became—in the aftermath of Zahniser, because there had been no one since then—Brower got wrapped up in his own ego too much—he could have done it. And I wish I could have been it. I feel very badly that it was not in me to be it either. Who could mesmerize people to believe that our political system works.

Sadly for both Doug Scott and the environmental movement, he was right. No John Kennedy was emerging from the ranks. Neither the Yale-trained lobbyists nor any of a score of Patagonia-clad Berkeley individualists could unite the movement. Even a redneck from New Mexico couldn't do it. In fact, that wasn't his goal. Foreman didn't believe that the system worked, and he sure as hell wasn't going to try to convince people that it did. Foreman thought Scott's pre-Vietnam, pre-Watergate sensibility was mere nostalgia. Brock Evans, who was older than Scott, thought it was something else, but he wasn't sure what. Evans was confounded by Scott's near-worship of Howard Zahniser. Not only had Zahniser died before Scott had a chance to meet him, but Scott's own political victories came at a time when the piecemeal Zahniser approach was already becoming obsolete.

Scott's vision may have been a trifle narrow, but he wasn't far off the mark when it came to Foreman. In 1986, Foreman still tended to believe his own rhetoric a bit too wholeheartedly. "I think Earth First! steps out of the traditional spectrum," he told a reporter. "People are rebelling against technocracy, the anthropocentric imperialism of Western civilization. Earth First! is made up of people who are really trying to get back to their roots as a tribal civilization. When you're trying to do something that radical, outside of civilization, it's going to flower in a lot of different ways.

"The majority of the people in Earth First! are of the sixties generation, but there are some very respectable older people. That's the thing I love the most, is when I give a speech and old people, like this old clodhopper at the Texas Pow Wow, come up to me afterwards and tell me how much they liked it." Rednecks, middle-class people, backwoods hippies, and young wanna-be hippies "with their wooden bowls and chopsticks and . . . their soggy vegetables" were all part of the tribe, said Foreman, preaching a tolerance he didn't feel in his heart. What he neglected to mention were the real misfits who were attracted to Earth First! Documentary filmmaker Jessica Abbe, who shot footage of the group in the early 1980s, characterized Earth First!'s founders as "brilliant" but said that many of their followers were "one step up from street people."

There was a another, perhaps related, drawback to the group's laissez-faire attitude that Foreman was only beginning to recognize. Early in 1986, someone sabotaged a timber sale in Montana. Foreman claimed that the saboteurs were not affiliated with Earth First!, although they had hung an Earth First! banner at the scene. Worse than that, Foreman thought that the unaffiliated monkeywrenchers had picked the wrong target.

"What happened in Montana was that some idiot went out and spiked some trees and trashed a piece of equipment, then hung up an Earth First! banner," Foreman said, his twang growing broader with each angry syllable. "They did it to a small local logger. He wasn't running a bad logging operation, not something we would have a problem with, and it really hurt the Montana group."

Although the Montana incident made him angry, there hadn't been enough of these incidents yet to temper Foreman's pride in Earth First!'s miraculous growth. The group's anarchistic makeup had helped it spread around the country like a weed. Earth First! had reached Texas, where a group of swinging nudist Austinites were staging sit-ins to stop the extinction of endangered cave bugs. California was riddled with Earth First! groups. Even New England was getting into the act.

"We just roughed it out on the Mexico trip," Foreman said in the late spring of 1986. "I think we had the self-restraint to let Earth First! develop itself. It's hard to let go and trust other people, to say, 'OK, start a local Earth First! movement. Go for it. Here are some ideas, but use your creativity.' Other environmental groups are terrified to do it."

Despite these words, by summer Foreman was having serious doubts about the movement, which seemed to be taking on a life of its own. Foreman's Frankenstein fantasies surfaced only occasionally, usually when he was with a close friend like Jim Eaton. At the California Rendezvous, Foreman and Eaton perched up on a hill surveying the scene they had helped create. It was time for the day's mass consensus meeting. Foreman and Eaton watched as the California Earth First!ers sat in a circle, arguing. They couldn't hear what was being said, but they could imagine it. Vegetarianism had become a hot topic. Discussions about it had a navel-gazing quality, featuring such questions as Do you eat meat or not? How do you feel about it? Sometimes the women complained that they had to act too pushy to get a spot singing around the campfire. They didn't want to act aggressive because that would be buying into the male paradigm. So could the men be more considerate? At other times, complaints would be made about such important policy issues as excessive midnight howling, sloppy beer drinking, or loose dogs. Consensus would eventually be reached on these important issues, but it could take hours. Policy decisions on environmental issues were reached the same way, with predictable results.

Neither Eaton nor Foreman said much, but each could guess what the other was thinking. Foreman was getting the idea that Earth First! might turn into yet another remake of the movie *Little Shop of Horrors*. It would be offbeat casting, but could Foreman be playing the mild-mannered clerk who stumbles across a man-eating plant? At first the clerk enjoys the fame that the plant's tremendous size brings him. He tries to control its nasty appetite for blood. When that fails, he becomes a one-man Red Cross. But it's not enough for the plant. It gets hungrier. It begins eating people. The plant racks up quite a score before it attacks the clerk's girlfriend, a bleached-blond Brooklyn broad with a heart of gold, and he musters up the courage to dispatch it to houseplant hell.

Grim thoughts like these silently hung in the air as the two men looked out over the baked California hills and off into the Pacific Ocean. Finally, Foreman half-jokingly suggested they go into town for a politically incorrect cheeseburger.

Later that night, Eaton, Foreman, and a few others sat around the campfire getting drunk and telling war stories. A few members of the younger generation stood or crouched behind them, cradling beers and listening. Several hundred feet away, a second group sat in a circle in a grassy meadow trying to figure out how to create a new culture. Jim Eaton remembers thinking how different the two groups seemed. Foreman felt it, too. The ex-anthropology major from the University of New Mexico still liked the *idea* of creating a tribe. But when it came right down to it, Doug Scott was right. Foreman was an old wilderness activist at heart. This was not his tribe.

Still, there were compensations. Foreman liked being famous, or at least semifamous. In his childhood, he had often heard Skip tell stories about famous war heroes. Invariably these anecdotes ended with Skip gaining the upper hand. It was odd that the tight-lipped Air Force pilot would reveal this minor sign of insecurity. But not so odd that his high-achieving son, the recovering nerd, would exhibit the same impressionable nature. In the late 1980s, Foreman began moving in celebrity circles. It was very seductive when he realized that his reputation had preceded him. He couldn't help letting you know that he had just had a chat with Wendell Berry or thinking that a coffee-shop waitress recognized him when she really just thought he sounded like John Wayne. But he protested that he was just a regular guy, "a middle-aged, middle-class suburbanite." Occasionally he even said—not too loudly—that he was thinking of pulling back from Earth First!

If fame was a source of ambivalence to Foreman, it was both a danger and an opportunity for Earth First! The group was starting to attract a frightening amount of press coverage in 1986. *The New York Times* and *The Wall Street Journal* both ran articles on Earth First! which focused on the Oregon timber wars. *U.S. News and World Report* ran a piece on eco-radicals in general. *Mother Jones* ran a short piece on Earth First! and a larger story on the future of the environmental movement by social critic Kirkpatrick Sale. The following year, the *Los Angeles Times*, *Newsweek*, *Esquire*, and *The Nation* all published feature stories about this strange bunch of westerners.

Attention from the print media was gratifying, but not ground breaking. For an environmental group to land on TV, now *that* was radical. So it was only appropriate for the most radical environmental group in the United States to wind up on television. (Sea Shepherd, the maverick Greenpeace offshoot, was wilder, but because it operated outside the twelve-mile limit—in more ways than one—and was far smaller, it tended to get less publicity.) The group was on TV everywhere, from *Good Morning America* and the NBC national news to local coverage in Houston, Tucson, Salt Lake City, Portland, Seattle, and a string of other mid-sized cities. Getting on TV made everyone feel great, as if they were really accomplishing something. Hardly anybody thought about whether a group of people who were routinely breaking the law really wanted this attention. Hardly anybody except Ed Abbey. In 1982, Abbey got curious about whether he had been subversive enough to earn an FBI file. When he used the Freedom of Information Act to find out, he discovered that the FBI had been watching him since 1947, when he was a student at the Indiana State Teachers College in Indiana, Pennsylvania. He had posted a signed notice on a bulletin board that urged men to protest the draft, arguing that the arms race and peacetime draft would lead to World War III. The notice was classic Abbey. "Send your draft card with an explanatory letter to the president," it helpfully suggested. "He'll appreciate it, I'm sure." Although Abbey was just twenty—he had received his honorable discharge from the U.S. Army only months before—his tone wouldn't sound very different in the 1970s or 1980s, at least when the subject was authority.

There was more to the story. In Abbey's case, life seemed to imitate art and vice versa with uncanny frequency. Although Abbey didn't know at the time that the bulletin board incident had earned him a spot on the FBI's 100,000 "Sort of Wanted" list, the fate of Jack Burns, *The Brave Cowboy*'s protagonist, turns on a similar incident. Jack Burns has an FBI record, too. The police chief who must hunt Burns discovers that the cowboy was wounded in World War II and briefly attended the State University in "Duke City, New Mex." where he was "known to have attended secret meetings of so-called Anarchist group. . . .

"In March 1946 was one of five signers of document posted on University bulletin boards advocating so-called Civil Disobedience to Selective Service and other Federal activities," the fictional report goes on to state.

Burns's politics are his undoing. It is only after his anarchist background becomes known that Burns's escape attracts attention. If the political element had never surfaced, Burns would have quietly faded into the pockets and folds of the canyon country. Instead, he is brought down by the evil, machine-worshiping General Desalius and the reluctant, gum-chewing sheriff, Morey Johnson. Burns literally is cornered and killed by the Machine—an out-of-control truck driven by a man completely out of touch with the land or his own body. When Burns dies, so does the quintessentially American idea of freedom that he embodies.

The Brave Cowboy was published in 1956, only two years after Congress censured red-baiting Senator Joe McCarthy. The McCarthyesque repression that hammered down on Abbey's fictional hero, Jack Burns, and his friend Paul Bondi in *The Brave Cowboy* is more dramatic than what Abbey experienced—in Abbey's case, the FBI's busiest period was ten months of scrambling after him while he was working as a clerk-typist for the U.S. Geological Survey in 1952, supporting himself while he finished *Jonathan Troy*. The FBI kept trying to find out if he was a communist but failed to turn up enough evidence to get him fired. He wasn't exactly a communist, of course; he was something even more subversive—an anarchist. The FBI says its investigation of Abbey ended in 1967, when Abbey was working in Death Valley as a school-bus driver.[5]

When he received his files, Abbey wasn't at all surprised to find that the FBI had been keeping an eye on him, said Clarke Cartwright, his widow. Abbey believed that First Amendment rights are frequently disregarded "if you speak out against your government," she said. He also didn't believe that the investigation had ended. "We assumed all along that our telephone was tapped and perhaps there was even a bug in the house," said Cartwright.

In 1986, Abbey predicted that the stiff sentence meted out to Howie Wolke was only the overture for a campaign of government repression against Earth First! He called Foreman and the other Buckaroos "heroes." "I think they're risking very much for what they believe in. It's likely that they will be in some sort of serious trouble sooner or later," he said.

It was all part of a struggle that was growing more intense as resources dwindled. In the 1960s and 1970s, environmentalists were successful in mounting what Abbey called "a delaying action." But in the 1980s, they found themselves increasingly unable to hold the line. Abbey said he had always been willing to sacrifice a political point for the sake of a good story—or a cheap gag. But cheap gags were getting harder to come by. "More and more of us feel we have our backs against the wall. It's getting harder to make a comedy of it," said Abbey.[6]

Foreman also occasionally thought about the possibility of reprisal. "It's real easy to get paranoid and think everybody is a cop," Foreman said in 1986. "The simple fact is, if you're gonna get somebody, you're gonna get them, whether it's Karen Silkwood getting run off the road or someone planting dope in my wood stove. But worrying doesn't help."

The bigger the movement got, the more danger Foreman was in. Foreman knew it. But as he later admitted, he knew it in his head, not his gut. It was that same old virus, the nothing-can-happen-to-me syndrome. When he did fantasize about something bad coming down, Foreman imagined a shoot-out in the Old West. He would go out in a blaze of gory glory. It would have to be that way. In true romantic fashion, Foreman had pledged himself to fight to the death. At least that's how the speech went. "Aldo Leopold said, 'Of what value are forty freedoms without a blank spot on the map?' " Foreman reminded people at the 1989 California Wilderness Conference. "He talked about those who loved wild things and sunsets. And for me, I agree with Leopold. I do not care to be a domesticated animal. So I can do no less than to look at the next twenty-five years and pledge my life, my fortune—meager as it is—and my sacred honor to try to restore ecological wilderness to the United States and to this planet and I think that's the new crusade that the entire environmental movement must embark on."

But Foreman hadn't been much more than a toddler during the McCarthy era. In the days of COINTELPRO—the FBI's covert campaign against the antiwar movement and the Black Panthers— Foreman had been, however briefly, a Marine. His sense of government persecution was an unrealistic combination of abstract intellectualizing and his melodramatic imagination.

In fact, Howie Wolke's heavy sentence was a bad sign. The idea of monkeywrenching alone was enough to give Earth First! a bad name among most of the people who lived in the rural communities surrounding national forests. But a specific kind of monkey-wrenching—tree spiking—made them positively livid. The threat of violence was a wild card. It made Earth First! famous. But it led even some environmentalists to regard them as traitors. "If Earth First! didn't exist, the oil companies would have invented it," was a typical comment. Even Foreman was unable to make up his mind about whether monkeywrenching did Earth First! more harm than good. But unlike Mike Roselle, he was honest enough to admit that, yeah, someone could get hurt. He was prepared to take the risk.

"As far as hard-core physical nonviolence goes, it's life denying," he said. "You corner anything and it's going to fight."

Foreman and most other Earth First!ers had the sense of crisis that is the common denominator for all radical action. Ed Abbey had cast the mold in his "Foreward!" to Foreman's book *Ecodefense*. "If a stranger batters your door down with an axe, threatens your family and yourself with deadly weapons, and proceeds to loot your home of whatever he wants, he is committing what is universally recognized—by law and morality—as a crime. In such a situation the householder has both the right and the obligation to defend himself, his family, and his property by whatever means are necessary. . . . The American wilderness, what little remains, is now undergoing exactly such an assault." As for monkeywrenching, Foreman's bottom line was this: "You're basing it on an ethic. It's not just mindless, angry vandalism. We minimize any possible danger, but when it comes down to it, I'm not philosophically nonviolent. These guys don't have to be cutting trees. They're doing it to make a buck."

Them's fightin' words. If the goal of Earth First! was to become "the forest defending itself" as Australian Earth First!er John Seed phrased it, then the group was succeeding. In the guise of the Buckaroos and their soggy hippie supporters, the forest wasn't just defending itself; it was rioting.

On May 8, 1987, a twenty-three-year-old timber worker in Cloverdale, California, was rushed to the hospital. His name was George

Alexander and his face looked like confetti. Alexander had been standing near a head-rig band saw at a Louisiana-Pacific lumber mill when its blade hit a sixty-penny nail. *Brrr. Contact.* A twelve-foot piece of steel flew through the air. It struck Alexander's face, shattering the Lexan face shield that hung down from his hard hat. It fractured his jawbone, severed his jugular vein, broke his upper and lower front teeth, and caused "multiple lacerations."

Nothing was ever the same for Earth First!

The story of Alexander's maiming was published in the *San Francisco Chronicle* on May 9. As the story was picked up by other publications, odd details began surfacing. Odd, that is, if you knew anything about Earth First! For instance, the log that was spiked came from a second-growth redwood tree. But usually Earth First!ers only cared about first growth—primeval forest, ancient forest, old growth. Then company loggers reported that a decapitated, skinned dog carcass was found on a tractor in the woods near the trees that had been spiked. Bad craziness.

When they heard the news on the radio, Mike Roselle and Karen Pickett were on their way up north to visit Karen's sister. They stopped at an environmental center in Garberville to try to find out what had happened. The rumor was that the culprit was a right-wing crackpot who owned land adjacent to the property where the trees were being cut. Later, a Marxist carpenter-turned-Earth First!er named Judi Bari said she found out that the accident had occurred because the mill's band-saw blade was old and unsafe. Even if these rumors were correct, it was too late. By the time Roselle's denial reached print, the damage was done. Press coverage of Earth First! took a radical turn to the right.

"Terrorists for nature proclaim Earth First!" ran the headline on the *Chicago Tribune* story. "Earth First! 'Fanatics' Try to Keep Things Wild" trumpeted the *Los Angeles Times*. What had gone wrong? What happened to the good-humored outlaws of *Outside* magazine's "Real Monkeywrench Gang"?

Herb Chao Gunther thinks he knows. Gunther is the resident boy genius at the Public Media Center, the politically correct advertising think tank in San Francisco where Jerry Mander eventually landed. To Gunther, part of the problem was the "accidental" nature of Earth First!'s development.

"A lot of other organizations—the Sierra Club Legal Defense Fund, the Sierra Club—very consciously planned their development, and they controlled the phases a little bit more," said Gunther. "Earth First! didn't. Early on the monkeywrenching gave them a boost because it got them attention that they would never have gotten otherwise. But then it started working against them."

Gunther, a round-faced man who is a nonstop talker and a powerful figure in progressive politics, believes political movements go through several phases. In the first phase, the movement consists of a small circle of people. This is the creative period, the era of Victorio's monument, Dave Foreman's memos, the first Rendezvous. The group is still defining itself.

In the second phase, the group begins to get attention. They crack the Glen Canyon Dam. "The media becomes fascinated with an unknown organization that claims to do radical direct action. As a small organization, it's not caught up in a lot of contradictions or controversies. They're easier to define. They're easier to project. It's a more elegant institution to write about or talk about."

In the third phase, the group becomes romanticized. Stewart McBride dubs them "The Real Monkeywrench Gang" in hip, macho *Outside* magazine. "In the growth of Earth First!, the movement, when it's defined in very romantic terms, there's not a lot of fact. There's no track record to speak of, no contradictions, no controversies, no real leadership struggles, no issues of policy. It's very easy to be an eco-warrior without ever having gone to war around anything." In this phase, there is a "mad rush" of people who have read about Earth First! in left-wing or obscure publications. They come to hear Dave Foreman or Mike Roselle speak. They attend a few Earth First! meetings. Maybe they join the road blockades in Oregon. The media's heavy artillery is wheeled out. Earth First! gets big-time attention, but the tone is still relatively uncritical. The organization attracts a lot more people. Real political debates begin.

By the time the fourth phase rolls around, the honeymoon is over. "All the illusions are gone and the media begins to take a harsh look," said Gunther. "People step back and say, 'Boy, these people are dangerous. They're crazy. They're eccentric. They're weird. I wouldn't want my daughter to go out with one of them . . .'

"Then the realization sets in that Earth First! really doesn't count for much in terms of actual change. It's symbolic."

Far from making it irrelevant, Earth First!'s symbolism is the reason Gunther thinks it's important. In 1986, Gunther offered to mount a direct-mail campaign for Earth First! He said he was motivated by a belief that the "raging debate" provoked by Earth First! is a necessary prerequisite for social change, both inside and outside the environmental movement.

Gunther met with Mike Roselle and Dave Foreman. He found himself in the unaccustomed role of trying to convince Earth First! to sign on with the Public Media Center. Usually environmental groups came to him for help. After all, Gunther's partner, Jerry Mander, had produced the famous ads that helped keep dams out of the Grand Canyon. With direct-mail honcho Richard Parker, whom Gunther jokingly calls "the Richard Viguerie of the Left," Gunther himself had helped create the incredibly lucrative Greenpeace direct-mail campaign featuring cute baby harp seals that were being clubbed to death for their pelts: "Kiss this baby goodbye" read the copy, beneath the heartrending photo of the white, furry harp seal, the environmental equivalent of big-eyed children painted on velvet. This 1976 campaign, which was light years more successful than anyone anticipated, had put direct mail on the map as an environmental tool and turned Greenpeace into a behemoth. With this track record and the low prices he was able to maintain because of Public Media Center's nonprofit status, Gunther rarely had to beg for clients. But this time, he was the one pitching.

"We sat down and said, 'Look, we helped create Greenpeace. We're disappointed in what Greenpeace has become. You guys are basically where the fire needs to be,' " said Gunther.

"We thought at the time . . . with *The Monkey Wrench Gang* and with the growing frustration with government not doing what it needed to do on the environment, that there would be the level of national support. The cynicism had grown to the point where people would support real, honest, authentic direct action. Earth First! would have been the Greenpeace of the eighties."

Herb Gunther may have been right. But he never found out. The Earth First!ers responded to Gunther fairly quickly. They said no.

"They came back to us and said, 'We can't do a direct mail because it's inconsistent with what we're about.' Because of the trees, and the paper. And we looked at them and we said, 'Well, we're not surprised by that decision. We'd like to argue with you about that. Sometimes there are higher and better uses for trees. If it doesn't go into direct mail, it goes in as toilet paper or in printing *The New York Times*.

" 'We think we can convince you that recruiting support for Earth First! so we can go out and save the planet is a higher and better use of those trees.'

"They just looked at us and said, 'No, we're just not going to get into it.' "

Impractical? Maybe. But Earth First! had been founded as an antidote to groups like Defenders of Wildlife, which spent 34 percent of its 1991 budget on overhead, including a hefty direct-mail campaign.[7] It wasn't just money but identity that was at stake. Mike Roselle was the lone dissenter. He wanted to make Earth First! a mass movement, a desire that set him apart from the movement's founding Buckaroos. Later, he would work with Gunther on small-scale media campaigns for California Earth First! But he was outvoted on the big question.

Herb Gunther was impressed with the integrity shown by Foreman and the others. Impressed, but . . . rueful. Gunther remains convinced that Earth First! could have had an even bigger constituency than the Sierra Club or the Wilderness Society. "Earth First! *does* things. It's visible. It also has a name and a face," said Gunther. Gunther still believes that if Dave Foreman had accepted his offer in 1986, he could have made him a star. Instead, 1987 came along and so did George Alexander.

Earth First! had already begun devouring itself. Tree spiking and other rowdy Earth First! habits had caused nasty internal rifts. Mountain climber Mike Jakubal had shown up in Corvallis, Oregon, where he rapidly became the local bad boy. He joined the Cathedral Forest Action Group, where civil disobedience activist Mary Beth Nearing was playing den mother to a bunch of weedy, overaged, eternal students and conscience-ridden community activists. Jakubal's antics soon got him kicked out of the group. He hadn't done much, just the standard tree-sit and a few slightly more in-your-face moves, like throwing sawdust on a Forest Service honcho's desk. All in all, he had gotten arrested more than a dozen times. If Corvallis had a "Ten Most Wanted List" he would have been at the top. It was a small town, after all.

After Jakubal's ouster, the Cathedral Forest Action Group (also known as CFAG, pronounced *See-Fag*) took a nonviolence pledge. No more monkeywrenching. Definitely no tree spiking. Bad juju. Bad press. Jakubal promptly went off and got himself arrested for sawing down a billboard with a reporter from a national magazine along to record the event for posterity.

Oregon home girls like Nearing weren't the only ones to decide that monkeywrenching didn't cut it. The 1988 Drug Omnibus Act, with its funny little rider about tree spiking, had taken the fun out of things. Suddenly this age-old tactic of Luddites and hard-ass union organizers had been declared a felony. Civil disobedience was also attracting unwelcome attention. Back in 1982, the Bisti badlands demonstration had caused little more than confusion. Five years later, Earth First!ers protesting at a Grand Canyon uranium mine were greeted by helicopters and police. Twenty-one people were arrested, including two who had chained themselves to the mine's head rig in the now-classic "Buggis Maneuver."

Earth First!'s actions had become so nettlesome to the timber industry that when a disputed old-growth stand called Millennium

Grove was left unattended for a few days in 1985, the president of Willamette Industries, Inc., took advantage of the lull to chop down thousand-year-old trees in record time, calling his decision a matter of "principle."[8]

Then there were the SLAPP suits—Strategic Lawsuits to Avoid Public Participation. In 1987, the Maxxam Corporation sued Northern California Earth First!ers for $42,000, claiming that a group of about 100 had "trespassed maliciously and to oppress" the company. This oppression consisted of six women dancing on a pile of redwood logs and a handful of tree sitters. The following year, six Earth First!ers who had chained themselves to a ninety-two-foot-tall yarder, a machine that helps remove trees from a logging site, also were SLAPPed. Even though the protesters had stopped work at a Kalmiopsis forest logging site for only a day, they were sued by the Medford Timber Corporation (MEDCO). The company, which had recently been taken over by a corporate raider, won $58,000 in civil damages against the environmentalists, who were dubbed "the Sapphire Six." The name came from the stretch of forest that they were trying to save. It certainly had nothing to do with jewelry—a private investigator hired by the company discovered that collecting on the judgment would be next to impossible. The activists didn't own anything, earn anything, or save anything besides trees.[9] Even that was debatable. Although Earth First! supporters from Mike Roselle to *Green Rage* author Christopher Manes argue that monkeywrenching has resulted in the cancellation of federal timber sales, nobody has ever been able to prove it. It's likely that a few sales have quietly died as a result of a combination of monkeywrenching and public outcry. But as the Millennium Grove incident proved, tree spiking could backfire. The overall effectiveness of monkeywrenching is practically impossible to assess. Certainly the Forest Service—like the Iran-Contra cowboys of the Reagan administration—would never admit that they had caved in to "terrorism."

In any case, Herb Gunther was probably right when he said that the significance of Earth First! was not in the number of trees it saved but in the debate it provoked. By 1987, the group's own internal debate was becoming toxic. At the Rendezvous, which was held that year at the Grand Canyon, Ed Abbey was surrounded by a group of people criticizing his stands on immigration and feminism—or what they perceived his stands to be. The old lion held his ground, but the event left an unpleasant taste in Foreman's mouth. Since the California Rendezvous the year before, he had been increasingly uncomfortable with Earth First! His anger over the incident grew as Abbey became ill in early 1989. For nearly ten years Abbey had been walking around with a disease called esophageal varices, which is common among alcoholics. Abbey got it after a thrombosis clogged his portal vein. Smaller veins grew around the damaged portal vein but they were too close to his esophagus and were prone to bursting. The fact that Abbey, a man whose literary voice had been so controversial, would be struck in the throat seemed to be not just an irony, but a gloomy defeat.

For several years, Abbey ignored the illness. Finally, he agreed to go to the doctor. After that doctor's visit, he quit drinking—or nearly did—because it aggravated his condition. For a long time he stayed in fairly good health. But each time his wife, Clarke, sent him off on a trip—Abbey still did solo hikes across the Cabeza Prieta lava flows and up in the Colorado Plateau—she knew that his blood vessels could give way and he could die alone on a bajada or up a steep mountain slope. Wisely, she tried not to think about it. As it turned out, the land that Abbey loved didn't betray him. The end was slower. In 1988 the Loefflers and the Abbeys spent Christmas together. Over the holidays Ed Abbey and Jack Loeffler planned a trip. Abbey wanted to go camping on his birthday, January 29. But when Loeffler arrived at Abbey's comfortable old house in the Tucson mountains with his bedroll and cookstove, Abbey said he didn't feel well enough to go out. Abbey "gave me the strangest look," said Loeffler. "I said, 'What's happening, Ed?' He said, 'It's getting close.' I said, 'Come on, man. We have millions of miles to walk.' He said, 'Yeah, God damn it, we do.' But we didn't."

Abbey and Loeffler postponed their trip until March. On March 6, Loeffler returned to Tucson. The two men went out to eat. They talked about where they would go on their camping trip. It would be a place they knew well, where black lava was stacked like the fortressed walls of a medieval town and bighorn sheep were the only creatures surefooted enough to run. "I knew that he was planning on dying," said Loeffler. "The idea had originally been that he and I would go camping and he'd die."

But the two men never made it out of town. Clarke came to Loeffler in the middle of the night. Ed was sick; he was really sick. Loeffler bundled Abbey up and took him to the hospital. For a while it looked as though he would die there. But he insisted on going home.

Not too many days later, Dave Foreman and Nancy Morton were called on a similar errand. Loeffler had gone back to Santa Fe. Ed had to go to the hospital and he didn't want an ambulance. He was too weak to get into the car and Clarke wasn't strong enough to carry him. Nancy and Dave took him to the hospital, Nancy monitoring his blood pressure. Clarke followed in another car with Doug Peacock while Lisa Peacock stayed with the children.

Once again, Abbey was treated and taken home. That was where he died.

That spring, a photocopy of Ed Abbey's handwritten letter to his wife, Clarke, circulated among some of their friends. It said:

CLARKE:—*Funeral instructions:* transported in bed of pickup truck and body to be buried as soon as possible after death, in a hole dug on our private property somewhere (along Green R., up in La Sals, or at Cliff Dwellers). No undertakers wanted; no embalming (for godsake!); no coffin. Just a plain pine box hammered together by a friend; or an old sleeping-bag, or tarp, will do. If site selected is too rocky for burial, then pile on sand and a pile of stones sufficient to keep coyotes from dismembering and scattering my bones. Wrap body in my anarchist flag. But bury if possible; I want my body to help fertilize the growth of a cactus, or cliffrose, or sagebrush, or tree, etc. Ceremony? GUNFIRE! And—A little music—

please: Jack Loeffler and his trumpet; the Riverine String Band, if available [this later got a line drawn through it] maybe a few readings from Thoreau, Whitman, Twain (something funny), Jeffers, and/or Abbey, etc: that should be sufficient. No speeches desired, tho' the deceased will not interfere if someone feels the urge. But keep it all simple and brief. Then—*a wake!* More music, lots of gay & lively music—bagpipes! drums & flutes! the Riverine String Band playing jigs, reels, country swing and polkas; I want dancing! and a flood of beer and booze! a bonfire! and lots of food—meat! corn on the cob! beans & chiles! cake & pie & ice cream & soda pop for the kids! gifts for all my friends & all who come—books, record albums, curios & keepsakes. No formal mourning, please—lots of singing, dancing, talking, hollering, laughing, and love-making instead. And I want my widow to take a new man as quick as she can find one good enough—for her. [Along the sides of the page he wrote:] (Disregard all state laws re burials.) (Hang a windbell nearby.) (Invite everybody! (we like))

Almost everyone who read the letter smiled through parts of it and cried through others. Abbey's death affected people deeply, even if they had only known him slightly. "Ed was the most individuated person I have ever known," said Jack Loeffler. Most people who knew him felt the same way.

A few years before, Abbey had taken up William Randolph Hearst III on his offer to be the *San Francisco Examiner*'s writer in residence. The old farm boy had gone to a sophisticated bar in San Francisco— it sounds like Tosca—where he was "served something hot, smooth, sweet, insidious," he wrote. "The decibel level is deafening; a roar of chatter comes from every side, violent music rises from the floor, from the walls, but all about me are the most distinguished-looking women I have ever seen—tall, blond, Nordic, elegantly dressed—not pretty but *handsome*—engaged in drowned, mute, but brilliant conversations.

"Perhaps it's all a mime, a dumbshow," Abbey writes. "Whatever the case, I am struck once again by the painful realization that there are worlds out there I shall never know, pleasures and refinements I could never understand. Not in Moab, Utah; not in Oracle, Arizona; not in a hundred years."

Yet he had spoken at Harvard. He had published a dozen books. He had revealed to people parts of themselves that they might otherwise never have known. He had shown them their place in the variegated river that links two continents, the human and the natural. He had shown them that "the wilderness is a valuable thing for its own sake. It also has a lot of symbolic value from a human point of view. It can mean freedom, liberty, spontaneity, the unplanned, unplannable progress of life. Wilderness also symbolizes, in my mind, the world that lies under the human world . . . and encloses it."

He had changed their lives.

Dave Foreman was flying home from a bird-watching vacation in Belize. He was standing at a phone booth at the Houston airport when he heard the news. For twenty-four hours, he cried. Then he went to the wake at Saguaro National Monument. In the green, surreal, underwater landscape of the saguaro desert outside Tucson, he cried some more. He mourned Ed Abbey and his own youth and then he made some decisions about his life.

Four hours north of Tucson, in the mile-high town of Prescott, Arizona, another man reacted to the news. Ronald Kermit Frazier noted the event in the diary he had been keeping for the FBI. "Abbey dead," he wrote. "Hooray!"

The
Lost
Boy

1986–Prescott, Arizona

THE ARIZONA TRAILER PARK is so sleazy it would be chic if it were
somewhere else. But it's not. It's stuck away on a back road of Prescott, Arizona. To the north is the giant irrefutable fact of the Grand
Canyon. As you drive south from the canyon, the land shears off like
clay-colored paper. It reaches a nadir in the blighted valley that is the
city of Phoenix. Prescott is somewhere between the two, and not just
geographically. It is a real American town, built around a lawn-clad
square where a band plays old Broadway show tunes on summer
nights. The adults speak softly in the dark in front of the big courthouse while children dart around the statue of a grimy-looking cowboy on horseback.

The cowboy is Bucky O'Neill, a bookkeeper–turned–Rough
Rider tragically killed by a sniper's bullet while using a south-of-the-
border latrine during the Spanish-American War. But make no mis-

take about it, Prescott is as much the New West as the Old. The city council is run by Republicans, but there are two health-food stores within walking distance of the town square. The rodeo comes to town each year, but the local bookstore owners who publish a peace and social justice newsletter on their Macintosh manage to remain oblivious to it.

The land itself is not quite desert and not quite forest. It is generic Lone Ranger and Tonto country, with skinny pinstripes of vanilla-scented ponderosa pine, long open patches of chaparral, dangling red penstemon, moon-faced orange globe mallow, here and there some cactus. But in the Arizona Trailer Park not a damn thing is growing, most of all not on the trellis that peels away from the manager's crumbling adobe house like a broken harp. Mexican illegals lounge on the porch, cans of beer linked onto their palms like vestigial digits. A white haze of dust hangs over everything.

Back when the trouble started, pure white roses floated on the upright trellis. A well-built thirty-seven-year-old drifter named Ronald Kermit Frazier breathed in their scent. Frazier was looking for a place to live. When the manager opened her front door, he hoped he had found it. Blond, blue-eyed Ilse Asplund was hardly the beer-bellied Ralph Kramden he expected to be in charge of such an operation. At first Frazier didn't register her features at all, just the sensation that the earth was crashing in around the bright center that was her smile. It surrounded him like the first really warm day of spring and made him feel—well, better than he could remember feeling for a long time.

Ilse was blinded by the sun glinting over Frazier's shoulder. When he walked in, she saw that he was handsome in an unremarkable way, with dark blond hair and regular features. The only remotely unusual thing about him were his deep-set eyes and high cheekbones, reminiscent of the century-ago Cherokee he claimed as an ancestor. Without much conversation, Frazier rented a trailer space. As he opened the door to go, he became a dark silhouette again, framed by the low afternoon sun like a leftover cowboy.

Of all the smooth-voiced Willie Nelson clones wandering around the New West, Ron Frazier probably came the closest to being a real denizen of the frontier. Frazier was a misfit who lived at the margins of society. He had spent his childhood in a small town near a big river in the western reserve of Ohio. Once this part of Ohio had been virgin territory. Then the land was doled out to New Englanders who had been burned out of their homes by the British in the War of 1812. These settlers cut and burned the forests to build farms, just as their ancestors had done a century before in states like Connecticut, Massachusetts, and Rhode Island. By the 1880s, the trees were gone.

By the time Ron Frazier was born, a second forest covered the countryside. The trees had been left alone long enough so that it resembled primeval forest—a dark, heavy curtain that hid a secret world. It was the world Ron Frazier escaped to when he was about fourteen. That was when his parents began a difficult, angry divorce. But it wasn't really the divorce that drove him out—it was his mother. Ron, the oldest of four kids, had always been close to her. His earliest memory was sitting on her lap, listening to Elvis sing "Wooden Heart." Even now, Frazier remembers the concatenation of his wide-open senses: the sound of the music; Elvis's voice, liquid and deep; the warmth of his mother's body.

When she changed, it was swift and unreasoning. She "freaked out" at any sign of Frazier's burgeoning masculinity. One day she noticed the veins in his arms popping out around his newly developed muscles. She thought something was wrong with him and became hysterical. His father tried to calm her, but he couldn't do much. He wasn't a sophisticated man, just an oil-field roughneck, and he often verged on violence. He and Frazier were buddies, but they didn't do a lot of talking.

As soon as he graduated from high school, Frazier left Ohio for good. When he got to Arizona he was still only seventeen. He passed through many of the state's weird small towns, places like Bowie and Wilcox. He picked cotton and fruit, hauled cement, did any menial labor he could find to earn a few bucks. Then he'd take the money he had saved—usually no more than $500—and go backpacking for a few months, stocking up on staples and hunting for meat. Sometimes he was so poor he would go for days eating only jerky. When he arrived at a town, he would haunt the public library. He read hungrily, but only about certain subjects. Prehistoric civilizations. Mechanics. He would assume a know-it-all air when discussing these things. There were few women, despite his good looks.

In 1979, he found his way to Bisbee, a southern Arizona mining town of steep, winding streets and ramshackle houses. The mine had long since closed. Now the town produced only long-haired freaks and artists. There was never any way to earn money in Bisbee, so Frazier would leave periodically to find work. He'd come back to hunker down for the winter, signing up for food stamps to get through the slow time. That was something the hippies had taught him to do. They also taught him to do drugs. He experimented with heroin and speed, but mostly he liked mind-expanding drugs like peyote and LSD. Frazier says he never hallucinated when he took acid. Instead, he would get an initial rush, which made him anxious. He'd calm himself down, and as the acid smoothed out, he'd get into a "clear" space. That's what he liked, getting into the "clear." He smoked pot every day for months, reputedly selling fairly small quantities to make his head stash, then he'd stop for a while. He read Nietzsche and listened to Jethro Tull, practiced his calligraphy, thought about art.

It was an odd life, but on the surface not so radically different from the lives of a lot of other people in Bisbee and places like it. Beneath the surface, Ron Frazier had his own reasons for staying outside mainstream society, as people generally do. Bits and pieces surfaced in town gossip. Some came to light in police records. Bisbee is a small town and there were incidents. Once Frazier was accused of molesting a little girl, one of the countless hippie children who roam the streets with dirty faces and flying hair. Frazier said he had only befriended her. No charges were filed, for whatever reason, but Frazier's popularity in Bisbee waned.

As the years passed, Frazier became more isolated. In 1983, he shot a gun into a van full of people. He thought the driver was out to get him. Maybe he was right, because no charges were filed this time, either. Once Frazier was accused of hitting someone's sheepdog.

But this incident was dropped, too. Frazier had such a passive, child-like demeanor, it is hard to think of him as violent. But drug-induced paranoia can do strange things to people. Bisbee police records show that Frazier once made a complaint against someone for "threatening and intimidating." He often felt people were bullying him.

In any case, the only time Frazier ever got convicted of anything was when he got caught with some peyote. That wasn't much of a black mark in Bisbee. By 1986 he was getting out of town, anyway. He had this idea about studying gunsmithing at the community college up in Prescott. He was already in his early thirties, and he wanted to make something of himself. Even drifters and losers are susceptible to the American dream. Frazier's dream was to build a home. During one lucrative year of working with heavy equipment, he had even managed to buy about twenty acres. But he owed a couple of thousand in back taxes and didn't know if he'd be able to hold on to it.

Frazier may have wanted a home, but what he got was a trailer. Actually, he got a little more. When he told Ilse he was a starving artist, she agreed to let him use an empty shed as a welding shop cum art studio. Frazier promptly painted a letter-perfect Mickey Mouse on the door. The bright cartoon face was a magnet for the trailer park kids, including Ilse's three-year-old daughter, Julia.

Ilse had helped out another drifter, as well. Mike Gooch was an eccentric fellow, a compulsive chain-smoker with missing teeth who seemed to know a lot about nature. Ilse let the scuzzy Gooch live in his Travelall truck just outside her dining-room window. He rigged up electricity from her house so that he could read at night.

This generosity was characteristic of Ilse. Ilse Washington Asplund was the daughter of two journalists, a headstrong romantic with an intellectual bent and too much empathy for her own good. A backslid southern belle, Asplund had bounced around several progressive colleges before winding up in Prescott. You couldn't help feeling that she was in search of something. Maybe it was her own fate. She wasn't sure what "it" was, but when she found pieces of it, she recognized them instinctively. The first time was at the age of eighteen, when she traveled to Taos on a ski vacation. She was with a doctor, the kind of guy she probably should have married. She shed the doctor but kept the Southwest in her mind for two years, until she could figure out a way to get back.

"You know, I had been to Europe and I had been to the East Coast, but I had never been out here. So I got off the bus in Albuquerque and I was all, hot damn, we're going to ski, and I looked around and it was just incredible, the silence just fell over me, this silence just fell over everything, and I just finally let go, and this feeling, I just can't describe it. And we rode all the way from Albuquerque to Taos on this bus and everywhere I looked it was me, turned inside out. This was home."

Ilse made her second big decision in 1982. She married Ken Asplund, a professor at Prescott College, a progressive school with an orientation toward environmental studies. Ken was a botanist, more than a decade older than Ilse. With Ken, Ilse thought she could get security without sacrificing the intellectual buzz she craved. Prescott College paid next to nothing, so the couple landed a gig managing the trailer park. Ilse worked, went to school, and in 1983 gave birth to Julia. In 1986 Adam was born. By that time, the couple was having serious problems. According to Ilse, Ken was a workaholic, emotionally distant, and not particularly interested in the children. Later Ilse said she would find out part of the reason for his diffidence about their family life—he was gay. In the meantime, she thrashed around, trying to salvage her identity.

As things grew bleaker with Ken, Frazier started looking more attractive to Ilse. But when she told her best friend, Peg Millett, about him, Peg thought Ilse had lost her mind. In certain respects, Peg's background was similar to Frazier's. Peg was the younger half sister of feminist author Kate Millett. Although they had never met, the two women shared the same father. He was a heavy drinker, and as a child Peg felt that there was only one safe place. The Sonoran desert outside her parents' Phoenix home was where she sang out loud and talked to the lizards and roadrunners that skittered across the sand. In her late teens, she left for good. She brought herself up the hard way, riding the rods as a fruit tramp, fishing on Alaskan trawlers, breaking wild horses all over the West. Her skill with horses even got her to Europe. She ran a riding stable at a resort in Norway for a few months, then took off to hitchhike through Scotland. She went to Europe three times in all, going to museums and buying cheap theater seats. She always came back broke. But her adventures kept her alive—even when they nearly killed her.

Peg's life changed when she moved to Prescott, probably in the same way that Frazier hoped to change his. She worked her way through Prescott College. She married a forest ranger named Doug Vandergon and lived with him in a rustic outpost called Palace Station. It was almost too good to be true. In 1985, she read an interview with Dave Foreman in *Mother Earth News*. Like Karen Pickett, she felt that she had found a voice to articulate her long-held beliefs. When she went to the Earth First! Rendezvous that summer, Peg felt instantly at home. She became friends with the Montana delegation, hard-partying frat-boy types who managed to be serious, hardworking environmentalists during the day. She also fell in with the good old girls in the Redneck Women's Caucus. At the Rendezvous, Peg did everything she had always wanted to do. She danced like a demon. She sang in her high, clear voice. No more beating her brains out for no-good country musician boyfriends. It was her turn. She enthusiastically threw herself into the quasi-spiritual activities that the cowboys disparagingly called woo-woo. She enjoyed the fact that she could kick shit with the best of them—she and Foreman got along well, for instance—but could pitch woo-woo with the New Age types, too.

Peggy and Ilse had become friends in January 1979. Ilse was working in the admissions office of Prescott College when Peg walked in covered with flour from the sourdough bread she had been baking. She told Ilse she had just heard about the school in a radio ad and wanted to apply. Here, she said, here's a picture of me when I was running a stable in Norway. Ilse smiled. Peg was just amazing; unsophisticated, but strong and direct. The two women quickly formed a close, almost symbiotic relationship. Ilse admired Peg's macho attitude toward life. Peg's opinion of Ilse vacillated between awe and condescension. With her two children and her unflinching ability to be vulnerable, Ilse personified the femininity that Peg had never felt safe enough to express. Ordinarily they reserved judgment about each other's men, the way women do in order to avoid conflicts of loyalty. But this time Peg wished she could say something. Peg thought Frazier was way beneath Ilse. He had that *look* in his eye, the blank, intense, thousand-yard stare. You could see him mentally switching gears all the time, but with a grinding noise; sprockets were missing from the chain. After all those years on the road, she recognized the type.

Even if Peg had cautioned her, Ilse probably wouldn't have listened. Her life with Ken was falling apart. One night, she found herself sitting on her front steps with Ron Frazier. It was a full moon, one of those summer evenings when time slips past you, the air is warm, there is a sudden intimacy. Ilse told Frazier about her problems with Ken. They talked about everything, about nature and politics and moral responsibility and their childhoods. Or at least Ilse talked about those things. It went on for hours, until Ilse realized it was midnight and rather abruptly said good night. For the first time, it occurred to Frazier that he might have a chance with her. He always thought that Ilse and Ken and their two beautiful towheaded children were the all-American family. Ilse had told him enough to convince him otherwise.

Things unraveled, with appropriately dubious spiritual overtones, on the weekend of the Harmonic Convergence. Ilse and Ken had planned a camping trip to the San Francisco Peaks, a range of high mountains between Prescott and Flagstaff. Frazier and Mike Gooch had both been invited.

Ilse got home from work and packed so that she would be ready when Ken got home. Sleeping bags were rolled on the floor like sausages, the baby was tucked up and ready to go in his Gerry pack, four-year-old Julia was fed and sneakered. It was already late when Ken arrived and announced that he wasn't going. Neither was Mike Gooch. Over Ilse's protests, Ken left the house. Zoned-out coincidence maybe, but Frazier appeared a few minutes later. Without talking too much about it, he swept up Ilse and the children and they drove out to the San Francisco Peaks. They camped in a high meadow, where Ilse breast-fed Adam to sleep. The two adults slept side by side, not touching until the second night.

They were lovers for about six weeks. In October Frazier told Ilse that he was tired of sneaking home at 5 A.M. to avoid trailer park gossip when Ken was on his cottonwood research expeditions. He gave her his ultimatum at Palace Station, the rustic compound where Peg lived with her husband Doug. With Peg just a few feet away taking care of her horses, Ilse told Ron Frazier that their relationship was over.

Soon afterward, Ilse separated from Ken Asplund. She became platonic friends with a man named Mark Davis. Davis had recently gone through a divorce himself. Red-haired and built like a wood stove, he was the kind of man who could sweep away almost anything or anyone in his path—or thought he could. He was intense, energetic, and, some people thought, too smart for his own good. Mark had a big heart, but his friends suspected that brutal beatings from his oil-company-executive father had permanently rewired his brain. His intelligence was like loose electricity, a tesla coil on LSD. After helping to start a counterculture drug rehabilitation center in Phoenix in the late sixties, he had migrated to the weird underbelly of Southern California hippie mysticism. He traded his Harley for a Sikh sheet, learned Kundalini Yoga, and somewhere along the line did the mundane stuff: married twice, fathered three kids, learned carpentry.

Ilse had first met Mark back in July 1987, when he showed up on her doorstep trying to connect with a ride to the Earth First! Rendezvous, which was being held only a few hours away at the Grand Canyon. Peggy had found a real niche in Earth First! and now Ilse thought she might, too. She had just heard about the uranium mine that was going to open on the rim of the Grand Canyon. What she was reading about the health effects of living close to uranium mines was shocking to her. She wasn't really paying much attention to Mark, although he sounded interesting. Peggy had told her that Mark was a hard-core monkeywrencher. Crazy but brilliant. He was a maverick, too. He wasn't really part of Earth First! The group's ideas were just more information to feed into his hyperactive mind, along with magazines like *Harper's* and *Scientific American*. He liked *Harper's'* intellectual Ping-Ponging of ideas, which was unfettered by any single philosophy. He was a big fan of the column written by the magazine's editor, Lewis Lapham. He also read a random assortment of poetry, fiction, spiritual writings, and science.

At the Rendezvous, Mark Davis stayed pretty much by himself. He said it was because he thought most Earth First!ers were lightweights. Davis had studied martial arts. He was pumped up about something called the warrior path. He knew the relative weight of life and death in the struggle between good and evil, when to strike and when to hold back. If, as ecologist Raymond Dasmann had written, World War III was the war of industrial humans against the earth, Davis knew which side he was on and he was ready to open fire. Every once in a while he would breeze through Ilse's campsite, keeping her company while she cared for her children. Mark had two daughters of his own. With children, he was strong and loving. It was only with other adults, when he wasn't in control, that he ran into trouble.

Around Christmastime, Ilse and Mark suddenly clicked. By then, Ken Asplund was long gone and Ron Frazier was history, at least as far as Ilse was concerned. It was awkward for Frazier, who was still hanging around the trailer park, wondering if anything would ever happen with Ilse again. The prospects didn't look good especially after the night he baby-sat for the kids so that Ilse could go out with Mark. When they got back, they politely kicked him out so they could be alone. But it was okay. Prescott in the eighties was the sixties all over again. Jealousy was out. Mark Davis and Frazier even became friendly. Frazier helped Mark buy a cutting torch and taught him how to use it. At first, Frazier didn't know what the target was. All he knew was that it was for an environmental cause. That was okay with Frazier, too. He thought environmentalists were rich, ignorant city people, but he loved nature. He had spent years backpacking in the forests and deserts, a lost boy. The physical world was real to him; human society contained only ghosts of his former pain. It wasn't just a cactus or a coatimundi that brought reality home. It was anything he could touch with his hands. He loved the poetry of big machines, their heft and size and kinetic energy. Instinctively, he knew how to fix them. And he knew how to break them, just like a child. He shared that knowledge with Mark Davis. He sympathized with Mark's radicalism, but mostly he just liked the attention. "There was a dynamic between us," he recalled later. "I would come up with the information and he would execute. . . . If Mark Davis had treated me a little bit more like a human being I would have stayed on his side."

Into this oddly matched group of ecosaboteurs wandered a Ph.D. botanist named Marc Andre Baker. A tall, gangly vegetarian, Baker was the quintessential absentminded professor. He was even brilliant in his field, an expert on cholla and acuña cactus. Baker's expertise was wide-ranging. Half his career had been spent in the desert and half in rain forests. In fact, Baker and his wife, Nicole, had just re- turned from Ecuador, where Baker's botanizing included ingesting large quantities of ayahuasca, a powerful hallucinogen used in Indian religious ceremonies. LSD and psilocybin mushrooms were inferior, earthbound highs compared to ayahuasca, according to Baker. It was just as well that the drug wasn't available in Prescott.

Nancy Zierenberg and Rod Mondt, Dave Foreman's friends from Chico, California, also arrived in Prescott that summer. Nancy always loved botanizing and bird-watching, but up until now Rod's career had kept them moving around. But that spring Rod said good-bye to both the Forest Service and the Park Service and began working in a Prescott sporting-goods store. Nancy decided that it was time to get involved in the environmental movement. She listed herself in the *Earth First! Journal* as a local contact person. In the spring, she organ- ized a picnic, where she met Peg Millett, who was the other Prescott contact. Mark Davis didn't come, but he called later to set up a meet- ing. Davis was thinking of starting a local environmental group called Yavapai Earthnet. He hoped it would be successful enough to get him out of the carpentry business.

———

Late on the night of October 4, 1987, a band of ecosaboteurs carried a heavy welding torch into the San Francisco Peaks. By the time they came down, so had the pylons that held up the main chairlift of the Fairfield Snowbowl. The owners of the resort, which had been operating on Forest Service land since the 1930s, were threatening to expand farther into the mountain range. They didn't seem to care that the San Francisco Peaks were sacred territory to several Indian tribes. This had been particularly annoying to Mark Davis; it exemplified everything that was wrong with industrial capitalism.

The Snowbowl was immediately notified that the lifts had been damaged. So were a dozen radio stations and newspapers, which refused to print the letter outlining the group's demands because they thought it would encourage the ecosaboteurs. They did report that a group calling itself EMETIC, the Evan Mecham Eco Terrorist International Conspiracy, was claiming credit for the incident, citing their opposition to the resort's expansion into sacred Indian territory. Almost immediately, Arizona governor Ev Mecham, the wacky right-wing car salesman who was later impeached after committing a series of blunders that indicated his utter lack of familiarity with the U.S. Constitution, declared that he had nothing to do with the group. The authorities were not amused. Neither was the Snowbowl. A $5,000 reward was posted for the perpetrators.

EMETIC's humor found a more appreciative audience at the Arizona Trailer Park. Ilse and Ron Frazier passed the newspaper back and forth that morning, laughing. Now Frazier knew how Mark was using the welding skills he had taught him.

In November, another letter arrived at the Snowbowl from EMETIC. Iisaw, the *nom de monkeywrench* of the group's leader, advised Snowbowl management that the lift had been sabotaged again. In fact, it hadn't been. But the company was forced to shut down briefly and spend money to find this out. EMETIC's jokers were on a roll.

There was only one problem. Ilse Asplund's house was being watched by the FBI. Tired of being broke and angry that nobody trusted him enough to let him in on the joke, Ilse's second-string trailer park protégé, the toothless, chain-smoking Mike Gooch, had contacted the authorities. For a short time, Gooch wore a wire provided by the FBI. But the only inside information he got was about good fishing holes.

The fissure first appeared when Marc Baker let slip a few ill-chosen words at a backyard barbecue in nearby Prescott Valley. His friend Harry Macey was complaining about carrying his two kids when they got tired of hiking. Baker ribbed him, saying if he thought that was bad, he should try carrying a cutting torch up the San Francisco Peaks.

Then, just two months after the second Snowbowl letter had been sent, the fissure turned into a crevasse when Mark Davis made his fatal, arrogant mistake. That winter Ron Frazier had been working for Jody Skjei, an old high-school friend of Davis's. He was also going to school full-time and, according to him, earning straight A's. But Ron Frazier's sense of reality, tenuous at best, was being shredded by megadoses of LSD—five, six, seven hits at a time. He became prey to delusions that Skjei was in love with him, even though she assured him this was not the case. Finally she fired him, complaining that he was coming to work stoned. They had a dispute over money and Frazier left a succession of threatening telephone messages on Skjei's answering machine. Mr. Hippie himself stepped in, Mark Davis, the old drug and alcohol counselor, mystic warrior, protector of women and children. Get into the martial arts, man, he told Frazier. Meditate. Learn to focus. Part of your brain isn't energized.

Even for Frazier, this was too much. Blandly agreeing, he waited until the trailer door closed behind Mark Davis's highly energized, meddlesome brain. Then he jumped in his old pickup and hightailed it down to the FBI office in Phoenix. There, for the first time in his life, Ron Frazier's dream came true. He found someplace he belonged.

The FBI was only too ready to welcome Ron Frazier into the fold. Agents had been watching Earth First! since the early 1980s. In 1981, an executive of the Salt River Project, the utility that operated the Glen Canyon Dam, had written a letter to the FBI's Terrorism Research Bomb Data Center. He asked for a "threat assessment or profile information . . . on a regional or national level, on a recurring basis . . . on a relatively new environmental group known as Earth First, which was formed in March, 1981 [the month they "cracked" the dam], and apparently espouses violent activity aimed at utilities."

From FBI records made available under the Freedom of Information Act, it is not clear if this letter provoked an investigation. But the following year Earth First!ers began their crusade to lampoon Interior Secretary James Watt. This time the FBI got to work.

Starting in 1982, the agency made periodic reports on Earth First! These reports were released to me in 1986 under the Freedom of Information Act, but all the names were blacked out. Still, they offer a way to track the FBI's interest in Earth First! For instance, on November 29, 1982, someone from Earth First! made an attempt to talk to Watt during a public appearance. When he was told to write a letter instead, the Earth First!er wrote warning Watt that oil and gas exploration or any other activities detrimental to wilderness would be "followed by civil disobedience." "If you continue to follow the Reagan administration's course it will harden our resolve to Block the Course," said the letter, which was signed by "Ned Lud [*sic*], Rocky Mtn. Regional Coordinator, Earth First!" Park police forwarded the letter to the FBI, along with photos obtained by the Colorado State Patrol. The FBI report continues, "[Name blacked out] further advised his office has a large file on Earth First [*sic*] which he described as a violence prone organization operating in the West and Southwest portions of the United States."

Reports from the Bald Mountain road blockades in 1983 sounded a saner note. They characterized the group as peaceful and environmentally concerned. Members of Earth First! were afraid that logging of Bald Mountain will "hurt the environment," one report stated. But another memorandum from this period was alarming. It was dated May 25, 1983—the date of the Glen Canyon Dam birthday celebration and Earth First!'s counterdemonstration, the canyon's funeral. It contained a synopsis of a U.S. Park Service report on a man in a canoe near Rainbow Bridge. The man was reportedly carrying a Ruger Mini-14 fitted with a scope. He was a member of Earth First! and had a record of problems in other parks, according to the rangers. Concerned about the safety of James Watt, Park Service cops confiscated the man's gun, telling him he could retrieve it later. He never returned. This appeared to be the same man Ken Sanders knew as the "sinister" Piton Pete, one of the scuzzy hangers-on who had been showing up whenever Earth First! staged a big whoop-de-doo. "He scared the bejesus out of me," Sanders recalled. "He had a truck that was loaded to bear, with weird radios and a satellite TV. I thought he was an agent provocateur." Sanders doesn't remember seeing him after the Glen Canyon funeral either.

The FBI reports seem to taper off after 1983. Coincidentally, or maybe not so coincidentally, that was the year James Watt resigned, leaving the Department of Interior a blander place. But a 1986 incident captured the FBI's attention once again. Arizona ecosaboteurs tossed a harpoonlike device over a power line, briefly interrupting transmissions from the Palo Verde nuclear generating station. A few months later an Earth First! rally was held in Tucson. The Palo Verde hit was mentioned, and someone in the audience shouted "Nice work!" to Dave Foreman and Roger Featherstone. From the stage, both men denied any involvement in the incident. Then Peg Millett made a smart-aleck remark about taking credit where credit was due. It probably meant nothing. For years, Dave Foreman had been telling everyone he was too visible to monkeywrench. But according to Ron Frazier, there was an undercover FBI agent in the crowd that night who wasn't about to take Foreman at his word.

So when Frazier walked in the door of the Phoenix FBI office in January 1988, the agents thought it was Christmas, Hanukkah, and the Fourth of July rolled into one. To Frazier's surprise, they said, "You're one of us, boy." The agents fitted him out with a snazzy lightweight reel-to-reel Nagra tape recorder and sent him home. Sources close to the investigation say that the FBI became convinced at this early stage that Foreman was at the center of an antinuclear conspiracy that had begun with the Palo Verde incident. This was the first real break in the case. It remains unclear exactly how it occurred. For instance, there is speculation that Frazier may have been inspired by the knowledge that Gooch had already turned informer. In any case, he quickly outdid his predecessor. To Frazier's surprise, Mark Davis almost immediately spilled his guts about plans for future monkeywrenching adventures. Frazier, the square-jawed, all-American psycho, was in deeper than he had bargained for.

"All I really wanted was the dirt on the Snowbowl and he starts telling me about the next project and Thermit (an incendiary powder)," said Frazier. "And I'm going no, please. No next project. No Thermit. I don't want to hear this."

Later he added, "I mean, all I wanted to do was snitch on Mark and get out. It was a chickenshit thing to do."

Chickenshit or not, Frazier did the job, ultimately receiving just under $54,000 over a three-year period. The FBI even allowed him to go to Seattle to work on the diesel engine of a boat belonging to the Sea Shepherd Conservation Society, the Greenpeace splinter group that was going around calling itself the Earth First! navy and ramming whaling boats. By this time Frazier had switched over to Yavapai College's diesel mechanics course, where he showed considerable aptitude. His skills did not go unappreciated by the Sea Shepherds, a navy whose fleet could be charitably characterized as rustbucket class. Frazier liked Sea Shepherd, too. His FBI handlers probably didn't realize how close Frazier was to shipping out for good on that trip. When he came back, he was still in their good graces. The best thing he had done, at least from the FBI's point of view, was introduce FBI undercover agent Mike Tait to Peg Millett at the Earth First! Rendezvous in Washington state in the summer of 1988.

By then Frazier's relationship with Mark Davis was eroding. In fact, Davis seemed to be cooling off on the idea of monkeywrenching altogether. His personal deity, which he simply referred to as "She," was telling him to mellow out, he told Frazier. For months Davis and Frazier had toyed with the idea of using Thermit to down power lines. Frazier kept having "trouble" locating the Thermit. Finally Davis gave up on the idea. It would be bad public relations, he decided. "Okay, so maybe it's a blessing in disguise not to have the

Thermit," Davis told Frazier. "The definition of the job is to do it so people will like that it's done and think about why."[1] Frazier couldn't figure out if Davis had stopped trusting him because he hadn't come through with the Thermit, or if Davis was really backing off from monkeywrenching. Frazier was losing whatever slender grasp he had on Ilse, too. But he still fantasized about "saving" her from Mark Davis by putting her to work for the FBI. They could work as a team—if he wasn't hooked up with FBI agent Lori Bailey by then. Bailey was a blond woman in her early thirties who looked like a younger, prettier Martina Navratilova. Frazier suspected that Bailey, who was in charge of the sting, had romantic feelings toward him. He also thought that the FBI wanted to promote him from informer to full-time agent.[2]

But Ilse was not the FBI's next target. Peg Millett was. FBI undercover agent Mike Tait—whose real name was Mike Fain—realized that of the four EMETIC outlaws, Peg was the easiest to manipulate. She had a weakness for cowboys, so Fain played the consummate Marlboro Man. He fit the part, being long legged, good with his hands, and emotionally retarded. Peg's husband, the forest ranger Doug Vandergon, didn't dance, so Peg and Fain went dancing together. When the relationship felt that it was getting too heavy, she fixed him up with her friend, a striking widow named Jane Chapman. But Peg kept seeing Fain, too. She was never physically unfaithful to Doug, but there was something intense and disturbing about her relationship with Fain. She began to read about codependence. Mike Fain had told her that he was an alcoholic, but he had never gone to AA. She thought he was what AA calls "a dry drunk"—someone who exhibits alcoholic behavior but doesn't drink. She thought that her own behavior was codependent; she kept trying to "save" Fain. She grew alarmed about the relationship, but instead of ending it, she redoubled her efforts to fix it.

Slowly and methodically, Mike Fain worked to gain the trust of the Prescott ecosaboteurs. For a long time, Mark Davis suspected him of being "a deep plant." He spent time with Fain but refused to discuss monkeywrenching. Davis thought Fain rather pathetic, but decided that he would help him, mentor him, get him out of his screwed-up, emotionally blocked, post-Vietnam rut.

Ilse was the only person in the group who was completely turned off by Fain. For one thing, he took up too much of Mark Davis's time. Their vaguely militaristic male-bonding routine—running up Granite Mountain at the crack of dawn and kick-boxing in the garage—made her want to puke. "I was a southern belle before I was an ecoterrorist, honey," she joked later. "If they wanted to get me, they should have sent a Jewish bon vivant."

Eventually it was not sweat and violence that caused Mark Davis to drop his guard. It was a lie told by a woman. As her marriage faltered, partly because of her husband's discomfort with her Earth First! activism, Peg Millett grew increasingly attached to Mike Fain. The emotional hold that Fain had on her after "confessing" that he was an alcoholic proved overpowering. Peg's father had been a drunk, a violent one. Ignoring a warning instinct, Peg resolved to rescue Fain from his strangled sensitivity, the way children try to mend their broken parents so that the parents can be there for them. She would get him in touch with the earth—and his own feminine side—by turning him into the world's greatest monkeywrencher. To convince Mark Davis that Fain was for real, she implied that Fain had committed a felony with her. Interestingly, the one she chose was trashing a bulldozer, the same kind of heavy equipment her father had operated. Davis believed her. Fain was in.

Between Fain and Frazier, the FBI had EMETIC pretty well taped up. Literally. More than 800 hours of mostly turgid conversations were recorded on body wires worn by Fain, Frazier, and a snitch named Katherine (or Catherine) Clarke, a woman with a throaty, resonant voice who volunteered at the *Earth First! Journal* office in Tucson. The house on Sosna Drive that Mark Davis and Ilse Asplund moved into in March 1988 was wired from floor to ceiling, including the telephone. Similar surveillance was conducted in Tucson. The feds recorded everything from kids playing and dogs barking to a couple making love on a kitchen table, an invasion they excused by saying they thought the people were eating soup.

All this work did not go unrewarded. On September 25, 1988, a power line leading to the Canyon Mine on the North Rim of the Grand Canyon was cut by EMETIC. This time, the Prescott monkeywrenchers had chosen a real cause. This was the uranium mine Ilse had found out about the summer before. When she researched it, she discovered that the mine was both a potential health hazard and a financial boondoggle. Uranium mines have been linked to obscenely high cancer rates in children. Because of the location of uranium deposits, Native Americans, who are often poor and unable to defend themselves through the political or legal process, are the most affected. In this case, the proposed mine threatened to contaminate the water supply of the Havasupai Indians. In addition, under the antiquated 1872 Mining Law, Energy Fuels Nuclear was paying only $100 for the right to gouge out uranium from national forest land. The Sierra Club and the Havasupai Indian tribe were in court trying to stop the mine from opening. If construction could be slowed, the lawsuits might have a better chance of succeeding.

According to an affidavit filed on February 23, 1989, FBI agents knew all about EMETIC's plan to hit the Canyon Mine *before it happened*. Yet they did nothing to stop it. Former prosecutor Ivan Abrams says the FBI was holding out for a bigger prize—Dave Foreman, whom they believed was the puppet master behind EMETIC. Abrams believes the FBI was wrong and the Earth First! case should have been prosecuted as a minor criminal matter. But by the time Abrams took the case, the government's decision had been made. Part of the problem was Mike Fain. Just like his cover story, the real Mike Fain had done hard time in Vietnam. He was considered a free spirit by his law-enforcement peers. He even called himself an environmentalist. Fain felt a troubling affinity for his subjects. Especially difficult was the romantic relationship that he began with Jane Chapman, Peg Millett's friend.

But Fain was also a serious Christian. He was shocked when Peg and Ilse took part in a women's ceremony at the Grand Canyon that included the old Druid rite of dripping menstrual blood on the earth. According to Abrams, Fain's biggest problem was that he was too rigid to modulate his training to fit a situation where he was infiltrating idealists instead of ax murderers. When it came down to it, Fain was a company man. He was even married to an FBI agent.

An inadvertently recorded conversation between Mike Fain and another agent seems to bear out the theory that the FBI was waiting to ensnare Foreman. Foreman was not "the guy we need to pop, I mean, in terms of an actual perpetrator," Fain told his buddy. "This is the guy we need to pop to send a message." Suddenly realizing his Nagra's spools were still spinning, Fain exclaimed, "Ohh, we don't need that on tape. Hoo boy."

The presence of an FBI informer in Tucson also indicates that the FBI was targeting Foreman. Cat Clarke made a concerted effort to befriend Dave Foreman's wife, Nancy Morton, whose radicalism was perhaps even harder edged than Foreman's. Like Morton, who was a nurse, Clarke worked in health care. Sometimes she moonlighted as a professional clown. She adopted many masks; her hair color changed almost as often as her makeup. Clarke struck members of Tucson Earth First! as bubbly, bouncy, and emotionally unstable. She told the Earth First!ers that she had been a bodyguard for a local Islamic cult leader named Kalifa. Kalifa was a former science adviser to Libya's Col. Muammar al-Qaddafi. He was an obvious subject for FBI surveillance, leading to later speculation that Clarke had a track record as a federal snitch. Kalifa was assassinated in 1990, several months after Clarke was expelled from the group. His assassin was never found. Soon afterward, Clarke attached herself to Earth First!, enthusiastically volunteering for sit-ins and trying to get people to monkeywrench with her.

Dave Foreman was going through his own personal crisis that spring. Sobered by intimations of mortality—including Abbey's death and a nasty bite from a brown recluse spider which forced him to spend the winter as an invalid—Foreman decided that his young Frankenstein had outgrown him.

"Abbey's death changed things for me. Ed could say outrageous things. He could be a gadfly. I realized that for twenty years, really all of my adult working life, except a year or two when I worked at a Zuni trading post, I'd been speaking on behalf of some environmental group. In that situation, you have to be careful what you say. By the time I hit that ten thousandth interview, I couldn't escape the feeling that I was pandering. Right now, I only want to speak for Dave Foreman," he said in the beginning of May 1989. Not long before, he had severed his formal relationship with Earth First!, handing over the ownership of the *Earth First! Journal* to a nonprofit organization composed of the newspaper's staff members. At Dave's urging, Nancy Zierenberg rented a white frame house in downtown Tucson and moved the *Journal*'s office out of the back bedroom of the Calle Carapan house. Although he stopped by the office nearly every day, Foreman's only visible tie to Earth First! was his public speaking, which provided his main source of income. But even "The Speech," Foreman's foot-stomping, rabble-rousing call to action, felt stale. He was bored and a little tired. His guard was down.

Just as he had manipulated Peg Millett to gain access to Mark Davis, Mike Fain was going to use Mark Davis to get to Dave Foreman. He had finally won Mark's trust, just as Mark's fantasies were reaching new heights of grandiosity. With Fain's help, Davis concocted a plan to knock down power lines to five nuclear facilities simultaneously. A grand gesture seemed like the only way out of a horrible depression that was settling in on Mark. He was backing out of his relationship with Ilse, using the excuse that "the warrior path" was too dangerous for women and children. He moved upstairs, leaving Ilse in the downstairs apartment. But the separation wasn't solving his problems. He often felt suicidal. In his FBI-taped conversations with Ilse, Mark fantasized about sacrificing himself for the good of the world, in one media-heavy kamikaze death strike. "It's like poker; you have to ante. My ante is my life," he swaggered.[3] But in reality Mark had trouble coordinating his complicated antinuke action. Despite his brilliance, Mark Davis was the kind of guy who couldn't balance a checkbook or run a business, much less organize the ecoradical version of the Strategic Air Command. Five nukes became three—the Palo Verde nuclear power plant in Arizona; the notorious Diablo Canyon plant in California, built on the San Andreas Fault;

and a military-grade plutonium-processing facility at Rocky Flats, Colorado, one of the most polluted places on earth. The whole operation had to be conducted with complete safety, Davis constantly admonished. Nobody was to be hurt, including the monkeywrenchers. It all sounded good, unless you knew Mark. He couldn't even get to Tucson without the FBI agent's assistance—his car was too much of a junker to make the four-hour trip. Mike Fain drove Davis down to Tucson twice to put the touch on Dave Foreman. Once Davis scored $500. But Fain was not allowed into the meetings between Foreman and Davis.

Then one day Mike Fain came to see Dave Foreman alone. He came to the Calle Carapan house. The two men spoke for a while, then went for a walk in the desert. As they left the quiet suburban streets behind and entered the saguaro forest, Fain told Foreman that Mark Davis was planning a practice session before the nuke job. For the warm-up, Davis wanted to down a power line connected to the Central Arizona Project, which was finally on its way to completion.

As the sun haloed the edges of the tall Sonoran Desert cactus, a plane flew overhead. Foreman, an Air Force brat, thought little of it. There was an Air Force base east of the city, and Tucson International Airport was only a few miles to the southeast. But this plane was different. It contained FBI agents who were using high-technology devices to monitor his conversation, in case Fain needed corroboration in court.

Fain said that hitting CAP was a bad idea. Foreman agreed. Fain continued to work him, repeating the same statements over and over like an expert fisherman hauling in a wary, battered old trout. Finally Foreman made one incriminating reply. "I think it's got to be real targeted and be directed at targets that will have some kind of impact," he said. "Like the nuclear thing, that might help prevent additional plants . . . But with the CAP thing we are essentially done in the United States with uh . . . large water projects."

Explaining that his personal finances were in bad shape, Foreman told Fain to see Nancy Zierenberg at the Earth First! office. A few months before, when Rod decided to attend graduate school at the

University of Arizona in Tucson, Foreman had offered Zierenberg a job as the *Earth First! Journal*'s merchandise coordinator. Foreman told the agent that the group was holding a yard sale and he might be able to score a couple of dollars from petty cash "to help fund you, you know, whatever work you wanna do." Still giving it the old school try, Fain asked if he could tell Mark Davis that the money was "not necessarily for the CAP." "That's fine," said Foreman.

It was May 13, 1989.

On May 31, Ilse Asplund lay asleep in the house she shared with Mark Davis deep in the woods outside Prescott. Her own children and Mark Davis's two daughters were in the house with her.

At 3 A.M. Ilse woke up, alarmed. She padded out to the living room, where she had left a sleeping bag on the couch for Peg. The bag was empty. She wondered what was going on but realized there was nothing she could do. She went back to bed and fell asleep. She dreamed about a jail cell. The floor of the cell was hard-packed dirt. She touched it with the flat of her hand. It was cool and dry. High above her head, there was a narrow window with bars. No light came in. Inside the cell it was quiet. Ilse breathed more slowly. She felt a sense of relief.

While Ilse dreamed, Peggy, Mark Davis, and Marc Baker were running from the FBI SWAT team at power pole number 40-1 outside Salome, Arizona. Baker went down first, stumbling and losing one of the ridiculous snowshoe-type devices that he had fashioned out of plywood and baling wire in an effort to disguise his footprints. He fell down and stayed down. A SWAT team member kept a gun trained on him until an interrogator led him away. Davis, too, was arrested quickly and without incident. Neither man was armed, although the FBI confiscated Baker's Swiss Army knife. It wasn't much of a weapon; its blade was broken.

Peg was not so easy to catch. She had one great advantage over her pursuers—lack of fear. The desert had always been her refuge; it didn't betray her. She instinctively knew which jagged rock would give way and which would hold beneath her feet, which cairns might hide a rattlesnake den. She also knew that the biggest threat to a human being in the wilderness is panic. Peg didn't panic. The woo-woo kicked in—all her meditation, the dreams about her power animal, the raccoon. She sank herself into her surroundings, *became* the rocks, the clean-smelling creosote, the paloverde arcing over the wash.

Peg ran all night. By the time the moon rose, she had outpaced the FBI agents, their helicopters, horses, and German shepherds. At dawn she reached asphalt. Over the past few hours she had assessed her situation, deciding that the only sensible course was to turn herself in. She stood placidly by the side of the road, waiting to be picked up. She was unmistakable, with her strong rooted legs, her long single braid, and her wire-rimmed glasses. One, two, three sheriff's cars whizzed by her. The hell with it, she decided, and stuck out her thumb. A little old man with a cooler full of sodas picked her up. They sipped cans of Tab all the way to the Pancake Inn on the outskirts of Prescott. The FBI didn't find her until afternoon.

About the time Peg was getting out of the car in front of the Pancake Inn, FBI agents were knocking at the door of Dave Foreman and Nancy Morton's house on Calle Carapan. After Nancy opened the door, they pushed past her into the couple's bedroom, swung open the door, and surrounded the bed where Foreman was sleeping. He opened his eyes to the blue-black gun barrels of three cocked .357 Magnums. The stunned Foreman took out his earplugs—there were noisy dogs on the block that year—and the FBI agents read him his rights. It was only later that Nancy realized the agents must have known the floor plan of her house.

At the same time that the FBI was crossing the threshold of the Calle Carapan house, another group of agents arrived at the house on Sosna Drive in Prescott where Ilse Asplund lived. This group included the investigation's team leader, Lori Bailey.

It was 7 A.M., and Ilse was getting her children and Mark's two daughters ready for school. Ilse was still in her nightshirt and the kids were looking for their shoes when Bailey and another woman grabbed her and marched her off to another room in the apartment. The frightened children were left sitting in a row on the couch while FBI agents went upstairs to search Mark's apartment for evidence. Downstairs, Ilse and Lori Bailey confronted each other. Ilse refused to speak to Bailey without a lawyer. "What would you like us to do with your children when we arrest you?" Bailey threatened. Matching her steel magnolia to steel magnolia, Ilse replied, "I'll deal with that when the time comes." Suddenly Ilse heard one of the kids crying. She ran out to the living room, where a beefy FBI agent was "guarding" the children, and ordered him upstairs. The FBI had a warrant to search Mark's apartment, not hers, she told him. At first the agent refused. But Ilse stood right in front of him until he reluctantly moved upstairs. Only when one of the kids piped up, "Mom, you're in your underwear!" did she notice she was still in her nightshirt.

After that incident, things calmed down. Bailey eventually gave up on getting Ilse to talk. She allowed her to get dressed and take the children to school. Under the scrutiny of a half dozen FBI agents watching from a second-floor balcony, Ilse loaded the car with the four kids and several bags of laundry. "She's loading something in the car," she heard one of them say. As she drove off, she comforted the stunned children, imagining the FBI agents searching through soiled socks and underwear.

Down in Phoenix, the FBI was having an easier time with Marc Baker. Baker was spilling at least part of his guts, telling them he had made a terrible mistake by following Mark Davis, even if he did agree with him in principle.

A few weeks later Prescott was hit by a violent summer rainstorm. Ilse was driving home when she passed Ron Frazier going the opposite way. They pulled over and talked for a minute, letting the monsoon heave big raindrops through their open car windows. Frazier told Ilse that he had just been out to her house looking for her. She asked him to follow her home so they could talk. As the storm beat against the windows of the Sosna Drive house like giant moth wings, Frazier confessed to being an informer. Ilse couldn't help smiling when he told her Lori Bailey had been furious at her recalcitrance on May 31. "She thought you would be easy," Frazier told Ilse. Even Peg had misjudged her the same way. On the night of the Canyon Mine hit, Peg told Mike Fain that she had been nervous as a cat while Ilse had been completely calm.[4]

But as Frazier kept talking, her satisfaction was replaced by fear.

"You are all terrorists, and I was in constant fear of my life," she reports that Frazier told her. "I had no choice but to go to the FBI or to pull a Rambo at an Earth First! Rendezvous."

Ilse sat at her kitchen table terrified, but she tried not to let him sense her panic.

"He was like a great white shark," she said. "Silent and deadly." She remembered Frazier trying to poach deer in the woods surrounding the Grand Canyon Rendezvous site. The woods were full of people who could easily be mistaken for game, particularly by a hunter tripping his brains out on LSD.

Ilse was indicted six months later.

It would be two years before the Arizona Five, as they came to be called, went to trial. In those two years, the sophisticated anarchy that had held Earth First! together broke down completely.

14   Vineland

She'd come down by the old 101 from the redwoods to the City, a teenage beauty with the same blue eyes and wolf-whistle legs her daughter would have, out on her own early because of too many mouths to feed at home. Her father, Jess Traverse, trying to organize loggers in Vineland, Humboldt, and Del Norte, had suffered an accident arranged by one Crocker "Bud" Scantling for the Employers' Association, in plain sight of enough people who'd get the message, at a local ball game, where he was playing center field. The tree, one of a stand of old redwoods just beyond the fence, had been cut in advance almost all the way through. Nobody in the stands heard saw strokes, wedges being knocked loose . . . nobody could believe, when it began to register, the slow creaking detachment from the lives around it as the tree began its descent. Voices found at last only reached Jess in time for him to dive out of the way, to save his life, but not his mobility, as the redwood fell across his legs, crushing them, driving half of him into the earth.

—Thomas Pynchon
Vineland, 1990

1990 – Northern California

THE BODY'S SHOCK MECHANISM IS A TURTLE moving at the pace of a hare. It pulls everything inward, shunting blood away from the extremities and pumping it furiously to the vital organs: liver, heart, brain. There is something else, too, a protective psychological film that drops like a loose window shade. For more than a year, Judi Bari could not remember the pain she felt when the pipe bomb went off in her car, shattering her pelvis. In her memory, her body was a distant island. She didn't hear the sound of sirens or smell her own burning flesh.

The only thing she did remember was straining to visualize the faces of her two daughters in an effort to make herself want to live. But sight failed her.

It was only later, when she was giving testimony in a lawsuit against the FBI for allegedly fumbling the investigation of the bombing, that Judi Bari remembered those first minutes of pain. Suddenly she heard the thunderous sound of the bomb. She was in her crumpled Subaru station wagon, begging the cops to lower the seat, not knowing one of its steel springs had been blown into her body. Floating in shock, she cried as they arranged her on a stretcher. She passed out for a few seconds, then came to, and that was the time she remembered once she got to the hospital. Pain beyond words, more brutal than she would have wished on the worst capitalist pig land raper in northern California. It made her want to die. But Judi Bari was going to live. This time.

Judi Bari's home lies between the Golden Gate Bridge and the Oregon border. The 400 miles of northern California coastline are fogged in, wild. Ice plants curl daggers over humped sand dunes. The dunes go on forever, like gray cities in a science-fiction movie about the overindustrialized overpopulated future that is turning final, banking before it lands with the unavoidable certainty but uncertain velocity of a plane running out of gas. There is a sense of borrowed time here on the vacant beach, its big transparent waves rocking the shore in a constant Einsteinian kinesis, the pulp mill belching a rainbow plume overhead. The plume is a leaky trail from logging roads that merge into a dense forest further inland. The beach is little more than a false front for tourists, a narrow bandage winding up the coast. The real northern California is in the deep woods, where big trees and bushy sensimilla plants are fed by the hot, bright summer sun and unremitting winter rains.

In the 1970s northern California was hippie heaven, an overflow valve for leftover leftists squeezed out by Nixon's accession and Carter's recession. Then the CAMP soldiers descended in their federal helicopters and camouflage pajamas, toting semiautomatic weapons and assorted paramilitary gizmos. The Campaign Against Marijuana

Planting turned Eden into a war zone. This was the war zone that Judi Bari happily walked into in 1986. Her background was typical, but Judi wasn't. She had gone to the University of Maryland, where she majored in antiwar protests and drugs. Like many Vietnam-era radicals, Judi was a pink-diaper baby. Her parents were linked not only by affection but by shared socialist ideals. Her mother, who is Jewish, was the first woman to graduate from Johns Hopkins University with a Ph.D. in mathematics. Her father is an Italian gem cutter. In college, Judi was not rebelling against her parents' values but against the hypocrisy that she believed they had adopted in order to function in society. When she toted home Mao Tse-tung's little red book, her mother admonished her, "Don't make the same mistake we did. Socialism in America has to be American." Bari took the advice to heart, but it would be a while before she actually used it, as an Earth First! organizer in California's timber and dope country. When she did, she would run up against the most brutal antienvironmental backlash in U.S. history.

If Judi Bari was an unlikely candidate for Buckaroo status, the man who introduced her to Earth First! appeared even more ill suited to the role. Darryl Cherney was a fast-talking Jewish guy from New York who had been a child actor in TV commercials. His indoor pallor and masses of dark, curly hair gave him the appearance of a Hobbit with bad habits. Darryl had made his pilgrimage to California in 1985, and California had not disappointed. A seemingly random encounter with a Native American hitchhiker named Kingfisher brought Darryl to the town of Garberville, a center for dope smuggling and environmental action. Not long after he arrived he found the offices of the Environmental Protection and Information Center, or EPIC, a grass-roots environmental group founded by an earlier generation of long-haired pilgrims. The EPIC activists were classic 1960s dropouts—a former real estate broker, an ex–legal secretary, the son of a Nobel Prize–winning physicist. They smoked dope, wore their hair in ponytails, and sported purple ties for press conferences. But the EPIC folks worked within the system, bringing a string of underfunded but remarkably successful lawsuits to stop log-

ging in California's old-growth forests. At the EPIC offices, Darryl
was struck by one of Earth First!'s "silent agitator" stickers, which
featured an updated version of the green fist logo Mike Roselle had
sketched after the Pinacate trip. That summer Darryl attended the
Earth First! Rendezvous in Colorado. The diminutive urban refugee
was "scared shitless" of all the big macho guys guzzling beer and
howling around the campfire. But when Darryl whipped out his guitar, he fit right in. Back in California he became the resident ecoradical, singing environmental folk songs that got airplay on local radio
stations. He even made it onto Doctor Demento's syndicated show.

Things really started happening when Darryl met up with a
bearded, handsome young reporter named Greg King in March 1986.
King had driven up to Garberville to cover his first demonstration, a
guerrilla tree planting on George Pacific land. He spotted Darryl in
the crowd of hippies waiting for rides outside the EPIC office. Darryl,
who gravitates toward reporters like a starving coyote to mice, lost no
time in getting to know King.

When he met Darryl Cherney, King had just won an award for
his investigative reporting on Louisiana-Pacific's operation in Sonoma
County, which lies between San Francisco and the timber empires of
Mendocino, Humboldt, and Del Norte. A banker's son, King had
grown up in Sonoma. Now he was getting interested in what was
happening farther north, where people were less sophisticated and the
action was rougher. He had read about Texas corporate raider Charles
Hurwitz taking over a family-run timber operation in Humboldt
called Pacific Lumber. For decades, Pacific Lumber had been a notable
exception to the aggressive harvesting practices of the region's two
other major landholders, Simpson and Louisiana-Pacific. Because of
its conservative cutting policies, PL owned more untouched redwood
forest than any company in California. Darryl and his local Earth First!
activists thought PL's old-growth holdings should be seized by the
state to become parkland. But the state would have to act fast. A report
commissioned by Hurwitz's corporation, Maxxam, was recommending that Pacific Lumber more than double its cut. If this advice was
followed, Pacific Lumber would become indistinguishable from the

region's other timber companies.¹ The company also could pay off the more than $500 million junk-bond debt that Hurwitz had incurred while buying the company.

It was a hell of a story. But to Greg King, it was more than a story. In the fall of 1986, King quit his newspaper job. He had just had his first look at Owl Creek Grove, a stand of old-growth red-woods owned by Pacific Lumber. After he saw it, journalism wasn't enough. He moved north to save the redwoods, even turning down an offer by a Sierra Club activist to run a weekly newspaper. He wanted to *do* something. With the help of deep-ecology popularizer Bill Devall, who taught at Humboldt State University, King and two students named Larry Evans and Todd Swarthout developed a proposal for a 98,000-acre wilderness complex. In keeping with their state-of-the-art ecological orientation, the proposal was designed to protect an entire watershed. The area included the largest contiguous piece of old growth still in private hands, a little-known 3,000-acre stand of ancient redwoods owned by Pacific Lumber. The land was off-limits to hikers, but King mapped it anyway, becoming the first environmentalist to enter the forest. It was an unbelievably pure rush. He felt like an explorer discovering a new world, an experience that had become increasingly rare in a world made smaller by technology and overpopulation. Yet it had been a formative event in the lives of many conservationists. Wilderness Society founder Aldo Leopold had experienced it when he entered the Sierra Madre in 1936 after a trip to Germany. In a single year, Leopold saw the extremes of human impact on the land, from the fully civilized to the fully wild. This stark contrast had a profound effect on his thinking.²

Another Wilderness Society founder, Bob Marshall, spent much of his short but intense life seeking out the pure wilderness rush. Marshall and his brother George were both under twenty-one when, with their guide Herb Clark, they became the first people to climb all forty-six Adirondack peaks over the height of 4,000 feet. Even with the heavy equipment of his era, Marshall routinely hiked thirty to forty miles a day. Alaska was his mecca. Nowhere else did Marshall find the undiluted experience of going where no man had gone before—probably. (In those days, wilderness hikers didn't stop to consider that their virgin land may have been the corner grocery store for prehistoric people.) "In many ways the greatest one day I have ever spent was the day we snowshoed up to the very head of Clear River and looked down over the top into the Hammond River watershed," Marshall wrote in his posthumously published book *Alaska Wilderness.* "The thrill of that look into unknown country and the thrill of being the first people ever reaching the head of a great river are things that stand out forever in a person's memory." Marshall died of mysterious causes while on a train from Washington, D.C., to New York. A police autopsy was unclear about the cause of death but showed evidence of leukemia and coronary arteriosclerosis. His friend and colleague Robert Sterling Yard believed Marshall's unremitting demands on his body hastened his death. There was evidence of a certain compulsiveness on Marshall's part. In Forest Service camps he was known for his eccentric habit of listing things. He not only wrote down information about his hikes; he also noted the average number of pancakes eaten by his fellow Forest Service workers. His boss called him enthusiastic, happy, eager to learn, and "a very odd chap." Nevertheless, his family-authorized biographer, James M. Glover, said Marshall was not driven to his death by neurosis but made a conscious decision to live at full throttle. He was thirty-eight years old when he died.

On his excursion onto Pacific Lumber territory, Greg King experienced a frenzy similar to Marshall's. In two days, he completed a rugged thirty-five-mile hike that was supposed to take twice as long. He couldn't stop walking. Even though he knew loggers had been on the property, he saw no sign of them. The forest was a giant's landscape of velvety redwoods and ferns as tall as a human being. King half expected to see a woolly mammoth drinking from the rock-strewn waters that crossed and recrossed his path on a heavily wooded ridge. "It was the Lost World, not just because I was lost, but literally, it seemed like walking from the present into millions of years ago," he said. The redwoods were Greg King's Pinacate Desert; they meant to him what Yosemite had meant to John Muir. In the following months, King led students on trespassing expeditions to map the forest, which he named Headwaters. By August, he was tree sitting with Corvallis-based Earth First! activist Mary Beth Nearing in a week-long protest that was eventually broadcast on the *Today* show and on *20/20.* The next year, King and the Humboldt State students completed their wilderness proposal, which they presented at a national conference on environmental restoration in Berkeley.

They had, as politicos say, an issue. In January 1988, Darryl organized a march on freezing-cold Wall Street to protest Hurwitz's takeover. Fifteen New York City protesters stood in a circle holding abandoned Christmas trees. They sang along with Darryl to the tune of John Lennon's song "Give Peace a Chance." "All we are saying, is give trees a chance." At Maxxam headquarters, a spokesman denied that the company was destroying a national treasure. But he admitted that increased logging was necessary to pay for the takeover.[3]

In October, a congressional report revealed "significant evidence" of insider trading in the takeover of Pacific Lumber by Maxxam Group, Inc. Pacific Lumber was one of fourteen takeover-related stocks named by the SEC in connection with the insider-trading investigation of Ivan Boesky and Drexel Burnham Lambert, Inc.

Only days before the Pacific Lumber takeover bid surfaced, two investment firms, the Jeffries Group and the Transcontinental Services Group, had purchased large amounts of Pacific Lumber stock. Later, members of the Jeffries Group would admit that they had been used as a front for convicted felon Ivan Boesky, although they admitted nothing specific about the Pacific Lumber transaction. The second outfit, Transcontinental Services Group, was headed by a friend of Hurwitz's named Stanley Cohen. Hurwitz's corporation, Maxxam, held 12 percent of the stock of Transcontinental, which was registered in the tax haven of the Netherlands Antilles. The report also stated that Stanley Cohen was a partner in the law firm representing Maxxam in the takeover.[4]

After the report was issued, Hurwitz and Cohen testified at a Congressional hearing on hostile takeovers. No significant action was taken against them. But Maxxam's troubles were far from over. Just as things were cooling off in Washington, trouble began in California. In 1988 and 1989, Pacific Lumber stockholders, including members of the family that had owned the company before Maxxam, brought two separate lawsuits contesting the takeover. The uproar wasn't confined to the company's upper reaches. Pacific Lumber mill workers became alarmed that increased production would put them out of a job. "It's incredible the amount of wood that's being cut. They're selling logs for export; they're selling logs to other mills. It's gluttony," said Pete Kayes, a ten-year PL employee. Another worker said, "I don't agree with the tree spiking or anything. But without trees there are no jobs."[5] The workers hired a San Francisco consultant and attempted, unsuccessfully, to buy out Charles Hurwitz.

This shining example of the New Greed was a perfect setting for Judi Bari's entrance. Darryl Cherney first met Judi in 1987 at a benefit concert. A few weeks later, they ran into each other at a local environmental center. Cherney was running for Congress, a classic Darryl move that generated more personal publicity than political heat. He asked Judi to make posters for a save-the-redwoods fund-raising campaign.

"The thing that attracted me to her was her incredible sense of humor," said Darryl. "She laughed like hell at my congressional campaign."

Bari agreed to do the graphics only if Cherney entertained her two-year-old daughter. He improvised a tune, winning over Judi's daughter—and Judi herself. In a lot of ways, it was a match made in hell, a clash of titanic egos. But until it ended a year and a half later, it was true love. Because Darryl was, in the words of one of Judi's friends, a "wimp," Judi could tap into her own softer, more emotional side when he was around. Darryl fed on Judi's intellect. Darryl, who had once been a flack for a record company, would always rely more on flash than analysis, but the couple seemed well matched politically.[6] Still, Darryl was forced to expend considerable time and energy persuading Judi to join Earth First! Like many women in the Bay Area (and elsewhere), Judi thought Earth First! was a bunch of rowdy, sexist assholes. On top of that, the group seemed to be getting a little stale.

John Davis had gradually taken over from Foreman as editor of the *Earth First! Journal*. The youthful Davis he had majored in environmental ethics in college. Under his direction, the *Journal* became mired in dull, theoretical discussions of deep ecology and long-winded scientific (or pseudo-scientific) articles on conservation biology. Although well-intentioned, Davis had the heavy-handed way with a blue pencil that is the mark of a young editor. The facts stayed in, but the author's voice got lost. By 1989, the *Journal* had lost more than its writers' voices and its sense of humor. It had also lost most of its audience in the mainstream environmental movement. "I still see it now and then," said Tom Turner, a former editor-in-chief of the Friends of the Earth publication *Not Man Apart,* now an editor for the Sierra Club Legal Defense Fund. "But I'm damned if I can read it."

Dullness was not the *Journal*'s only problem. When the articles weren't tedious, they tended to be offensive. *Journal* articles on AIDS, immigration, and Third World famines were provoking an outcry from people who ordinarily would have looked favorably on Earth First! As they struggled to contort deep ecology into an all-encompassing worldview, Earth First! writers like Christopher Manes were coming up with theories that took it to absurd lengths. Manes's 1987 article, written under the pseudonym Miss Ann Thropy, began with the statement "If radical environmentalists were to invent a disease to bring human population back to ecological sanity, it would probably be something like AIDS." Manes was careful to mention that it was merely coincidental that AIDS hit the homosexual population first. But his celebratory attitude toward the epidemic was partly based on the dumb contention that AIDS would wreak enough havoc to spell the end of industrial civilization. Failing that, Manes gloated over the fact that the epidemic promised to reduce human population.

Most environmentalists would agree that population reduction is desirable. Some would even agree that diseases like AIDS may be nature's response to humans overrunning the planet. But few would manifest such enthusiasm for this particular method of solving the problem. "As radical environmentalists, we can see AIDS not as a problem, but a necessary solution (one you probably don't want to try for yourself)," wrote Manes, whose tasteless echo of Hitler's "final solution" was either unconscious or a joke. If it was a joke, most people didn't get it. Manes compounded his sins by flourishing references to Voltaire and using the word *effect* when he meant *affect*. The juxtaposition of pretentiousness and sloppy writing only made the whole thing more offensive.

Ed Abbey could get away with making immodest proposals. Manes couldn't. It was a question of tone as well as content. Instead of sounding like a modern-day Jonathan Swift using exaggeration to make a point, this new breed of radical sounded insensitive, immature, and possibly dangerous. Worst of all, they sounded pompous. The heyday of the Buckaroos was long past.

Manes's article was followed by a string of equally controversial polemics. For a few months, the pages of the *Earth First! Journal* became a national refuge for crackpots. To be fair to John Davis, he was virtually prohibited from turning down articles from any faction of Earth First! A bunch of anarchist "mutualists" who had rudely confronted Ed Abbey at the 1987 Grand Canyon Rendezvous strutted their stuff in an article titled "Alien-Nation." The anarchists accused Earth First! of racism, sexism, and "the worst kind of wild west imagery." Yet another AIDS article suggested that Gaia's own immune system might be lashing out against human beings, not merely for being too prolific but also for killing whales. The author, a lawyer named Daniel Conner, wrote that he hoped a cure for AIDS would be found. But he prayed that Gaia would not respond by hurling something more terrible at us, like Big Nurse straight-arming a javelin toward her cowering charges.

These articles, along with Abbey's immigration piece and a few ill-considered remarks by Foreman about famine in Ethiopia, sent the American Left into a feeding frenzy. "When I tell people how the worst thing we could do in Ethiopia is to give aid—the best thing would be to just let nature seek its own balance, to let the people there just starve there, they think that is monstrous. But the alternative is that you go in and save these half-dead children who will never live a whole life. Their development will be stunted. And what's going to happen in ten years' time is that twice as many people will suffer and die," Foreman told deep-ecology popularizer Bill Devall in an interview conducted as the two men sat at the top of Growler Peak in the Cabeza Prieta National Wildlife Refuge in southern Arizona.

After Devall's interview was published, social ecologist Murray Bookchin took Foreman to task, both in print and in person. So did dozens of other people, who told Foreman that the displacement of traditional agriculture by cash crops for First World markets was a major reason for African famines. But population was one of Foreman's hobbyhorses. He boasted that he had married the only two women who disliked children more than he did. He had gotten a vasectomy "for ethical reasons" and it irked him that Earth First!ers were "having children right and left." There were quite a few people who agreed with him. This segment of Earth First! bore an odd resemblance to modern-day Shakers. The women got tubal ligations and the men got vasectomies. To the people who agreed in principle that overpopulation was bad but held more moderate views, the phenomenon smacked of self-mutilation.

But Foreman's views were not illogical. The doubling of human population over the next fifty years was a truly frightening concept. It didn't make sense to have children if you were an environmentalist, but most people settled for having one or two children rather than three or four. As for the starving Ethiopians, Foreman's solution also made sense—in strictly logical terms. But a civilization that lets its children starve to death hardly seems worth saving. The callousness of Foreman's remarks obscured what many Americans considered to be the real issue—cutbacks in funding for international population-control by successive Republican administrations whose policies were being dictated by the religious right.

Because he was the prime spokesman for Earth First!, Foreman was attacked for the AIDS and immigration articles, as well as for his own remarks about Africa. His response to the criticism was unclear. Sometimes he apologized for his insensitivity, as he did onstage with

Murray Bookchin in New York City in November 1989. At other times, he would dodge the question and reassert his allegiance to a less brutal form of deep ecology. He even wrote a defense of Abbey's article on illegal immigration. Foreman's opening anecdotes are vivid pictures of life on the U.S.-Mexican border, full of color and compassion. At the end he shifts tone, defensively reiterating Abbey's wistfully impractical recipe for dealing with the immigration problem. ("Stop every campesino at our southern border, give him a handgun, a good rifle, and a case of ammunition, and send him home. He will know what to do with our gifts and good wishes. The people know who their enemies are.") The awkwardness of this well-meaning defense is unmistakable. Even Abbey presumably knew that his immigration essay was meant to be thought-provoking satire, not policy analysis.

In general, Foreman's uncomfortable tossing and turning gave him away as an "old wilderness activist" who appeared to be out of his depth—or at least too far away from his home turf. One of his mentors, Celia Hunter, whose progressive political views sprang from her Quaker background, found Foreman's public statements incomprehensible. Years before, she had judged him better suited to the "rough and tumble" of New Mexico politics than to the patrician hallways of Washington, D.C. But even if his worldview was colored by his down-home roots, she didn't understand why his intellect seemed to balk at anything that sounded Liberal with a capital *L*. The poet Gary Snyder, who had given his qualified support to Earth First! since the group's inception, believed that Foreman had never stopped running long enough to think things through. Whatever his reasons, Foreman made himself vulnerable to criticism, not just from outsiders but also from within Earth First! The carping was even more emotionally exhausting than FBI persecution. Christopher Manes, the author of the controversial AIDS article, avoided most of the flak because he had written under a pseudonym.

Despite these offenses, Judi let Darryl convince her to join Earth First! "I had problems with Earth First!" she said. "I was against tree spiking, and I was appalled by this male macho image and their anti-labor attitude. I thought it was disgusting." But Cherney convinced her. "Darryl said to me, 'Look, you can either start a new group from scratch, or you can join Earth First! and the timber companies will quake in their boots.' I realized there was something to that. Also, Earth First! is very decentralized. I realized we could make our group any way we wanted."[7]

It was inevitable that Judi Bari's Earth First! would be very different from Dave Foreman's. About the only thing that Judi shared with the old-line Buckaroos was a sense of humor. For one thing, her political experience was in labor organizing, not in the conservation movement. In the mid-1970s she had dropped out of college and put her socialist ideals into practice by becoming a blue-collar worker and a union activist. For seven years she worked at the Washington Bulk Mail center in Largo, Maryland. She published an underground newsletter called *Postal Strife,* satirizing the official publication, *Postal Life. Postal Life* had the postal eagle; *Postal Strife* had the postal buzzard. At one point, Judi and a group of workers smuggled in a researcher for columnist Jack Anderson so he could see how unsafe machines were mangling the mail. The resulting nationally syndicated article carried a headline that Bari coined—"YOU MAIL 'EM, WE MAUL 'EM."[8]

Judi used *Postal Strife* as a way to consolidate her power. Managers, it seemed, were more afraid of ridicule than outright insubordination. As a shop steward, she was able to end the mail center's mandatory overtime policy. She was so effective that some of her black coworkers called her "Mafia Mama" in a joking reference to both her Italian name and her clout.

Legends grew up around Judi which suggested that she didn't need the Mafia to act tough. A janitor with a reputation for sexual harassment interrupted her when she was talking to a fellow shop steward named Joe Cuppy in the lunchroom. When Bari didn't respond, the janitor put his arm around her and touched her breast, saying to Cuppy, "Judi really doesn't like men, does she?" In a reflexive action, she decked him with a karate punch. He hauled himself up and threatened her. But Bari kept talking. That was how she was, incredibly intense. She had been about to make a point and nothing was going to stop her. Over the next several weeks, the janitor continued making threats. A protective phalanx of workers silently surrounded Judi every time he walked by.[9]

Clearly Judi Bari was not your average gal—neither your average female blue-collar worker, usually a tough breed, nor your average female Earth First!er, an even tougher one. Her unaffected warmth drew people to her, but her abrasiveness was hard for some people to handle. In 1979 she married a fellow union organizer named Mike Sweeney and moved to Santa Rosa, California. She had two children and participated in antinuclear and Central American demonstrations. She didn't quite fit in with the mellow Sonoma County left-wingers, who tend to sound as if they're trying to overthrow the government while on Quaaludes. "It was hard for me to deal with Judi's anger," one of her girlfriends told a reporter. "She's a hostile person. She knew the world was fucked up."[10] In 1988, after she and her husband began building a house up north in the heart of dope and tree country, Judi's marriage dissolved. She got a job working for David Raitt, the brother of singer Bonnie Raitt, who owned a construction company called California Yurts. Each day she commuted to work, her little car surrounded by fully loaded logging trucks. It was 1988, a ten-year high for logging in California. Suddenly she put it together. "I was putting the siding on this house and it was just this beautiful stuff—this redwood was like twenty feet long with no knots and this tight grain— and a light bulb went off in my head. And I went to the bookkeeper and said, 'Is this old-growth redwood?' and he said, 'Oh yeah, the salesman told me this stuff is a thousand years old.' I began to become really obsessed with the forest."[11]

Soon Bari was bringing the same intensity to environmental issues that she had once focused on union organizing. At a wealthy client's housewarming party she presented him with a photo of a clearcut to show how ancient redwoods had been sacrificed for his house. Instead of throwing Judi out, he hung the photo up. This act was similar to

Earth First! guerrilla theater, but not quite the same. Judi's move had that nasty edge; personal, gritty. But it was close enough for rock and roll.

It was a good time for Judi to jump on Earth First!'s Pleistocene Go-Kart. Mike Roselle, the Buckaroo most sympathetic to Bari's left-wing views, had been living in California since 1984. Half of the *Journal*'s subscribers also lived in California, where the movement was expanding its range into new environmental issues. For example, Roselle was working on the boycott of Burger King. The fast-food empire was being targeted for encouraging rain forest destruction because of its use of low-cost Latin American beef. Randy Hayes and another environmentalist named David Cobb had been trying to get Friends of the Earth to take on the rain-forest issue for years. But their efforts were stymied by the group's financial problems. In 1984, Hayes, who had helped Toby McLeod film the cracking of the Glen Canyon "Damn," finally decided to launch his own environmental group, the Rainforest Action Network. Mike Roselle pitched in, designing RAN's stationery and coordinating its activities with Earth First! David Brower, who had an infallible instinct for important new ideas, also supported Hayes. So did movement advertising man Herb Gunther. After a stint in a closet-sized room at Gunther's nonprofit Public Media Center in San Francisco's North Beach neighborhood, the Rainforest Action Network moved into the offices of Earth Island Institute, the group that Brower had formed after Friends of the Earth ousted him in 1985. By 1992, Hayes and his twenty-member staff were operating out of a spacious two-story corner office just across the street from Earth Island Institute and a few blocks from the group's original cubbyhole at the Public Media Center.

Not long after Rainforest Action Network was formed, California ecoradicals glommed onto another up-and-coming issue, genetic engineering. On April 24, 1987, Earth First! ecoraiders yanked out a patch of 2,000 strawberry plants in Brentwood, California. The strawberries had been treated with a genetically engineered form of bacteria called Frostban or ice-minus, a Vonnegut soundalike substance that was designed to retard frost. The genetic-engineering company that owned the ice-minus patent, Advanced Genetic Sciences, had been stopped from testing their product in several other California communities. Before the Brentwood test, San Francisco Earth First!ers and Green Party members had collected 1,200 signatures on an antitesting petition in Brentwood, which has a population of 5,600. But neither the county supervisors nor the state court would stop the test. The strawberry sabotage continued for the next year or two, but eventually the company was able to complete its work.

As usual, monkeywrenching's real clout rested in the realm of public relations. The Brentwood strawberry incidents, which attracted national media attention, vividly illustrated author and social critic Jeremy Rifkin's more reasoned arguments about the dangers of unleashing biotechnology before its potential impacts on the environment were understood.

In 1989, Earth First! began tentatively to establish links with hunt saboteurs. In the spring, a group of college women decided to parachute into British Columbia to protest a wolf hunt. They called themselves the Wolf Action Group (WAG) and were following in the footsteps of their mentor, Captain Paul Watson of the Sea Shepherds. At the last minute one of their leaders, Sue Rodriguez-Pastor, allowed herself to be bribed out of the jump by her stepfather, a successful Bay Area attorney who offered to put up the cash for a lawsuit. The other young women made the jump, but it was Rodriguez-Pastor's stepfather's legal offensive that stopped the hunt.

Although the Wolf Action Group ultimately relied more on the traditional tool of environmental groups—the goodwill of the rich—than newfangled in-your-face radicalism, it was notable for being one of the first organizations to plant itself in the area where animal rights and radical environmentalism overlap. This overlap is limited. Animal-rights activists care about individual animals, but most radical environmentalists would probably be happy to personally sacrifice ten dogs or cats if it meant saving a single endangered desert tortoise. Nevertheless, in the late 1980s uneasy alliances grew up between these two new wings of the environmental movement. Of course, not all Earth

First!ers were willing to embrace their new partners, who tended to be either weird, female, or vegetarian—and sometimes all three.

But Mike Roselle was a quick study—longtime Bay Area environmental journalist Angela Gennino called him a walking sound bite—and it wasn't long before he picked up on the new ideas that were floating around the environmental movement. The innovative spirit of West Coast environmentalism appealed to him, but there was something else that kept him hanging around. When he arrived in California in the fall of 1985, he crashed at a house that belonged to the local Earth First! contact person. Karen Pickett, who had gotten to know Roselle when she participated in the Bald Mountain blockades, lived in a rustic cabin in Canyon, a hippie community preserved along a back road in a honeycomb of plastic East Bay suburbs. A few months later, on an Earth First! excursion to Mexico, Roselle and Pickett fell in love. Roselle became a fixture in California. Eventually he and Pickett got married.

Northern California Earth First! had a unique constituency. It was a combination of students, hippies, gays, back-to-the-land white trash, disaffected dope-smoking loggers, and a sprinkling of misplaced intellectuals. The crusade that they adopted in 1990—saving the redwoods—should have been easy. The redwood forest was already acknowledged to be one of the wonders of the world. In fact, most people thought the redwoods had already been "saved." But only about 100,000 acres—5 percent—of the original two million acres of virgin redwood forest were still standing. About 76,000 acres were in parks. The rest was in private hands. Coming from the East helped Judi realize that the reason there was *any* old growth left in the West was the recent vintage of European settlement. The largest remaining stand of old-growth forest in New England was less than 100 acres. There was only slightly more in the Great Smokies. But here in northern California Judi could feel the frontier rushing up against the last ragged fringes of real wilderness. As usual, the wilderness was losing. Already the redwood gene pool had been permanantly altered.[12] Under the circumstances, there was a certain irony in the tree's Latin name, *Sequoia sempervirens,* which means "always living." With its soft, deep red bark and its ability to regenerate out of fire, the redwood made a good symbol for the Jungian principle of the feminine. Bari's political choices reflected her belief that contemporary culture splits off male and female traits. The feminine is virtually ignored while the masculine is overvalued. Bari wasn't the only one. A growing chorus of ecofeminist thinkers was linking diverse issues, including the ill treatment of livestock animals, to a male-driven culture of technology and death. The environmental consequences of this split were obvious. Dave Foreman had made the connection, too, although these days his inclinations might lead to shooting a range cow rather than lining a stable with straw. Foreman's quirks aside, the Earth First! bumper sticker that he had helped design and market, "Subvert the Dominant Paradigm," was a perennial best-seller. To Judi, and eventually to thousands of demonstrators who came to the North Coast in the summer of 1990, the cutting of redwoods, the largest trees in the world, became emblematic of how the culture of domination was choking life out of the planet. The fight to save the last redwoods took on overtones of a jihad.

When Judi held a powwow at a local diner with loggers and truckers, she explained her philosophy. "The first question they asked us was, 'Are you communists?' I answered, 'No, I'm much more radical. Communists only want to redistribute wealth in society; we want to have an entirely new society that's based on achieving a stable state with nature instead of exploiting the earth.' "

Bari's Californicated hippie utopianism would eventually set her at odds with the old-line Buckaroos. Not that they didn't share her vision of utopia. They just didn't believe it was possible. California optimism is like a night-blooming flower that fades as the sun rises over the motels of Reno, Nevada. A more familiar view of America returns when the traveler is faced with neon signs, nicotined rugs, and lurking teenage runaways. The rows of organic lettuce, colorful Guatemalan wristbands, and bottles of diamond-clear Japanese designer water degenerate into a half-remembered, low-calorie dream. Innovation is frowned upon. Rugged independence is prized; support groups are not. Foreman's days of touting tribal unity were over. By the time Bari joined Earth First! in 1988 he had securely wrapped himself in his pessimism. His goal was to save enough wilderness for a biologically diverse gene pool to survive the inevitable Armageddon.

Bari thought Foreman was failing to realize that wilderness did not exist in a vacuum. When asked to define their differences, Bari called herself an agnostic.

> It seems as though this whole thing is going to end in fire immediately. That's the religious view we've all been taught. But I don't know whether it will or not. I was raised nonreligious, with a Catholic father and a Jewish mother. . . . I do know that the earth cannot support this society. I don't know whether there's going to be a precipitous end or whether there's going to be a slow, grinding thing like Africa. That's why I feel that preserving wilderness in chunks isn't enough, although it needs to be done. Any chunks of wilderness can be destroyed by ozone or greenhouse or drought or also just by the pressures of this society. Anything that's left, hey, when they run out of old growth on private land you think they're not going for the parks? Or when they run out of Forest Service? They're goin' for the parks. It's only just a political boundary that says this is public and this is private.

In late 1989, Judi found an issue that combined social change with environmentalism. A community activist named Anna Marie Stenberg told Bari about a PCB spill at a Georgia Pacific mill in Fort Bragg. Bari and Stenberg brought the workers' case to OSHA, which initially ruled that the company had "willfully exposed" the workers to PCBs. When the workers failed to gain compensation, Bari, Stenberg, and Darryl Cherney recruited them to the environmentalist cause.

To Dave Foreman and most of the other founding Buckaroos, the idea of a worker-environmentalist alliance was repugnant. They believed that timber workers were responsible for their environmentally destructive acts. Judi felt that Foreman should blame the corporate bosses who were really in control, not the grunts. The clash may have revealed more about Foreman's working-class background and Judi's middle-class one than it did about the timber workers. In any case, Judi believed that her campaign to organize Louisiana-Pacific workers was the perfect riposte to the timber industry's charge that "environmentalists want to take your jobs away."

Darryl and Judi had a great time putting together their minority alliance of timber workers and environmentalists. Judi would play her fiddle and Darryl would rock out on acoustic guitar, shouting out lyrics in his thin, hoarse voice. Then Judi would get down to business: staging workshops to rally workers under the twin banners of Earth First! and the Industrial Workers of the World or Wobblies. To someone with Bari's intellectual rigor and black sense of humor, the Wobblies were the ultimate labor union. They were, in the purest sense, the radicals of the trade union movement. (The etymological origin of the word *radical* is the Latin word *radicis,* which means "going to the root of things.") Back in the early part of the century, the Wobblies had called for workers to seize the means of production. In its heyday, the IWW attracted between 5,000 and 10,000 members. It was about the same number of followers as Earth First! would later draw; perhaps it is the threshold for a radical group in the United States, not a friendly place for radicalism or for political ideologies in general. Like Earth First!'s, the Wobblies' clout was out of proportion to their numbers. They used music, art, and stickers, which they called "silent agitators" to get their message across. Their philosophy of "One Big Union" included blacks and women. They didn't believe in contracts, because they felt that contract negotiations drained the energy of union leadership. Instead, they favored "direct action" in the tradition of the English food riots. It was the Wobblies (and the prospect of some spare change) that Dave Foreman had in mind when he developed the bumper stickers and T-shirts, aka "snake oil and trinkets," sold by Earth First! It was also the Wobbly tradition, along with Foreman's interest in anthropology, that helped shape Earth First!'s mix of culture and politics.

In the case of the Wobblies, government repression was inevitable. In January 1914, one of the union's prominent leaders and songwriters, a man named Joe Hill, was arrested for murdering a grocery clerk. Despite a lack of direct evidence, he was convicted. The case became known all over the world. Ten thousand letters of protest were sent but failed to prevent Hill's execution on November 19, 1915. But Hill managed to get in the last word. Giving Joan Baez one of her best lines, he wrote to Wobbly leader Big Bill Haywood before his death, "Don't waste any time mourning. Organize."[13]

The government's dislike for the Wobblies increased as World War I intensified. In 1917, the government arrested 165 IWW leaders for conspiring to hinder the draft, encourage desertion, and intimidate people in connection with union disputes. In a statement that could just as easily have been made by a black political activist in the Vietnam era, one IWW man told the court: "You ask me why the IWW is not patriotic to the United States. If you were a bum without a blanket; if you had left your wife and kids when you went west for a job, and had never located them since; if your job had never kept you long enough in a place to qualify you to vote; if you slept in a lousy, sour bunkhouse, and ate food just as rotten as they could give you and get by with it; if deputy sheriffs shot your cooking cans full of holes and spilled your grub on the ground . . . how in hell do you expect a man to be patriotic? This war is a business man's war and we don't see why we should go out and get shot in order to save the lovely state of affairs that we now enjoy."[14]

All the defendants were convicted, juries not taking kindly to draft resistance, especially during wartime. Their punishment was not as severe as Jack Burns's in Abbey's novel *The Brave Cowboy*, who died in pursuit of freedom from nationalistic constraints. But it was enough to crush the movement for most practical purposes. The judge gave the defendants heavy sentences and fined the IWW $2,500,000. Big Bill Haywood, the Wobblies' most charismatic leader, jumped bail and fled to Russia, where he remained until his death ten years later. (He was reincarnated as a pseudonym for Dave Foreman's coauthor of *Ecodefense: A Field Guide to Monkeywrenching*.) After World War I, the Wobblies limped along, showing enough vigor in 1925 to convert Bob Marshall to socialism after he saw the improvements made by the union in Pacific Northwest lumber camps. But by the 1980s, the IWW consisted of little more than a home office in the Midwest and a few doddering Socialists.* Judi Bari set out to change that.

Bari actually won some converts. But even her minor success threatened the fragile equilibrium of northern California timber country, where working-class people were feeling squeezed from all directions. Mills were closing and in 1990 Louisiana-Pacific announced it was opening a new plant in Baja California, Mexico, that eventually would employ up to 1,000 people. The Baja mill, which was on the coast, would be well situated to process timber from Latin America when domestic wood ran out.

This phenomenon was nothing new. Historically the timber industry had cut and run. Moving from east to west, loggers scythed their way across the United States in the 1800s, leaving a wasteland of decimated forests and inspiring Gifford Pinchot to form the U.S. Forest Service to safeguard against such abuses in the future. He was only temporarily successful. By the 1980s, timber companies were once again practicing rape and run. The only difference was that now they were working on a global scale, taking advantage of lower wages and fewer environmental regulations in Third World countries. By 1992, Louisiana-Pacific had closed more than half a dozen Northern California mills, sold another half dozen to a spin-off company, and laid off about 1,000 workers. Partially processed logs were being shipped to Mexico from company docks in Samoa, California. When they arrived, they were planed and set out to dry by workers whose daily wages were only a little more than what U.S. workers earned in an hour.

The toll for California workers was not just financial. At Pacific Lumber, employees worked mandatory overtime to keep up with in-

---

* The elderly Wobblies included Edward Abbey's father, Paul Revere Abbey, who had outlived his son and was proprietor of a rock shop in Home, Pennsylvania, until his own death in 1992.

creased production. Two workers died and several were injured in the four years following the takeover. After the second death, a lumber handler said, "They're working us too hard. When you get tired and don't stay alert all the time, you do things you probably wouldn't do again . . . people don't pay as much attention as they should."[15]

Loggers averted their eyes from injuries caused by overwork. They looked away from the ever-expanding clearcuts. Instead they kept their gazes firmly trained on their car payments and mortgages. In any case, most of them were offended by smelly hippies who looked like trolls from Trollhatten telling them that their whole way of life was wrong.

But the pressure wasn't just coming from hippies. The real threat to the timber industry was the U.S. Fish and Wildlife Service, which in 1990 succeeded in having the northern spotted owl declared a threatened species. As the controversy over the owl grew, so did the timber industry's public-relations budget. By 1987, Pacific Lumber had already hired the notorious Washington, D.C., public-relations firm of Hill & Knowlton, whose client list reads like a Who's Who of Third World dictatorships, to gussy up its image.

Pacific Lumber wasn't the only timber company going on the offensive. The situation in northern California was ripe for exploitation by the so-called Wise Use movement. This bigger and better Sagebrush Rebellion was supported by industry, right-wing groups, and fundamentalist Christians. Suddenly environmental backlash groups seemed to be everywhere. One of the slickest is the Center for the Defense of Free Enterprise, a direct-mail and right-wing publishing organization run by Alan Gottlieb and Ron Arnold. The more visible partner, Ron Arnold, is a PR man with a Mennonite fringe of facial hair who is fond of declaring that his goal is to "destroy the environmental movement once and for all." Ironically, Arnold is a former member of the Sierra Club. A cynic might reflect that his change of heart could be traced to his rumored links to the financial empire of Sun Myung Moon.[16] Arnold's partner, Alan Gottlieb, is a major fund-raiser not only for the Wise Use movement but also for the gun lobby, which is his favorite cause, according to an investigative article by Jon Krakauer in *Outside* magazine. "A significant portion of the money winds up in Gottlieb's pocket as well," wrote Krakauer, "in the form of profits from the companies that perform the mailings and publish the books." Gottlieb is a convicted felon who did time for filing false income-tax returns. While he was in prison, his employees accused him of misusing foundation funds for personal gain and sued him for racketeering and conspiracy to defraud.

Chuck Cushman is another movement guru. He is head of the National Inholders Association, whose members own land that falls within the boundaries of national forests. Often the land had been in their families for generations, but now the government was trying, gently, to get them to follow new rules, or in some cases, sell out. Cushman, who looks a lot like Dave Foreman if you added twenty years and twenty pounds, travels around the country advising Wise Use adherents to videotape environmentalists as a form of intimidation.

By the early 1990s, the Wise Use movement claimed three million members. A member of the Bush staff, David McIntosh, spoke in support of their cause at their annual meeting. Renegade Sierra Clubber Ron Arnold crisscrossed the country, giving rousing speeches— including one to the American Newspaper Publishers' Association in Washington, D.C.—about the "sword" of antienvironmental justice whose purpose was to kill its enemies. Not surprisingly, violence against grass-roots environmentalists increased in this climate. A Florida woman told a *60 Minutes* reporter that men angered by her local group's attempt to police industry had retaliated by raping her, burning her with a cigar, and slashing her face with a razor. Fistfights broke out in upstate New York. In Ohio, a woman drawn to environmental activism after her child died of leukemia was pelted with rocks until she was unconscious.[17]

To Dave Foreman and other veteran activists, these attacks were nothing new. The memory of architect Buzz Yuins had never left Foreman. While Foreman was still working for the Wilderness Society, Yuins's corpse had been found tied to a tree not far from his home in Alpine, Arizona. The cause of death was listed as a heart attack, but Foreman believed that antienvironmentalist rednecks had killed Yuins by tying him up and torturing him. Now he had no doubt that the same people who had called Sierra Clubbers "green niggers" back when Brock Evans was still working as a field representative in the Pacific Northwest had gotten organized in a frightening fashion. It was as if the Ku Klux Klan had become a viable third party, with big corporate money, a raft of slick spokespeople, and a national political strategy.

Partly, the strategy consisted of co-opting the tactics of the environmental movement. This was outlined by a former California state senator, right-wing Christian, and state gun lobby founder named H. L. Richardson. Richardson is so far to the right that he accuses Strom Thurmond of being too compromising. In the late 1980s, the newly appointed head of the California Timber Association distributed copies of a Richardson speech to his membership as a position paper. It urged good Christians—and industry supporters—to go on the offensive by adopting the "confrontational" and organizational political tactics of their opponents.

The burgeoning Wise Use movement would hardly neglect northern California's high-profile political troubles. It wasn't long before a whole slew of "grass-roots" timber support groups sprang up from the San Francisco Bay to the Oregon border. Some acknowledged receiving industry funding; others refused to reveal who their supporters were. As Richardson had outlined, these pro-timber "citizens' groups" were modeled on the hundreds of grass-roots environmental groups formed as a response to the Reagan administration's neglect of environmental issues in the 1980s. They had heartland-inspired names like the Yellow Ribbon Coalition and W.E.C.A.R.E. These groups were clearly organized along class lines. For instance, W.E.C.A.R.E. occupied office space in the Eureka Chamber of Commerce and its members included prominent business and civic leaders. The Yellow Ribbon Coalition was the workingman's front group. Although it was supposedly a grass-roots operation, its plentiful printed signs were handed out in the mills. There was even an Earth First! takeoff called Mother's Watch. Mother's Watch specialized in pranks that went beyond Earth First!'s essentially good-humored jibes. These included impersonating Judi Bari on the telephone and printing fake Earth First! literature. As its name might suggest, Mother's Watch was an all-female group. It was headed by a classic redneck woman. She was not a long-haired western cowgirl like Peg Millett, but the real thing: an obese, brightly dressed woman with the crinkly hairstyle that is the result of the kind of bad perm perpetrated by hairdressers in every small town in America. Her name was Candy Boak. Boak was tough, angry, and intelligent. She came from the same generation as the hippied-out single mothers that Judi had attracted to the movement. A wary mutual respect existed between the two groups, but even those most sympathetic to Boak couldn't help feeling that Mother's Watch represented something ugly and dangerous, Earth First!'s evil twin.

The male version of Mother's Watch was even more sinister. The Sahara Club was a collection of off-road-vehicle users from Charlie Manson's playground, the Mojave Desert. The Sahara Club was the brainchild of two burly dudes named Louis McKey, aka the Phantom Duck, and Rick Sieman. In the early eighties, the Bureau of Land Management got McKey's dander up when it stopped the annual Barstow-to-Vegas dirt-bike race. The agency had found that 90 percent of the mammals along the racecourse were either getting wiped out or fleeing after hordes of exhaust-puffing dirt bikes rammed through the fragile desert. The year after the ban was instituted, McKey, under his Phantom Duck pseudonym, led a pack of outlaw racers booming through the closed-off racecourse. The next year, the BLM backed down and allowed the race.

Earth First! decided to take matters into its own hands. In 1987, half a dozen amateur engineers stayed up all night plugging a culvert with creosote-soaked railroad ties. The next morning 300 dirt bikers took off with a roar that sounded like a fleet of Concordes. As their wheels dug in, a dust cloud rose higher and higher, until the desert became temporarily invisible. When it cleared, the bikers realized they were riding straight toward a barrier of Day-Glo survey tape and a sign saying "Fuck the Duck."

It wasn't long before the Phantom Duck counterattacked. In 1988,

McKey and Sieman found the money to publish a newsletter. It featured articles like this one, headlined "FAGGOTS IN THE FOREST."

> In this day of "enlightenment", we are supposed to be tolerable [sic] of "alternate lifestyles". Well, at the Sahara Club, our values are very much old-fashioned and we call 'em as we see em. Anyway, it has come to our attention that the Sierra Club has a special chapter call [sic] GAY AND LESBIAN SIERRANS! This group, made up entirely of fruitcakes, has things like *"moonlight hikes" and "buddy backpacking trips."* Yessiree. Just don't bend over to sniff the flowers as you hike with this fun-loving group. If you want an idea of just how huge the queer membership is in the Sierra Club, give their Homo Hotline number a call and just listen to the activities these Virus Vampires have planned: [phone number].

Along with homophobia, infantilism, and violent tendencies, the Sahara Club's articles of faith included the theory that Earth First! was funded by the Sierra Club. This conspiracy theory also was touted by Pacific Lumber's president, a tough Australian named John Campbell.[18] This was no coincidence. Despite its patrician flavor, W.E.C.A.R.E., which Campbell supported, "networked" with the Sahara Club. The groups shared both information and mailing lists. If you were a member of W.E.C.A.R.E., you would receive an action alert in the mail when the Sahara Club was waging a letter-writing campaign and vice versa. W.E.C.A.R.E., which has since changed its name to the Alta California Alliance, also was linked to other so-called Wise Use organizations.[19]

Pacific Lumber and other timber companies probably didn't need to funnel so much money into W.E.C.A.R.E. and other phony grassroots groups. People in northern California already were running scared. The region had always suffered cyclical unemployment. Even when times were good, they weren't *that* good. Loggers weren't like blue-collar workers in Detroit who earned more than $20 an hour. Many timber companies, including Pacific Lumber, were nonunion.

The unions that did exist were feeble compared to their urban counterparts. Veteran loggers considered themselves lucky if they earned $15 an hour. Many timber workers made as little as $7.50 an hour for doing work that was dangerous even without tree spikers.

In fact, the Redwood Empire should have been called the Sensimilla Empire. The only ones getting rich in northern California were the dope growers. Mindful of their reliance on community goodwill, most made sure to inject money into the local economy. But when the CAMP helicopters arrived, the growers went underground. Thanks to federal dope eradication efforts, storefronts were boarded up, folks holed up at home with their Uzis, and northern California reverted to its status as a colonial dependent. Then, in the midst of dealing with this recession, northern California residents all of a sudden found a hobble on their only other cash cow, the timber industry. Trying to explain that global economics were to blame for their problems was like talking nuclear physics to a boar as it charged toward you with spears sticking out of its hairy hide. It didn't take long for things to get ugly.

First it was hate mail. Its source has still not been determined, but the ugly, homophobic ranting reeked of the Sahara Club. In fact, the Sahara Club newsletter had published the Earth First! contact list, inviting its readers to " 'reason' with them about the errors of their ways." The group also paid a visit to the North Country to teach a dirty-tricks workshop, which members of Mother's Watch attended.

Whoever they were, the authors of these letters were prolific. There were two main versions of the letters. One was sent to men, the other to women. The one received by approximately a dozen female activists in California (including people who were not affiliated with Earth First!) read like this:

> It has come to our attention that you are an Earth First! lesbian whose favorite pastime is to eat box lunches in pajamas . . . this kind of behavior is to be expected of lesbians like you, since we have been observing Earth First! freaks like you for some time. Not only have we been watching you . . . but we

also know and have distributed your phone number [which they include] to every organized hate group that could possibly have hostile tendencies toward ilk of your kind. No longer can sleazy dikes like you operate with impunity through the guise of anonymity. We know who you are, where you live, and continue to home in on you . . . but you don't know who we are. . . . Rest assured . . . that we shall not be indiscriminate in our actions against the spineless, invertebrate members of Earth First! To the contrary, we will specifically hunt down each and every member like the lesbians you really are.

The letters were signed by the "Committee For The Death of Earth First! Brought to you by Fed Up Americans for Common Sense." Men received similar letters accusing them of being "Earth First! fellatio expert(s) who suck dicks in outhouses."

In Tucson, the *Earth First! Journal* staff received reports of letters like these from 1987 until 1990, when they resigned en masse over political disputes and the *Journal* moved up to Missoula, Montana. California Earth First!ers received more threats than anyone else, with Judi Bari topping the list. Bari routinely got threatening phone calls and nasty misspelled missives. But the harassment wasn't confined to California, or even the West. "Dear Faggot" letters were sent to Earth First! activists as far away as Maine. Rod Mondt, who had worked as a Park Service law enforcement ranger, noticed that the period over which the letters arrived coincided with the FBI's undercover investigation. Mondt, Foreman, and the newspaper staff speculated endlessly over their source. Could the FBI have infiltrated the Sahara Club? Was the agency actually *funding* the right-wing nuts? The FBI had been involved with radical right-wing groups in Southern California before. In 1976, an informer named Howard Berry Godfrey told the *Los Angeles Times* that the FBI had paid him to participate in two right-wing groups in San Diego, the Minutemen and the Secret Army Organization. SAO member Jerry Lynn Davis said of Godfrey, "There were times we could not have existed without his financial

support. You might say we were a federally funded antipoverty program for the right wing." In January 1972, a young woman was shot
by a man riding in a car driven by Godfrey. Her family later sued the
FBI for hindering the investigation. Godfrey also testified that he had
sold explosives to an SAO member who bombed an adult movie
theater. These revelations raised serious questions about FBI complicity in the illegal activities of the right-wing groups that they were
investigating.[20]

On their most paranoid days, Mondt and the others wondered if
the FBI was sending the letters itself. COINTELPRO documents released as a result of a Socialist Workers Party lawsuit had revealed that
the FBI manufactured press releases and inflammatory cartoons to un-
dermine the 1960s antiwar movement. These flyers and press releases
were not unlike the material being circulated to make Earth First!
look bad. For instance, the Sahara Club newsletter published a diagram
that was supposedly a reprint from an Earth First! publication. It
showed how to build a booby trap that could injure or even kill a
motorcyclist or off-road vehicle user. The diagram was completely
spurious, but convincingly aped the *Earth First! Journal*'s format. Even
more suspicious was the appointment of Richard Held as special agent
in charge of the bureau's San Francisco office. The son of an FBI
agent, Held had been deeply involved in the FBI's COINTELPRO
investigations of the Black Panther Party and the American Indian movement. As a bureaucratic entity, COINTELPRO, short for
"counterintelligence program," had long since been officially moth-
balled. But the bureau still funneled $35 million a year into something
called "domestic counterterrorism."

Before the arrests of Foreman and his codefendants, Earth First!ers
contacted the FBI about threats that they were receiving. The FBI
told them that no crime had been committed, according to Mondt's
wife, Nancy Zierenberg, who was working as the *Journal*'s merchandise coordinator, and Kris Summerville, the paper's business manager.

"What made the whole thing so odd is that we had never gotten
any hate mail before," Zierenberg said. "We did get sort of a funny
fan letter from Squeaky Fromme—remember she was one of those

Manson girls?—from some federal prison somewhere, but that was it. Pretty amazing, when you think about it, because EF certainly was controversial. Then all of a sudden, all those letters. It was creepy."

For the northern California people, it was more than creepy. It was downright scary. The first violence occurred in the summer of 1989, when Earth First! staged a demonstration at a Calpella, California, lumber mill. The Earth First!ers were demonstrating against the chipping of young trees, pecker poles in logger's slang, to make pressed-wood products. According to Judi Bari, it was a peaceful demonstration, with no civil disobedience or illegal activity of any kind. Then someone in the crowd began revving a chainsaw. Bari says there were about forty police officers present. "They all just turned their heads away," she said.

Things were getting gnarly, and Greg King made them worse. "You're not gonna need such a big bar on your chainsaw anymore now that all the old growth is gone," he scoffed to a logger. The logger told him to get lost or he would "slap" him. Greg cockily replied, "You're not going to hit me." Wham! Greg went down. He had broken the first law that hippies learn in the Redwood Empire. Do *not* make smartass remarks about the size of a logger's equipment.

Greg and the others tried to get police to arrest the man who had decked him, but they refused. Weeks later, he was able to file charges. The logger pleaded guilty.

Earth First! wasn't exactly winning friends and influencing people in northern California. Judi's 1988 appearance at a pro-choice rally at a Planned Parenthood clinic had set the confrontational tone. The clinic was going to be the first place in Mendocino County to offer abortions. Operation Rescue, Randall Terry's militant national anti-abortion group, was threatening to appear for the grand opening. In the meantime, homegrown weirdos were harassing the clinic staff. Bill Staley, a former Chicago Bears linebacker with a walleyed My Lai stare, reportedly threatened to rape the clinic's director so she would have his child.

Too indignant to be worried about her personal safety, Judi tried to rally support for the clinic from Earth First! groups. At every meeting, she says, at least one guy would say, "It's not an Earth First! issue." Not an Earth First! issue? Population control? A few female Earth First!ers took her side, along with one or two "feminist men." Finally, she made her case at a lesbian coffeehouse. "None of the lesbians told me it wasn't a lesbian issue," she says, disgusted.

With her eclectic band of supporters surrounding her, Judi sang a song whose humor was so harsh it shocked even some of the people who agreed with her. Its lyrics were set to the tune of "Will the Circle Be Unbroken."

Betty Lou, she got pregnant,
and was addicted to 15 drugs,
she went down to the abortion clinic,
and was accosted by right-wing thugs.

(chorus)
Will the fetus be aborted,
bye and bye, lord, bye and bye,
there's a better world awaiting,
in the sky, lord, in the sky.

Bridget had two kids already
and an abortion is what she chose
the Christians showed her a bloody fetus
she said, that's fine I'll have one of those.

(chorus)

Reverend Broyles★ hated abortion,
but for a peaceful end he searched,
he said we'll never bomb your clinic,
we said we'll never bomb your church.

★ Reverend Broyles was a local Baptist minister.

(chorus)

There's so many starving children
and living in the streets is tough,
there's five billion of us already,
don't you think that is enough?

Nobody questioned the Earth First!ers' bravery. But some questioned their integrity. *California* magazine reporter Jonathan Littman suggested that Judi, who relished telling reporters about her affinity for fat joints she called "hooters," let herself be used by a dope grower whose business had been short-circuited by a small-scale timber operation:

> In August 1989, Bari and Cherney decided to blockade an access road to 300 acres being logged by Doyle Lancaster in Whitethorn, part of Humboldt's pot-growing region. The Lancasters, unlike Pacific Lumber or Louisiana-Pacific, were "gyppos"—small-business owners who do contract logging for the giant timber corporations and local mills. The Lancaster property was mainly oaks, madrones, Douglas firs and a few redwoods. There was no virgin old growth.
>
> Yet it was the second time the Lancaster family had been blockaded. Bari says the Lancasters were asking for it: "This really shitty gyppo was filling in streambeds, shooting guns off, logging on neighbors' pieces of land and speeding their trucks." She claims that outraged neighbors asked for Earth First! "reinforcements."
>
> "I know why we were targeted," says Gladys Lancaster. "This guy, he targeted us because he and a pal were growing pot on that property for years." When the Lancasters submitted their harvest plan in the spring of 1989, the Department of Forestry surveyed the property and found black irrigation pipe, fertilizer and fences—telltale signs of a pot-growing operation. The timber-harvest preparations made it impossible to

plant that season's marijuana crop. "They [the pot growers] lost access," says Lancaster.

Soon after, the Lancasters lost a Caterpillar to "monkey wrenching." Lancaster says the displaced pot grower bragged that he knew who had poured abrasives into the tractor's engine. On the day of the blockade, the pot grower was there with Bari and Cherney.

What Littman didn't appear to know was that pot was a minor consideration in Whitethorn. The town was Humboldt County's hub for the production of crank, also known as speed, crystal meth, or methamphetamine. In fact, right in the middle of the demonstration two businessmen demanded to cross the blockade to get to their lab. When a protester was crazy enough to try to stop them, they whipped out their semiautomatics, put the pedal to the metal, and ran the blockade.

The other thing Littman left out of his account was that an actual environmental issue was entangled with all this sleazy drug activity. The land under dispute ran along the banks of a tributary to the Mattole River. For almost a decade, back-to-the-landers had been lovingly restoring the Mattole to its former salmon-spawning glory. Their painstaking work was one of the cornerstones of the new environmental restoration movement. According to Greg King, the Lancasters were recklessly bulldozing along the streambed, even creating an illegal land bridge across the tributary itself. The stream was silting up under the depredations of the big Cat, King said. This was exactly what the Mattole folks had been trying to correct with their sandbags and laboriously hand-built rock retaining walls.

The difficulty of sorting out the motives of Bari, Cherney, and the others is not unusual in northern California, where dope is so entwined in the culture that local ministers bemoan the effects of a CAMP-inspired dip in the drug trade. In any case, whatever the moral passions and lapses that led up to the day of the Whitethorn demonstration, it ended up being an unlucky one even by funky northern California standards. It started peacefully enough, if somewhat obnoxiously, with Bari and Cherney reviving an old Commander Cody favorite to mock the blockaded truck driver—"Here I sit, all alone with a broken heart. Well, I took three bennies and my semi truck won't start. . . ." But the demonstration soon turned into a brawl. In the melee, David Lancaster, the son of the owner of the small logging outfit, allegedly broke the nose of Mem Hill, a woman in her fifties who was generally agreed to be completely nonviolent. After Hill had been injured, Earth First!ers jumped David Lancaster, said Judi Bari. "We were just basically restraining him, maybe a little kick and punch on the way, but . . . and then his brother got out a gun and shouted out, 'You fucking commie hippies, I'll kill you!' "

When the Mendocino County sheriff's department arrived, they took Lancaster's statement—he said he had hit Mem Hill by mistake —but wouldn't talk to the Earth First!ers, Bari said. Despite Hill's broken nose, the district attorney refused to press charges against David Lancaster.

Mendocino County was beginning to resemble a post-hipster version of the Hatfields and McCoys. But this was only the beginning of the trouble for Earth First! A day or so after the Whitethorn incident, a logging truck rear-ended Judi's car. The passengers included Darryl Cherney, Judi's friend Pam Davis, Pam's two young sons, and Judi's two daughters. According to Judi, her car was slammed so hard it reeled off the road and collided with another truck. The impact of this second collision pushed Judi's car into the porch of a bar. All the adults got whiplash. The kids mostly got scared. "One of them got glass cuts in her face and there are still scars that you can see. They're pretty light but they're still there. Other than that, they were sore a little bit. . . . Kids are made out of rubber," said Judi.

After the three vehicles smashed to a halt, everyone had a chance to look around. According to Judi, she recognized the truck that hit her as the same one she had been blockading at Whitethorn. After the accident, the driver appeared shocked. "Oh, God, I didn't know there were kids in the car," Judi says she heard him say. After thinking about that one for a little while, Judi decided to sue.

The back injury Judi suffered in the crash was serious enough to get her state disability payments. The accident put her out of commission as a carpenter, but that was only temporary. Her subsequent failure of nerve could have been permanent. But her courage returned after a trip to the Highlander Center, a venerable leftist institution in Knoxville, Tennessee. Since the 1930s, Highlander had been training political activists, including union organizers and civil-rights leaders like Martin Luther King, Jr., and Rosa Parks. At Highlander, Bari met people who had braved multiple assassination attempts without backing down. She saw gruesome pictures of strip mines, which struck her as not unlike clearcuts. She returned to California sobered, but with renewed commitment.

In the winter of 1989, Bari concentrated on working with the Georgia-Pacific employees who had been exposed to the PCB spill. "We had Earth First! activities certainly but not the kind of intensity we usually do during the summer," she said. "I never compromised the Earth First! side to work with the workers. What I did was seek out progressive enough workers so that they could handle that. I was the best-known Earth First!er in the area so any worker that met with me knew that's who they were meeting with. They still were willing to meet with me and work with me, which I thought was pretty damn incredible.

"There's some real radicals out there. They're just mostly scared to death. But there's some workers out there that I would call Earth First!ers. In fact, they don't need a book by Dave Foreman to tell them how to monkeywrench. They already know how *all* that machinery works. Actually there's more worker sabotage than there is Earth First! sabotage around here."

As Judi got more immersed in organizing for the IWW, Darryl faded out of the picture. According to Judi, "Workers have built-in bullshit detectors," and Darryl, whose stock in trade was PR, sent them into the stratosphere. Before long, Judi and Darryl were history, at least in a romantic sense. Judi and her friends, a cohort of downhome dope country mamas, were deliberately blowing the stereotype of Earth First! as a boy's club. In the process, Judi was starting to eclipse Darryl and Greg King. King didn't care, but Darryl was another story. Darryl needed attention the way Judi needed her late-afternoon hooter. He had always run off hyperkinetic actor's energy. Now, in the face of a barrage of death threats, he seemed to be unraveling. In March 1990, Darryl smugly told *60 Minutes* reporter Ed Bradley that if he contracted a fatal disease, "I would definitely do something like strap dynamite on myself and take out the Glen Canyon Dam. Or maybe the Maxxam building in Los Angeles after it's closed up for the night."

If the staff of the *Earth First! Journal* had been Jewish, they would have collectively exclaimed, "Oy vey!" as they watched their erstwhile colleague dive-bombing himself—and by extension, the whole group—into a deep, dark canyon, failing even to scrape the sides of the Glen Canyon Dam or the Maxxam corporation in the process. Probably figuring that an apology was in order, Darryl hastily flew to the Sonoran Desert to "cool out." He stopped over in Tucson, where the forces of reason no doubt attempted to lock the barn door after the horse had already gotten out and whinneyed loud enough to make Mr. Ed look like a demure newborn foal.

To Bari, Darryl's *60 Minutes* gaffe was merely a distraction. She and Darryl were organizing Earth First!'s biggest show ever, a series of mass protests called Redwood Summer. In January, a hustling hippie named Walking Rainbow buzzed through town. In a weak moment, Judi agreed to meet with him. As he babbled, something made Judi pay attention. Walking Rainbow kept talking about how the forests needed a mass movement, just like the civil-rights movement. He kept saying that trees had rights. Walking Rainbow wasn't the first person to come up with this idea. In the early 1970s, an essay by Christopher D. Stone called "Should Trees Have Standing?" had become a landmark in environmental law. In the 1972 Mineral King case, Sierra Club Legal Defense Fund attorneys used Stone's revolutionary concept that if trees were going to be injured, they could be plaintiffs. The U.S. Supreme Court disagreed—with at least one notable exception, William O. Douglas, the liberal outdoorsman who had been influenced by Stone's essay.

In the 1980s, deep ecologists also proselytized about the idea that nature had rights. So did Dave Foreman, when he compared mon-keywrenching to the Boston Tea Party. But it took Roderick Nash, a historian at the University of California at Santa Barbara, to finally spell it out. Nash had written *Wilderness and the American Mind*, a classic book on the evolution of the wilderness idea in American culture. In his 1989 book, *The Rights of Nature*, he characterized American history as a process of continually expanding rights. He outlined the progres-sion from the rights of man to the rights of animals—and finally to the rights of nature itself. He wrote favorably about Dave Foreman and Earth First!, giving them academia's Good Housekeeping seal of approval. Nash's book and the enthusiasm of *The End of Nature* author Bill McKibben were as close as Earth First! would come to establish-ment recognition—or even comprehension.

The fact that Walking Rainbow and Roderick Nash were on the same wavelength was incongruous, but not wholly coincidental. There was something in the air. Judi Bari was part of it, too. Instinctively, Judi thought of concentration camps when she tried to describe the destruction of ancient redwoods. Pacific Lumber's mill had been built in the late 1800s. Diffuse green light filtered through its high-vaulted fiberglass ceilings. It was not unlike a Gothic cathedral—or the dim gas chambers portrayed in World War II movies. Outside, a machine lifted huge redwood trees, one after another, out of a holding pond and rolled them into a giant saw blade. As the red dust flew, it was impossible not to think of the mill as a romantically lit slaughterhouse.

Judi brought Walking Rainbow and his idea to the local environ-mental center. A committee formed to organize a series of major rallies called Redwood Summer, which would be punctuated by more typ-ical Earth First! actions, such as blockades, tree-sits, and, of course, a smattering of ecotage. At a panel in March, millworker and union activist Gene Lawhorn abruptly changed his planned speech after he heard Judi playing fiddle on the song "Spike a Tree for Jesus."

"I said if you really want to build bridges between timber workers and environmentalists, you should denounce tree spiking," Lawhorn said. "At that moment Judi got up and said, 'I agree with Gene.'" According to Lawhorn, someone went outside to tell Mike Roselle about the exchange. He had "a heart attack" Lawhorn reported, but once he got over his shock, he agreed that California Earth First! should renounce—not denounce—monkeywrenching, at least for the duration of Redwood Summer.

"I wasn't with Earth First! then," Lawhorn recalled. "I was just a wood products worker who was starting to speak out about environmental issues and was starting to get heat about it.

"It's not like Foreman says in his book. There's not Plexiglas protecting the workers. There's a lot of open space. I looked down once (after a sawblade hit something) and there were little pieces of shrapnel around my feet."

On April 11, 1990, after a few weeks of heated debate, Northern California Earth First! pledged a moratorium on tree spiking. Redwood Summer would resemble the civil rights campaigns Judi had learned about at the Highlander Center. "Partially it was in response to what had happened last year," Bari explained. "Very suddenly, within one year's time, they got very violent towards us and there were three incidents of real overt violence in which people were hurt. They [these incidents] were not investigated, they were not prosecuted. . . . It was a problem for me. How could I, as an organizer, bear . . . I felt a responsibility for leading people into actions in which they were likely to get hurt."

After the nonviolence pledge, Dave Foreman fired off a letter outlining his disagreement with their decision but avoiding an open split. Foreman wasn't happy with events in northern California, but most of the time he was too busy preparing for his trial to worry about it. Not only had his cause attracted the Big Cowboy Kahuna Gerry Spence, but it had also enlisted the help of a less well known attorney named Sam Guiberson. Guiberson was a rotund ex-hippie who had once wanted to be a filmmaker. When his prestigious Houston family ran low on funds, he went to law school instead. With his familiarity with recording devices and counterculture-inspired interest in government surveillance, Guiberson became one of the country's foremost wiretapping experts. While Judi rallied the troops in California, Foreman, Nancy Morton, and a dozen volunteers spent over a year commuting to Guiberson's comfortable Galveston beach house, where they transcribed close to 800,000 pages of taped evidence.

The FBI case wasn't the only thing holding Foreman back. He simply didn't think that Redwood Summer was a good idea. Foreman had joined David Brower in a 1986 demonstration against the Maxxam takeover; and at the 1989 California Wilderness Conference, organized by his old friend Jim Eaton, he spoke favorably of Greg, Darryl, and Judi's attempt to go after private landowners. Although the concept might have offended a strict libertarian, Foreman's devotion to the environment outweighed ideology. There was even a precedent for the Pacific Lumber campaign. Early in his career, Bob Marshall, the socialist founder of the Wilderness Society, had attempted to reform private forestry. Marshall changed his approach when he decided that government acquisition of land would be more effective. Nevertheless, regulation of private forestry had become institutionalized since Marshall's day. Of course, there was a vast gulf between the approach of Northern California Earth First! and the usual process of government regulation, especially in California, where the state Department of Forestry was dominated by a mode of thought that hadn't changed since the post–World War II housing boom.

While Foreman recognized the need for reforming the state's regulation of private lands, he felt that the national forests in California were a more pressing issue. These forests, which contained far more old growth than did private land, were constantly being eroded by salvage logging and other operations that took advantage of regulatory loopholes. Redwood Summer seemed like a distraction from the less dramatic process of fighting the Forest Service, using channels for public dissent that already existed.

In any case, the fact that the state's regulatory board needed reform was not exactly news. The smart, underfunded hippies who ran EPIC out of Garberville were desperately trying to get a statewide reform initiative called Forests Forever on the November 1990 ballot. Their original plan had been to try for the 1992 election. But trees were being cut so fast that they decided to go for it in 1990. They knew it would be tough. Not only was the timber industry an economic

Goliath, but the Sierra Club and other environmental groups were working on their own ballot initiative, which was nicknamed Big Green. Big Green took the kitchen-sink approach to environmental reform. It contained at least one provision for every businessman in the state to hate, including major pesticide reforms that were revving up the state's formidable agriculture lobby. What was significant to the EPIC hippies, though, was the fact that Big Green's forestry-reform provision was much weaker than theirs. The Forests Forever initiative was the last best hope to save the redwoods. And if it passed, it would reorganize the antediluvian decision-making process of the California Department of Forestry along ecological lines.

Foreman knew that Redwood Summer could deal a deathblow to EPIC's already dicey chances. The timber industry's sophisticated PR machine was working overtime to blend EPIC and Earth First! in the public's consciousness. Yet Redwood Summer's organizers refused to believe that their campaign might be counterproductive. This blindness to strategy was a new phenomenon in Earth First! Until now, Earth First! had refrained from mowing down other environmentalists with friendly fire. Even though the group had criticized moderates, its members had been practical enough to realize the limits of being a gadfly. Most of them worked hard to fulfill a strategic role that advanced the practical, if more limited, agenda of the mainstream groups. Although the high-level conspiracy imagined by Wise Use supporters was fictional, informal links often did exist between Earth First!ers and local mainstream activists. In northern California this relationship was being blown apart. Darryl was particularly dense when it came to knowing his enemies. He could barely be convinced not to stage a sit-in at the Save the Redwoods League, a group founded in 1918 which was still active in forest protection in California.

Despite Darryl's peccadilloes, it was pretty clear to Foreman that Redwood Summer was a done deal. He supported the northern Californians in public, but privately he stepped back. In Mike Roselle's view, Foreman was copping out. The relationship between the two men had been worsening for some time. For one thing, Nancy Morton didn't get along with Roselle. Ron Kezar felt that she didn't particularly like him, either. Morton could be charming, but when she disliked someone she was merciless. Some members of Earth First! respected Nancy's toughness; others nicknamed her Nancy Reagan and accused her of channeling her own formidable ambitions through her husband's career. "I don't consider her a player," said a prominent female Earth First! organizer. "She just doesn't have the judgment, although she's intensely loyal to Dave."

But Nancy thought she was a player; and she didn't like being crossed. If nothing else, she had proved her loyalty during the lean years of the mid-1980s by supporting the Earth First! household in Tucson with her demanding work as a trauma nurse. Ron Kezar had been able to reach a working accommodation with her, so he stayed within Foreman's inner circle. But Roselle couldn't hack it. He blamed Dave, not Nancy. Dave avoided confrontation so assiduously it sometimes interfered with his ability to communicate. It was inevitable—and maybe unfair—that Nancy would take up the slack.

"A lot of people say Nancy is the problem," Roselle responded, when asked about his difficulties with Foreman. "I'm not going to blame Nancy because I think Foreman needs to accept responsibility for his actions. Dave isolated himself."

Roselle was exaggerating, but he was not completely off base. Professionally, Foreman was reaching out to conservation biologists and to environmentalists working on innovative, small-scale projects that stirred the few remnants of optimism he had managed to salvage from twenty years as an environmentalist. But personally, Foreman was circling the wagons. After all these years of crowd pleasing, he found himself withdrawing to a smaller circle of friends. Closest to him was his inner circle of uncritical supporters like John Davis, Rod Mondt, and Nancy Zierenberg. Then there were the hard-drinking western writers, hairy-chested men like Charles Bowden, William Kittredge, and Doug Peacock.

Roselle fit neither of these descriptions. Part of the problem may have been his emotional instability. Roselle was drinking and smoking dope more than ever. His marriage to Karen Pickett had broken up fairly quickly and he was back to moving from city to city and from relationship to relationship. On the other hand, Foreman and the other Buckaroos had settled down. At Howie Wolke's wedding, Louisa Willcox remembers Howie telling her that if they hadn't all calmed down, they'd probably be dead by now.

Although his emotional maturity might be lagging, politically Roselle may have been outgrowing both Earth First! and Dave Foreman—and he wasn't doing it gracefully. He had learned first-hand about international environmental issues, traveling to Southeast Asia and Latin America under the aegis of the Rainforest Action Network. In 1987, he began working for Greenpeace. He spent enough time in Washington to grow disillusioned with big-budget environmentalism. Eventually he spent four months in a South Dakota jail for dropping a Greenpeace banner protesting acid rain down the faces on Mount Rushmore.

After four months of incarceration, something crossed over in Roselle. He became angry, but that passed. As he reached his late thirties, Roselle became even more committed to the vagrant lifestyle of a political agitator. His tolerance for bullshit became nonexistent. His loyalty to his old friends was even scarcer. He criticized Foreman and his cadre of supporters for not keeping up with the rapid changes in the environmental movement. Foreman's failure to clearly refute charges of racism and sexism genuinely appalled him. But the vehemence of his attacks on Foreman seemed to come from something deeper and more personal. He accused Foreman of using the *Earth First! Journal* for his own ends and dubbed his supporters "Foreman-istas." Foreman stonewalled, refusing to be drawn into a dispute or even to talk things over. Roselle kept hammering away, telling everyone who would listen that the Arizona contingent was too isolated, both culturally and geographically, from the rest of Earth First! "They live in a Western movie," he said bitterly.

Roselle's biggest beef was control of the *Earth First! Journal*. He estimated the *Journal*'s budget at about $200,000 a year. He said that he couldn't understand where all the money was going, since the drab-looking paper couldn't cost that much to produce. Roselle correctly assumed that some of the cash was being selectively funneled to activists, which gave Foreman a strong power base within the organization. With some justice, Roselle charged that the *Journal* needed fresh air. It had been exciting from 1980 until 1985, when the mainstream press was ignoring environmental issues. But after *Time* magazine ran its "Planet of the Year" issue in 1989, the situation changed radically. Not only was the mainstream media covering the environment more, but the advent of desktop publishing was spawning a whole new generation of cheaply produced, well-designed environmental publications. The *Journal*'s layout and graphics, which always had ranged from clumsy to awful, ceased to be a quaint reference to the group's affinity with the era of cave paintings. After trying and failing to assert influence on the paper, Roselle gave up. Instead he established his own power base, insisting on using the *Journal*'s mailing list to raise money for his Direct Action Fund.

He may have grabbed a purse string or two, but Roselle hadn't found a way to resolve his differences with Foreman. In his view, Foreman's whole clique was failing to acknowledge the rifts that were weakening the group.

"The generational differences are obvious," he said. "I think they're even apparent between Foreman and Kezar and myself. Foreman grew up in a time before the civil-rights movement, before the women's movement. I mean, it was just a few years that he missed it, but that's important. You're talking about your juvenile years when you really are picking up how to deal with society. So he carries that air about him.

"Abbey was worse, but Abbey was older. You get young people now, like we get eighteen-, nineteen-year-old kids, even if they're rednecks you're not gonna hear them use racial slurs and you're not gonna hear them talk about women in the way the older generation would. Because times have changed somewhat. Now I'm not sayin' there are not these fossilized individuals out there that can't tell the difference. There are certainly those individuals out there. But we don't get them in Earth First!"

As Foreman evaded Roselle's attempts to talk about their problems, Roselle grew increasingly hurt and frustrated. When Foreman finally tried to shake hands with him at an environmental conference, Roselle walked away. He said that he felt the gesture was meaningless, because Foreman still refused to have a substantive discussion with him.

Ironically, the two men seemed to be in accord on environmental issues. While the pragmatic Bart Koehler and other mainstream environmentalists were lobbying for a Montana wilderness bill that appeared to be the best of a series of very bad compromises, both Foreman and Roselle unequivocally said that the mainstream guys were wrong: the bill should be dumped. As for Redwood Summer, Roselle was too savvy not to realize the strategic problems it posed. His attitude was simply more tolerant. "I would like to see us focus more on public lands," he said. "I would have liked to see us (Northern California Earth First!) focus on public lands a long time ago, but most of the activists have wanted to really concentrate on redwoods. This was a day of reckoning."

By April 1990, the day of reckoning was approaching at a velocity terrifying to Judi Bari. In late March, she says, Louisiana-Pacific mill workers asked her to organize a demonstration at a Mendocino County Board of Supervisors meeting. On April 4, she appeared before the supervisors with a group of mill workers, IWW members, and Earth First!ers. They called for the seizure of timber company land under eminent domain.

After the meeting, she said, "I very much got the feeling the line had been crossed." Within a few days, she began receiving death threats in the mail. Two fake Earth First! press releases calling for violence were circulated to the media. The right-wing radio station in nearby Fort Bragg seemed to be mentioning Bari's name almost daily. The pressure kept up for at least a month. During that time, Darryl did what Darryl did best: turned up the heat. In early April, he circulated an Earth Day poster. In the foreground were two Cro-Magnon Earth First!ers hefting monkeywrenches. In the background was a bulldozer. "EARTH NIGHT 1990," it announced. "GO OUT AND DO SOMETHING FOR THE EARTH . . . AT NIGHT."

Someone apparently took his advice. On the night of April 22, a wooden transmission tower was sawed through and 92,000 people in Santa Cruz and Watsonville lost power for several hours. The next morning, a 100-foot metal tower slammed down and the area was blacked out again. These events generated particularly strong feelings because the area had been hit so hard by the big earthquake of October 1989. Santa Cruz is a pastel-colored university town on the central California coast. For twenty years it had been a stop on the underground railroad for hippies, a bastion of progressive politics and hallucinogenic drugs, and a magnet for surfers. The power-line hit was rumored to be of local origin, but even Santa Cruz subversives thought that it was in poor taste to exhume the trauma caused by the earthquake so soon and for no discernible reason.

Darryl's involvement in the Santa Cruz incident may have been limited to his inspirational poster. But Darryl's own Earth Day was far from uneventful. At 4:30 in the morning, he was in a Marin County phone booth, dialing the home phone number of every reporter he knew. In front of him, a group of Earth First!ers were dangling a banner from the Golden Gate Bridge, which links Marin County to San Francisco. Apparently Darryl's publicity reached not only journalists, but the authorities, too. In a matter of minutes, Darryl was hustled off to jail. Darryl said it was the Oakland police who searched his car, not the Marin County cops. "I thought FBI," he said. "We knew the FBI was big in Oakland."[21]

Back in the north country, Darryl's poster was mysteriously showing up on loggers' doorsteps. Threatening letters—one with a crudely drawn hangman's noose—kept arriving. Judi finally became frightened and called Dave Foreman for advice. According to Judi, he said, "You're a hero. A hundred years from now people will remember you." Then he told her to talk to Rod Mondt, who could advise her on security precautions. A few days later, she says she was asked to appear before the Mendocino County Board of Supervisors to explain the violence that had occurred in the timber conflicts.

When Judi arrived at the county offices on May 2, she said she was greeted by "a lynch mob" of gyppo owners, low-level managers, and security personnel. Once the meeting started, she held up her most recent piece of hate mail, a photo of herself on which the crosshairs of a rifle had been superimposed. "Violence isn't being directed at workers. It's being directed at us," she said, provoking hoots and yells from the audience. As she stalked out, a supervisor named Marilyn Butcher said primly, "Judi, you've brought this on yourself."

After the meeting, the death threats abruptly stopped. Judi met with the loggers who had attended. She won the respect of most of them. A few even decided to support her cause. Close up, she was less threatening. She had a ready sympathy and a certain rough charm. Then, on May 9, a pipe bomb exploded in a Louisiana-Pacific mill in Cloverdale. Police investigated the incident, but it was barely noticed in the furor over Redwood Summer.

Redwood Summer wasn't just rocking the establishment; it also was seriously straining the meager organizational resources of Earth First! Fortunately for the roughly 3,000 demonstrators who showed up, a Berkeley-based group called Seeds of Peace stepped in. Seeds of Peace had provided logistical support for a string of civil-disobedience actions at the Nevada Test Site, as well as for the Great Peace March across America in 1987. The group was staffed by pros like James McGuinness, a fortyish Brooklyn boy who enjoyed stopping in Vegas to play the slots and drink imported beer after playing cat and mouse with authorities at the test site. The no-bullshit practicality of people like McGuinness was a much-needed antidote to the Earth First!–inspired chaos.

Seeds of Peace could handle the crowds. It was Judi and Darryl's job to draw them in. The couple began touring colleges to drum up support for the first big demo, a protest against log exports which was going to be held at a Louisiana-Pacific mill on June 20. On Thursday, May 24, they had a gig booked in Santa Cruz. The night before, they drove down to Berkeley to meet with Seeds of Peace. They crashed at separate houses in the East Bay. It was close to noon when Judi and Darryl left for Santa Cruz. Less than fifteen minutes after they drove off in Judi's Subaru, the bomb exploded.

Who bombed Judi Bari? When the shouting quieted down and the big rains started that winter, a documentary filmmaker named Stephen Talbot and a journalist-cum-private-eye named David Helvarg tried to find out. Coincidentally, Talbot, like Cherney, was a former child actor. Talbot had been a regular on the old *Leave It to Beaver* series. He looked the part, with a toothy grin and an affable manner. But he had also been head of Wesleyan University's SDS chapter in 1968. Among his other interests, Talbot was a mystery buff who had named his son Dashiell. It was easy to see why Bari's story intrigued him. Helvarg's political credentials were just as good. He had seen active duty as a journalist in Central America and written tough investigative articles on environmental issues. Bari trusted both of them. No less a personage than Bruce Anderson, the intellectual ex-Marine who owned the muckraking newspaper the *Anderson Valley Advertiser,* expected their film to be "The Definitive Mendo Movie."

Talbot and Helvarg's documentary aired on San Francisco's public television station KQED in the spring of 1991. The documentary profiled a number of suspects in the bombing. One was Irv Sutley, a bearded, potbellied gun freak and known informer. He had taken photos of Judi Bari with an Uzi, ostensibly as a joke for a record-album cover. After the bombing, he sent it to local police stations. Another was the ex-linebacker Bill Staley. There was some speculation that Staley, the militant anti-abortionist who had threatened the Planned Parenthood clinic's director, was the author of a bizarre letter that had been sent to a local newspaper on May 30. The letter, which was signed by someone calling himself "The Lord's Avenger," claimed responsibility for the bombing of Judi and Darryl. The author also claimed to have set what Judi called "the test bomb" at the Cloverdale mill back on May 9. The letter was sent to reporter Mike Geniella of the *Santa Rosa Press Democrat.* Geniella, who was later removed from the timber beat, had done some of the best investigative reporting on the North Coast timber wars. As published by the *Press Democrat,* the letter read:

> I built with these Hands the bomb that I placed in the car of Judi Bari. Doubt me not for I will tell you the design and materials such as only I will Know. I come forward now emboldened by the Spirit of the Lord to spread the Message spoken by the bomb so that All will hear it and take into there [*sic*] Hearts. This woman is possessed of the Devil. No natural Woman created of our Lord spews Forth the Lies, Calumnies and Poisons that she does with such Evil Power. The Lord cleared my vision and revealed this unto me outside the Baby-Killing Clinic when Judi Bari smote with Satan's words the humble and Faithful servants of the Lord who had come there to make witness against Abortion. I saw Satan's flames shoot forth from her mouth her eyes and ears proving forever that this was no Godly Woman no Ruth full of obedience to procreate and multiply the children of Adam throughout the world as is God's Divine Will.

> Let the woman learn in silence with all
> subjection. But I suffer not a woman to teach,
> nor to usurp the authority over the man,
> but to be in silence.
> —Timothy 2:11

> . . . This possessed demon Judi Bari spread her Poison to tell the Multitude that trees were not god's Gift to Man but that Trees were themselves gods and it was a sin to cut them. My Spirit ached as her Paganism festered before mine Eyes. I felt the Power of the Lord stir within my Heart and I knew I had been Chosen to strike down the Demon. But my Faith was Weak and I was Deaf to His Words as he instructed me. The Devil Hissed into my other ear that I should use Cunning and turn Judi Baris [*sic*] poison against her . . . I dared not Strike

at the demon herself. No, instead the Devil moved my hand
nto bomb in Cloverdale to bring infamy down on Judi Bari . . .
The Lord told me Use no Indirection. The Lord had shown
me that his Work needed no Subtergufe [*sic*] and must be clear
and Visible in the eyes of all. I was His Avenger. The demon
must be struck down. The Light filled me and my Faith was
impregnable. Great joy Filled me I set to work.

The righteous shall rejoice when he seeth
the vengeance: he shall wash his feet in the
blood of the wicked.
—Psalms 58:10

   I put the bomb in her car whilst she was at the meeting
with the loggers. The wicked shall know no Refuge. . . . For
two nights and two days the [bomb] stayed until the Demon
was joined in her car by the VERY SAME man who had
helped her Mock and Insult the Faithful outside the Abortion
Clinic that day years ago. PRAISE GOD!

Wherefore be ye not unwise, but understanding
what the will of the Lord is.
—Ephesians 5:17

   But if you Heed not his Warning and go into the forests
to do Satan's Bidding surely you will Suffer the Punishments
of demon Judi Bari.

I will early destroy all the wicked of
the land; that I may cut off all wicked doers
from the city of the Lord.
—Psalms 101:8

   I HAVE SPOKEN. I AM THE LORD'S AVENGER.[22]

The *Press Democrat* received the letter on May 29 and turned it
over to the FBI. Agents asked the newspaper to excise the letter's
technical information about the manufacture of the two bombs.

"There is enough detail in this letter that we are obviously looking at it very seriously. It would indicate at this point that someone had very good knowledge of both devices," said FBI agent Barry Mawn. However, Mawn said, it was also possible that the letter was the handiwork of a prankster who had done some "lucky guesswork."[23] Earth First!ers also speculated that the tone of religious zealotry in the Lord's Avenger letter could be a smokescreen.

Judi's ex-husband, labor organizer Michael Sweeney, was another suspect on Talbot and Helvarg's short list. Several years before, Sweeney had led an unsuccessful antigrowth campaign against an airport expansion. When the airport was nearly destroyed by an arson fire triggered by a complicated electronic device, Sweeney was a prime suspect. Judi was not implicated in the arson, according to Talbot and Helvarg. The documentary team reexamined the arson case onscreen, providing a compelling argument that authorities should at least consider Sweeney's possible involvement in the Earth First! bombing. The suggestion infuriated Judi, who tried to force Talbot to cut this section before the documentary aired. She accused him of sexism, charging that he was ignoring the political implications of the attempt on her life in favor of a sordid domestic violence scenario. She also complained that Talbot had failed to include among his suspects Mendocino county's radical right-wingers, who had banded together in a group called Blue Light.

Despite Judi's anger, the documentary team had done her at least one great service. "Who Bombed Judi Bari?" provided convincing evidence of Judi and Darryl's innocence. It helped balance the early news coverage, which had been weighted heavily in favor of speculation that Judi Bari and Darryl Cherney had known about the bomb.

Television coverage of the story was damaging, but a series of articles in the Oakland *Tribune* practically convicted the two radicals on the basis of information that later turned out to be false. In the first weeks after the bombing, veteran cop reporter Harry Harrison and investigative reporter Paul Grabowicz clearly had the inside track, probably because of Harris's long relationship with the Oakland police. The day after the bombing Harris and Grabowicz wrote that "law enforcement sources said investigators are convinced Bari and Cherney were transporting the explosive device when it went off at about 11:50 A.M."

The following day, the two reporters wrote a second major story. In this article they beat out the rest of the Bay Area media by outlining the evidence against Bari and Cherney. Once again, their information came from unnamed "law enforcement sources." According to the *Tribune's* sources, the pipe bomb had been in the backseat of Bari's car, covered by a guitar case. This indicated that Bari knew the bomb was there, reported the *Tribune.* In addition, finishing nails "identical to ones used in the bomb" were found elsewhere in the car. Similar nails also were found during a search of one of the suspect's houses in the Garberville area, the *Tribune* reported. There was more. Duct tape and wire "that resembled that used in the bomb also was found in Cherney's van and house and in Bari's house."[24]

Getting this information was quite a coup for the *Tribune.* The only problem was that it was all either wrong or misleading. In the following weeks, the facts emerged. The bomb had been under Judi's seat, not in the back of the car. The finishing nails came from a batch so large that it was impossible to trace them. The fact that the duct tape and wire were "similar" was simply irrelevant.

As the story evolved, it became apparent that Oakland police had been feeding *Tribune* reporters false information. A staff member of the congressional subcommittee that watchdogs the FBI said the Oakland police had been in charge of the investigation for the first month. When Oakland's theories didn't pan out, the FBI took over. "The primary culprits in fingering Judi and Darryl were clearly the Oakland police department, not the FBI," the staff member said. However, the subcommittee's chair, Congressman Don Edwards, said he was disturbed by the fact that Cherney and Bari were identified as suspects partly because of the FBI's analysis of forensic evidence—the matching nails and the bomb's location—which later proved to be false. Edwards blamed the Oakland police for manipulating the FBI. Earth First!ers were not so quick to exonerate the feds. Eventually they would bring a lawsuit against the FBI Special Agent in Charge,

Richard Held. But in the meantime, they fired off letters to Edwards, hoping to provoke an investigation.

The only reason Congressman Edwards was showing any interest in the case was that Mike Roselle liked strong, dynamic women with independent careers. (This may have been the most convincing evidence of the generational division that he claimed existed between him and the other Buckaroos.) Roselle's new girlfriend, Claire Greensfelder, was a fifth-generation Californian who had been a Democratic political activist for almost twenty years. After the bombing, she persuaded Congressman Ron Dellums to hold a press conference calling for an inquiry into the FBI's handling of the case. Dellums followed up with a letter to Edwards. (A similar letter was sent by the heads of the Sierra Club, the National Wildlife Federation, Friends of the Earth, the National Audubon Society, and the National Parks and Conservation Association. This letter had no effect whatsoever, which doesn't speak well for the environmental lobby's much-lauded political clout.)

Edwards received an oral briefing from the FBI, but he failed to launch a full-fledged investigation. Even though Edwards didn't insist on Congressional action—which at least one staff member thought was warranted—the FBI was put on notice. It was a far cry from the previous year, when the FBI's congressional liaison had called Edwards's office to brag about Foreman's arrest. The FBI's other recent counterintelligence campaign, an investigation of Central America support groups, had led to problems when the agency was linked to illegal break-ins. The EMETIC arrests were used as an example of playing by the rules—targeting criminal incidents rather than a whole movement. "The FBI was on the defensive and using this as an example of how they did it right," said the committee staffer.

Then Foreman and his attorneys released the transcript of Agent Fain's remarks about busting Foreman, not because he was an "actual perpetrator," but to "send a message."

"Since then, some of that [the FBI's claim to playing by the rules] has unraveled," commented the staffer rather drily.

After the bombing, the circumstances of Foreman's arrest came under renewed scrutiny. Edwards would be keeping a close watch on the trial. A congressional investigation was still possible.

For several weeks, Judi was too sick even to think about the FBI. Led by Karen Pickett, Earth First!ers held a vigil outside Oakland's Highland Hospital while Judi waffled in and out of consciousness. When she was awake, she noticed a pervasive, disturbing odor. Eventually she figured out where it was coming from. Gunpowder and shrapnel were clinging to her long, reddish brown hair. For ten days, she begged the hospital staff to rinse it out, but they refused, telling her that she was too weak to be moved. Up north, Redwood Summer was continuing. But for those first few weeks, Redwood Summer in the Bay Area consisted of providing support for Judi. Darryl had escaped with only minor injuries.

"There's somebody with me twenty-four hours a day. If I wake up crying, there's somebody to hold my hand, and I don't even always know the person, but there's always someone here, and I really appreciate it," she told the *Anderson Valley Advertiser*'s feisty editor Bruce Anderson three weeks after the bombing.

When Anderson told her the bombing had been covered nationally, Judi joked, "Some people will do anything to be famous. . . ." Anderson replied, "I know Darryl wanted to get on TV, but [laughter] . . . that may account for the placement of the device."

Quite seriously, Bari responded, "No, Darryl, first of all, has some of the least mechanical skills of anyone I've ever known. I once tried to hire him to hang sheet rock and found him to be unemployable, because he didn't know how to hammer." To anyone who knew Darryl, this was a convincing argument. But to Judi, there was an equally compelling one. "Darryl loved me," she told Anderson. Case closed, just like Mike Sweeney's. Judi may have been a woman's woman, with a healthy contempt for male foibles, but her belief in the bonds she had forged with certain men was unshakable.

This deeper side of Judi surfaced frequently during her slow recovery. She was still funny and obnoxious, with a penchant for calling young trees pecker poles and talking about smoking hooters. But she had come close to death and for many months she remained cloaked in the silent intensity of that experience. It would take years to assimilate what had happened. "The nights are hard," she said. "I get terrified at night."

By the end of the summer Bari was walking again, using a pair of crutches. Surgeons told her that they could not operate on her pelvis; her nerves and bones were so jumbled up that surgery could paralyze her. Her pelvis looked like a kaleidoscope. Her coccyx looked like "cottage cheese." Her right foot was paralyzed from the ankle down. She could not walk long distances or sit for long periods of time. "As the day goes on, I get more and more prone," she joked. When asked if she could have a regular sex life again, Bari was uncharacteristically silent. Finally she answered in a neutral tone. "That's the last thing I'm thinking about," she said. Then she changed the subject to her children.

Redwood Summer went on without Judi. There were four big demonstrations and about a hundred arrests. Occasionally there were flashes of violence, sometimes initiated by protesters. In September, screaming demonstrators pounded at the windows and doors of a building where timber officials were meeting. As the officials departed, protesters flailed at the windows of a car carrying Pacific Lumber president John Campbell, the tough Australian ex-surfer who had made his fortune in America by marrying the boss's daughter. As the car continued on its path, one protester flung himself on the hood. Campbell, either unfazed or too shocked to react, kept driving until the speed of his car caused the protester to tumble onto the pavement.

No trees were saved by Redwood Summer, but thousands of students were initiated into counterculture politics. The California Department of Forestry got a new director who showed signs of breaking the agency out of its usual role as a rubber stamp for the timber industry. Over the next few years, a bill designed to save Headwaters Forest inched through Congress. By September, Judi Bari was helping to organize Redwood Summer's sequel. Its catchy title—Corporate Fall—proved that Judi's mobility had suffered but not her wit. Once again, her cleverness was lost on her opponents. This time thugs threatened to burn down her house. In November, both of California's environmental ballot initiatives, Forests Forever and Big Green, lost at the polls.

Splitting
the
Sheets

*To carry out this program it is exigent that all friends of the wilderness ideal
should unite. If they do not present the urgency of their view-point the other
side will certainly capture popular support. Then it will only be a few years
until the last escape from society will be barricaded.*

—Bob Marshall
"The Problem of the Wilderness," 1930

*For a few years they were left in peace, forgotten by a world that seemed, for
all they could tell, to have forgotten itself—and then the gates of the citadel
were opened and certain men came forth with aspirations far more grand than
those of farmers and herdsmen and hunters. The oldest civil war of all, that
between the city and the country, was resumed.*

—Edward Abbey
Good News, 1980

July 1989–Ann Arbor

DAVE FOREMAN CLIMBED ONTO THE STAGE at the Sierra Club's International Assembly. He wore a tweed sport jacket, not a Fuck Bechtel T-shirt. There wasn't a monkeywrench in sight. He didn't need one. Thanks to the FBI, Dave Foreman's fifteen minutes of fame had begun.

As soon as he opened his mouth, speculation that Dave had been cowed by the FBI vanished. In a matter of minutes he won the audience over. His astonishing talent for getting up close and personal with a crowd remained intact.

His message hadn't changed much, either. He talked about the legacy of the club's patron saint, John Muir. Foreman obviously identified with the romantic Scot careening off into the glacial wilderness of his own soul. After all, he was a diehard romantic himself, a lobbyist who had abandoned his trade, announcing that he could no longer lock "my heart in a safe deposit box and replace my brain with a pocket calculator."

Then Foreman talked about the modern-day Sierra Club. By building on David Brower's model of political activism, it had become the best environmental lobbying group on Capitol Hill. But when it refined its political skills, the club lost something. It left for dead the northern spotted owl—and the old-growth forests of the Pacific Northwest—because its leaders judged the timber industry impossible to defeat. Would the Sierra Club also hang back from the issues of overpopulation, species extinction, global warming?

In the early eighties, Foreman had jokingly touted himself as a write-in candidate for the Sierra Club Board of Directors. Now, more seriously, he called for a revolution within the ranks. By returning to the idealism of its early leaders, the Sierra Club could advance the environmental debate beyond realpolitik.

"One of the alternatives I'd like to offer is that the Sierra Club learn a little humility. I remember a number of years ago at a conference in Africa on environmental problems around the world some people came up with the idea that instead of a Peace Corps, what we need is a reverse Peace Corps. Instead of North America and Europe teaching the rest of the world how to live, we needed some Australian aborigines and bushmen and Eskimos and Kayapo Indians and Penan tribespeople to come to teach us how to live."

Here, Foreman was interrupted by loud applause.

I think too often the American environmental movement thinks that since we started environmentalism we know how to do it and every other environmental group in the world needs to learn from us.

Well, I think we can learn from the Australian Conservation Federation and the Australian Wilderness Society, which are the mainstream groups in that country and which have practiced nonviolent civil disobedience to stop dams.

Why doesn't the Sierra Club try that? I think we can learn from the Kayapo Indians, from the Penan tribespeople. . . . I want to say that the greatest honor I have ever received was finding out that the Penan tribespeople had several copies of my book, *Ecodefense*. I think I have learned more from them, and from the Kayapo and that kind of courageous resistance than I can from anything else.

I would like to challenge the Sierra Club to confront the crisis we're in. The most prominent ecologists in the world today say we may face the loss of one-third of all species. Michael Soulé, founder of the Society for Conservation Biology, tells us that vertebrate evolution may be at an end. Think about it. Let it sink in.

We aren't talking about scenery. We aren't talking about aesthetics. We aren't talking about non-motorized, primitive, recreational opportunities. We're talking life. We're talking about three and a half billion years of life on this planet. The whole flow and flowering and blossoming of evolution on this planet for a longer time than any one of us can imagine. The activities of this generation could truncate that whole flowering, that whole blossoming. . . .

We are involved in the most sacred crusade ever waged on earth.

It is time to hold the line, Foreman told the crowd. You are the ones who can do it. You are the elect, the chosen. It is you who are the heirs of John Muir, the mountaineering comrades of David Brower.

We have to have a ferment of ideas where we can come up with wild and crazy and provocative things because the problems facing us today are so overwhelming that if we stay in the same straight and narrow of ideas and reflection then we aren't going to get anywhere. We'll be going down the same path of destruction that we've been on for 10,000 years of civilization.

The job of the Sierra Club is not to come up with the good, solid, pragmatic compromises that can pass Congress. The Sierra Club should never support a bill that can pass Congress. . . .

At this point, Foreman is drowned out by applause.

Our job is to be constant advocates of wilderness and ecological sanity. We pay congressmen and bureaucrats to make compromises. But unless we hold their feet to the fire, just like Exxon holds their feet to the fire, the compromises are all going to be the other way.

Instead of being insulted, the audience gave Foreman a standing ovation.

Not everyone stood. Behind his bushy walrus moustache, Doug Scott was working himself into a rage. Foreman had called the Sierra Club the "most important environmental group on earth." Then he delivered a blueprint for destroying the group's credibility. "The Sierra Club should never support a bill that can pass Congress"? Without the Sierra Club and other mainstream groups, environmental bills would *die* in Congress. Industry-sponsored legislation would be virtually unopposed. If the Sierra Club was ever crazy enough to take Foreman's advice, everything Doug had worked for would be destroyed.

Environmentalists are not noted for their ironic distance. Doug simply couldn't take Foreman's comment for what it was, a piece of rhetoric, a metaphor, a goad. He was too earnest and the stakes were too high.

"Doug almost as a point of pride doesn't wear his heart on his sleeve," said Tim Mahoney. "But the environmental movement was his whole life. He's fascinating, and shy in his own way. He has inspired people, not on a mass level, but to play the inside game. It probably bothers him that he's never received the accolades that Dave and others have. He cares just as much, but he believes the torch bearers can mislead and he strikes out at them."

Scott believed that Foreman and his followers in Earth First! were destructive to the environmental movement. To add to his catalogue of sins, Foreman had just implicitly but very publicly trashed Doug's entire insider's career with his idiotic remarks. Particularly galling was the fact that he had done it at Scott's alma mater, the University of Michigan. This was where Doug had first volunteered for the Wilderness Society. He had been among the students who started Earth Day here. It was in Ann Arbor, too, that he had submitted his master's thesis on Howard Zahniser, the mentor who died before Doug got a chance to meet him.

As he schmoozed at the conference, Doug stopped now and then to scribble a few notes for his own speech. He didn't have to agonize. The Sierra Club's conservation director was a deft and experienced orator: not as gifted as Foreman, but animated by his own brand of passion. It was the passion of the conservative Edmund Burke, not the romantic vision of Rousseau. But it was passion nonetheless. "I'm fed up with these people who think these things [environmental laws] are just tools, just lifeless pieces of paper," he said in an interview about a year later. "So what if Congress gets all excited and in a huge backlash guts the Endangered Species Act? Well, that is a species of arrogant, self-indulgent, head-in-the-sandism that just drives me crazy. If environmentalism is radical, it won't have a social consensus around it and it won't work. It won't last. We've hardened the lines in a way that I think is terribly unfortunate. I think it will have dire implications for trees down the line. More than I could say, I wish I had been smart enough to see a way to head that off. But I think we're in the hands of the fates."

When it was his turn to address the crowd, Scott's first priority was responding to Foreman's dictum that the Sierra Club should not support any legislation that could pass Congress.

"We've engaged in a good deal of discussion about what would be ideal in ideal circumstances," Scott told the crowd in his reedy but powerful voice. "But we also have the world of reality. In the world of reality, the Congress will be voting on an imperfect bill on the Tongass National Forest." Scott was referring to the ground-breaking reform bill that Bart Koehler was finally herding through the legislative process with the help of both the Audubon Society and the Sierra Club. It was a dig at Foreman. Look at what Bart's accomplishing, he seemed to be saying. How many trees have you saved with all your rhetoric?

Then Scott really let 'er rip. Dave Foreman's line sounds good, but only to people who don't think very deeply, said Scott. In the world of reality, you don't get to play if that's the attitude you bring to the bargaining table. Activists have to realize what they're giving up when they adopt radical tactics, he told the audience.

"This is what being an effective environmentalist might be like," he said. "Get on the phone. Write a letter. If not ignore, at least pay proper disrespect to your own bureaucracy. What we are talking about is *individual political action.*"

Scott went on to give his boilerplate pep talk, about the individuals who had made a difference in the environmental movement. These people had worked doggedly for slow, incremental progress. They were the real heroes. They had locked up wilderness and it had stayed locked up. They had forced government agencies to consider the environmental consequences of their actions. Together, thousands of environmentalists had altered the country's conscience.

Doug got a standing ovation for his speech, too. But the skinny rear end of one white-haired ectomorph remained firmly attached to his rickety auditorium chair. David Brower was appalled by Doug's attack on Foreman. He also vehemently disagreed with his message. Scott's Horatio Alger optimism struck Brower as absurd. Scott actually believed that things were getting better, that there was a "net gain."

In the 1970s, Scott had won legislative protection for more land than anyone since Howard Zahniser. He had steered the Alaska National Interest Lands Act and the Endangered American Wilderness Act through Congress. But twenty years later, he exemplified a frightening complacency. After the conference David Brower wrote a letter to him. "Can you tell this alleged what's-his-name-reincarnate, what has driven you from the damn-the-torpedoes man you were for the Alaska Coalition?" Brower asked. Then he outlined a view of the Sierra Club's role that resembled Dave Foreman's more than Doug Scott's.

> My thesis is that compromise is often necessary but that it ought not originate with the Sierra Club. We are to hold fast to what we believe is right, fight for it, and find allies and adduce all possible arguments for our cause. If we cannot find enough vigor in us or them to win, then let someone else propose the compromise. We thereupon work hard to coax it our way. We become a nucleus around which the strongest force can build and function.

Brower rattled off a mind-numbing list of the club's dips into compromise, starting back in 1938 when he was working for the club half-time at $75 a month. Then he offered an outline for a major campaign to save the old-growth forests of the Pacific Northwest. It was prefaced by this paragraph:

> Then I get to the crisis of the ancient forests and the club's role that is so faltering that SCLDF [the Sierra Club Legal Defense Fund] had to come to the rescue of the trees by hiring a lobbyist. And I think of the rude treatment of Dave Foreman, a club-invited speaker whom the assembly audience had admired for his courage, courage which gives the club a field to be bolder in, which the club should be grateful for.

David Brower's letter was copied so many times it became an epistolary Tribble. Brower himself gave it to the Sierra Club's new executive director, Michael Fischer. He liberally sprinkled it among his legion of friends and supporters. They passed it out to dozens of reporters. The odd thing was, Scott said Brower never sent it to him. Scott saw it, of course. He couldn't help being hurt by what Brower had written. Certainly he was humiliated by the manner in which the letter had fanned out among their mutual friends, acquaintances, and colleagues.

In the end, Doug decided not to reply. "I wrote draft after draft and spent days fuming," he said. "Then I decided, this is bullshit. I would not dignify it with a response. I think it is self-revealing bullshit. . . . I think early on something snapped in him and he had to have sycophants around him.

"If I had written to Dave I'd have said, 'You know, Dave, you stopped having a useful feedback loop when people started standing up before your speeches as well as after them.' That's a real bad thing. I hope nobody ever gives me a standing ovation before they've heard what I had to say."

The whole pissing match gave Dave Foreman something new to think about. He began to see a parallel between his dispute with Scott and the falling out between John Muir and Gifford Pinchot in 1916. Eureka! The Hetch Hetchy argument was still going on, the same old environmental carcass waking up and shaking itself, wearing Gore-Tex these days instead of canvas. Unlike Scott, the early conservationist Gifford Pinchot came from a Gilded Age background so aristocratic it is hard even to imagine in an era of mass culture. Yet Pinchot entered government as a reformer. He convinced Teddy Roosevelt to start the U.S. Forest Service in order to stop the ransacking of the frontier by a few greedy entrepreneurs. Like Roosevelt—and Doug Scott—he was a firm believer in the greatest good for the greatest number.

Pinchot's relationship with Muir was problematic. At first, the two men were friends and allies. But when the Hetch Hetchy dam was proposed, Pinchot waffled. The 1906 earthquake had ignited a chain of fires that practically leveled San Francisco. Fearing another disaster, the people of the city wanted a steady, cheap supply of water. Building a dam at Hetch Hetchy was only one of several possibilities, but it was favored by businessmen and a handful of corrupt politicians who stood to make a profit from it. Eventually Pinchot joined their side.

It was ironic that the aristocratic Pinchot was dominated by the ideology of the masses. Muir, whose childhood had been emotionally and materially impoverished, recognized that physical discomfort could be survived, but spiritual loss could not.

Pinchot's betrayal of the wilderness ideal, which far outweighed any compromises Doug Scott might have made in his career, was sadder because of his great contributions to forestry reform and because of Muir's advanced age. It was a bad ending for a friendship between the two founders of American conservation. It opened a rift that would widen until its fissures undermined the structure of the modern environmental movement.

If Doug was a latter-day Pinchot, then Foreman was Muir's most recent reincarnation. Dave Foreman's affinity with John Muir explained a lot of what was happening to him these days. Several years before, he had read *The Pathless Way,* a book by Michael P. Cohen. Cohen's book looked beneath the surface of the bearded patriarch's life story. It provided Foreman with insight into Muir's transformation in the wilderness, which began with a near-death experience. Just a month before his twenty-ninth birthday, Muir was temporarily blinded by an industrial accident. After he recovered, he abandoned a promising career as an inventor and manufacturing executive. He made his "Thousand Mile Walk to the Gulf" which he later recounted in a book. On the trip he picked up an illness, probably from a mosquito, which would reappear throughout his life during times of stress. But this journey was merely an opening, the initial stage in Muir's process of self-definition. It wasn't until Muir reached the western edge of the United States that he found the transcendence he was seeking.

"The West of which I speak is but another name for the Wild; and what I have been preparing to say is, that in Wildness is the preservation of the World. . . . The most alive is the wildest," Thoreau had written in his essay "Walking."

Stripped of his past, Muir found a new sense of self in the West. In Yosemite, he had the paradoxical experience of defining a new self and at the same time feeling a greater sense of connectedness to other creatures. Only then did Muir make the decisive break from his father's dour, repressive God. He found his own god, the intelligent force behind the harmonious processes of nature.

In his forties, Muir's life changed dramatically. He married the richest girl in Martinez, California, and turned her inheritance into a profitable orchard. Now and then, he retreated to his "scribble den" on the third floor of their elegant house and turned out a best-selling book. When his health and spirits drooped, his wife would order him into the mountains, where he would miraculously regain his desire to live. He became friends with a Scottish painter named William Keith, whose San Francisco studio he frequented. Once the Sierra Club had formed, Muir went on the group's hiking trips. Like many writers, he was a compulsive talker. In 1909, as he walked down from Glacier Point with William Howard Taft, Taft teased him for being so enthusiastic. Michael Cohen writes that Muir's childlike quality was simultaneously genuine and part of a "calculated charm" which he used for political purposes.[1]

As he grew older, Muir diluted the purity of his wilderness message. He became an enthusiastic advocate of bringing visitors to national parks. His rationale was that if more people learned about nature, they would want to protect it. In 1912 he even advocated building roads through Yosemite. On the subject of a railway line near the Grand Canyon, he wrote: "In the presence of such stupendous scenery [trains] are nothing." He compared trains and automobiles to beetles and caterpillars and, in Cohen's words, "his language revealed a grudging willingness to accept the beginnings of industrial tourism."[2]

Muir was over seventy years old when Model A cars began cranking along the edges of the American wilderness. He probably could not have foreseen the world that existed by the time his biographer became a Sierra Club trip leader in the 1970s. Cohen's experience led him to believe there is a gap between the mountain world and the world of Washington, D.C., that cannot be bridged by brilliant talk or good intentions. Although certain observations leave him vulnerable to charges of elitism, Cohen's account reflects the process of an environmentalist losing his illusions:

> Muir's politics, to the extent that he was capable of manipulating the circumstances, were carried out in the mountains. Men like Roosevelt and Taft, Burroughs and Harriman, came to his world in Alaska and Yosemite. Muir did not go to Washington, or even to Sacramento, unless he had to. This *was* important. Mountain thinking was different, and so consequently was mountain society. If only the conversion in the wilderness could be made strong enough, it would be carried back to the lowlands and change the cities. All of this suggested that the Sierra Club Outing carried the possibility for a re-creation of human society.
>
> When I worked on Sierra Club Outings, there was still hope that the outings would enlist the "support and cooperation" of the participants. The air was alive with it. How could people fail to gain something after camping for two weeks in the company of Norman Clyde? There was a place on a Sierra Club Outing for a young man like George Dyson, a place where he could get away from his father's obsessional vision of a nuclear-powered escape from a polluted and overpopulated world. He could find a congenial group, a cult of revolutionaries who believed that our own world was our only world, and one worth saving. Even doctors and lawyers became something different when they went into the wilderness; they learned a new set of manners and a new set of values. That was the promise of the Sierra Club and of Muir's kind of Sierra Club Outing politics. Americans could sense, for a while, what it meant to be at home in Nature, and then they would write to their congressmen.
>
> The dream of the Sierra Club Outings had always been essential to Sierra Club politics, but the reality of the outings suggests something else. People haven't always gotten along

with each other, and there have been frequent moral conflicts between the younger crews and the older campers over precisely the question of what constitutes the "right manners of the wilderness." On one trip we invited along two boys, nine and eleven years old, from the Oakland ghetto. Duke and John. They were miserable. They missed the television set and even the noise of traffic. They could not understand why sane adults would want to spend any time out in that wilderness. We were shocked to discover firsthand that the taste for wilderness was culturally determined, a privilege enjoyed only by the sons and daughters of a certain comfortable class of Americans. One could cultivate a sense of utopian community on the outings only by beginning with a group of people who already agreed closely about certain basic values. Mountain thinking and mountain politics were not likely to become a ground swell in the evolution of American culture and politics. The Sierra Club Outing had always been designed to appeal only to middle- and upper-class people. And it worked effectively only within those groups. The most popular crew members, not surprisingly, were the young men who had gone to elite prep schools like Phillips Exeter and Choate. The doctors, college professors, and lawyers loved them.[3]

Like Muir, Foreman had thrown away a promising, if conventional, career. He had gone on his own journey of self-exploration. It involved more booze and less apparent introspection than Muir's, but he had defined his role in the world. He had also defined his limits. One of them was the one hundredth meridian, the line separating East from West. From obscure outposts like Ely, Nevada, and Chico, California, Earth First! had managed to alter the views of people who ran things from Washington, D.C., Boston, and New York. Foreman was at ease in his world. When he remarried, he chose a woman who was comfortable sharing his outlaw status.

As the pressure increased in the months leading to his trial, Dave

Foreman drew closer to Cohen's conclusion. He could not be a democrat "with a small *d*" as Doug Scott claimed to be. He did not want to be part of a mass movement. The rapt quality of his audiences terrified him.

More than ever Foreman wanted to retreat to his own scribble den and write, to drink and talk and hike only with people he trusted. The FBI tapes included painful passages. His friend Peg Millett had been recorded calling him a paternalistic asshole. Mark Davis spent more time figuring out how to manipulate Foreman into funding his revolutionary fantasies than he did considering the consequences of his actions. Foreman had created a monster. The monster had turned on its creator.

The irate anarchists who had surrounded Ed Abbey at the Grand Canyon Rendezvous in 1987 were the advance guard of an obnoxious army. Barely a month after Foreman's arrest in 1989, Mike Jakubal, the wild young mountaineer who had invented tree sitting, burned the American flag at the Earth First! Rendezvous in the Jemez Mountains of New Mexico. The incident was prominently featured in the media. Foreman was disgusted. From the start, he had deliberately wrapped Earth First! in the American flag. Patriotism was a subject on which Foreman and Doug Scott were in perfect accord. "A movement's got to be brain dead to let the American flag get away from it as a symbol," said Scott. "Brain dead." Nancy Morton felt even more strongly about the Jakubal incident, but for personal reasons. Still freaked out about the FBI's invasion of her home, she spread the word that Jakubal was a government plant. Her accusations created even more paranoia and divisiveness. But there was no other way she could understand such an ill-timed, destructive act.

These days when he made public appearances Foreman often was confronted by hecklers. Invariably they were Earth First! members. The gentlemanly Foreman would respond as genially as possible, then go home muttering about the bad manners of the younger generation. In July 1990, not long after the New Mexico rendezvous, *The Nation* and the *Anderson Valley Advertiser* ran an interview with Mike Roselle that broke records for vituperation. When Roselle claimed that the press had given Earth First! a raw deal, his interviewer, Alexander Cockburn, pulled him up short.

COCKBURN: But Mike, Foreman's and Abbey's statements weren't misinterpreted or taken out of context.

ROSELLE: No, they weren't. They stand on their own, and they are recognized as being racist, extremely ignorant and insensitive. There's big debate in the grass roots of Earth First! over these issues. The problem is that Foreman doesn't want to discuss the issues any more. He feels his words speak for themselves and he's been misinterpreted. So the rest of us are left hanging and we have to deal with this dirty laundry that Foreman has left all over the place and to defend ourselves on positions we don't even have. Any effort to resolve this has been met by the stubborn opposition of the current editors of the *Earth First! Journal*, John Davis and Dale Turner, two people [in Tucson] not involved with the grass roots of Earth First! and hand-picked by Foreman. There's a lot of bitterness right now in Earth First! about the total loss of control of the paper and how, as grass roots organizers, we haven't been able to address the most important issues. When we walk into the offices of the local peace committee some place and want some help on old growth, we don't want to have to answer for David Foreman's statements on immigration or his position on the future of tribal people in Ethiopia. Foreman has announced his retirement and continues to say that he doesn't speak for the movement. Unfortunately, he gets a lot of phone calls from the media and they don't know that, and I don't think he makes it clear to them. I think he's become a liability to us . . .

It was a clear invitation to resign. Ten years before, Foreman had been in a similar position, at odds with the new regime at the Wilderness Society. Since tossing aside his career as a lobbyist, Foreman had been free, but poor. In the early 1980s, he unhesitatingly sold his land in

Glenwood to fund Earth First! He lived in a house owned by his wife. For a long time, he hadn't even owned a tent. He had spent most of his adult life wearing black T-shirts with monkeywrenches on them and geeky surplus camouflage duds from the local Army-Navy store.

With the notoriety of his arrest, Foreman's long scramble for cash looked as if it might be over. His speaking fee doubled, jumping from $1,500 to $3,000. He got a respectable advance from a major publisher for his memoirs, *Confessions of an EcoWarrior*. He was on a roll.

But somewhere along the way, Foreman's list of dependents had grown. When his sister Roxanne's marriage went bad, he hired her to run his mail-order book business. Roxanne and her three kids moved into the Calle Carapan house. Eventually Foreman's mother, who was ill with emphysema, began to spend part of the year there, too. Dave and Nancy moved to a nearby apartment. The whole ménage balanced on Dave's fragile notoriety. When the book business was bad, both households were jeopardized.

When Roselle's interview was published, Foreman set aside these considerations and decided that he wasn't afraid to start over. He might have mellowed, but he wasn't ready to mimic John Muir's transformation into a gelded patriarch. Foreman's vision of Earth First! was being sullied by anarchist shoplifters, by rude North Country mamas, and bratty adolescent boys. He wasn't going to rationalize. He wasn't going to try to fit in. Dave Foreman was a military brat. He knew how to move on. Maybe he was addicted to it. He was an entrepreneur, a loner, and, most of all, a purist who couldn't bear it when his creativity ran up against a dead end. John James Audubon had been similarly compelled by his "Great Idea," the depiction of every single American bird caught in a state of uncanny, frozen intensity.[4] Foreman's romantic view of the West was not unlike Audubon's ecstatic vision. The wilderness aesthetic existed outside cheap squabbles and self-righteous pedantry. This was Bob Marshall's theme in his essay "The Problem of Wilderness," the most commanding argument for the wilderness aesthetic ever written. The experience of wilderness is unanchored in the historic stream, according to Marshall. Nothing stands between the aesthete and experience; no other aesthetic experience so completely fills the spectator's senses. "There can be no extraneous thoughts—no question about the creator of the phenomenon, its structure, what it resembles or what vanity in the beholder it gratifies. 'The purely esthetic observer has for the moment forgotten his own soul,' he has only one sensation left and that is exquisiteness," Marshall wrote in 1930.[5] Marshall did not duck charges of elitism but faced them head on. He argued that the amount of wilderness was tiny in proportion to the country's vast carpet of roads and stores and telephones. Financial losses accruing from wilderness protection could easily be offset by better stewardship of the land already under cultivation.

But Marshall's most compelling argument was the exaltation of his prose when he described wilderness. It was this purity of feeling, transcendent but transitory, that drove him to a full life and an early death. It also kept Foreman on the move. Years before, he and Debbie Sease had gone to see *Lawrence of Arabia*. Blinking from the glare of the streetlights, they left the movie theater talking about the film. Debbie thought that Lawrence must have been crazy, even if his masochistic embrace of extremes allowed him to accomplish the impossible. Dave loved the movie unconditionally and was outraged at Debbie's unimaginative caution. He was ready to throw on white robes and start the long march.

It was ten years later, and he was ready to do it again. It could have been that he was tired of not fitting in. Or perhaps he was just stubborn, impatient, and egotistical. All he knew was that he was getting the hell out.

There was one problem. If Foreman ditched, it would look like he was trying to save his ass. Gerry Spence had agreed to defend him only after Foreman promised to keep rabble-rousing. Tough, Foreman decided. He talked to Spence on the telephone. Then he sat down with Nancy Morton. Together they wrote a corny but heartfelt Dear John letter to their Baby Frankenstein. "Dear friends," it began. "We feel like we should be sitting at the bar of a seedy honky-tonk, drinking Lone Star, thumbing quarters in the country-western jukebox, and writing this letter on a bar napkin." The letter lovingly embraced what the anarchist mutualists had disparagingly called "the worst kind of Wild West imagery." It also affirmed Dave and Nancy's commitment to a "biocentric" view of the world—and people. "A good metaphor, we think, for Earth First! over the last decade is that of a generalist species in a new habitat with many available niches. . . . Oftentimes, external environmental stresses push a generalist species toward faster differentiation into separate, specifically adapted sister species. This is what has happened to us in Earth First! Those given to better exploiting the different niches of monkeywrenching, direct action, and conservation biology have been diverging. . . . Splitting the sheets is not pleasant but staying together with irreconcilable differences is worse."

Dave and Nancy's letter didn't quite get the circulation of David Brower's, but it managed to make its way into the hands of Mike Roselle and Doug Scott. "I think we should be careful about using biology to understand human things," said Roselle, mindful of the split between leftists and deep ecologists. He couldn't resist one last parting dig at Dave. "It's like using the Bible to expound on politics."

Scott's reaction was kinder. It was almost as if he were welcoming Dave back into the fold. "I think it's the best thing Dave ever wrote," he said. "I wouldn't be surprised if there were tear stains on the original letter."

Still nostalgic for the legacy of Howard Zahniser, Doug added, "The single most tragic thing is that the Wilderness Society that I knew in the sixties and seventies no longer exists. . . . Dave would have been a different person, a happier person [if it did]."

But the heyday of the Wilderness Society was long gone. Doug Scott spoke the truth when he said that the environmental movement's greatest gain was America's increased awareness of environmental issues. But the growth of conservation into a mass movement had diluted the message of Aldo Leopold and Bob Marshall. Rock-and-roll rain-forest benefits with performers like the Grateful Dead, Madonna, and Sting were deceptive. Even a real environmental vice president could only gloss over the fact that the real game is hardball and the good guys are always losing. Ed Abbey had turned out to be right when he said that conservationists never "gain" anything. "In two or three years the other side is back again," Abbey noted. Eventually a compromise is reached. The result is inevitably loss—of biodiversity, wilderness, a sense of freedom. "I'm in favor of genuine compromise," Abbey said. "If you build a dam, remove one."[6] In the preface to *Beyond the Wall*, he went further:

> Let us save the 2 per cent—that saving remnant. Or better yet, expand, recover and reclaim much more of the original American wilderness. About 50 per cent would be a fair and reasonable compromise. We have yielded too much too easily. It is time to start shoving cement and iron in the opposite direction before the entire nation, before the whole planet, becomes one steaming, stinking, overcrowded high-tech ghetto. Open space was the fundamental heritage of America; the freedom of the wilderness may well be the central purpose of our national adventure.[7]

Radicals like Abbey weren't the only ones who saw the movement's effectiveness eroding. Foreman's ex-wife Debbie Sease had watched it happen from the inside. Even after Sease became one of the few female policymakers on the Sierra Club staff, she kept a stuffed deer head protruding from her office wall to remind her of the Buckaroo Bunkhouse days. To Sease, the antienvironmental backlash unleashed by the Reagan administration grew more subtle—and more effective—during the Bush presidency:

> The clear-cut good guy/bad guy model that Watt provided was replaced. Watt said, "I'm a born-again man who's going to trash the environment. I'm going to take back the west for the states." It's clear-cut; he was just a beacon of radicalism.
> And Hodel . . . I can remember the first meeting I had with Hodel before he was confirmed. He took out this piece of paper. He put a line at the top and a line at the middle. He said, we can all agree that some things definitely ought to be

protected. And we can all agree that some things definitely ought to be exploited. He said, what I want to spend my time doing is talking about the things that maybe should and maybe shouldn't. I want to narrow the debate.

Well, in fact, that's the difference between him and Watt. Watt talked about things that shouldn't be exploited. Therefore, he did a lot to create a public consciousness of the public lands and those kinds of issues outside of the local western environment. It made him very ineffective.

Hodel, by leaving aside things that everybody agreed shouldn't be developed, managed to get a lot more damage done. So we were dealing with a more subtle threat.

The pro-active Bush administration was not satisfied with Reagan's policy of not-so-benign neglect. The man who had run for office promising to serve as "the environmental president" tried to cut back wetlands protection, sabotaged tougher gas-efficiency requirements for automobiles, supported weakening the Endangered Species Act, and sided with the coal industry in pressing to dismantle enforcement of strip-mining laws. In 1992, Bush's agriculture secretary, Edward R. Madigan, made a proposal that would have practically eliminated citizen input from the forest-planning process. With the backing of Vice President Dan Quayle's antienvironmental star chamber, the Council on Competitiveness, Madigan proposed to end administrative appeals of forest plans. If his proposal had been adopted, environmental opposition would have been limited to the far more costly option of lawsuits.

The environmental movement was not just being attacked by its traditional pro-business opponents. The movement's efforts to negotiate in the hostile climate of successive Republican administrations provoked savage attacks from its own left wing. It wasn't just wilderness purists like Brower and Foreman who were down on groups like the Sierra Club, the Wilderness Society, the National Audubon Society, and the National Wildlife Federation. So were urban antipollution groups. "We can't get funding from the national environmental groups for our work," said Linda Campbell, director of Southern Women Against Toxics, in Livingston, Alabama. "They're nowhere to be seen in our fights." Critics called the big groups the Gang of 10, a term that originated in the late 1980s, when the heads of the mainstream groups began meeting in Washington, D.C., on a regular basis to keep one another informed on their respective activities. Increasingly, gang members heard complaints that they were sleeping through World War III.

"What seems to be selling out is trying to get something done in a very rough situation," said Audubon's Brock Evans, who was probably the most responsive of any top-level official to grass-roots concerns. "It struck me last summer that we're being savaged on the right and attacked on the left and maybe the center cannot hold."[8]

It all got to be too much for Doug Scott. Not long after David Brower's letter splashed down, he made his escape plans. By November 1990, Scott had left the Sierra Club. If he had anticipated the election of Bill Clinton and Al Gore, perhaps he might have stayed on, hoping for a replay of his triumphs during the Carter administration. But the election was too far away to call. He took a job as the head of a small theater company on San Juan Island, a green, unspoiled community full of trees in the Pacific Northwest.

These days, most of the Buckaroos were in semiretirement, too. Ron Kezar had long since repaired to the garden spot of Ely, Nevada, where he worked his way into a sinecure with the Bureau of Land Management. His fire-fighting job allowed him to keep up with his various hobbies, including writing the odd article for the *Earth First! Journal,* usually a polemic on the bombing and polluting that the Department of Defense was inflicting on the public lands.

Howie Wolke had benefited from the boom in ecotourism. His guide service, Wilderness Horizons, had finally become lucrative enough to support him and his small family, which included Marilyn's two children from a previous marriage. Being a founder of Earth First! didn't hurt. Celebrities like Grateful Dead guitarist Bob Weir signed up for Howie's trips, lured by his aura of outdoorsier-than-thou radicalism. Occasionally Howie would surface in the politics of the northern Rockies, mostly as a supporter of Alliance for the Wild Rockies, a group whose tactics and ecosystem-oriented wilderness proposals fell somewhere between those of Earth First! and the mainstream groups.

Even mainstream hero Tim Mahoney had gone to ground. After his RARE II wilderness bill triumph in 1984, Mahoney had become the Sierra Club's point man on Alaska. The battle over oil exploration on the coastal plain of the Arctic National Wildlife Refuge was the last big frontier of the wilderness war. It wasn't over when Mahoney resigned in the late 1980s, but it didn't look as if it was going to be over for a long time and Mahoney was tired. He became that ubiquitous Washington species, a consultant, and taught college classes on the history of the environmental movement. He also became, of all things, a Sierra Club volunteer. In that capacity, Mahoney served as an unpaid unofficial adviser to less experienced environmentalists.

Mike Roselle and Bart Koehler were probably the most active of the Buckaroos. Roselle spent the end of the 1980s traveling around the country organizing demonstrations for Greenpeace. Their emphasis on direct action rather than philosophy suited him. But sometimes being part of an organization—even a relatively loose and disorganized one such as Greenpeace—was too much. In early 1990 he left Greenpeace to man the phones for Redwood Summer. Roselle still was an Earth First!er at heart, but there wasn't much he could do while the Foremanistas kept control of the *Earth First! Journal.* By Thanksgiving he and Claire Greensfelder were preparing to move to Washington, D.C. Roselle was going to rejoin Greenpeace as a roving agitator, and Greensfelder would direct an antinuke campaign.

Roselle wasn't the only Buckaroo acknowledging the pull of Washington, D.C. Even though he was an official Alaskan now, Bart Koehler had spent quite a bit of the late 1980s in Washington. It wasn't just that he didn't like the cold weather, although some of his friends joked that this had something to do with it. The real reason was that Bart was riding straight to the happy ending of the corniest cowpoke movie ever made, "The Tongass Trail." His cubbyhole at the Audubon Society's Washington office was bursting with inspirational totems. Photocopies of old sepia portraits of western outlaws. A certificate of appreciation from the Alaska Peace Officers' Association. A framed piece of glass with a yellow Post-It smacked on it. (Someone had written "SEACC's window" on the Post-It.) A photo of Ed Abbey. A Rosie the Riveter poster with the headline "WE CAN DO IT!" A pinup of pitcher Nolan Ryan. A color photo of Bart and Howie with Mardie Murie, the widow of Wilderness Society founder Olaus Murie. A ripped, impaled, and sadistically tortured copy of *People of the Tongass*, the propaganda book printed by Ron Arnold and Alan Gottlieb's Wise Use group, the Center for the Defense of Free Enterprise.

Go, team!

The most important thing on the cubbyhole's wall was the Tongass trail map. Magic Markers of every color imaginable traced the metaphorical journey of the Tongass Timber Reform Act. Like the grizzled, over-the-hill Texas Rangers in *Lonesome Dove*, the Tongass Rangers had herded this little puppy from the Rio Grande all the way north to the promised land. It had slunk its way through the Metzenbaum Morass. It had climbed Mt. Wayburn. It had hitched a ride on the Mitchell Ferry, climbed up the Wirth Waterfall, passed the Bittersweet Grasslands, hiked the Bennett Johnston Canyon and made it all the way to the White House (Lawn) rose garden by the banks of the Chinook River. (Chinook is the town near the Milk River where the Lonesome Dove cowboys ended up, not to mention the name of the only beer brewed in Alaska.)

In November 1990, the Tongass reform bill landed on Bush's desk. Mirabile dictu, he signed it. Bart won the Alaska Wildlife Federation's Olaus Murie Award, and SEACC was named Conservation Group of the Year by the National Wildlife Federation. After seven years of steady work, he had engineered a deal to stop logging in a stretch of forest that was bigger than the state of New Jersey. On the eve of final congressional approval for his reform bill, Bart downplayed his achievement to the press, calling it a "bittersweet result . . . [but] balanced and fair." Privately he crowed about his victory. If he had learned anything from his years with Earth First!, it was how to harness the power of regular people to change the terms of debate. Bart's coalition was not just made up of environmental activists of the Saab and Land Rover genre but also included fishermen, sportsmen, and Native Alaskans. His tiny staff had, in Doug Scott's words, "done what the Sierra Club does better than we do." They had traveled through the Lower 48 states with a slide show and a good rap, generating reams of letters to Congress. In Bart's words, they had forced Alaska's unwilling congressional delegation into the fray, fought, and ridden away with their best horses.

For the next few months, Bart holed up on Admiralty Island with his wife, Julie. Occasionally, the phone would ring. It was usually one of his friends congratulating him or an environmental group trying to woo him away from Alaska. The months passed. Winter on Admiralty Island grew whiter and more silent. Bart stayed home, building fires in the fireplace and playing his guitar. On clear days, he paddled out in a kayak to watch for humpback whales and listen for the sharp cries of eagles. Bart wasn't in any rush. He had waited a long time for this.

High
Noon

1991—Prescott, Arizona

IT WASN'T EASY TO PISS OFF NANCY ZIERENBERG. The Earth First! merchandise coordinator was a rangy, clear-eyed woman with a deep laugh and a healthy disregard for authority. She had an outdoorsy kind of beauty that would be spoiled by makeup and high heels. Z's easygoing nature made her the most well liked person in Earth First! Except for her general disgust with the U.S. government's environmental policies, she didn't get angry often. When she did, it was big. A little bit like a tectonic plate moving fast, and in your general direction.

It was the night before the Earth First! trial was going to begin. Around nine o'clock, Sam Guiberson, one of Foreman's two defense attorneys, shoved a pile of wrinkled shirts into Nancy's arms. "Just take them to the office and call the dry cleaners," he told her, in a tone that left no room for argument.

Nancy raised an eyebrow and walked off. Where the hell did Guiberson think he was? Paris? He'd be lucky to find a pizza in Prescott this time of night. Just for the hell of it, she made a couple of calls. She struck out, of course. Then she started asking around. The Foreman camp had rented a bank of apartments in a housing development on the outskirts of town. She knocked on door after door. No one had remembered to bring an iron. Finally she got around to the R.V. that Nancy Morton's parents had driven out from California. Nell Morton had brought along one of those miniature stripped-down travel irons. Nancy Zierenberg plugged it in and got to work, trying to coax herself into being tolerant. After all, Sam was under a lot of pressure. The defense team was depending on his expertise in wiretapping. Guiberson had made a career out of convincing juries that government agents psychologically manipulated people to say things that sounded incriminating on tape. A former documentary filmmaker, he had used his own expertise with technology to achieve a command of evidence that overshadowed his opponents'. It was Sam's Byzantine computer program that gave the defense instant access to an intimidating crush of transcripts and motions. Sam was indispensable in other ways, too. His to-the-manner-born Texas affability had cast him in the role of go-between. When the feds wanted to take care of business, they called Sam.

As if the ordinary pressures of the case weren't enough, the disarray of Guiberson's personal life had spilled over to his work. Until shortly before the trial, he had been dating his legal assistant. When he announced his engagement to another woman, she abruptly resigned both positions, leaving Sam cowering under a microchip blitzkrieg.

By the time Nancy returned with his shirts, Sam had calmed down enough to take a good look at her face. He had the sense to thank her effusively, acting suitably abashed when he realized that she had ironed the shirts herself.

The summer was filled with these vignettes of barely controlled chaos. Short tempers, stress, and most of all, paranoia, kept everybody wired. Foreman popped tranquilizers. Guiberson nearly went broke.

The wife of one attorney had a baby. Another lawyer's wife was diagnosed with a rare, usually fatal cancer. Peg Millett got divorced. So did Marc Baker. Ilse Asplund broke up with her new boyfriend and fought with her mother. And Mark Davis . . . well, Davis got frenetic.

By the time the trial started, Davis had switched lawyers three times. First he fired Tom Hoidel, the head of the public defender's office. Hoidel's sin was showing enthusiasm for a plea bargain, which could include the proviso that Davis testify against Foreman. This caused Davis to suspect Hoidel of complicity with the FBI. Then Davis hired Dick Eiden, a left-wing lawyer from Southern California who knew virtually nothing about the case. Eiden went along with Mark's idea of using a strategy called the necessity defense. The necessity defense is based on the idea that the defendant was operating under a higher moral law, which led him to break the lesser human law. It was a strategy popular with political activists, particularly Catholic Rambos in the Ploughshares movement who pulled stunts like breaking into defense plants and pouring blood on missile nose cones. There was only one problem with it. Judges despised it. The necessity defense was a sure ticket to martyrdom.

When they discovered Eiden's approach, Guiberson and Foreman's other lawyer, Wyoming trial attorney Gerry Spence, frantically filed a series of motions to sever Foreman's case from those of the other defendants. The motions were denied, one after another. To their relief, Davis eventually tired of Eiden, too. At Spence's urging, Wellborn Jack, Jr., a brilliant but eccentric lawyer from Shreveport, Louisiana, popped up to take Davis's case. Jack was so intense that he positively twitched with agitation, his small, marionette body unable to take the ferocious jolts of energy pumped out by his brain. Davis had met his match. Ilse Asplund stopped worrying—at least about that aspect of the case. "This is perfect," she thought. "Mark finally found a lawyer as crazy as he is."

Davis wasn't the only one taking potshots at his own foot. There was the small matter of Gerry Spence's motion. Nothing was wrong with it per se. Like everything else that Spence wrote, it was quite eloquent. There was just the little matter of Spence's calling the judge Bloomfield when his name was really Broomfield.

When jury selection began, Foreman realized that something more serious had gone awry. The jury pool was so big it practically overflowed the Federal-style courtroom. But the fact that there were over one hundred potential jurors provided scant comfort. Each one seemed to have worked for the U.S. Forest Service, the Salt River Project, or a local sheriff's department. Every man had a National Rifle Association bumper sticker on his pickup truck; they watched sports on TV and didn't read books. The women had cotton candy hair, and the last book they had read was the Kitty Kelley biography of Nancy Reagan. "I haven't been around so many rednecks since I left Louisiana," muttered the AP stringer covering the case.

Someone had definitely screwed up. Months before, when the four Prescott defendants complained that they couldn't afford to relocate, Spence and Guiberson had agreed to switch the trial's venue from Phoenix to Prescott. Prescott was a nice little town, and nobody in his or her right mind would want to spend a long, hot summer in Phoenix. But when they agreed to press for the change, Foreman's attorneys had assumed that the jury would be drawn exclusively from Yavapai County, where Prescott was located. They were counting on Prescott's New West transplants and affluent retirees to provide them with an understanding jury. They didn't realize that the jury would be culled from the five counties surrounding Prescott, which were so conservative that air routes had to be redirected so that people from New York or California wouldn't go into culture shock just flying over them. As jury selection droned on, they all realized what a mistake they had made. They found themselves grateful for slim pickings, like the Apache, Navajo, and Hopi reservations. Maybe they could dig up at least one juror who considered the federal government capable of malfeasance. That would be enough for a hung jury.

After opening statements by the prosecution and defense attorneys, the prosecution would be presenting its case. Later, the defense would get its chance. Because of last-minute casting changes, the prosecution's show promised to be a combination of the McCarthy hearings and *Reefer Madness*. While the defense was scrambling to iron shirts and straighten out spelling errors, the prosecution had been churning through its own chaos. The original prosecutor, a lawyer named Steven (Mad Dog) Mitchell, who had the reputation of not being terribly competent, had been replaced by a man named Ivan Mathew. Then Mathew was replaced by a bright, ginger-haired fellow named Ivan Abrams. Abrams was a former antiwar activist from Pittsburgh whose politics had slipped to the right over a decade of working as a federal prosecutor. In December 1990, Abrams drafted a second superseding indictment that stretched the definition of conspiracy to include Foreman in virtually every criminal activity of EMETIC. In this document, the government indicted Ilse Asplund, who had so far remained out of the case. Asplund reportedly was indicted in order to pressure Davis to make a deal. The indictment was a killer piece of legal work. Not long afterward, Abrams awoke to a midlife crisis. Riven by self-disgust—and distaste for the government's handling of the Earth First! case—he resigned to enter private practice.

That left Roslyn Moore-Silver. The best adjective to describe Moore-Silver is severe. She was deadly pale beneath an early Faye Dunaway mane of blond hair. When she pinned her hair up in a French twist, she revealed a deliberate strip of brown underneath. The Disney movie *101 Dalmatians* had been rereleased that summer. Moore-Silver's two-tone dye job and baleful manner inspired the press pool to nickname her Cruella de Vil. Most of her peers in the legal community considered Moore-Silver terminally uptight. She had a reputation for getting so hung up on details that she lost sight of the larger canvas. But she was clearly single-minded enough to twist the neck of a cute Dalmatian puppy if circumstances required. Years before, a fellow attorney had been amused when he kept running into her in the Maricopa County law library in the middle of the night. "We'd be the only people there at two in the morning. I was there because I was ripped on drugs. She was there because she was such an incredible world-class grind," he said with a laugh.

The Earth First! trial was a big deal for Moore-Silver. The federal prosecutor's office was being criticized for ignoring Arizona's political corruption. The Earth First! case was an opportunity to deflect this criticism with a flashy national cause célèbre. Moore-Silver pulled out all the stops. On the day of her opening statement, she wore a dress-for-success, 1970s-style power suit in patriotic shades of red, white, and blue. Only someone from Phoenix would get within a city block of this fashion felony, much less wrap it around her body. She even brought a visual aid—a large sketch pad with phrases like "Anarchy and Revolution" and "Eco-Terrorism" written in big block letters with a Magic Marker. Two FBI agents sat at the prosecution table with her. They were Lori Bailey, the young Martina Navratilova look-alike who had been in charge of the case, and the FBI tape-meister, Keith Tollhurst, a standard-issue, pug-nosed all-American boy. That first day, Moore-Silver reportedly alienated Bailey when she told jurors, "Miss Bailey will be my Vanna White, if you will." Bailey utilized her FBI training to remain stone faced while she flipped from one page of the sketch pad to another.

In her opening statement, Moore-Silver made it clear that she was taking the hardest line possible. "This is going to be a long trial," she told the jury. "But this is not a complex case.

"What is this case about?" she asked rhetorically. "Very simply, this is a case about monkeywrenching. . . . Monkeywrenching, ladies and gentlemen, is terrorism."

Dave Foreman was sitting behind the defense table like a middle-aged schoolboy in his shiny new suit and cowboy boots (sans muleshit this time). Heads swiveled as Moore-Silver pointed him out, calling him a preacher. But she didn't call him a preacher of a pantheistic religion, which, in an odd way, he was. "This man is the preacher of ecoterrorism," Moore-Silver told the jury. Like a preacher herself, Moore-Silver used the measured cadences of call and response. "What is this case about?" she screamed. "This case is about . . . [Vanna flips the chart] 'ANARCHY AND REVOLUTION.' *Ecodefense*, Foreman's field guide to monkeywrenching, was filled with sabotage techniques for bedeviling businesses and the government."

Dave Foreman had never looked so swashbuckling. He had always been a nerd in cowboy's clothing, a ninety-seven-pound weakling who had taken the Charles Atlas course but kept his butterfly collection by his bed. In Moore-Silver's cosmology he had finally made it to Lucifer status, the fallen angel who did ". . . outshine/Myriads though bright" in *Paradise Lost*. Not bad for a shitkicker from New Mexico.

Mark Davis had been promoted, too. He had become a "mastermind." The epithet had been bestowed by a credulous Peg Millett in an idle conversation that just happened to have been taped by the FBI. For three years, Davis "perfected them [techniques] into the dangerous monkeywrenching techniques used in this grand plot," Moore-Silver advised the jury. Grand plot? One of Davis's worst sins was designing the acronym EMETIC, which stood for the Evan Mecham Eco Terrorist International Conspiracy. Of course, Davis had later changed "terrorist" to "teasippers." In EMETIC's second letter to the Fairfield Snowbowl, "Iisaw" had explained the situation:

> In passing it seems necessary to clear up some of the confusion surrounding our name. We would like to state clearly here and now that we firmly support Governor Mecham in his courageous battle against the militant liberal faggots trying to hound him from office. He has done more in a few months to slow economic growth in Arizona than EMETIC could hope to with years of dedicated conscientious destruction. If he is recalled, and someone competent elected, then Arizona's rampaging business community will be free to return its full attention to the process of turning one of the loveliest places on earth into a giant shopping mall.
>
> We aren't really terrorists. We refuse to do anything that will physically injure anyone. We just needed a T word to make the acronym work.

Back to so-called reality.

"You see? These defendants even called themselves terrorists. . . . Of course Evan Mecham had nothing to do with these acts. It was a red herring to pull people away from who was actually committing these acts," Moore-Silver intoned. Du-uh.

Listening to the prosecutor, it was easy to get the impression that the monkeywrenchers' worst sin was having a good time. True, there was something a little sick about the rush that people got from monkeywrenching, or even from civil disobedience. But Moore-Silver made it sound as if the rush, not the act, was illegal. "It was willful. It was more than willful," she said. "It was *gleeful*. You will learn, ladies and gentlemen, that these people thought these acts of destruction were fun."

Heaven forfend.

After Moore-Silver's performance, a veritable Rockettes chorus line of defense attorneys lined up at the podium to make their opening statements. The first to speak was Mike Black, a former Miami federal prosecutor who had become a drug lawyer in Phoenix. Black was a tough, garrulous good old boy from South Dakota who had taken Peg Millett's case because she reminded him of his little sister, a speech therapist also named Peggy. Black tried to insist that Gerry Spence go first, but it would have been a hot day in the Himalayas before Spence gave up star billing. He was the Bull Goose Looney of the legal Rockettes, and he'd let you know about it in three seconds flat. When push came to shove, Black backed down.

Black promised to mount a true nineties defense. Part of his entrapment argument was based on the fact that Peg Millett was the child of an alcoholic. By claiming to be a recovering drunk in search of help, Mike Fain exploited her vulnerability. Ironically, when Black's real-life sister had pointed out to him that their family was similar to Peg's, Black replied that he preferred to stay in denial, if that's what the hell it was. Perhaps mentioning Peg's vulnerability as the daughter of an alcoholic was his roundabout method of acknowledgment. In any case, Black resembled nothing so much as an elder brother defending his baby sister against a gang of hoodlums.

Next, Mark Budoff, a handsome, nattily dressed man with chiseled features, gave a low-key statement on behalf of Ilse Asplund. Budoff's presentation would get more dramatic as the trial went on. After Bu-

COYOTES AND TOWN DOGS

doff, Skip Donau, the Tucson lawyer known for his representation of the Bonanno Mafia clan, did his schtick. Donau's great strength was thinking on his feet. Spontaneously, he decided to use Moore-Silver's own sketch pad to refute her point-by-point. He even asked Baker to flip the pages for him. The respectful tone he used toward his client contrasted sharply with Moore-Silver's ill-considered Vanna White remark. It was "*Doctor* Baker this" "*Doctor* Baker that." Dr. Baker pitched in by trying to look the part. He had cut his hair and shopped at the Salvation Army for some straight-looking clothes. In keeping with Donau's contention that he was a respectable—if absentminded—scientist who had half unwittingly stumbled into this gang of eco-outlaws, Marc sat a few feet apart from the other defendants. As the trial swirled around him, he seemed absorbed in reading *The State of the World* and other suitably sober-minded environmental tomes. It was a good routine. Since getting cleaned up, the six-foot-five Baker looked almost statesmanlike, a latter-day Abe Lincoln. No one had ever questioned his intelligence or his talent for botany. His friends even said that he had matured after his arrest—as much as he was ever going to.

After Donau was finished, Wellborn Jack, Jr., pulled out all the stops. He invoked religious imagery like Jimmy Swaggart in a three-piece suit, getting down on the good foot in the way that only a Southerner can. Jack's most memorable line was delivered when he cast his client, Mark Davis, as an impotent dreamer. His best-of-trial aphorism came not from Flannery O'Connor or any other practitioner of southern Gothic but revealed itself as a straight shot from the streets of New York, courtesy of the city's top mouthpiece, Jimmy Breslin. "This was the Monkey Wrench Gang That Couldn't Shoot Straight," Wellborn told the court. Observers familiar with the facts of the case silently breathed the word *Amen*.

After Jack's presentation, court recessed at the suggestion of the defense. The afternoon was wearing on, and it was obvious that Gerry Spence didn't want anything to break his rhythm once he got started. Everyone in the courtroom was aware of his reputation. He had never lost a case, and many of his cases had been sure losers. His clients were regular folks: a Wyoming sheriff accused of murder, a Miss America contestant who claimed to have been maligned by a satirical article in *Penthouse* magazine. Karen Silkwood's family. Imelda Marcos . . . well, not exactly a little guy, but to Spence she was a victim, too. At least, that's what he convinced the New York jury to believe. He had won huge awards for his clients in civil cases. Many were reversed on appeal, but the legend was untarnished. Everyone in Prescott expected Spence to work a miracle, not just for Foreman, but for the other defendants, as well. Peg Millett, not exactly a fan of male authority figures, had been charmed and awed by Spence when he took her to lunch. He told her that in college he had vacillated between becoming an opera singer and studying law. Peg could identify with Spence's artistic sensibility; her arrest had given a big boost to her singing career. His humongous ego failed to offend her. Peg herself drove friends crazy with wild oscillations between grandiosity and poor self-esteem. All in all, she was quite taken by Spence's forceful, fatherly personality. "He reminds me of George Washington," she said, possibly prompted by a defense strategy of invoking the flag.

As charismatic as Spence was, the real star of the show was going to be Dave Foreman. The trial's climax would come when Foreman used his awesome powers of persuasion to save his own neck on the witness stand. If Spence couldn't work a miracle, Foreman surely could. Everyone was waiting for it. When David Brower came to Prescott to drum up support for the defendants—Doug Scott would have gotten perverse gratification knowing that Brower received a standing ovation both before he spoke and afterward—he announced that this was going to be "the trial of the century." The outcome would reveal the future of the environmental movement, Brower told a wholesome crowd of Birkenstock-shod young people, most of whom were associated with one of the three colleges in Prescott. Ilse Asplund saw the trial in even larger terms. She was a direct descendant of George Washington and Thomas Jefferson, and her sense of connection to the political philosophies that shaped the Constitution was strong.

"In some sense, it's about a mode of government that came out of the French Enlightenment and worked out its destiny on this wild continent," she said in a late-night conversation early in the trial. "There are two questions here—of our constitutional rights and the rights of the land."

While most of the legal team would be trying to prove that the FBI had violated their clients' civil rights, Spence would be trying to raise the other question that Asplund said concerned her. "How will our form of government deal with the sacredness of the land?"

Foreman and the warm, eloquent Asplund were the only defendants who were going to testify. The other four were too obdurate and fringy. With the heroic figures of Spence, Foreman, and Asplund on one side and Roslyn Moore-Silver's cartoon sketches of deviltry on the other, the trial's political imagery outweighed its legal issues. Moore-Silver's predecessor, Ivan Abrams, thought that the whole thing should have been treated as a minor case of criminal mischief. Instead, it was a clash of symbols.

As befits a symbolic clash, the trial progressed at a stately pace. Everyone knew that they would have to wait for Foreman's star turn. But as it turned out, they waited for Spence, too. As the prosecutor and the other defense attorneys sweated and strained at their opening statements, Spence sat quietly at the far end of the defense table taking notes with the uncanny concentration of a Sioux warrior with a penchant for kingly Stetsons. The most talking Spence had done was at a benefit picnic held the Sunday before the trial began. As he posed onstage with an American flag, Spence sounded pompous, paternalistic, and practically silly. But when he finally approached the podium to deliver his opening remarks, an amazing transformation overtook the Bull Goose Looney, the Big Kahuna of Litigation. On the grander scale of the courtroom, staginess became intimacy. The man who acted like a bull elk in rutting season in the corridor became a kind, trustworthy authority figure. "Together we're going to get to the bottom of this," the Great White Father assured the jury. Then he showed them a time line—with careful elisions—that proved beyond a shadow of a doubt that his client couldn't possibly be guilty. The confusing welter of evidence miraculously rearranged itself. The Wizard whipped out his crystal ball and there it was—Kansas, in all its homespun glory.

Dave Foreman was bathed in the rosy light of Spence's rhetoric. He managed not to cringe in his uncomfortable courtroom seat when Spence suggested that the sensitivity of this newfangled Marlboro Man stopped barely short of quiche eating. No longer proud Lucifer, Foreman was "a fierce-looking man with the sloppy, mushy heart of a puppy." Hyperbole aside, Spence had obviously spent time analyzing his client's character. He even borrowed a leaf from Foreman's own history book, intimating that Foreman was being punished for being a nonconformist "as many of our leaders have been," including Washington, Jefferson, John Brown, and Henry David Thoreau. Spence's explanation of Foreman's apparent willingness to go along with Davis and Fain's nuke scheme accurately reflected Foreman's emotional style. Although he could be sharp-tongued with his intimates, Foreman generally went to great lengths to avoid contradicting people. Instead, he gently led them to discover their mistakes themselves. His avoidance of confrontation verged on the neurotic; it had sent Mike Roselle bouncing off the walls. It wasn't inconceivable that Foreman would have grunted assent to just about anything that Mike Fain said.

Spence gave a masterful performance, but it was the last aria that he would sing for this particular jury. For the next several weeks the prosecution plodded away at establishing the facts of the case. They seemed to be fighting a war of attrition, calling the same dull witnesses from the Fairfield Snowbowl and the Canyon Mine to elucidate the same dull details from every conceivable angle. It was only after weeks of devastating boredom that they called Ron Frazier to the stand.

The prosecution had worked its own kind of magic on its star witness. Frazier had been transformed from a hippie survivalist into Charlie Brown. For one thing, Special Agent Keith Tollhurst had taken him shopping. He wore a brown corduroy sport jacket and a tie. His hair was mostly combed. His face looked freshly scrubbed. If it hadn't been for a certain air of discomfort, an indefinable sense that the pieces didn't quite fit together, Frazier might have looked like an FBI agent instead of an informer.

Once Frazier started testifying, the trial switched channels, flipping from *Dragnet* to *The Outer Limits* with disorienting alacrity. Frazier looked okay, but he acted weird. He waited an Alabama minute before answering almost every question. In those interminable pauses, he would stare at the ceiling or at the floor in a spaced-out way, as if a prompter were feeding him lines. Whoever he, she, or it was, they were doing a good job. Frazier said all the right things, testifying that he had first contacted the FBI because he was worried that Mark Davis was a danger to Ilse's children. He also talked about a confrontation with Dave Foreman at the 1988 Rendezvous. Frazier was unloading packed garbage bags from the back of a pickup truck when Dave Foreman walked over and asked him what he was doing. "I order you to put those bags back on the truck," Frazier quoted Foreman as saying. Frazier told the jury that he had clicked his heels together and raised his hand in a Nazi salute and said, "*Jawohl, Herr Presidente.*" Foreman jumped onto the truck, his face swollen with anger. Frazier said that he grabbed Foreman, admonishing him "not to get violent."

"He seemed to deflate then," Frazier told the courtroom.

This was the only time Foreman smiled in court, apparently at the absurdity of Frazier's story. Under cross-examination, Frazier would admit that he had been the one throwing a tantrum. When Foreman appeared, Frazier was tossing garbage out of the back of the pickup, yelling, "You goddamn Yuppie bastards. If you can haul this garbage in, you can haul it out." But that was later. For now, Frazier was conscientiously earning the FBI's $54,000.

Later that day, Mark Davis talked about how well prepared Frazier seemed to be. "Oh, yeah," Davis said. "There's no doubt about it. He's buffed."

Frazier's unconventional training program was revealed under cross-examination by Wellborn Jack. In a variation on the CIA's alleged use of psychics to get information from dead agents, the FBI had flown Frazier to a Texas hypnotist. The FBI claimed that the hypnosis was to jump-start Frazier's memory of a name. Jack said that the FBI's real aim was "memory hardening," a subtle form of brainwashing that would strengthen Frazier's testimony in court. While in Texas, Frazier told the FBI psychiatrist that he felt guilty about betraying Ilse. The FBI psychiatrist helped him get rid of his guilt, Frazier said. He expressed his gratitude to the psychiatrist, calling the hypnosis "a growth experience." But Frazier's voice was uncertain. He claimed that he had never been unconscious during the hypnosis. Yet in his exchange with Jack he sounded like a child, or a zombie.

"You weren't brainwashed, were you?" Jack asked.

"I don't think so."

"You were finding some new friends though?"

"I had already."

"The FBI."

"Yes."

Eerie as it was, this exchange revealed only one side of Frazier's personality. Another side was revealed in the moment that everyone had been waiting for, whether they knew it consciously or not. Frazier was asked about his relationship with Ilse Asplund. Sitting directly in front of her, he told the packed courtroom about the circumstances of their intimacy; Ken's abrupt cancellation, how he had shown up with his sleeping bag, the camping trip to the high meadow in the San Francisco Peaks. We got close, Frazier said. We stayed "close" for a month and a half.

Sam Guiberson watched Ilse. She was staring at Frazier, who rigidly avoided her gaze. Tears ran down her face.

The next day, Ilse came to court with an impassive expression. She was wearing a sleeveless black turtleneck. Underneath it she wore a black brassiere. Stripped of her privacy and dignity, all she had left was this secret gesture of defiance.

After Frazier's testimony about Ilse, the defense lawyers felt an even stronger stake in the case. They were a talented bunch, and it didn't take them long to tear him apart. "It will be like peeling an onion," Wellborn Jack, Jr., crowed. "I think we may have an actual case of multiple personalities."

First there were the drugs. Frazier had done more than his fair hippie's share. "I could tell he was fried. I met with him, and the FBI and was appalled. I instantly knew here was a very . . . odd individual," said former prosecutor Ivan Abrams. When it became obvious that the defense was going to bring up his drug use, Frazier balked. Could the FBI guarantee immunity if he answered questions about drugs? For some reason, Moore-Silver hadn't anticipated this problem. Fearful that his refusal to testify under cross-examination would result in a mistrial, his government handlers told him to get a lawyer. He hired a local attorney, who negotiated a deal with the sheriff's office. Then Frazier proceeded to tell the judge that he had used a medicine chest of mind-altering substances, including peyote, LSD, heroin, barbituates, speed, and marijuana. Although he had been arrested only once, for peyote, he was known as a pot dealer in Bisbee. Oops, there's one more thing. Frazier had been tripping on LSD during the Rendezvous. He was stoned on several tabs of acid when he took Ilse's daughter for a walk. He might have been high during his famous run-in with Foreman. Judge Broomfield ruled that the jury could hear about Frazier's drug use. The accusations of child molesting, beating a sheepdog, and firing a gun into a van full of passengers in Bisbee were not allowed into evidence, although when the jury was out of the courtroom, Spence thundered about the government's irresponsibility in letting a possible child molester baby-sit for Ilse's children.

Wealthy drug lawyer Mike Black showed great gusto in moralizing about Frazier's drug use. He even waved a paper cup, asking if the government had given Frazier a drug test (they hadn't) and not-so-subtly implying that now might be a good time to correct that oversight. There was some speculation around the courtroom that Frazier, who certainly seemed to be in some sort of Thorazine-inspired trance, might be on medication to keep him calm. Then again, he probably wasn't the only one.

Assistant U.S. Attorney Tom Simon, playing good cop to Roslyn Moore-Silver's bad cop, found himself in the odd position of defending Frazier's drug use. Whether or not LSD affects perception is a matter of opinion, Simon asserted. It was an ironic position for the government to take in the era of Just Say No.

Simon tried hard, but Frazier's cover of normalcy had been blown. Of course, his former friends weren't exactly refugees from the cast of *The Brady Bunch*. One of the FBI tapes contained Mark Davis's long, vague explanation of the mysterious "She" who wanted him to lay off monkeywrenching for a while. Unfortunately, Davis was not referring to the role played by bombshell Ursula Andress in the justly famous B movie made from the H. Rider Haggard novel. He was speaking about his personal New Age deity who appeared to him in the form of a bird.

Davis and Peg Millett were especially prone to New Age maunderings. But they were eccentric, not crazy. Frazier had true difficulty in distinguishing between fantasy and reality. This was especially true where women were involved. He testified that he had tried to implicate Ilse, hoping that he could bring her into the FBI fold—and, who knows, perhaps back into a relationship with him. "She's already helping us, albeit unwittingly," wrote Frazier in a diary he kept for the FBI. "I feel that I am preparing her in this way to help us consciously at a propitious time." Actually, Ilse was the only defendant who seemed to know how to keep her mouth shut around Frazier. Under his repeated prodding, her standard line had been, "That's between you and Mark."

By then the jurors shared Abrams's opinion of Frazier. He was an odd duck, to say the least. But in a flash of pure inspiration, Skip Donau cast the informer in a larger context. First Mike Black softened him up. Like a butcher pounding veal, Black hammered him with questions about his pseudonyms, Victor and Stilson. The meaning of Stilson became clear soon enough. It was oil-field slang for a monkeywrench. Frazier had used Stilson as his pseudonym with Earth First! In fact, his FBI bosses had chastised him for writing a letter under that name to the *Earth First! Journal* that began "*Achtung,* neanderthals" and used the Phoenix FBI office as a return address. But nobody knew why Frazier had chosen Victor to use as a code name with the FBI.

Black's repeated questioning failed to elicit an answer from Frazier. But it pulled up a connection in Donau's mind. When it was his turn to question Frazier, he asked him to hold the cutting torch he had helped Mark Davis buy. Then he asked Frazier if there was a brand name on the torch. Frazier answered affirmatively. When Donau questioned him further, he said the brand name was Victor. Frazier admitted that he had once owned a Victor torch himself. It had been his favorite torch.

Stilson and Victor. Frazier had named himself after tools. Tools kept machines alive. He loved big engines the way other people loved poetry, paintings, or their best friends. Earth First!—and Dave Foreman, a klutz who couldn't fix a carburetor if his life depended on it —were trying to destroy these machines. Frazier was the nightmare that Ed Abbey hadn't lived long enough to dream up. It wasn't the evil General Desalius in Abbey's post-apocalyptic novel *Good News* who would destroy rebellious Nature. It was a grunt. A fucked-up mechanic.

"Do you consider yourself a tool, Mr. Frazier?" Donau asked.

"No."

"Do you consider yourself a tool of the government to ensnare the people named in this indictment?"

Quietly. "No."

Everybody was waiting for Dave Foreman to take the stand. By the end of Frazier's testimony, the trial had lasted almost three months, and the prosecution was only half finished. In August, the court recessed for a week. After the break, Mike Fain, the shadow man who had infiltrated Peg Millett's life, would be taking the stand. He had already been spotted around the courthouse, dodging photographers and hightailing it up to the third-floor office where the prosecution was camping out. Cameras weren't allowed in the courtroom, so it was possible that his cover would remain semi-intact even if he took the stand. But would the FBI's case?

Attorney Skip Donau had grown up in the border town of Nogales, Arizona. It is a depressing little town just across the international line from a crime-ridden, dilapidated Mexican city. Even though Donau's family had been well-off, growing up there had helped him develop a certain kind of street smarts. He had his own stubborn set of morals—for instance, he had refused the government's fee as a court-appointed attorney because he believed it would be hypocritical to take money from the enemy. But as the defendants wryly pointed out, this moral stand made their lives more difficult because they had to scramble to meet his expenses. But Donau couldn't be persuaded. His mind worked like a cruise missile. When the recess began, this became an advantage. He sensed that Frazier's bizarre performance had given the defense a temporary edge. Waiting for Fain to take the stand could be advantageous. But it also would be risky. Fain was a pro. His only weakness would be on the entrapment issue. Entrapment was a tough call, especially with a jury that believed in Mom, Apple Pie, and Big Brother. If the entrapment line didn't fly, the case was over. Nearly all the defendants, except Foreman and possibly Ilse, had already convicted themselves on tape. Despite his jumbled personality, Frazier had convincingly corroborated the taped evidence. Mark Davis and Peg Millett were guilty as hell. Marc Baker had been caught red-handed at the CAP pole and had probably gone on at least one Snowbowl hit. It was a good bet that Ilse Asplund had been along on the Canyon Mine incident. That couldn't be proved, either, but she risked going down on the broad charge of conspiracy, which could include merely knowing about EMETIC's activities. Under the harsh 1988 federal sentencing guidelines, each defendant faced a minimum of five years for each charge. The only one who was almost certainly going to walk was Foreman. There wasn't enough evidence against him, even on conspiracy charges.

Donau presented the idea of a plea bargain to the defendants. It was a touchy subject, because each defendant's situation was different.

The government's case against Foreman was so weak, Donau thought he could negotiate him out of serving any jail time. Mark Davis would probably have to accept a sentence of more than five years. The others were scattered in between.

Up until now, they had overcome fear, grudges, and tremendous personality differences to stick together. Each of the Prescott defendants had turned down deals to testify against Foreman. Marc Baker, who was regarded as the most likely to fold, had been pressured the most. Baker had the most to lose, with his career in botany and two young children. But Mark Davis was also vulnerable. He was an acute claustrophobe. In the county jail he had suffered constant anxiety attacks and lost forty pounds. He had children to think about, too. Davis was unstable in many areas, but he was a devoted father. Separation from his daughters was nearly unbearable.

There were other pressures on Davis. He and Dave Foreman couldn't stand each other. Privately, Davis hinted that Foreman was more involved in EMETIC than the tapes showed. If Foreman had implicated himself in untaped conversations with Davis, Davis could turn the whole trial on its head. It must have been tempting. Davis resented Foreman's success, considering him a smooth-talking hypocrite. Foreman had taken a hard line on monkeywrenching in the 1986 interview with deep ecologist Bill Devall, saying, "I think the worst thing you can do if you consciously break the law and are caught is to whine about it. Accept the consequences. Welcome the consequences. But don't do something and then try to get out of it." Now Foreman was doing his damndest to save his own neck. Nevertheless, Davis never seriously considered turning state's evidence. Most of the time he was willing, almost eager, to be a martyr.

Ilse was ready to tough it out, but the decision was harder for her. During the trial her mother announced that she did not feel up to caring for Ilse's two children. Ilse's ex-husband grudgingly agreed to care for one of the kids. But separating the children was inconceivable. Adam and Julia had grown more dependent on each other since the traumatic events of 1989. A foster home was a nightmarish thought. Julia still woke at night asking Ilse if the FBI was going to take them away. When the subject of the trial was mentioned, four-year-old Adam shut off like a little freckled light bulb.

Mark Davis had sacrificed domesticity two years before to embark on a "warrior path." This time, he made a different decision. He told Ilse to go along with Skip's plea bargain deal. As he turned forty, Mark Davis finally seemed to be learning that one woman and her children could be more important than playing war for women and children in the abstract. But in some ways the lesson came too late. During the recess, he and Ilse ran into each other on Thumb Butte, a hiking spot outside Prescott. As they talked, Mark found himself surrendering to Ilse in a way he had never done while they were together. He talked about turning forty, confiding to her his feelings of failure. Ilse reassured him. Keep fighting, she told him. Just learn to fight another way. For a few days after their encounter, Mark thought the relationship had come alive again. But it was just one of those flashes of intimacy that occur when there is nothing left to lose.

Foreman's decision was more complicated. His acquittal was almost as good a bet as his codefendants' convictions. But the trial was not living up to its promise as the environmental case of the century. The media were ignoring it. It might look better to a few hard-core environmentalists if Foreman stuck it out, but the personal cost, both financial and emotional, would be tremendous. He was deeply in debt. The strain was affecting his marriage. He felt himself becoming bitter and depressed. It was worse for the others, of course. Peg Millett was facing certain conviction with a possible sentence of ten years or more. Three months after Judi Bari was bombed, Foreman had denied feeling responsible for the people he attracted to Earth First! Now he seemed to have changed his mind. Foreman said that while he was making his decision he'd thought about something Ed Abbey had written. "Never sacrifice a friend to a cause," he paraphrased, as the reporters dutifully took notes. Foreman agreed to be part of the package.

On the last day before the recess, Skip Donau approached the prosecution with his deal. To his surprise, they were willing to accept most of it. The deal was based on the defendants pleading guilty to charges linked to the 1987 Snowbowl incident. (The first sabotage of the Snowbowl had occurred before more stringent federal sentencing guidelines went into effect.) But the prosecutors were not willing to let Foreman plead out to a misdemeanor. Neither were they willing to make a deal that didn't include every defendant; it was all or nothing. During the week-long break, Guiberson guided the two camps through intense negotiations. Once the plea bargain was under way, Gerry Spence bailed. He had done his best to put U.S. environmental policy on trial. He had delivered a fine soliloquy on the antiquated mining laws that allowed the Canyon uranium mine to operate on federal land without paying a cent into the treasury. He had talked about forests and whales and grizzly bears. But his client's political beliefs were not on trial. Spence wasn't hitting the right notes. Wellborn Jack had been slightly more on the mark. But both attorneys were performers, not negotiators. Their involvement was over. Now it was up to Sam Guiberson, Dave Foreman, and the local tough boys.

On the first day of negotiations Dave Foreman was called to the judge's chambers. Sitting at a long table was the prosecution team, which included Assistant U.S. Attorney Tom Simon, a mild-mannered regular kind of guy; Roslyn Moore-Silver; and Daniel Fromstein, a ferret-faced lawyer from the Justice Department's anti-terrorism section. The FBI was lined up along another side of the table. To Foreman's surprise, the bureau was not just represented by Lori Bailey and Keith Tollhurst. Mike Fain was there, too.

Since the busts, the FBI had denied being out to get Foreman. Yet none of the other defendants had been invited to this meeting. Foreman's central role became even more apparent when Moore-Silver got to the point. In effect, the prosecution wanted Foreman to recant—to disavow monkeywrenching, and to endorse the FBI's actions.

At last. To the people in Judge Robert Broomfield's book-lined chambers, it was as if the events of the past two years had compressed themselves into this final moment. They watched as Foreman drank it in. Then he spoke. He told the prosecutors and the FBI exactly what he was willing to do. He would no longer advocate monkeywrenching, but he refused to disavow it.[1] He would never, never endorse the FBI's actions. He talked about how it had felt when the FBI stormed into his house and pointed their guns at his wife. He told them what it was like to face death at the hands of your own government. The audience was tiny, but it was the most important performance of his life.

Foreman won most of his points. There would be no recanting, although he would avoid the subject of monkeywrenching. In return, he agreed to plead guilty to a felony conspiracy charge. His sentencing would be delayed for five years. At the end of five years, his charge would be reduced to a misdemeanor. Mark Davis received a six-year prison sentence. Peg Millett got three years. Mark Baker got six months. Ilse Asplund got a one-month sentence.

At her sentencing, Ilse delivered a carefully prepared speech that left courtroom observers in tears. She referred to her two children, who were dressed up and sitting in the front row. She said the FBI's threats to take her children away on the morning of May 31 consti tuted true "terror." She, too, refused to recant.

"They [my children] must know that there's a range of life that cannot be reduced to merchandise . . . and they must know that I will guard that for them," she said.

"The government has already won. They've sent their message," she told Judge Broomfield. "I'm tired and I'd like to go home."

That remark could just as easily have been made by Foreman. He spent the next few months finishing a new edition of *The Big Outside*, the atlas of roadless areas that he had compiled with Howie Wolke. He made few public appearances. With his usual insensitivity to bleeding-heart liberals, he called the trial a tar baby and swore he was letting it go. But he seemed practically obsessed with it. He suspected that he was being followed. Moore-Silver was hauling him into court again. The FBI was keeping him on a leash. The mail-order book business was in the pits, which added to his gloom.

Eventually Foreman fell back into his routine. In the two years he waited for his trial to begin, he had founded a new environmental group with Rod Mondt and John Davis. The Wildlands Project was going to be a network of grass-roots groups devoted to saving entire ecosystems. The goal sounded familiar to anyone involved in the early days of Earth First! Mike Roselle said Foreman hadn't come up with any new ideas since his benchmark article in *The Progressive*. But those ideas had been good ones. Although remnants of most major ecosystems had been protected, they weren't large enough to sustain biodiversity. Now regional groups had come up with innovative ways to approach that goal, like wilderness corridors to preserve migration and breeding routes.

Foreman said he was growing tired of tearing down his tent and starting over. He hoped The Wildlands Project would be an organization that he could live with for the rest of his life. It wouldn't be as flashy as Earth First! But that had been a different time. With a sympathetic administration about to take office, there was no longer fuel for the rage and frustration that had helped create Earth First!'s guerrilla politics. Or maybe it was just that Foreman's political style had changed. His basic beliefs were the same, but he was less of a rebellious adolescent. He was convinced that Mike Roselle's biggest problem with him was that he was no longer a party animal.

Earth First! was still full of party animals, and Mike Roselle was still keeping up with them. In the spring of 1992, he finally got control of the *Earth First! Journal,* which was being published out of Missoula. At first, it appeared that Roselle had won only a Pyrrhic victory. Nobody seemed to be reading the *Journal* except a handful of diehard activists. The most dynamic, sophisticated Earth First!ers had moved on, usually to form small groups that offered a no-compromise alternative in local and regional land disputes.

Then, all at once, Earth First! revived. New groups formed in the United States. People in England calling themselves Earth First! fastened their heads to heavy equipment with bicycle locks, à la the long-dead but not forgotten Buggis. As for the real monkeywrenchers, these lone, wild wolves of environmentalism were not about to be deterred by a plea bargain or even by the breakup of the old Earth First! It wasn't these isolated individuals that federal agents and prosecutors worried about. It was the man who had the power to make monkeywrenching a national pastime.

For ten years, Dave Foreman had gotten away with saying fuck you to the U.S. government. In a way, it was a tribute to the country's concept of freedom that he had lasted so long.

He came out of hiding in the spring. At first he spoke only to small, sympathetic audiences. These days, he made cracks about being a capitalist and shilled for his own books. He told people that he hadn't been Mr. Monkeywrench for a long time. It was both self-serving and true. One of his first gigs was in Phoenix, at a panel called "Humankind's Responsibility to the Environment." He hadn't delivered a speech in months. But he wasn't nervous. He never got nervous. If he had still believed in a god, he would have said it was his god-given gift. It came to him as naturally as food or sex or running in the desert. He walked up to the podium.

Before he could speak, the crowd stood. They drowned him in applause.

Acknowledgments

VERY SIMPLY, this book could not have been written without Dave Foreman. As a journalist, I appreciated finding a source with such an engaging intellect. Even rarer is a political figure who exhibits a high degree of honesty without regard to self-interest. Dave is all of that. He is also generous, patient, and very funny. His memory for facts belongs in the *Guinness Book of World Records*.

All of the Buckaroos told great stories. Thanks to Ron Kezar, Bart Koehler, Mike Roselle, and Howie Wolke. Judi Bari, Jim Eaton, Susan Morgan, Karen Pickett, Ken Sanders, Debbie Sease, and Louisa Willcox provided necessary perspective.

I am grateful to Doug Scott for trusting me to convey some of the knowledge that he acquired during almost thirty years in the environmental movement. Tim Mahoney also patiently helped educate me, as did Brock Evans and Brooks Yeager.

To Rita Deanin Abbey, thanks for following your instincts. I also want to thank Ilse Asplund, Roger Featherstone, Lorane Foreman, Rod Mondt, Roxanne Foreman Pacheco, and Nancy Zierenberg for their patience and friendliness.

Many of my friends are writers who care about the environment. Diana Hembree was the first to suggest that my magazine article could be turned into a book. I am only one of many journalists who have benefited from her sensitivity, generosity, and ethics.

Since 1985 Angela Gennino has been sharing her hilariously un-varnished views of the environmental movement with me. She con-sented to be one of this manuscript's early readers, even dragging it along the Ho Chi Minh trail. When I needed to hear it, she told me it was all worth it.

Ariel Rubissow contributed to this book in so many ways that it's difficult to express my thanks adequately. Her writing gave me mo-tivation to improve my own and her friendship helped teach me how to live.

Frances Taliaferro was kind enough to allow this 1960s TV kid to borrow her impeccable literary conscience for a second time. Bruce Kirmmse has been a teacher and a friend for almost twenty years. He helped provide the intellectual backdrop for this book and made val-uable suggestions after reading the manuscript. The novelist Susan Lang-McMonagle also read an early draft. Her careful editing was an act of real friendship and her uncompromising moral perspective was useful and thought-provoking. When I could not be in two places at the same time, Rebecca Rosen worked briefly, but very effectively, as my research assistant. My editor, David Stanford, helped shape this book from the beginning. His humor was as valuable to me as his farsightedness.

Patricia Damery deserves special thanks. Her perfect emotional pitch, which I may or may not have been able to achieve in the foregoing text, nonetheless helped it to be written.

Clarke Abbey, Ivan Abrams, Gloria Billings, Chuck Bowden, Pe-ter and Cheryl Bradt, Charles West Conner, Chris Cutler, Mark Dowie, the Duthie Family, Nancy Evans, Marc and Marnie Gaede,

Julian Hayden, Alison Humes, Barry Kaiser, David Kaplan, Daniel Lynch, Craig MacCraiger, Terry McDonell, Bill McKibben, Tom Miller, Sigrid Nunez, Laurence Orme, Adrianne Rankin, Stuart Rickey, Gary Snyder, Ellin Stein, the whole Elizabeth Stinson–Hoyt Dingwall ménage including Cosmo and the tree, Stephen Talbot and David Helvarg, Tom Turner, Eric Twachtman, David Rains Wallace, Lloyd Van Brunt, and Ira Wolfman all provided insight and encouragement.

Several people and organizations made contributions that kept this project going. My mother, Barbara Berkall, became a partner in this book, both emotionally and financially. *Coyotes and Town Dogs* was finished in a reasonable amount of time because of her help and because of assistance from my cousin Benita Tall Kaplan, whose generosity recalls the second definition of the word in the third edition of the *American Heritage Dictionary: "nobility of thought or behavior; magnanimity,"* which her father would no doubt have memorized had this edition been published in his day. I am also grateful to the Ira-Hiti Foundation for Deep Ecology; Blue Mountain Center; Esta and Lewis Ress; and the Center for Investigative Reporting. I wish to express my support for the National Writers Union, which is working to get writers a living wage.

Notes

All quotes in Coyotes and Town Dogs *are taken from the author's interviews, unless otherwise noted. These primary source quotes are noted below only when the origin is unclear in the text.*

CHAPTER 1

1. Bernard De Voto, "The West: A Plundered Province," *Harper's*, August 1934, 355.

2. All quotes in this passage are from Richard Hughes and C. Leonard Allen, *Illusions of Innocence: Protestant Primitivism in America, 1630–1875* (Chicago: University of Chicago Press, 1988).

3. Michael Lacey, "Inside the Deal," *New Times*, 21–27 August 1991, 5.

4. Curt Meine, *Aldo Leopold: His Life and Work* (Madison: University of Wisconsin Press, 1988), 228.

CHAPTER 2

1. "Mood Is Joyful as City Gives Its Support," *New York Times,* 23 April 1970, A30.

2. Bill Lawren, "Once Aflame and Filthy, a River Shows Signs of Life," *National Wildlife,* February–March 1990, 24.

3. *Newsweek,* 26 January 1970.

4. " 'Teach-In' to Save the Earth," *Reader's Digest,* April 1970, 111.

5. *Time,* 4 May 1970, 16.

6. *Newsweek,* 26 January 1970.

7. Scott interview, January 1990.

8. "Angry Coordinator of Earth Day," *New York Times,* 23 April 1970, A30.

9. *Time,* 4 May 1970, 16.

10. *Time,* 4 May 1970.

11. Both quotes from *New York Times,* 23 April 1970, A30.

12. *Time,* 4 May 1970, 16.

13. "Veteran of Earth Day 1970 Looks to a New World," *New York Times,* 16 April 1990, B8.

14. David Rains Wallace, author of *Bulow Hammock: Mind in a Forest,* Sierra Club Books, 1989, used this image of wilderness.

15. *Time,* 4 May 1970.

CHAPTER 3

1. Daniel Grossman, "Neo-Luddites: Don't Just Say Yes to Technology," *Utne Reader,* March–April 1990, 44–53.

2. Peter Matthiessen, *Indian Country* (New York: Viking, 1984), 97.

3. For detailed accounts of this story, see Wiley and Gottlieb's *Empires in the Sun,* Fradkin's *A River No More,* Martin's *A Story That Stands Like a Dam,* and Reisner's *Cadillac Desert,* all listed in the bibliography.

4. Jack Loeffler, *Headed Upstream: Interviews with Iconoclasts* (Tucson: Harbinger House, 1989), 167.

5. Alvin Josephy, "The Murder of the Southwest," *Audubon,* July 1971, 57.

6. Marjane Ambler, *Breaking the Iron Bonds: Indian Control of Energy Development* (Lawrence: University Press of Kansas, 1990), 222.

7. Janet Cuthbertson, "Ecotage!" *Heresies* 13. Cuthbertson lists her sources as *Newsweek,* 5 October 1970 and 11 January 1971; Sam Love and David Obst, eds., *Ecotage* (New York: Pocket Books, 1970).

8. Tom Miller, "What Is the Sound of One Billboard Falling?" *Berkeley Barb,* 8–14 November 1974.

CHAPTER 4

1. Dennis M. Roth, *The Wilderness Movement and the National Forests* (College Station, Tex.: Intaglio Press, 1988), 34.

2. Ibid., 30.

3. Merritt interview, January 1991.

4. Brock Evans, "Two Roads North," *Sierra Club Bulletin,* November–December 1974, 19.

5. Interview with Julie McDonald, Sierra Club Legal Defense Fund staff attorney, March 1991.

6. Ibid.

7. Roth, *The Wilderness Movement and the National Forests,* 48–49.

8. Ibid.

9. Ibid., 51. Other sections of this account are drawn from an interview conducted with Doug Scott in January 1991.

CHAPTER 7

1. Wallace Stegner, *The Uneasy Chair* (Salt Lake City: Peregrine Smith Books, 1988), 292.

2. Ibid., 302–4.

3. "Study Finds Profits in Grazing Subleases," *New York Times,* 25 October 1992.

4. Unless otherwise noted, all the information on grazing comes from Denzel Ferguson and Mary Ferguson, *Sacred Cows at the Public Trough* (Bend, Oreg.: Maverick Publications, 1983).

5. Aldo Leopold, *The Sand County Almanac with Essays from Round River* (New York: Sierra Club and Ballantine Books, 1971), 197.

6. Phillip Fradkin, *A River No More: The Colorado River and the West* (Tucson: University of Arizona Press, 1984), 74.

7. Gary Snyder, *Axe Handles* (San Francisco: North Point Press, 1983).

8. Edward Abbey, *Cactus Country* (New York: Time-Life Books, 1973), 153.

9. William, Hartmann, *Desert Heart: Chronicles of the Sonoran Desert* (Tucson: Fisher Books, 1989), 12.

10. Ronald L. Ives, "The Pinacate Region, Sonora, Mexico," Occasional Papers of the California Academy of Sciences, 28 August 1964, 8–9.

11. John C. Van Dyke, *The Desert* (Salt Lake City: Peregrine Smith, 1980), xiv. Republished recently by the University of Arizona Press.

12. Ibid., 84.

13. Ibid., 93–94.

14. Ibid., xiv–xv.

15. Ibid., 108. Thanks for some help with this section to Ruby Mattson, gnostic scholar and dream analyst.

16. John Muir, *Thousand Mile Walk to the Gulf,* ed. William F. Bade (1916; reprint, Boston: Houghton Mifflin, 1917), 354; quoted by Michael P. Cohen in *The Pathless Way: John Muir and American Wilderness.*

17. Bart, who is now married, claims that when he actually got Marta alone he feigned a stomachache, smiled in a sickly way, overpaid, and left as soon as possible.

CHAPTER 8

1. David Quammen, "Bagpipes for Ed," *Outside* magazine, June 1989, 25.

2. Marc Reisner, *Cadillac Desert* (New York: Penguin, 1987), 293–99.

3. Stephen Fox, *The American Conservation Movement: John Muir and His Legacy* (Madison: University of Wisconsin Press, 1985), 275–76.

4. Reisner, *Cadillac Desert*, 293.

5. Russell Martin, *A Story That Stands Like a Dam* (New York: Henry Holt and Company, 1989), 182.

6. Ibid., 62.

7. Phillip Fradkin, *A River No More* (Tucson: University of Arizona Press, 1984), 231–32.

8. Martin, *A Story That Stands Like a Dam,* 261. Later, Goldwater would join with Congressman Mo Udall to pass a strong Arizona wilderness bill.

9. Ibid., 266.

10. Ibid., 292.

11. Ibid., 171.

12. Larry McMurtry, *In a Narrow Grave: Essays on Texas* (Albuquerque: University of New Mexico Press, 1968), 25.

13. Karen Evans, "The Monkeywrench Guy," *New Age Journal,* January 1985, 43.

CHAPTER 9

1. Michael McCloskey, "Twenty Years of Change in the Environmental Movement," *Society & Natural Resources: An International Journal* 4, no. 3 (1991), 273–84.

2. *Facts on File,* 8 April 1983.

3. Paul Brinkley-Rogers, "Protest Fails to Wrench Visit," *Arizona Daily Star,* 20 May 1983, A1.

4. Parts of this account are drawn from Tom Miller's article, "James Watt and Friends, Live Onstage," in the Phoenix, Arizona, weekly newspaper *New Times,* 25 May–1 June 1983 issue.

5. Charles Bowden, "Dave Foreman! In the Face of Reality," *Buzzworm* 2, no. 2 (March–April 1990), 48–49.

6. Suzanne Winckler, "Stopgap Measures," *The Atlantic,* January 1992, 78.

7. For an account of this event, see Peter Wiley and Robert Gottlieb, *Empires in the Sun* (Tucson: University of Arizona Press, 1985), 54–74. Originally published by Putnam in 1982.

CHAPTER 10

1. Dennis M. Roth, *The Wilderness Movement and the National Forests 1980–1984,* Forest Service History Series, U.S. Forest Service pamphlet FS-410, August 1988, 54–55.

2. Peter Matthiessen, *Indian Country* (New York: Viking, 1984), 68–72.

3. Catherine Caufield, "The Ancient Forest," *The New Yorker,* 14 May 1990, 71.

CHAPTER 11

1. This information comes from a series of interviews with Tom Atzet, an ecologist at the Siskiyou National Forest in Oregon.

2. Dennis M. Roth, *The Wilderness Movement and the National Forests* (College Station, Tex.: Intaglio Press, 1988), 25.

3. Dennis M. Roth, *The Wilderness Movement and the National Forests 1980–84,* Forest Service History Series, U.S. Forest Service pamphlet FS-410, August 1988, 26, 37.

4. Catherine Caufield, "The Ancient Forest," *The New Yorker,* 14 May 1990. Caufield is using biomass figures from *Secrets of the Old Growth Forest* by David Kelly.

5. Peter Matthiessen, *Indian Country* (New York: Viking, 1984), 170.

6. *Deep Ecology: Living As If Nature Mattered* was published in 1985 by Gibbs M. Smith, Inc., Peregrine Smith Books, Layton, Utah.

7. Bron Taylor, "The Religion and Politics of Earth First!" *The Ecologist,* November–December 1991, 259.

8. This section draws from Rik Scarce's book, *EcoWarriors,* published in 1990 by the Noble Press, Chicago; *The Rights of Nature: A History of Environmental Ethics,* by Roderick Frazier Nash, published by The University of Wisconsin Press in 1989; and interviews with Mark DuBois and Catherine Fox.

9. Caufield, "The Ancient Forest," 72.

10. Ibid., 61.

11. Ibid., 69–70.

12. Interviews with Tom Turner, Sierra Club Legal Defense Fund, 1990, 1992.

CHAPTER 12

1. Jacobs also runs a tiny antigrazing environmental group called Free Our Public Lands!, whose main function seems to be sending out fact sheets and printing bumper stickers. *Waste of the West* can be obtained by writing to Lynn Jacobs at P.O. Box 5784, Tucson, Arizona 85703. Individual copies are $28. By my calculations, that works out to be about $1 a pound.

2. Howard Zinn, *A People's History of the United States* (New York: Harper Perennial, 1990), 277, 280–89.

3. Bernard De Voto, "The West: A Plundered Province," *Harper's,* August 1934, 355.

4. Jane Kramer, *The Last Cowboy* (New York: Pocket, 1977), 22.

5. "FBI Tracked Abbey for 20-Year Span," *Arizona Daily Star,* 25 June 1989, 1.

6. Author's interview with Edward Abbey, 1986.

7. "Report Card Time: Doling Out the Marks on 14 Leading Environmental Groups," *Outside,* December 1991, 62–63.

8. Dan Wyant, "Logging of Ancient Trees Starts," Eugene, Oregon, *Register-Guard*, 1 April 1986, 1.

9. Christopher Manes, *Green Rage* (Boston: Little, Brown, 1990), 206.

CHAPTER 13

1. Transcript of FBI tapes.

2. Any information not otherwise cited in the preceding passage is from an interview with Ron Frazier conducted in Bisbee, Arizona, in October 1991.

3. Michael Lacey, "Inside the Deal," *New Times*, 21–27 August 1991, 8.

4. FBI transcripts of surveilled conversations among EMETIC members.

CHAPTER 14

1. These companies weren't exactly role models, having been cited for about 40,000 environmental violations over a six-year period, mostly for dumping untreated waste in the Pacific Ocean. "Slide Over, Hazelwood: Make Room for the New Dirty Half-dozen," *Outside*, December 1991, 64.

2. Curt Meine, *Aldo Leopold: His Life and Work* (Madison: The University of Wisconsin Press, 1988), 368.

3. "A Street Filled With Angry Trees," Dennis Duggan's "New York Diary" column, New York *Newsday*, 14 January 1988, 9.

4. Thomas E. Ricks and Daniel Hertzberg, "Ex-Jeffries Aide May Have Parked Stock for Hurwitz, Congressional Report Says," *Wall Street Journal*, 5 October 1987.

5. "PL Workers Dream of Ownership," *Eureka Times-Standard*, Eureka, California, 15 September 1988, 1.

6. This section is based on Jonathan Littman's article "Peace, Love . . . and TNT," *California*, December 1990, 82–89, 128–29, and on interviews with Judi Bari and Darryl Cherney by the author.

7. Stephen Talbot, "Earth First! What Next?" *Mother Jones*, November–December 1990, 77.

8. Ibid., 76.

9. This account was first published in Jonathan Littman's article in *California* magazine. In an interview, Judi Bari filled in additional details which somewhat altered the tone of the anecdote.

10. Littman, "Peace, Love . . . and TNT," 86.

11. Talbot, "Earth First! What Next?," 77.

12. Interview with John LeBlanc, extension forester, Department of Forestry and Resource Management, University of California, 25 March 1992.

13. Howard Zinn, *A People's History of the United States* (New York: Harper Perennial, 1990), 327.

14. Ibid., 364.

15. Clark Mason, "Hike in Mill Mishaps, Workers Say," *Santa Rosa Press Democrat,* 22 May 1989.

16. Information about Ron Arnold and Ron Gottlieb from "Brown Fellas" and "Brown New World" by David Quammen, *Outside,* December 1991, 50–53, 68–72, 114–16.

17. This information was broadcast on *60 Minutes,* October 1992. The Center for Investigative Reporting, which contributed research to the broadcast, also published a story about attacks on environmentalists in the fall 1992 issue of its publication *Muckraker.*

18. Interview with Campbell, September 1990. Campbell, who had married the daughter of the former chief executive of Pacific Lumber, was a supporter of the Maxxam takeover.

19. Information about links between the Wise Use groups from an interview with Paula Langager, W.E.C.A.R.E. staff member (now Alta California Alliance), Eureka, California, September 1990.

20. Narda Zucchino, "Ex-FBI Informer Describes Right-Wing Terrorist Role," *Los Angeles Times,* 26 January 1976, 1.

21. This quote, along with some factual details of this period, comes from Jonathan Littman's article in *California,* "Peace, Love . . . and TNT."

22. "Letter Widens FBI Probe," *Santa Rosa Press Democrat,* 1 June 1990, 1.

23. Ibid.

24. Harry Harris and Paul Grabowicz, "Bomb Victims Jailed," *Oakland Tribune,* 26 May 1990, 1.

CHAPTER 15

1. Michael P. Cohen, *The Pathless Way: John Muir and American Wilderness* (Madison: University of Wisconsin Press, 1984), 319.

2. Ibid., 307.

3. Ibid., 320–21.

4. Adam Gopnik, "Audubon's Passion," *The New Yorker,* 25 February, 1991, 96–104. Gopnik described the look of Audubon's birds as one of "ecstatic animation."

5. Robert Marshall, "The Problem of Wilderness," *Scientific Monthly,* February 1930, 141–48.

6. Interview with Edward Abbey, 1985.

7. Edward Abbey, *Beyond the Wall* (New York: Henry Holt and Company, 1984), xv.

8. Keith Schneider, "Selling Out? Pushed and Pulled, Environment Inc. Is on the Defensive," *New York Times,* 29 March 1992, sec. 4, 1.

CHAPTER 16

1. "I would no longer overtly advocate monkeywrenching, because that was what I had already decided. I wanted to push conservation biology—pushing monkeywrenching at the same time only confused the message," Foreman wrote.

Bibliography

Abbey, Edward.
Fiction:
> *Jonathan Troy*. New York: Dodd, Mead and Co., 1954.
> *The Brave Cowboy: An Old Tale in a New Time*. 1956. Reprint. Albuquerque: University of New Mexico Press, 1977.
> *Fire on the Mountain*. 1962. Reprint. New York: Dial Press, 1982.
> *Desert Solitaire*. 1968. Reprint. New York: Ballantine, 1979.
> *Black Sun*. 1971. Reprint. Santa Barbara: Capra Press, 1981.
> *The Monkeywrench Gang*. 1975. Reprint. Salt Lake City: Dream Garden Press, 1985.
> *Good News*. New York: E. P. Dutton, 1980.
> *The Fool's Progress*. New York: Henry Holt and Company, 1988.
> *Hayduke Lives!* New York: Little, Brown, 1990.

Nonfiction:

Cactus Country. New York: Time-Life Books, Inc., 1973.

The Journey Home: Some Words in Defense of the American West. New York: E. P. Dutton, 1977.

Abbey's Road. New York, E. P. Dutton, 1979.

Down the River. New York: E. P. Dutton, 1982.

Beyond the Wall. New York: Henry Holt and Company, 1984.

One Life at a Time, Please. New York: Henry Holt and Company, 1987.

Ambler, Marjane. *Breaking the Iron Bonds: Indian Control of Energy Development.* Kansas: University Press of Kansas, 1990.

Austin, Mary. *The Land of Little Rain.* New York: Penguin Books, 1988.

Bowden, Charles. *Blue Desert.* Tucson: University of Arizona Press, 1988.

———. *Killing the Hidden Waters.* 1977. Reprint. Austin: University of Texas Press, 1985.

Brown, David E., and Carmony, Neil B., eds. *Aldo Leopold's Wilderness.* Harrisburg, Pa.: Stackpole Books, 1990.

Cohen, Michael P. *The History of the Sierra Club 1892–1970.* San Francisco: Sierra Club Books, 1988.

———. *The Pathless Way: John Muir and the American Wilderness.* Madison: University of Wisconsin Press, 1984.

Cronon, Bill. *Changes in the Land: Indians, Colonists, and the Ecology of New England,* 2d. ed. New York: Hill and Wang, 1984.

de Tocqueville, Alexis. *Democracy in America.* New York: New American Library, 1956.

Devall, Bill, and Sessions, George. *Deep Ecology: Living As If Nature Mattered.* Layton, Utah: A Peregrine Smith Book, Gibbs M. Smith, 1985.

Eastlake, William. *Go In Beauty.* 1956. Reprint. Albuquerque: University of New Mexico Press, 1980.

Ferguson, Denzel, and Ferguson, Mary. *Sacred Cows at the Public Trough.* Bend, Oreg.: Maverick Publications, 1983.

Foreman, Dave. *Confessions of an Eco-Warrior*. New York: Crown Publishers, 1990.

———. *Ecodefense*. Tucson: A Ned Ludd Book, Earth First! Books, 1985.

———, with Murray Bookchin. *Defending the Earth*. Boston: South End Press, 1990.

———, with Howie Wolke. *The Big Outside*. New York: Crown, 1992.

Fox, Stephen. *The American Conservation Movement: John Muir and His Legacy*. Madison: University of Wisconsin Press, 1985.

Fradkin, Phillip. *A River No More: The Colorado River and the West*. Tucson: University of Arizona Press, 1984.

———. *Sagebrush Country*. New York: Alfred A. Knopf, 1989.

Gilliam, Harold. *Voices for the Earth*. San Francisco: Sierra Club Books, 1979.

Glover, James M. *A Wilderness Original: The Life of Bob Marshall*. Seattle, Wash.: The Mountaineers, 1986.

Gordon, Suzanne. *Black Mesa: Angel of Death*. New York: John Day Co., 1973.

Grey, Zane. *Desert Gold*. New York: Bantam, 1990.

Hartmann, William K. *Desert Heart: Chronicles of the Sonoran Desert*. Tucson: Fisher Books, 1989.

Jacobs, Lynn. *Waste of the West: Public Lands Ranching*. Tucson: Lynn Jacobs, 1991.

Kittredge, William. *We Are Not in This Together*. Port Townsend, Wash.: Graywolf Press, 1984.

Kramer, Jane. *The Last Cowboy*. New York: Penguin Books, 1977.

Kroeber, Theodora. *Ishi, Last of His Tribe*. New York: Bantam, 1978.

Kropotkin, Peter. *Mutual Aid*. 1902. Reprint. Boston: Extending Horizons Books, 1955.

Leopold, Aldo. *A Sand County Almanac*. 1948. Reprint. London, Oxford, New York: Oxford University Press, 1968 (special members' edition for the American Museum of Natural History).

Loeffler, Jack. *Headed Upstream: Interviews with Iconoclasts*. Tucson: Harbinger House, 1989.

Manes, Christopher. *Green Rage.* New York: Little, Brown, 1990.

Martin, Russell. *A Story That Stands Like a Dam: Glen Canyon and the Struggle for the Soul of the West.* New York: Henry Holt and Co., 1989.

Maser, Chris. *Forest Primeval: The Natural History of an Ancient Forest.* San Francisco: Sierra Club Books, 1989.

Matthiessen, Peter. *Wildlife in America.* New York: Penguin Books, 1978.

————. *Indian Country.* New York: Viking, 1984.

————. *In the Spirit of Crazy Horse.* New York: Viking, 1992.

McKibben, Bill. *The End of Nature.* New York: Random House, 1989.

McMurtry, Larry. *In a Narrow Grave: Essays on Texas.* 1968. Reprint. Albuquerque: University of New Mexico Press, 1987.

McPhee, John. *Encounters with the Archdruid.* New York: Farrar, Straus & Giroux, 1971.

Meine, Curt. *Aldo Leopold: His Life and Work.* Madison: University of Wisconsin Press, 1988.

Nash, Roderick Frazier. *Wilderness and the American Mind.* New Haven: Yale University Press, 1982.

————. *The Rights of Nature: A History of Environmental Ethics.* Madison: University of Wisconsin Press, 1989.

Peacock, Douglas. *The Grizzly Years.* New York: Henry Holt and Co., 1990.

Pynchon, Thomas. *Vineland.* New York: Little, Brown and Co., 1990.

Reisner, Marc. *Cadillac Desert.* New York: Viking Penguin, 1986.

Roth, Dennis M. *The Wilderness Movement and the National Forests.* College Station, Tex.: Intaglio Press, 1988.

————. *The Wilderness Movement and the National Forests 1980–1984.* Forest Service History Series, U.S. Forest Service pamphlet FS-410, August 1988.

Snyder, Gary. *Turtle Island.* New York: New Directions, 1974.

————. *The Real Work.* New York: New Directions, 1980.

————. *The Practice of the Wild.* San Francisco: North Point Press, 1990.

Stegner, Wallace. *The Uneasy Chair: A Biography of Bernard De Voto.* 1974. Reprint. Salt Lake City: Peregrine Smith Books, 1988.

————. *The Sound of Mountain Water.* Lincoln: University of Nebraska Press, 1985.

Stewart, George R. *Earth Abides.* New York: Fawcett Crest, 1949.

Thoreau, Henry David. *Ktaadn.* New York: Tanam Press, 1980.

Twain, Mark. *Roughing It.* New York: New American Library, 1962.

Udall, Stewart. *The Quiet Crisis.* New York: Holt, Rinehart and Winston, 1963.

Van Dyke, John C. *The Desert.* Salt Lake City: Peregrine Smith, Inc., 1980.

Wallace, David Rains. *The Klamath Knot.* San Francisco: Sierra Club Books, 1983, 1984.

————. *Bulow Hammock: Mind in a Forest:* San Francisco, Sierra Club Books, 1988.

Wild, Peter. *Pioneer Conservationists of Western America.* Missoula, Mont.: Mountain Press Publishing Co., 1979.

————. *Pioneer Conservationists of Eastern America.* Missoula, Mont.: Mountain Press Publishing Co., 1986.

Wiley, Peter, and Gottlieb, Robert. *Empires in the Sun: The Rise of the New American West.* 1982. Reprint. Tucson: University of Arizona Press, 1985.

Wister, Owen. *The Virginian.* 1902. Reprint. New York: Pocket Books, 1979.

Wolfe, Linnie Marsh. *Son of the Wilderness: The Life of John Muir.* Madison: University of Wisconsin Press, 1973.

Zinn, Howard. *A People's History of the United States.* New York: Harper Perennial, 1990.

Index

About the Author

Susan Zakin grew up in New York City and has lived in New England, California, and Madagascar. Her articles have appeared in *Vogue, Salon, Sierra, Amicus Journal*, and *The New York Times*. Her syndicated newspaper columns appear in newspapers throughout the American West. She lives in Tucson, Arizona.